# The Best of
# an Almanac of
# Words at Play

Willard R. Espy

# The Best of
# an Almanac of
# Words at Play

Willard R. Espy

Merriam-Webster, Incorporated
Springfield, Massachusetts

## A GENUINE MERRIAM-WEBSTER

The name *Webster* alone is no guarantee of excellence. It is used by a number of publishers and may serve mainly to mislead an unwary buyer.

*Merriam-Webster*™ is the name you should look for when you consider the purchase of dictionaries or other fine reference books. It carries the reputation of a company that has been publishing since 1831 and is your assurance of quality and authority.

Copyright © 1999 Willard R. Espy

*Library of Congress Cataloging in Publication Data*

The best of An almanac of words at play / Willard R. Espy
    p.    cm.
    Brings together the best and most memorable entries from both An almanac of words at play and Another almanac of words at play.
    ISBN 0-87779-145-7 (alk. paper)
    1. Literary calendars. 2. English language—Lexicology—Anecdotes. 3. Play on words. 4. Word games. I. Espy, Willard R. Almanac of words at play. II. Espy, Willard R. Another almanac of words at play.
PN6075.B47 1999
793.734—dc21                                     9914620
                                                                         CIP

Printed and bound in the United States of America

123456QPV010099

## EPIGRAPH

Doubt, dishonor in the crowd;
    Government by fool or crook;
Acid rain and atom cloud—
    All's absurd, and so's my book.

(This is written for effect:
    Do not take me at my word.
Though the rest may be correct,
    My book's silly, not absurd.)
                    —W.R.E.

# PREFACE

THE BEST OF AN ALMANAC OF WORDS AT PLAY is a collection of the most memorable and entertaining entries appearing in Willard Espy's two earlier almanacs, *An Almanac of Words at Play* (1975) and *Another Almanac of Words at Play* (1980). According to the original plan for this book, Willard Espy was to approve the list of selections made by Merriam-Webster editors; sadly, however, Willard Espy died on February 20, 1999, shortly before the selection process was complete, and so securing his final approval of the contents of this book was not possible. The responsibility, then, for what has been included in this collection lies with the editors of Merriam-Webster, who were guided both by the Espy sensibility, as they came to know it, and by their own understanding of what is most likely to appeal to a new generation of readers.

The new volume preserves the organization of the preceding volumes. There is an entry for each day of the year, including February 29, and every effort was made to keep entries near to the date to which they were assigned in the earlier volumes. Some entries take the forms of puzzles and quizzes, and answers are provided at the back of the book. The front matter includes a remembrance of Willard Espy by Paul Dickson, who provides a fascinating look at the man himself, his many accomplishments, and the role Espy played in helping to develop the current level of public interest in wordplay.

The editors of Merriam-Webster are grateful to those who helped make this book possible. First, of course, we thank Louise Espy for the help she provided with this volume and for the role she played in creating the preceding almanacs. She "meted out patience or impatience as the situation required," Espy says in the first *Almanac*, thus aptly describing the ideal collaborator for a book like this. We also want to thank Faith and Ross Eckler, publishers of *Word Ways: The Journal of Recreational Linguistics*, not only for the material from that journal that is used here but also for maintaining their unique publication over the years. Willard Espy was a long-time fan of *Word Ways*, as revealed in the entry for August 2, and he would have rightly insisted that the role of the Ecklers be properly acknowledged in these pages.

Over the years, Willard Espy was assisted by an army of volunteers who sent him material and proposed ideas for entries, and we want to acknowledge their contributions as well. Their names are too numerous to list in full, and many unfortunately are no longer known, but there are a few names that we think

Willard Espy would have especially wanted us to mention: Louisa and Paul Bonner, Dmitri Borgmann, Sandy Choron, William Cole, Don Davidson, Charles F. Dery, Carolyn S. Foote, Martin Gardner, Richard Eddes Harrison, Barbara Huston, Richard Lederer, Louis Phillips, Peter Prescott, Alistair Reid, William Safire, and Will Shortz.

Production responsibilities for this book were shared by many at Merriam-Webster. Jennifer N. Cislo prepared the manuscript for the data-entry staff, consisting of Georgette B. Boucher and Florence A. Fowler. Technical direction for the data entry was provided by Stephen J. Perrault. Design, typesetting, and proofreading activities were managed by Thomas F. Pitoniak, under the direction of Madeline L. Novak. Proofreaders included Michael G. Belanger, Anne Eason, G. James Kossuth, Michael D. Roundy, Adrienne M. Scholz, Kory L. Stamper, and Linda Picard Wood. We also thank Paul Dickson, friend of Willard Espy and of Merriam-Webster, for the sound advice and valuable guidance he provided throughout the creation of this book.

John M. Morse
Publisher

# INTRODUCTION

The first thing you noticed about Willard Espy was the way he presented himself. His mane of white hair, carefully waxed moustache, boutonnieres, and elegant attire set him apart, even in his beloved Manhattan. As often as not, he was seen in perfectly pressed white suits, giving many the impression that they were in the presence of a dashing but older Tom Wolfe. One writer said his spiffy wardrobe was "something between Maurice Chevalier and the old *Esquire* magazine."

"One gets the feeling," wrote Heywood Hale Broun in the foreword to Espy's book, *Thou Improper, Thou Uncommon Noun,* "that he has an attention span measurable at somewhere between one and two martinis, and that his work, whatever it is, is something frivolous which begins at 10:30 a.m. and ends in the signing of a few letters before he goes to his club at noon."

Looks, however, can be deceiving: Willard Espy worked very hard at being Willard Espy. In a diverse series of books and in his life as a journalist, publicist, essayist, wordsmith, and poet, this native of Oysterville, Washington, wrote about things that really mattered to him, especially his ties to the Pacific Northwest. His stirring memoir *Oysterville: Roads to Grandpa's Village* is about what was important to the man, but he was also captivated by what he termed "the utterly unimportant," most especially wordplay.

The groundwork for his career in wordplay came in 1967, while he was lying on the beach at East Hampton, New York (he later noted that, in this case, one should not say groundwork but sandwork). He wrote a verse around a series of four anagrams using the letters a, e, i, d, s, r, and p, and he came up with this:

> When I _ _ _ _ _ _ _ to be a father,
> You _ _ _ _ _ _ _ my willingness to bother,
> Now you _ _ _ _ _ _ _; never knew
> I'd leave the _ _ _ _ _ _ _ to you.

Solved, the puzzle did exactly what Espy intended it to do, which was to "throw a little white light on the human condition."

> When I aspired to be a father,
> You praised my willingness to bother,

Now you despair; never knew
I'd leave the diapers to you.

Over the following weeks, he incessantly composed more of these anagram-matic puzzle-poems which were later dubbed "Espygrams." Later that year, when he and his wife Louise visited London, he submitted them to *Punch*, the humor magazine where, owing to his persistence, they were accepted at about $16 a verse. That sale, which later ended up as an episode in a book entitled *How I Made the Sale That Did the Most for Me*, began his career as a master player in what he called "the game of words."

Each week for more than two years one of his verses was published in *Punch*, and before long (1971), he had published the first of many books of wordplay and linguistic oddities, called *The Game of Words*. In the introduction to the book he invents his own metaphor for dealing with words as domestic animals: "Housebreak your words while they are still too young to know better. When you take one for its exercise, curb it, or the neighbors will become angry. Be considerate but firm. Teach your words to sit, lie, stay, fetch. Reward them for obedience and cleverness with a dog biscuit or, in the case of catty words, with a sardine." He cautions us not to be frightened by words lest they learn to ig-nore our commands. "But," he adds, "if they respect you, they will like you, and if they like you, there is nothing in their power that they will not do for you. For a few rare people they not only roll over and play dead, but walk on their hind legs."

The epitome of this attitude came in a pair of Espy books: *An Almanac of Words at Play* (1975) and *Another Almanac of Words at Play* (1980). Each book contained 366 entries, one for each day of the year (including an extra day for leap year), and they created something of a sensation. The original *Almanac* sold more than 100,000 copies and worked its way onto the *New York Times* best-seller list. The critics loved it. The *New York Times* said, "If you harbor an affection for the magic of words, you cannot help delighting in the prestidigita-tions of Willard R. Espy, a man who pulls words out of the air the way a ma-gician plucks pigeons from his pocket. . . ." The *Atlanta Constitution* called it "a year-round valentine, a recurring Christmas present, an eternal birthday gift for all who fall under the charm of words deftly used."

By the time *Another Almanac* came out the endorsements were pouring in. "This new almanac is a treasure," said Leonard Bernstein, and Isaac Asimov added, "Espy's joy in letters, words and language is absolutely contagious."

These books created a new climate for words, and soon more and more peo-ple came to see words the way Espy did . . . as units of play. The many suc-cessful books of wordplay that have followed since, coming from many talented writers, owe part of their success to the public's love affair with words that Espy helped kindle with these two books.

This new book, *The Best of an Almanac of Words at Play*, brings together the best and most memorable entries from both *An Almanac of Words at Play* and *Another Almanac of Words at Play*. It is intended to introduce a new gen-eration of word lovers, gamesters, and devotees of light verse to what Espy him-self, in the introduction to the original *Almanac*, called "the verbal vagaries."

* * *

Willard Espy passed away in February 1999, at the age of 88, just as this new anthology of almanac entries was being prepared for publication. I had first had the pleasure of meeting Willard Espy in 1986 at, appropriately, a Wonderful World of Words weekend at the Mohonk Mountain House at Lake Mohonk, N.Y. We became reacquainted about a month before his death, in his Manhattan apartment, and, despite the fact that he was terribly ill and his eyesight was failing, he was the same Willard Espy I had met years earlier—elegant, witty and still possessed of that unmistakable voice that always seemed perched on the edge of laughter. He was most pleased about this new work, and before he passed away, Louise sent a note saying that Willard Espy approved of its title.

If you're still not sure what "verbal vagaries" are, read on. This book is filled with them, and you'll soon get the idea. My only suggestion is that you keep in mind something that Willard Espy said in his introduction to the first *Almanac*—that words should not be taken too seriously. "Treat words," he said, "the way such wise men as Lewis Carroll, W. S. Gilbert, Ogden Nash, and Cole Porter treated them: as a gorgeous joke."

Paul Dickson

# DEFINITION OF TERMS

**ABC language.** A substitution of like-sounding letters, digits, or symbols for words or parts of words. AB C D goldfish.

**Acronym.** A word formed from the initial letters of a name, as NATO from North Atlantic Treaty Organization; or by combining parts of a series of words: *radar* for *ra*dio *de*tecting *a*nd *r*anging, for instance.

**Acrostic.** A composition, often in verse, in which one or more sets of letters, as the initial or final letters of the lines, taken in order, form a word or words.

**Anagram.** A word or phrase formed by reordering the letters of another word or phrase: *opts, pots, tops, spot, post.*

**Anguish languish.** Words so arranged so as to evoke overtones of other words: *Ladle Rot Rotten Hut* for *Little Red Riding Hood.*

**Bout rimé.** A couplet in which an inappropriate rhyming line is added to a famous first line. Called in English "rhymed endings" or, by Richard Armour, "punctured poems."

**Chain verse.** One in which the last words, word, or sound of each line is the first of the following line: "Alas, alas / A lass I knew / Knew an ass / Ask not who."

**Charade.** A kind of riddle, in which each syllable of the word to be guessed, and sometimes the word itself, are enigmatically described.

**Clerihew.** A humorous four-lined unscanned verse dealing with some unknown person. Named after its inventor, Edmund Clerihew Bentley.

**Echoing verse.** One in which the refrain of each stanza echoes the end of the preceding line.

**Équivoque.** A passage which, according to the way it is read, can have two or more meanings. If the second meaning is risqué, an équivoque is also a double entendre.

**Lapsus comicus.** A risible slip of the tongue.

**Lipogram.** A composition lacking a certain letter or letters. The 50,000 word novel *Gadsby,* by E. V. Wright, has no *e.*

**Macaronic.** A passage, generally a verse, mingling two or more languages.

**Palindrome.** A word, phrase, verse, or sentence that reads the same forward or backward: *a man, a plan, a canal, Panama.*

**Pangram.** A verse, sentence, phrase, or the like, containing all the letters of the alphabet. Pangrammatists are still trying unsuccessfully to use each letter only once and make sense.

**Pig latin.** A jargon in imitation of Latin, as *og-day atin-lay* for Dog Latin.

**Rebus.** A riddle composed of words or syllables depicted by symbols or pictures that suggest the sound of the words or syllables they represent.

**Rhopalic.** A snowballing line or passage in which each successive word has one more syllable (or word) than the last.

**Spoonerism.** An unintentional transposition of sounds, often the opening sounds, of words: a *bl*ushing *cr*ow, say, for a *cr*ushing *bl*ow.

**Stinky pinky.** A noun modified by a rhyming adjective, as lazy Maisie.

**Univocalic.** A writing containing only one vowel: "Persevere, ye perfect men; ever keep the precepts ten."

# JANUARY

## 1 JANUARY

### Jangled Janet

The following old rhyming calendar should get you through this year, but apparently not through next:

#### JANET WAS QUITE ILL ONE DAY

JANet was quite ill one day.
FEBrile troubles came her way.
MARtyr-like, she lay in bed;
APRoned nurses softly sped.
MAYbe, said the leech judicial,
JUNket would be beneficial.
JULeps, too, though freely tried,
AUGured ill, for Janet died.
SEPulchre was sadly made;
OCTaves pealed and prayers were said.
NOVices with many a tear
DECorated Janet's bier.
　　　　　　*—Author Unknown.*

The verse below is for anyone who may have awakened with a headache this New Year morning:

#### JANGLE BELLS

JANgle bells, jangle bells, jangle all the way!
FEBrifuge, aspirin, start this New Year's day.
MARk me down for a clown— I had the whole gang over;
APRicot brandy's what left me with this hangover.
MAYbe I erred to try whiskey laced with rum;
JUNiper potions were drunk *ad libitum.*
JULep's sinful when a skinful has a vodka chaser;
AUGht of saki leaves me rocky the ensuing day, sir.
SEPtic all alcohol is—the stuff of devils:
OCTopods, elephants, joined my New Year revels.
NOVelties from D.T.'s pall; I end my lay
DEClaiming I shall stay dry this whole New Year's day.
　　　　　　*—W.R.E.*

# 2 JANUARY

## *An ABC Proposal Comes to O*

My brother Edwin used to say I was so lazy I was bound to wind up as a minister. Ironically, it turned out to be Ed who devoted his life to religion, and Ed is one of the hardest-working men I know. But he was right; few people are lazier than I. When I approach a revolving door, I wait for someone to give the first push.

ABC is a lazy man's language. One digit or one letter of the alphabet can replace a whole word. Take this ABC love song:*

### A PROPOSAL

O FE dear, what XTC
I MN8 when U IC!
Once KT 1 me with her I's;
2 LN I O countless sighs.
'Twas MLE while over Cs.
Now all 3 R nonNTTs,
4 U XL them all U C
U suit me FE 2 a T.
　　　　　*—Louise J. Walker*

This ABC passage is elegant:

U O a O but I O U;
O O no O but O O me;
O let not my O a O go,
But give O O I O U so.
　　　　　*—William Whewell*

The sense begins to emerge when you reflect that an O may be just that; or oh; or owe; or a cipher; or a zero; or an aught; or a naught.

Having mastered Whewell, you will find the following octet as simple as, say, ABC.

Oy OO thO he O
2 On an OO. OO bO
An OO but he never thO
He'd O the OO dealer O
For the OO OO bO.
Say, has OO's OO brO
OO O that OO sO?
OO's OO's good for nO.
　　　　　*—W.R.E.*

---

* The original of this has disappeared from my files, and I fear my reconstruction may have some errors.

OIC

I'm in a 10der mood today
    & feel poetic, 2;
4 fun I'll just — off a line
    & send it off 2 U.

I'm sorry you've been 6 o long;
    Don't B disconsol8;
But bear your ills with 42de,
    & they won't seem so gr8.
            *—Anonymous*

# 3 JANUARY

## *One Week*

The year had gloomily begun
For Willie Weeks, a poor man's SUN.
He was beset with bill and dun
And he had very little MON.
"This cash," said he, "won't pay my dues,
I've nothing here but ones and TUES."
A bright thought struck him, and he said,
"The rich miss Goldrocks I will WED."
But when he paid his court to her,
She lisped, but firmly said, "No THUR!"
"Alas!" said he. "Then I must die!"
His soul went where they say souls FRI.
They found his gloves, and coat, and hat;
The Coroner upon them SAT.
            *—Carolyn Wells*

# 4 JANUARY

## *Sweet Hernia*

There is no flaw to be found in words save perhaps that they generally mean something. Walter de la Mare suggested that many essentially beautiful and evocative words have missed their vocation. *Linoleum*, for instance, might be a charming old Mediterranean seaport. Though a transposition of meanings is not as diverting as sheer meaninglessness, it will do for a starter. Familiar words shift identities here:

## SWEET HERNIA

Sweet Hernia on the heights of Plasticine
  Sings to the nylon songs of Brassière;
The very aspirins listen, as they lean
  Against the vitreous wind, to her sad air.
I see the bloom of mayonnaise she holds
  Colored like roof of far-away Shampoo
Its asthma sweetens Earth! Oh, it enfolds
  The alum land from Urine to Cachou!
One last wild gusset, then she's lost in night . . .
And dusk the dandruff dims, and anthracite.
                                        —*Edward Blishen*

# 5 JANUARY

### *A Man Beyond*
### *Sea-Duction*

(To fully appreciate the truth of the following verse, you must understand that I was reared in a tiny Washington state hamlet named, with good reason, Oysterville. When I tell you I find oyster beds uncohabitable I know whereof I speak.)

*I*
*Do not roister*
*With an oyster*
*I*
*Like my*
*Bed dry*
*An oyster*
*Moister*
*The wetter*
*The better*
*I*
*Find wet beds uncohabitable*
*Which is why*
*The moist*
*Oyst*
*And the dry*
*I*
*Are incompatible.*
                                        —*W.R.E.*

# 6 JANUARY

## *My S's Grow S's*

Some words ending in *s* change to quite unrelated words if another *s* is added:

"My s's grow s's, *alas!*" cried *a lass;*
"My *handles* turn *handless*, my *bras* turn to *brass.*
A girl who *cares* deeply is quick to *caress;*
She dreams of the *posses* whose love she'd *possess;*
An *as* with an s is an *ass*, and no less
When *asses* add s's, those *asses assess.*
Add s's to *mas* and they worship at *mass;*
Add s's to *pas*, and the pas make a *pass.*
—*W.R.E.*

The verse below, one of the most famous of puzzles, takes advantage of the s plus s oddity. The word involved is one of those I have cited.

A word there is of plural number
Foe to ease and tranquil slumber.
Any other word you take
And add an s will plural make;
But if you add an s to this
So strange the metamorphosis:
Plural is plural now no more
And sweet what bitter was before.
—*George Canning*

# 7 JANUARY

## *May Eagles Lacerate Eternally*

*Rhopalon* is Greek for a club which thickens from the handle to the head. A rhopalic verse is composed of lines in which each successive word has more syllables than the one before:

May eagles lacerate eternally
Your liver, overproud Prometheus!
Your fiery offering, predictably,
Has rendered humankind vainglorious.
—*W.R.E.*

Remove the limitations imposed by meter and rhyme, and rhopalics can swell to the size of the club that Theseus used to kill Procrustes. This example by Dmitri Borgmann adds letters instead of syllables:

I do not know where family doctors acquired illegibly perplexing handwriting; nevertheless, extraordinary pharmaceutical intellectuality, counterbalancing indecipherability, transcendentalizes intercommunications' incomprehensibleness.

# 8 JANUARY

### What's Yours, Fella?

This is hash-house vocabulary. The more terms you recognize, the more deplorable your eating habits.

1. Draw one!
2. Gimme a shimmy!
3. Side of French!
4. Mickey with a wreath!
5. Mike and Ike!
6. Chocker hole and murk!
7. Arizona!
8. Clean the kitchen, red lead!
9. One on the city!
10. A Coney Island!
11. Garibaldi!
12. BLT, hold the mayo!
13. Whistleberries and hounds, a pair!
14. Bossy in a bowl!
15. Stir two! Wheat!
16. Black and white!
17. Straight Kelly!
18. Eighty-one!
19. Novy on a B!
20. Adam and Eve on a raft!

—*Leonard R. N. Ashley*

# 9 JANUARY

### Suffix the Little Prefixes to Come unto Me (Comparatively Speaking)

Stop, Esther, stop! I quite concur:
Comparatives are suffixed *er*.
Comparative of *cow* is *cower;*
Comparative of *bough* is *bower.*

And I agree it's manifest
Superlatives are suffixed *est*.
*Digest* means "*dig* excessively,"
And *zest* is maximum of *z*.

Yet *er* can prefix, too, my doe;
Thus, *ergo* means "one up on *go;*"
And *ermine*'s easy to define:
"Another's fur that's more than *mine*."

As prefix, *est* retains its touch;
*Estate* comes out as "*ate* too much."
You, *Esther* dear, I long have prized
As "woman apotheosized."
—W.R.E.

# 10 JANUARY

## Marblehead and Athol

Detractors of Governor Chubb Peabody of Massachusetts said three cities in the state were named after him—Peabody, Marblehead, and Athol. Scarcely as brilliant a disparagement as this tirade by Henry IV against Sir John Falstaff:

> Why dost thou converse with that trunk of humours, that bolting-hutch of beastliness, that swoln parcel of dropsies, that huge bombard of sack, that stuffed cloakbag of guts, that roasted Manningtree ox with the pudding in his belly, that reverend vice, that gray iniquity, that father ruffian, that vanity in years?

Charles Lamb once joined in hissing a play he had written, to avoid being recognized as the author. Later he wrote to a friend:

> Mercy on us, that God should give his favourite children, men, mouths to speak with, discourse rationally, to promise smoothly, to flatter agreeably, to encourage warmly, to counsel wisely: to sing with, to drink with, and to kiss with: and that they should turn them into mouths of adders, bears, wolves, hyenas, and whistle like tempests, and emit breath through them like distillations of aspic poison, to asperse and vilify the innocent labour of their fellow creatures who are desirous to please them. God be pleased to make the breath stink and the teeth rot out of them all therefor!

Other insults:

### THE CURSE

*To a sister of an enemy of the author's
who disapproved of "The Playboy"*

Lord, confound this surly sister,
Blight her brow with blotch and blister,
Cramp her larynx, lung, and liver,
In her guts a galling give her.
Let her live to earn her dinners

In Mountjoy with seedy sinners:
Lord, this judgment quickly bring,
And I'm your servant,
—*J. M. Synge*

### ON JACOB TONSON, HIS PUBLISHER

With leering looks, bullfac'd, and freckled fair,
With two left legs, and Judas-colour'd hair,
With frowsy pores, that taint the ambient air.
—*John Dryden*

### TO SERGIUS

Thou'lt fight, if any man call Thebe whore:
That she is thine, what can proclaim it more?
—*Sir Charles Sedley*

### TO AN ACQUAINTANCE

Thou speakest always ill of me,
I always speak well of thee;
But, spite of all our noise and pother,
The world believes nor one, nor t'other.
—*Anonymous*

# 11 JANUARY

## *Clitch, Clitch, Clitch*

Complained England's Ernie Bevin of England's Aneuran Bevan: "All 'e ever says is clitch, clitch, clitch, clitch."

Cliché, which started life as a printer's term for a stereotype plate,* has come to mean "a phrase that has lost precise meaning by iteration." Yet communication in the absence of clichés is as inconceivable as breathing without air. If we had to freshen every utterance, most of us would be unable to communicate at all—with a few exceptions such as Bill here:

### AN ORIGINAL CUSS

A real original, I think,
My friend Bill can be termed;

---

* For that matter, see what happened to stereotype!

A smoker, not inveterate,
A drinker, not confirmed,
A hail fellow, but not well met,
A realtor, but no Babbitt;
I never knew a cuss like Bill
For cutting loose from habit.
—*Keith Preston*

I give you some run-of-the-mill (cliché!) clichés. If you can develop fresher expressions that make the point better, please send them to me.

Go the whole hog
A pretty kettle of fish
The acid test
Move heaven and earth
Beauty is only skin deep
There's the rub
His own worst enemy
A foregone conclusion
He sank like a stone
It is not all black or white
His heart was in his mouth
He drank like a fish
Root and branch
Lock, stock, and barrel
May the best man win
A tower of strength
Castles in the air
Hit the ceiling

And there are some clichés that nobody ever gets quite right. Peter Donchian, who composed the list below, says that to have even three of them right is something of an accomplishment, whereas to get them all you need to be a pedant.

1. Pride goeth before _____.
2. To _____ the lily.
3. A little _____ is a dangerous thing.
4. A penny for your _____.
5. Music hath charms to soothe a _____.
6. Imitation is the sincerest _____ flattery.
7. Ask me no questions, and I'll tell you no _____.
8. Give him an inch, he'll take _____.
9. Variety's the _____ of life.
10. _____ is the root of all evil.
11. Water, water, everywhere, _____ drop to drink.
12. I only regret that I have but _____ for my country.

# 12 JANUARY

## First Lines

If you read aloud the first sentence or two of any well-known book, saying "blank" for proper names, chances are that George Axelrod can identify the book. He has hit the jackpot sixteen times in a row. He stumped Edmund Wilson with this one: "First sentence, blank. Second sentence, 'No answer.' Third sentence, blank."

A variation is to identify the title of a book from its first sentence. See how many titles and first sentences you can match here.

1. If you want to find Cherry-tree Lane all you have to do is ask the Policeman at the crossroads.

   A. *The Great Gatsby,* Scott Fitzgerald

2. Nobody could sleep.

   B. *Swann's Way*, Marcel Proust

3. In the late summer of that year we lived in a house in a village that looked across the river and the plain to the mountains.

   C. *Darkness at Noon,* Arthur Koestler

4. Call me Ishmael.

   D. *Catch-22*, Joseph Heller

5. Arms and the man I sing.

   E. *The Good Earth,* Pearl Buck

6. You don't know about me without you have read a book by the name of *The Adventures of Tom Sawyer*, but that ain't no matter.

   F. *The Stranger*, Albert Camus

7. Call me Jonah.

   G. *1984*, George Orwell

8. The cell door slammed behind Rubashov.

   H. *The Metamorphosis,* Franz Kafka

9. My father's family name being Pirip, and my Christian name Philip, my infant tongue could make of both names nothing longer or more explicit than Pip.

   I. *Moby Dick*, Herman Melville

10. As Gregor Samska awoke one morning from uneasy dreams he found himself transformed in his bed into a gigantic insect.

    J. *The Naked and the Dead*, Norman Mailer

11. It was love at first sight.

    K. *A Tale of Two Cities*, Charles Dickens

12. For a long time I used to go to bed early.

    L. *Mary Poppins*, P. L. Travers

13. Mother died today.

14. It was Lung's marriage day.

15. In my younger and more vulnerable days my father gave me some advice that I've been turning over in my mind ever since.

16. It was the best of times; it was the worst of times.

17. I will begin the story of my adventures with a certain morning early in the month of June, the year of grace 1751, when I took the key for the last time out of the door of my father's house.

18. Happy families are all alike; every unhappy family is unhappy in its own way.

19. When the present century was in its teens, and on one sunshiny morning in June, there drove up to the great iron gate of Miss Pinkerton's academy for young ladies, on Chiswick Mall, a large family coach, with two fat horses in blazing harness, driven by a fat coachman in a three-cornered hat and wig, at the rate of four miles an hour.

20. "Take my camel, dear," said my Aunt Dot, as she climbed down from the animal on her return from High Mass.

21. It was a bright cold day in April, and the clocks were striking thirteen.

M. *Farewell to Arms*, Ernest Hemingway

N. *Cat's Cradle*, Kurt Vonnegut

O. *The Aeneid*, Virgil

P. *Huckleberry Finn*, Mark Twain

Q. *Vanity Fair*, William Makepeace Thackeray

R. *Towers of Trebizond*, Rose Macaulay

S. *Great Expectations*, Charles Dickens

T. *Kidnapped*, Robert Louis Stevenson

U. *Anna Karenina*, Count Leo Tolstoy

# 13 JANUARY

## Rubber Baby Buggy Bumpers

I murmured to myself:

> "If I fell on a felon feloniously,
> Who's the felon—the felon I fell on, or me?"

In the first flush this seemed a passable tongue twister, but of course it is not—it's too easy to say. By contrast, try to say rapidly, "The sixth sick sheik's sixth sheep's sick."

If your memory goes back as far as Prohibition, this snatch from a tongue-twisting verse by Newman Levy may strike a nostalgic chord:

> If you stick a stock of liquor in your locker,
>   It is slick to stick a lock upon your stock,
> Or some joker who is slicker's going to trick you of your liquor . . .
>   If you fail to lock your liquor with a lock.

Martin Gardner's collection of tongue twisters includes "rubber baby buggy bumpers," "bug's bad blood," and "the sinking steamer sunk." He adds: "Also well known is the skunk that sat on a stump; the skunk thunk the stump stunk, but the stump thunk the skunk stunk. Some are on the blue side, such as the curious cream-colored cat that crept into the crypt, crapped, and crept out again. It is said that a famous radio actor once refused a detective role when he learned that one of his lines would be 'Show me the chair Schmidt sat in when he was shot.' 'Whip gig, whip gig, whip gig' and 'troy boat, troy boat, troy boat' are both exceedingly difficult to repeat many times. An amusing children's catch is to challenge someone to recite 'Betty Boop, Betty Boop, Betty Boop' rapidly. After about the fifth 'Betty Boop,' wave your hat and shout, 'Heigh ho, Silver!' "

# 14 JANUARY

## *One Man's Abdomen*

My mother initiated a boy into certain nuances of the English language. Years later, a man grown, he returned to town and thanked her. "For one thing, Mrs. Espy," he said, "you made me realize how important pronouncination is."*

Pronouncination is important indeed to WQXR, the radio station of *The New York Times*. If you apply for an announcing job there, be prepared to read this passage aloud, and correctly:

> The old man with the flaccid face and dour expression grimaced when asked if he were conversant with zoology, mineralogy, or the culinary arts. "Not to be secretive," he said, "I may tell you that I'd given precedence to the study of genealogy. But, since my father's demise, it has been my vagary to remain incognito because of an inexplicable, lamentable, and irreparable family schism. It resulted from a heinous crime, committed at our domicile by an impious scoundrel. To err is human . . . but this affair was so grievous that only my inherent acumen and consummate tact saved me."

---

*Which reminds me that I read long ago (where? in *St. Nicholas? The Youth's Companion? The Saturday Evening Post?*) this couplet:
> *The boy who calls a creek a crick*
> *Was sick for three whole days last wick.*

WQXR's pronunciation of the disputable words (and how do you pronounce "disputable," WQXR?):

| | | | |
|---|---|---|---|
| flaccid | FLACK-sid | inexplicable | in-EX-plic-able |
| dour | DOO-er | lamentable | LAM-entable |
| grimaced | gri-MACED | irreparable | ear-REP-arable |
| conversant | KON-ver-sant | schism | SIZ-m |
| zoology | zoh-OL-o-ji | heinous | HAY-nus |
| mineralogy | miner-AL-o-ji | domicile | DOMM-i-sil |
| culinary | KEW-li-ner-y | impious | IM-pee-yus |
| secretive | see-KREE-tiv | err | ur |
| precedence | pre-SEED-ens | grievous | GREEV-us |
| genealogy | jan-e-AL-o-ji | inherent | in-HERE-ent |
| demise | de-MIZE | acumen | a-KEW-men |
| vagary | va-GAIR-y | consummate (adj.) | kon-SUMM-it |
| incognito | in-KOG-ni-toe | | |

If you made only four or five mistakes you may (or may not) be hired. But wait a minute: Even if you pronounced all the words wrong, you may be just as right as WQXR is.

Forget the myth that the pronunciation a dictionary lists first is any more acceptable than those it lists second and third. They are all correct.

Webster's unabridged dictionary, the second edition, says it is all right to pronounce dour DOW-er, culinary CULL-i-neri, precedence PRESS-e-dens or PREE-se-dens, genealogy jen-e-AL-o-ji or jee-ne-AL-o-ji. (Jan-e-AL-o-ji, the WQXR choice, is not given. A misprint, perhaps?) Webster's recognizes in-cog-NEE-toe, and puts va-GARR-i before va-GAIR-i. The American Heritage Dictionary likewise accepts DOW-er, CULL-i-ner-i and PRESS-e-dens. It accepts either jee-ne-AL-o-ji or jen-e-AL-o-ji, and blesses the pronunciation of the AL as ALL.

It approves of pronouncing grimace GRIM-is, conversant con-VER-sant, inexplicable in-ex-PLIK-able, lamentable la-MEN-table, schism SKIZ-m, mineralogy min-er-ALL-ogy, secretive SEE-kre-tiv, domicile dom-i-SILE or dome-i-SILE, vagary VAY-gar-y. (Va-GAIR-i, bet on by WQXR [and me] does not win, place, or show.)

So not to worry when you don't sound like WQXR. One man's AB-do-men is another man's ab-DOUGH-men.*

# 15 JANUARY

## Interminable Words

When Henry Carey wrote:

> Aldiborontiphoscophornio!
> Where left you Chrononhotonthologos?

---

* How often have you caught others, or been caught yourself, on the pronunciation of polopony?

he was paying tribute to the perennial, silly fascination of long words. Such words arrive occasionally at my desk, and I have to pay for the extra postage. Louis Phillips sent me *antielectrophotomicrographically*, a thirty-two-letter giant; Eric J. Bowen sent *pneumonoultramicroscopicsilicovolcanoconiosis*, which has forty-five letters. This list is from *Word Ways*:

| | |
|---|---|
| 27 | honorificabilitudinitatibus |
| 28 | antidisestablishmentarianism |
| 29 | trinitrophenylmethylnitramine |
| 30 | encephalomyeloraddiculoneuritis |
| 31 | dichlorodiphenyltrichloroethane |
| 32 | hepatocholangiocystoduodenostomy |
| 33 | tetradecamethylcycloheptasiloxane |
| 34 | supercalifragilisticexpialidocious |
| 35 | azaazoniapentacyclotricosaundecaene |
| 36 | dihydroxyphenylethanolisopropylamine |
| 37 | praetertranssubstantiationalistically |
| 38 | dioxinodioxinobenzopyranobenzopyrylium |
| 39 | hepaticocholangiocholecystenterostomies |
| 40 | dinitrotetramethyldiaminodiphenylmethane |
| 41 | tetradecahydrotetrazoloazacyclohexadecine |
| 42 | dibenzenotetrabenzotetraarsacyclohexadecin |
| 43 | spironaphthotriazoleoxaazabicyclononatriene |
| 44 | dithiatetraazapentacyclotricontatetradecaene |
| 45 | pneumonoultramicroscopicsilicovolcanoconiosis |
| 46 | bistetramethylenetetrahydrofurodihydropyrazine |
| 47 | dispirocyclopentaphenanthrenedioxolanedioxolane |
| 48 | lewdningbluebolteredallucktruckalltraumconductor |
| 49 | trepignemanpenillorifrizonoufresterfumbledtumbled |
| 50 | spirodioxabicyclononaneepoxycyclopentaphenanthrene |
| 51 | osseocarnisanguineoviscericartilaginonervomedullary |
| 52 | spirofuraniminomethanocyclopentapyrrolotrithiazepine |

—*Rudolf Ondrejka*

Hunter M. Leach is the latest to remind me of the Welsh place name Llanfairpwllgwyngyllgogerychwyrndrobwllllantysiliogogoch, fifty-eight letters. Comedian Red Skelton is credited with discovering the longest word of all—the one that follows "And now a word from our sponsors."

# 16 JANUARY

## *Knock Up*

"The use of this term by Englishmen in America is fraught with danger," says Norman W. Schur, "like the use of fanny by Americans in England. A respectable American will take great pains to avoid knocking up a lady friend, as he understands the term, because in his country it is an indelicate expression for getting a lady into a delicate condition. In England [it] is a far less serious matter. All it means there is to *wake* people *up*."

But not quite all. He adds that *knock-up* in England also may be the equivalent of American *warm-up* (in sports), and of throw together, as in "Come along to lunch, we can always *knock* something *up* in a hurry."

He does not, however, mention *knocked-up* as a synonym for exhausted, common in nineteenth-century England and, I believe, still extant. Says Jane Austen in *Mansfield Park:* "This will be a bad day's amusement for you, if you are to be knocked up" . . . "And but for Mr. Crawford and the beauty of the weather, [she] would have been knocked up now" . . . "The first division of their journey occupied a long day, and brought them, almost knocked up, to Oxford."

*Knock up* can also mean to accumulate. *The Listener* tells of people going reluctantly into the world "to knock up a bank balance."

# 17 JANUARY

## *Malo, Malo, Malo, Malo*

It is a marvel that four identical Latin words can be plausibly translated into a complete and complicated English sentence, yet *Malo malo malo malo* means, believe it or not,

> I would rather be
> in an apple tree
> than a bad man
> in adversity.

The first *malo* is "I prefer"; the second is "apple tree"; the third is "bad man"; and the fourth is "hard times." Case endings presumably supply "in," "than," and "in." But I suspect Lester E. Rothstein is right when he says in *Enigma*: "Even with the addition of prepositions plus the word *quam*, 'than,' the phrase is so ambiguous that it would have been Greek to any classical Roman."

# 18 JANUARY

## *Enter: Sir Benjamin Backbite*

To "mull," in English dialect, is to muddle or fumble. The Berry Brothers, still notable London wine merchants, in the eighteenth century sent the dramatist

Richard Brinsley Sheridan—too promptly to please him—a "mulled up" bill. He wrote back:

> You have sent me your Bilberry,
> Before it is Dewberry.
> This is nothing but a Mulberry,
> And I am coming round to kick your Rasberry
> Until it is Blackberry
> And Blueberry.

In Sheridan's dramas he employed surnames to let the audience know whether it was expected to cheer, boo, or ridicule his characters. *The School for Scandal* featured such as Sir Peter Teazle, Sir Oliver Surface, Sir Harry Bumper, Sir Benjamin Backbite, and Lady Sneerwell, not to mention Careless, Snake, and Crabtree. Congreve's *The Way of the World*, in the same spirit, starred Fainall, Witwould, and Petulant. The manservant was Waitwell; the woman servant, Foible. John Gay populated *The Beggar's Opera* with such as Peachum, Lockit, Filch, Jimmy Twitcher, Crooked-fingered Jack, Mrs. Coaxer, Mrs. Vixen, Betty Doxy, Jenny Diver, and Suky Tawdry.

The verses below refer to characters from three Restoration plays:

> *The Beaux' Stratagem (Farquhar, 1707)*
>
> Sullen's a sorehead, and Scrub does the hall;
>     Aimwell and Archer throw darts at the wall;
> Gibbet's a highwayman; Bagshot's the same;
>     Cherry's been plucked, and requires a new name.

> *Love for Love (Congreve, 1695)*
>
> Pray tell me, Foresight (gullible old male!) if
>     Tattle still would wed his Mrs. Frail if
> Her fondness for the other sex were tattled
>     By Scandal, who beneath the rose has prattled
> That Valentine will have to go to jail if
>     Sir Sampson Legend won't pay Snap the bailiff?
> (Foresight does not reply; the old man's rattled.)

> *The Provok'd Wife (Vanbrugh, 1697)*
>
> Who's that man in a woman's suit?
>     Sir John Brute!
> What is Heartfree thinking of?
>     Falling in Love!
> Constant's constant; yet he thrives
>     Wooing wives.
> *Treble is singing and Rasor is shaving;*
> *Bully and Rake are the ones misbehaving.*
>                                       —W.R.E.

# 19 January

### It All Deep Ends

English contains homonyms by the thousands—caul and call, hail and hale, pear and pair, and the like. Many words have inner homonyms as well. They sound like a series of shorter words strung together, the parts having no relationship in meaning to the whole. Words-within-words may make an eerie kind of sense:

| | |
|---|---|
| Come, passion | Loan sum |
| Purr, puss | Shall owe |
| No bull | King dumb, seek king, kick king, |
| Gas so lean | croak king |
| Die a tribe | Promise sorry |
| Deep lore | Pole light |
| Grew some | Whore id |
| Fall turd | Vow well |
| Judge meant | Tack tile |
| Free dumb | Sexed aunt |
| Junk shun, miss shun, | Suck core |
| sex shun | Thor axe |

Break up your syllables as suits you best. *Fertilize* translates as *fur till eyes*, *fur till lies*, or *fertile eyes* (only the last of the three is worth keeping); *depart* becomes either *deep art* or *deep part*, and so on.

You might enjoy seeing how many words you can find that change in sound and sense if you separate them into two or more parts: *warbled* into *war bled*, *areas* into *are as*, etc.

You may find ten, or a hundred, or a thousand. It all deep ends.

# 20 January

### A Squirming of Snakes

My brother Edwin, running barefoot across newly mown hay, found himself surrounded by a squirming of snakes—scores of the things, long and black and thick, with narrow yellow or red stripes running down their backs. They were harmless enough in all conscience, but nightmarish to a ten-year-old boy. He was too terrified even to call out, and several minutes passed before our father, riding the haymower, glanced over his shoulder and saw the boy frozen in place. Pop unhitched a horse, leaped astride, and galloped to the rescue, sweeping his son to safety with one arm.

One evening Ed encountered a stinking of skunks. He was pitching hay down from the mow under the barn roof, intending to distribute it among the cows enstanchioned below, when his fork thrust into live flesh. From the smell of him when he arrived home, a whole family of skunks must have been benighted in that hay mow.

"A squirming of snakes" and "a stinking of skunks" are improvised examples of the application of collective nouns to beasts.* Such collectives (called also venereal nouns, Venus having been goddess of the hunt) have found permanent niches in the English language. Though there can be either bees or flies, for instance, and herds of cattle, whales, or seal, there can be a kindle only of kittens, and a litter only of pups. Each of the following collectives is limited to a single family of animals:†

1. A shrewdness of _____
2. A rout of _____
3. A sounder of _____
4. A brood (or clutch) of _____
5. A cete of _____
6. A flock (or flight) of _____
7. A leap of _____
8. A nye of _____
9. A sloth of _____
10. A doylt of _____
11. A school (or shoal) of _____
12. A clowder of _____
13. A drove of _____
14. A down of _____
15. A troop of _____
16. A skulk of _____
17. A muster of _____
18. A gaggle of _____
19. A covey of _____
20. A pod of _____

# 21 JANUARY

## If He Doth Love Me

A curious rhetorical device is the équivoque, in which one radically changes the meaning of a passage by the shift of as little as a comma. Take this example:

> If he doth love me, then no more
> He dreams of others' kisses.
> If he doth love me, then no more
> He misses other misses.

Re-position the commas, and a darker view emerges:

> If he doth love me then no more,
> He dreams of others' kisses.
> If he doth love me then no more,
> He misses other misses.
>
> —W.R.E.

I saw this two-column headline in the sports section of *The New York Times*:

**JOHNSON, ON HIS RETURN,**
**SORRY FOR LEAVING GIANTS**

---

* See 9 September, 19 November. And be sure to read James Lipton's delightful *An Exaltation of Larks.*
† Except as noted in the answer section.

Then I spread the page, and discovered that the full headline took up three columns and read:

## RANDY JOHNSON, ON HIS RETURN, NOT SORRY FOR LEAVING GIANTS

The second of the two poems below says the opposite of the first, purely through changes in punctuation:*

### THE PESSIMIST
That deep red rose—I see its thorn.
I just ignore the scent that's borne.
To me it's nothing. I deplore
Those scratches that I got before.
I just complain about the pain.
A lot I think of beauty's gain!

### THE OPTIMIST
That deep red rose I see;
Its thorn I just ignore.
The scent that's borne to me—
It's nothing I deplore!

Those scratches that I got—
Before I just complain
About the pain a lot,
I think of beauty's gain.
—*Mary Youngquist*

The following verse might be termed a Freudian équivoque:

*MANICdepressant*
SOMETIMES I'M HAPPY
sometimes i'm sad,
SoMeTiMeS i'M HsAaPdPY.
—*Kim Dammers*

# 22 JANUARY

## *John Hancocks*

"When I was a child," recalls autograph collector Charles Hamilton, "there was a story in the local paper saying that some guy had repeatedly written to Rudyard Kipling and never got a reply—until he learned that Kipling got five dol-

---

* For an acrostic équivoque, see 27 February.

lars a word for his manuscripts, and he sent him a check for five dollars. Kipling sent back a one-word unsigned reply: 'Thanks.' Well, this appealed to me immensely. At the time, I was getting ten cents a week from my father for hauling out our furnace ashes, so I sent Kipling a dime, explaining its origin. He sent back a signature. And I was hooked."

Today Hamilton has the most valuable private collection of autographs there is, including these. See how many of the signatures you can identify.

1. Outspoken diplomat

10. Leading leaper

2. The Blue Angel

3. Mideast mastermind

12. Famous Minnesotan

11. Son of Don Brando

13. Thespian famed for his trans-world trip

4. The Sundance Kid

14. "Notorious" for his dimpled chin.

5. Nancy's "Special K"

15. An auld acquaintance

16. Cinderella, Italian style

6. Famous plumber

7. The père of a famous trio

17. Mime's the word

8. European statesman

9. Siamese potentate, once

18. Yankee Doodle Dandy

# 23 January

## *A Fishy Story*

Here is a fishy story.

There was once a brilliant sturgeon on the staff of the community health fishility. He was, in fact, one of its flounders. Wiser than Salmon, a fin fellow who would never shrimp from his responsibilities, he was successful and happy; he always whistled a happy tuna. One day, one of his patients, a mere whipper snapper, told the sturgeon that his medical theories were full of abalone, and started trouting around telling everybody that the sturgeon's treatments had made him more eel than he had been, and then actually conched him with a malpractice suit!

Well, the sturgeon was in a real pickerel. The board demanded his oyster. But the case smelt to high heaven, so the judge denied the plaintiff's clam. The board tried to hire the sturgeon back, but by then he had hit the bottlenose pretty hard, and the end of our shad tail is that the sturgeon wound up on Squid Roe. Buoy! Isn't that a fine kettle of you-know-what?

—*James Thom*

# 24 January

## *Ever See a Sand-Blind Titmouse?*

Many are sand-blind who never saw sand; the prefix corrupts the obsolete prefix *sam-*, meaning "half." The humble in "humble pie" was once *umble*, the umbles being the less attractive meats of a slain deer—heart, liver, and entrails. *Purlieu* derives not, as would seem reasonable, from French *lieu* (place), but from Old French *puraler* (to go through). Rosemary is used as if it meant the "rose of Mary," but its source is *ros marinus* (sea-dew). London's Rotten Row is a a distortion of *route du roi*. The spade in your bridge hand is no spade, but a sword; it comes from Spanish *espada*. The sire of bully is not bull, but Dutch *boel* (a lover):

> I kiss his dirty shoe, and from my heart-strings
> I love the lovely bully.
> —*Twelfth Night*

The titmouse, from *tit* meaning "small," and *mase*, a variety of bird, is no rodent, nor is it mammalian. Nitwits may lack wits but whether they have nits is an open question; this *nit* comes from a German dialect term meaning "not." The *cheese* in "big cheese" comes from the Hindi word *chiz*, meaning "thing."

All these are *hobson-jobsons*—foreign or forgotten expressions assimilated to familiar English words. For instance:

- *Cleopatra's needle* (brought to the Thames Embankment from Alexandria in 1878) was found in the capital of the Egyptian queen, but is otherwise unconnected with her; it was originally set up by Thothmes III 1500 years before she was born.
- *Ventriloquism* derives from the mistaken notion that the voice of the ventriloquist proceeds from his stomach.
- *Blindworms* can see, and they aren't worms; they are legless lizards.
- *Dutch clocks* were first of German, not Dutch manufacture.
- *India ink* originated in China.
- *Turkeys* are native not to Turkey but to North America.
- *Guinea pigs* are not pigs, but cavies from South America. (No, Virginia, *Guinea* is in Africa; *Guiana* is in South America.)

# 25 JANUARY

## *Be Friendly, Borgmann*

An English writer, juggling the letters of *Spiro Agnew*, discovered he had written *grow a penis*. *Dame Eleanor Davies*, a prophetess in the reign of Charles I, was anagrammed into *never so mad a ladie*, and *Queen Victoria's Jubilee* became *I require love in a subject*. Richard Edes Harrison turned singer *Beverly Sills* into *Silvery Bells*. Most of the collections in the two following sets, which came to my attention respectively in books by J. Newton Friend and Dmitri A. Borgmann, appear also in Howard W. Bergerson's *Palindromes and Anagrams*, and doubtless elsewhere. (The origins of most anagrams are lost in antiquity.) Anyhow, try your hand at transposing each word or expression below into some apposite letter arrangement (*angered*, for instance, into *enraged*).

1. Agitator
2. Constraint
3. Determination
4. French revolution
5. Misanthrope
6. Parliament
7. Train

1. The United States of America
2. The eyes
3. Is pity love?
4. Abandon hope all ye who enter here
5. A sentence of death
6. A shoplifter
7. Circumstantial evidence
8. Spring, summer, autumn, winter
9. The countryside
10. Anagrams
11. Lawyers
12. Punishment
13. Compassionateness
14. Conversation
15. Desperation
16. Endearments
17. Negation
18. Panties

—*Dmitri A. Borgmann*

# 26 January

## The Astonishment of Words

I have a tin ear for languages; I read the subtitles of foreign films.

But even with my kitchen-French and pig-German, I was able to get gloriously drunk on Victor Proetz's book of familiar English poems side by side with translations in French and German.

"How do you say 'Yankee Doodle' in French," wondered Mr. Proetz, "in case you can? Does 'The snail's on the thorn' get to be about an escargot? How do they say 'Houyhnhnm' and 'Cheshire Cat' and things like that in German? How can you keep a phrase like 'La Belle Dame sans Merci' in a French translation of the poem from being lost in the surrounding French? And how, in God's name, can you possibly say 'There she blows.' "*

Mr. Proetz went to and fro in the earth collecting translations, and mewed them into *The Astonishment of Words*, which he did not live to see in print. But he did discover something joyous:

"The complete success of some of these translations is incredible. They have weathered all the agony of change and have come through it in full bloom. A few, a very few . . . have actually improved on their way through hell."

Some examples:

### FROM "JABBERWOCKY"

English:
    One, two! One, two! And through and through
      The vorpal blade went snicker-snack!
    He left it dead, and with its head
      He went galumphing back.
                    —*Lewis Carroll*

French:
    Un, deux, un, deux, par le milieu,
      Le glaive vorpal fait pat-à-pan!
    La bête défaite, avec sa tête
      Il rentre gallomphant.
              —*Translated by Frank L. Warrin, Jr.*

German:
    Eins, Zwei! Eins, Zwei! Und durch und durch
      Seins vorpals Schwert zershnifersnück.
    Da blieb es todt! Er, Kopf in Hand,
      Gelaumfig zog zurück!
              —*Translated by Dr. Robert Scott*

---

* One dubious French solution: "Elle siffle!"

### FROM "TO A MOUSE"

English:

Wee, sleekit, cowrin, tim'rous beastie,
  O, what a panic's in they breastie!
Thou need na start awa sae hasty
  Wi' bickering brattle!
I wad be laith to rin an' chase thee,
  Wi' murdering pattle!
            —*Robert Burns*

French:

Petite bête lisse, farouche et craintive
  Oh, quelle panique dans ton sein!
Tu n'as pas besoin de te sauver si vite
  Et d'un pas si précipité!
Je me répugnerais de courir après toi
  Avec le cuvoir meurtrier!
        —*Translated by Leon de Wailly*

German:

Klein, furchtsam Tierchen, welch ein Schrecken
  Erfüllt dein Brütschen, so durch Hecken
Und Furchen dich zum Lauf zu strecken?
  Bleib! Nicht so jach!
Nicht setz ich mit dem Pflügerstecken
  Grausam dir nach!
        —*Translated by Ferdinand Freiligrath*

### FROM "THE TIGER"

English:

Tiger, tiger, burning bright
In the forests of the night,
What immortal hand or eye
Could frame thy fearful symmetry?
        —*William Blake*

French:

Tigre, tigre, brûlant éclair
Dans les forêts de la nuit,
Quel oeil, quelle main immortelle
A pu ordonner ta terrifiante symétrie?
      —*Translated by M. L. and Philippe Soupault*

German:

Tiger, Tiger, lohendes Licht,
Das durch die Nacht der Wälder bricht,

Welches Auge, welche unsterbliche Hand
Hat dich furchtbar in dein Ebenmass gebannt?
—*Translated by Mela Hartwig*

# 27 JANUARY

## *V. B. Nimble, V. B. Quick*

*Science, Pure and Applied by V. B. Wigglesworth, F.R.S.,
Quick Professor of Biology in the University of Cambridge.
—A talk listed in the B.B.C. Radio Times*

V. B. Wigglesworth wakes at noon,
Washes, shaves, and very soon
Is at the lab; he reads his mail,
Tweaks a tadpole by the tail,
Undoes his coat, removes his hat,
Dips a spider in a vat
Of alkaline, phones the press,
Tells them he is F.R.S.,
Subdivides six protocells,
Kills a rat by ringing bells,
Writes a treatise, edits two
Symposia on "Will Man Do?",
Gives a lecture, audits three,
Has the Sperm Club in for tea,
Pensions off an aging spore,
Cracks a test tube, takes some pure
Science and applies it, finds
His hat, adjusts it, pulls the blinds,
Instructs the jellyfish to spawn,
And, by one o'clock, is gone.
—*John Updike*

# 28 JANUARY

## *How Do You Say Bicister, Micister?*

The second Earl of Leicester sat silent in the House of Lords for sixty-seven years; the third, for thirty-two; the fourth, for twenty-three. The fifth and present earl, Thomas William Edward Coke, held his silence for twenty-two years and then made his maiden speech, as follows: "I hope we shall use safer chemicals in place of those which have devastated the countryside."

Gabby Tommy, his family calls him.

It is an astonishment to an American that any Englishman dares open his mouth at all. The proper names alone should be sufficient to tongue-tie him. Lord Drogheda, head of the *Financial Times*, is called *Droyda;* Beauchamp Street is *Beetcham;* the Marquess of Cholmondeley is *Chumbley;* Magdalen College is *Maudlen;* and St. John is *Sin-jon.* Herbert Mayes tells me Alnwick is pronounced *Anick,* Hargham *Haarfan,* Terfilian *Treveelan,* and Zwill, most unaccountably, *Yool.*

Darryl Francis reports these English and Scottish pronunciations:

| THE ENGLISH PLACE NAME | THE ENGLISH PRONUNCIATION |
|---|---|
| Abergavenny | aber-genny |
| Leominster | lem-ster |
| Cirencester | sis-e-ter |
| Churchtown | chow-zen |
| Uttoxeter | uck-ster |
| Godmanchester | gum-sister or gon-shister |
| Wymondham | win-dum |
| Jervaulx | jar-vis |
| Amotherby | amer-by |
| Pontefract | pom-fret |
| Lympne | lim |
| Mousehole | moo-zel |
| Ulgham | uff-am |
| Ulverston | oo-ston |

| THE SCOTTISH PLACE NAME | THE SCOTTISH PRONUNCIATION |
|---|---|
| Kircudbright | ker-koo-bree |
| Balquhidder | bal-widder |
| Dalziel | dee-ell |
| Borrowstounness | bo-nes |

# 29 JANUARY

## *Vile Vodka*

This quatrain will show you how countdown verses work:*

> Who of vodka distilled from potoooooooo† partake,
>   Heed this warning;
> You'll be jolly at night, but ooooooooooo when you wake
>   In the morning.

---

\* See also 3 August.
† There was once an English racehorse named Potooooooooo.

The first line is easy to decipher: eight o's are lined up there, so clearly the word you are after is, by sound, *potatoes*. But what about those eleven o's in the second line? Well, eleven is a greater number than eight, is it not? So:

Who of vodka distilled from potatoes partake,
    Heed this warning:
You'll be jolly at night, but morose when you wake
    In the morning.

—*W.R.E.*

This is a cross between a countdown verse and an ABC verse:

### FAREWELL, A LONG FAREWELL TO ALL MY PROTESTANT ETHIC

Day-day mis-tune-tune-tune-tune John ignores, 2 8
Morrow-morrow joys, which he CCCC as great;
Get-get-get-get that if his TTTT were a curse,
His TTTTTTT and TTTTTTTT must be worse.
The future he tell-tell-tell-tell sounds fine; but he
Go-go-go-go it-it-it-it sake present XTC—
Bid-bid-bid-bid himself all actions apt to please.

*My* rule is this: Time's lock-lock-lock-lock meant CC.
What's here UUUU I mean UU; I reach
4 surf that phosSSSS on the beach
No less than sweet AAAA and aging-aging-aging-aging;
All are YYYY men's use EE life's stings.
John's sight-sight-sight-sight not 4 me; I give my praise
Pleasure-pleasure not morrow-morrow but day-day.

—*W.R.E.*

### MITIGATION

So der der der der der der der der der der the night,
So der der der der der der der der der der the voice of the dove,
Who can blame the young wight
If he der der der der der der der der der der his lady his love?

—*W.R.E.*

# 30 JANUARY

### *Say, Who Will Write a Pun My Stone?*

Not all mourners are prevented by grief from punning on the name of the dear departed. A headstone for John Rose and family, for instance, bears the legend "This Grave's a Bed of Roses." Other punning epitaphs:

## ON ARCHBISHOP POTTER

Alack, alack and well-a-day;
Potter himself is turned to clay.

## ON JOHN CAMDEN HOTTEN*

Hotten
Rotten
Forgotten
—*George Augustus Sala*

## ON EMMA AND MARIA LITTLEBOY

Two littleboys lie here.
Yet strange to say
The littleboys
Are girls.

## ON A MUSIC TEACHER

Stephen and time
Are now both even:
Stephen beat time
Now time's beat Stephen.

## ON MRS. NOTT

Nott born. Nott dead.
Nott christened.
Nott begot.
Lo here she lies
Who was
and who was Nott.

# 31 JANUARY
## *Wede and F.P.A.*

Let me tell you why the following verses are signed "Wede."

At the age of four I fell in love with a twelve-year-old boy named Aquila. We were inseparable. Wherever Aquila went, I followed: through the hayfields, the stands of huckleberry, the alder trees, the gorse; through the marshes; along the ocean surf; out onto the sand flats of the bay.

The locals first called us Aquila-and-Willard, liking the echo; and when they learned that Aquila's nickname was Quede, they said Quede-and-Wede. I don't know why Aquila was nicknamed Quede, though.

---

*An English book publisher termed a "pirate" by Mark Twain.

When I was one-and-twenty, no use to talk to me, and bound to be a poet, I signed my verses "Wede."

In those days, an aspiring poet's dearest dream was to be published in F.P.A.'s legendary newspaper column, "The Conning Tower." For two years I sent F.P.A. an incessant sighing stream of verses on blighted love and the inevitability of the grave—topics which I continue to treat, albeit more gingerly, to this day. I light a candle to F.P.A. each January 31 because January 31, 1934, was the day he first printed one of my verses. He used five in all, and I clipped and filed them with trembling hands. Here are two of them.

Make a fellow feel old, don't they?

*From the New York Herald Tribune*

### COQUETTE

Out of gladness first I sung
Into Beauty's ears;
Beauty fled my tinkling tongue,
Weeping silver tears.

Later sang I out of love,
Sang that one was fair,
Conjured Beauty to approve;
Beauty was not there.

Sang I then on bated breath
Music overcast
With a sorrow sweet as death;
Beauty heard, and passed.

When I hushed my bootless tongue,
Finding peace more meet,
Beauty, wench-like, smiled; and flung
Daisies at my feet.

—WEDE
*17 April 1934*

### "I WOULD TO GOD THAT I MIGHT FIND A PHRASE"

I would to God that I might find a phrase
Telling the slow decay of life alone;
How loss of her has damned my flesh and bone
To walk with ghosts, and endlessly reblaze
The dimming landmarks of our dozen days.
Could I have changed the end if I had known,
Leaving a wish unspoke, or path ungone,
That foredecreed the sundrance of our ways?

Some be indeed who profit from each jot
Superimposed today on yesterday,
Setting their course by period and blot
Until the page is filled, or put away;
I can but stand bemused, staring across
The irrevocability of loss.

—*WEDE*
*29 October 1934*

# FEBRUARY

## 1 FEBRUARY

### What a Friend We Have in Cheeses

*"Poets have been mysteriously silent on the subject of cheeses."*
*—G. K. Chesterton*

What a friend we have in cheeses!
For no food more subtly pleases,
Nor plays so grand a gastronomic part;
Cheese imported—not domestic—
For we all get indigestic
From the pasteurizer's Kraft and sodden art.

No poem we shall ever see is
Quite as lovely as a Brie is,
For "the queen of cheese" is what they call the Brie;
If you pay sufficient money
You will get one nice and runny,
And you'll understand what foods these morsels be!

How we covet all the skills it
Takes in making Chèvre or Tilset,
But if getting basic Pot Cheese is your aim,
Take some simple kurds and wheys, a
Bit of rennet—Lo! you've Käese!
(Which is what, in German, is a cheese's name.)

Good lasagna, it's a-gotta
Mozzarella and Ricotta
And a lotta freshly grated Parmesan;
With the latter *any* pasta
Will be eaten up much faster,
For with Parmesan you'll find a charm is on.

Ask Ignacio Silone
What he thinks of Provolone,
And the very word will set his eyes aflame;
Then go ask the bounteous Gina
Her reaction to Fontina—
If you raise your eyes, you'll see she feels the same!

A Pont-l'Évèque *au point!* What ho!
How our juices all will flow!
But don't touch a Pont-l'Évèque beyond that stage,
For what you'll have, you'll surely find
Is just an overfragrant rind—
There's no benefit to this *fromage* from age.

Claret, dear, not Coca Cola,
When you're having Gorgonzola—
Be particular to serve the proper wines;
Likewise pick a Beaune not Coke for
Pointing up a Bleu or Roquefort—
Bless the products of the bovines and the vines!

Ave Gouda! Ave Boursault!
Ave Oka even more so!
Ave Neufchatel, *Saluto* Port Salut!
And another thing with cheeses—
Every allied prospect pleases—
Ah timbale! Ah Welsh Rabbit! Ah fondue!

And we all know that "Say cheese" is
How a cameraman unfreezes
A subject in a stiff, or shy, or dour way;
There's no other food so useful,
So bring on a whole cabooseful
Of the stuff of life! The cheeses of the gourmet!
—*William Cole*

# 2 FEBRUARY

## *"I'm Dying," He Croaked*

Croakers, invented and named by Roy Bongartz with the help of his wife and selected friends, are Tom Swifties in which a verb rather than an adverb supplies the pun. Some Croakers supplied by Mr. Bongartz to the *Saturday Review:*

"We've taken over the government," the general cooed.
"My experiment was a success," the chemist retorted.
"You can't really train a beagle," he dogmatized.
"That's no beagle, it's a mongrel," she muttered.
"You ought to see a psychiatrist," he reminded me.
"That's my gold mine!" he claimed.
"But it was mine!" he exclaimed.
"And I used to be a pilot," he explained.

"The fire is going out!" he bellowed.
"Bad marksmanship," the hunter groused.
"Another plate of steamers all around," he clamored.

Mr. Bongartz also introduces double-worded Croakers:

"I've got a new game," mumbled Peg.
"I spent the day sewing and gardening," she hemmed and hawed.
"I was in a riot in Paris," he noised abroad.
"My bicycle wheel is melting," he spoke softly.

# 3 FEBRUARY

### Identity Problem in the Mammoth Caves

O pendant stalactite,
　　Deposit crystalline,
Insensate troglodyte
　　Shaped of accreted brine,

Aspire you still to pierce
　　That upright stalagmite
Who in a million years
　　Your love cannot requite?

And if indeed your drip
　　With ardor one day fill her,
And bring you lip to lip,
　　And make you two one pillar . . .

Still, how can you be sure,
　　O pendant stalactite,
If you are you, or her—
　　An upright stalagmite?

　　　　　　　　—W.R.E.

# 4 FEBRUARY

### The Other Point of View

Whether or not the grass looks greener from the other side of the fence, says
*Word Ways*, at least it looks different:

From a clock's point of view the hands move counterclockwise.
From a chicken's point of view every egg is poached.
The sun never rises on the British Empire.
The tardy worm avoids the early bird.
Babe Ruth struck out 1,330 times.
A hen is only an egg's way of making another egg.
The way they are making things today, antiques will be things of the past
 in the future.
It may be garbage to you, but it's bread and butter to the garbage collector.
How come there's so much month left at the end of the money?

# 5 FEBRUARY

## The Half-Warmed Fish

Whether Dr. Spooner made all the accidental sound transpositions attributed
to him is doubtful; Bergen Evans credits him with only one spoonerism: "half-
warmed fish" for "half-formed wish." Still, he has the name, and may as well
have the game. Some of his alleged transgressions:

- Calling on the dean of Christ Church, he inquired, "Is the bean dizzy?"
- To a group of farmers, he began, "I have never before addressed so many
  tons of soil."
- Visiting a friend who had just acquired a country cottage, he congratulated
  him on his "nosey little cook."
- He hailed the "tearful chidings" of the gospels, and asked the congregation
  to sing with him "From Iceland's Greasy Mountains."

H. Allen Smith* cites the following spoonerisms by TV and radio announcers:

- One announcer asked, "Why not try Betty Crocker's poo seep?" and another
  said the fog was "as thick as sea poop." ("Soo peep" is a splendid spoonerism, too.)
- Milton Cross described the "Prince of Pilsen" as "the Pill of Princeton"; Jerry
  Lawrence said, "You will know the King and Queen have arrived when you
  hear a twenty-one-sun galoot"; an emcee, introducing Walter Pidgeon, said,
  "Mr. Privilege, this is indeed a Pidgeon"; a Los Angeles announcer wanted
  his audience to "get the best in bread," but transposed; Fred Hoey opened a
  broadcast with "Good afternoon, Fred Hoey, this is everybody speaking"; a
  cooking expert started her recipe for vichyssoise with "first you take a leek"
  (a fake spoonerism, but too delicious to ignore).

*Charles F. Dery brought Mr. Smith's collection of spoonerisms to my attention.

Other spoonerisms in the Smith collection:

"I'm getting my soles half-shoed after I have a cough of cuppee."
. . . "The thot plickens" . . . "The Indian died and went to the
happy grunting hound" . . . "Give me a jar of oderarm deunder-
ant."

Says Mr. Smith of the last-quoted item: "That's what I call a snooperism!"

# 6 FEBRUARY

## Telling Hearth from Earth Is Tough Stuff, Suzy

The verse below, called to my attention by Jean Libman Block, was devised by
a group of Britishers after World War II to help the multination personnel of
NATO pronounce English properly. Since some of the examples were so British
that they would puzzle an American as much as any other foreigner, I have
made a few changes.

> Dearest creature in creation,
> Spelling's not pronunciation.
> Hear, my Suzy, how diverse
> *Corpse* from *corps* sounds, *horse* from *worse!*
> Trip *among* my *songs, young* dear;
> *Tear* your hair, and shed a *tear*
> As I keep you, *Suzy, busy,*
> Till your *heated head* grows *dizzy*
> Saying *heart*, and *beard*, and *heard;*
> *Dies* and *diet; lord* and *word.*
>
> *Rounded* like to *wounded's* written;
> *Sword* to *sward; retain* to *Britain.*
> What? Do *early, dearly,* plague you?
> They're no worse than *vague* and *ague,*
> *Lose, ooze, use.* Since you must speak,
> Say *break* and *steak,* but *bleak* and *streak;*
> *Cloven, oven; how,* but *low;*
> *Rowed,* but *plowed; shoes, does,* and *toe.*
> Watch for Anglo-Saxon trickery
> In *daughter, laughter; chores, Terpsichore;*
> In *scour, tour, pour;* in *measles, aisles,*
> *Exiles, similes, reviles;*
> *Amen* and *stamen; war,* and *far;*
> *Scholar, solar,* and *cigar;*

*Anemone*, and *bone*, and *one*;
*Lichen, richen, benison;*
*Scene; Melpomene.*

Say *signed*

But *signet; wind,* but *mind.*
*Billet's* right, but so's *ballet,*
*Wallet, mallet,* and *chalet.*
Say with me *blood, flood, food, stood;*
*Bull,* and *dull,* and *mould,* and *should;*
*Toward* and *forward, cowed* and *owed;*
*Viscous, viscount; broad,* and *load;*
*Petal, penal; grieve,* and *sieve;*
*Friend,* and *fiend; alive,* and *live.*
Say, too, *Rachel; moustache; ache;*
*Seven; Heaven; heave.* Now make
Note of *hallowed* and *allowed;*
Of *people, leopard; towed,* and *vowed.*

Mark how lightly "o" shifts over
From *move* to *love,* and so to *clover.*
Say *leeches, breeches; wise, precise;*
*Chalice,* but *police* and *lice.*
*Unstable, constable* are plain;
So *certainly* and *ascertain.*

*Principle, disciple* form;
*Chair, chaise, chaos; worm* and *storm;*
*Ivy, privy; query, very;*
*Famous, clamour; fury, bury;*
*River, rival; tomb, bomb, comb;*
*Doll* and *roll* and *some* and *home;*
*Demise* and *premise; stranger, anger;*
*Dour* and *four; devour* and *clangour.*

The short for *Geoffrey* must be *Geoff.*
Say *zephyr, heifer, chef,* and *deaf.*
In *actual* and *interdict*
And *verdict,* use the *c*; you're licked.
Though, if you use it in *indict.*
In this, as *victual, c's* not right.
Remember: utter *gaunt,* but *aunt;*
*Font, front, wont; want, grand, grant.*
Say *finger, singer, ginger;* pause
O'er words like *gauge* and *mauve* and *gauze.*
Toss back and forth in *badinage*
*Age,* and *foliage,* and *mirage.*

Rhyme not *alien* with *Italian,*
Or *dandelion* with *battalion;*
Or *sea, idea, guinea, area;*
Rhyme not *Maria* with *malaria.*
Say *rally,* but *ally,* say *fever,*
But *ever; leisure, skein, deceiver;*
*Canary, granary; preface, efface;*

*Phlegm, phlegmatic; glass,* and *bass;*
Say *large;* say *target; gin, give, verging;*
Say *ear,* but *earn,* and *scour,* but *scourging;*
*Youth, south, southern; cleanse,* and *clean;*
*Doctrine, turpentine, marine;*
*Scenic, Arabic, landau,*
*Science, conscience, Arkansas;*
*Monkey, donkey.*
                              Say *endeavor,*
*Asp, grasp, wasp;* say *fever, sever.*

Suzy, though you've studied so,
You must take one final blow.
Is the proper rhyme for *tough*
*Though, through, plough, cough,* or *enough?*
*Hiccough* has the sound of *cup.*

Suzy, better give it up.


# 7 FEBRUARY

### *Many a Malapropism*
### *Has Flown under the Bridge*

In *Tom Brown at Oxford* an old farmer, bruised by a fall from a ladder, reports the verdict of the doctor who examined him:

"A zem'd to zay as there wur no bwones bruk—ugh, ugh—but a couldn't say wether or no there wasn't some infarnal injury—"
"Etarnal, Simon, etarnal!" interrupted his wife; "how canst use such words afore the young ladies?"

And again:

"Wut's to hinder thaay tryin' ov 'un, if thaay be minded to't? That's wut I wants to know."

"'Tis wut the counsellors call the Statut' o' Lamentations."
"Wutever's Lamentations got to do wi't?"
"A gurt deal, I tell 'ee. What do's thou know o' Lamentations?"
"Lamentations cums afore Ezekiel in the Bible."

Malapropisms continue their merry way. Some are apocryphal, as is, I suspect, the story of the landowner who said he proposed not to plant his property, but to measure it by leaps and bounds. His wife asked the gardener to put in a bed of saliva. "Fine," he agreed; "and while I'm at it I'll plant spittoonia for the border."

But many a malapropism is genuine. James Thurber's cook said one of her brothers "works into an incinerator where they burn the refuge"; a second brother had just passed his "silver-service eliminations"; and her sister got "tuberculosis from her teeth and it went all through her symptom."

A newspaper refers to the Duchess of Windsor as a "grievous widow." Another says that Isaac Asimov, author of more than a hundred books, "attributes his profligacy to the fact that he can type 90 words a minute." A Democratic politician, asked whether he is encouraging Teddy Kennedy to run for President, replies, "I haven't made any ovations to him, and he hasn't made any to me." Pierre Salinger describes John F. Kennedy as "a vociferous reader." Andrei Gromyko of Russia tells *The New York Times* that "a lot of water has flown under the bridge since the war." A wife says proudly, "My husband is a marvelous lover . . . he knows all the erroneous zones."

As IRS commissioner, Johnnie Walters cut the word "spouse" from his income tax instructions because too many people thought he was talking about a water fountain.

Some malapropisms from the collection of columnist Don Duncan: "He communicates to work"; "No phonographic pictures allowed"; "We arrived at our predestination"; "she apologized affluently"; "relapse and enjoy it."

Norton Mockridge collected thousands of the monsters in *Fractured English*. A dip-in:

> The English language is going through a resolution. . . . I was so surprised you could have knocked me over with a fender. . . . Now that we have teen-agers, we've been renegaded to the back seat. . . . Everything is going to rot and ruin. . . . A wealthy typhoon. . . . He's a busy-buggy. . . . He treats me like the dirt on his feet. . . . It sure is good to be back on terra cotta again. . . . My father is retarded on a pension. . . . White as the dripping snow. . . . He uses millinery brushes, and my sister uses massacre on her eyes. . . . I rode an alligator to the top of the Empire State Building. . . . Frances has beautiful hands, and some day I'm going to make a bust of them. . . . He used biceps to deliver the baby.

After a radio interview with sportscaster Jack Buck, Yogi Berra received a twenty-five-dollar check as an honorarium. "How the hell long have you known me, Jack?" he grumbled. "How could you spell my name like that?" The check was made out to "Bearer."

# 8 FEBRUARY

## *Mots d'Heures: Gousses, Rames*

My daughter Joanna, working for a book publisher, brought home a forty-page volume, *Mots d'Heures: Gousses, Rames,* explaining that it was in an extinct French dialect, and that she knew I was interested in that sort of thing. Well, I could make neither head nor belly nor tail of that book. I could not even understand the title, much less the verses inside. They certainly *looked* like French, but that was as far as it went. And though the elaborate annotations were in English, I could make no sense of them either.

Only when I tried reading the verses aloud did I realize that there was a familiar ring to them. At last the answer came like a *coup de tonnerre.* "Mots d'Heures Gousses Rames:" Mother Goose rhymes! Of course! How obvious!*

In self-defense I will say that I have shown that book to dozens of friends, and only one of them realized without prompting that the verses consisted of French words arranged so as to approximate English sounds.†

I give you two of these *rames,* with the original notes. Read them *à haute voix,* with an accent as bad as mine, and you will realize that you have known them all your life:

### OH, LES MOTS D'HEUREUX BARDES

> Oh, les mots d'heureux bardes
> Où en toutes heures que partent.[1]
> Tous guetteurs pour dock à Beaune.[2]
> Besoin gigot d'air
> De que paroisse paire.[3]
> Et ne pour dock, pet-de-nonne.[4]

1. Minstrels were no doubt a happy lot, and it is not surprising that France, a cradle of wit and culture, could turn them out in such numbers that they came and went on an almost predictable schedule. As one came in by the portcullis another left by the oubliette.
2. Beaune. Town in the Côte-d'Or, 11,000 pop., famed for its wines and mustard. It is not a port, therefore, why should everyone watch its docks? Certainly it does not have any particular renown as a center of contraband.
3. This must refer to the Côte-d'Or, a peerless parish indeed. Rich in some of the finest vintages of France and, if we are to believe the previous line, a great lambing country.
4. Pet-de-nonne. An extremely light and fluffy pastry. Although any decent housewife would ask for them without hesitation at her favorite pâtisserie, delicacy forbids a direct translation here.

---

*When the author, Luis d'Antin Van Rooten, died, his obituary failed even to mention that he was author of this intricate Franglish jape.
† Matt Huston, a twelve-year-old without a word of French, glanced at the title and understood it instantly.

### ET QUI RIT DES CURÉS D'OC?

Et qui rit des curés d'Oc?[1]
De Meuse raines,[2] houp! de cloques.[3]
De quelles loques ce turque coin.[4]
Et ne d'ânes ni rennes,
Écuries des curés d'Oc.[5]

1. Oc (or Languedoc), ancient region of France, with its capital at Toulouse. Its monks and curates were, it seems, a singularly humble and holy group. This little poem is a graceful tribute to their virtues.
2. Meuse, or Maas, River, 560 miles long, traversing France, Belgium, and the Netherlands; Raines, old French word for frogs (from the L., *ranae*). Here is a beautiful example of Gothic imagery; He who laughs at the curés d'Oc will have frogs leap at him from the Meuse river and
3. infect him with a scrofulous disease! This is particularly interesting when we consider the widespread superstition in America that frogs and toads cause warts.
4. "Turkish corners" were introduced into Western Europe by returning crusaders, among other luxuries and refinements of Oriental living. Our good monks made a concession to the fashion, but N.B. their Turkish corner was made of rags! This affectation of interior decorating had a widespread revival in the U.S.A. at the turn of the century. Ah, the Tsar's bazaars' bizarre beaux-arts.
5. So strict were the monks that they didn't even indulge themselves in their arduous travels. No fancy mules nor reindeer in *their* stables. They just rode around on their plain French asses.

# 9 FEBRUARY

## *Variable Verbs*

A boy who swims will soon have swum,
But milk is skimmed and seldom skum,
And nails you trim, they are not trum.

When words you speak those words are spoken,
But a nose is tweaked and can't be twoken,
And what you seek is seldom soken.

If we forget, then we've forgotten,
But things we wet are never wotten,
And houses let cannot be lotten.

The goods one sells are always sold,
But fears dispelled are not dispold,
And what you smell is never smold.

When young a top you oft saw spun,
But did you see a grin e'er grun,
Or a potato neatly skun?
—*Anonymous*

Use each of the following past tenses, all looking like products of ignorance, correctly in a sentence:

| | |
|---|---|
| 1. Flied | 6. Shined |
| 2. Hanged | 7. Spitted |
| 3. Leaved | 8. Sticked |
| 4. Letted | 9. Treaded |
| 5. Ringed | 10. Weaved |

—*Richard Lederer*

# 10 FEBRUARY

## *The American Traveler*

Robert H. Newell wrote this verse around the time of the Civil War. I have dropped fourteen stanzas that deal with places in states other than Maine.

To Lake Aghmoogenegamook,
    All in the State of Maine,
A man from Witteguergaugaum came
    One evening in the rain.

"I am a traveler," said he,
    "Just started on a tour,
And go to Nomjamskillicock
    Tomorrow morn at four."

He took a tavern-bed that night,
    And with the morrow's sun,
By way of Sekledobskus went,
    With carpet-bag and gun.

A week passed on; and next we find
    Our native tourist come
To that sequester'd village called
    Genasagarnagum.

So back he went to Maine straightway,
    And there a wife he took,
And now is making nutmegs at
    Moosehicmagunticook.

# 11 FEBRUARY

## *My Weight, Sir, You Must Not Survey*

A univocalic—a passage using but one of the five vowels—is difficult to arrange, unless you keep it short:

> Weep, weep.
> Then sleep
> Deep, deep.

Easier is the lipogram, which drops one vowel from each passage. The following lipograms retain the sound of the deleted vowel:

No A:

> My weight, sir, you must not survey.
> Sir, weigh me not—no weigh, no weigh.

No E:

> Snow falling fast. On snowy quai
> A Spanish miss shows how to ski.
> What sport, slaloming vis-à-vis
> Such fair companion! . . . *Si, ah, si!*
> But lacking ski-facility
> I wind up upsy-daisily.

No I:

> Why doth the eyeless fellow cry?
> Why, so would you, had you no eye.

No O:

> Il y a une lettre
>    Que je ne puis
> Pas permettre
>    Ici.
> Elle s'entend
> En
> Eau
>         Beau
>             Bateau
>                 Chateau
>                     Chapeau
>                         Plateau
>                             Tableau
> Et
> (En anglais)                                   Sew.

No U:

> A Vowel living in my town,
> Heard oftener than written down,

Gives voice in words like *brew, eschew,*
*Do, drew, anew,* and *interview.*
I now declare this Vowel Moot,
And Ban it from the Alphaboot.
—*W.R.E.*

# 12 FEBRUARY

### *Spaghettibird Headdress*

Anguish languish, popularized by the late Howard L. Chace, is a form of punning in which words overlap to give an impression of other words, as clouds assume forms according to the fancy of the observer. Take, for instance, these:

| | | |
|---|---|---|
| heresy | warts | firmer |
| ladle | warts | once |
| furry | welcher | inner |
| starry | altar | regional |
| toiling | girdle | virgin |
| udder | deferent | |

Now read the list aloud, listening for the overtones:
"Here is a little fairy story told in other words, words which are altogether different from the ones in the original version."
You knew it all the time.
The anguish languish that follows is appropriate to this date:

### SPAGHETTIBIRD HEADDRESS

bar Labour Ham Winking

Fors oar in shaving ear she goes, awful fodders broad fart hunter dish consonant hay noon action, corn sieved inebriety and addict hated tutor preposition dot omen or crated inkwell.

Non wiring caged integrate cymbal wart, tasting wither damnation, our runny gnashing, socking seed end sod defecated ken logging door. Worm head honor grape batter veal doff fat whore. Wave counter defecator potion audit felled azure vinyl roasting piece fort hose hoe hair gater wives tit tat gnashing mike leaf. Assault her gutter footing in pepper dot weigh shoe duties.

Budding awl archer since, weaken opt defecate, weekend not concentrate, working ought hello disk round. Depravement, livid indeed, hue straggle deer, heft cancer traded hit, pharaoh buff harp

burp hours tatter distract. Twirled wheel ladle node orlon ram
umber wad wheeze hay year, buttock an if veer fork add catered
hairdo done finest walk witch day hoof otter heft dust floor show
nobody at fenced. I doze rudder forest tubing hair debtor catered
tuba grape tusk rim onion beef harass—dot form tease own
whored did, wheat aching greased dim notion tutor cows far wish
dig rave do lustful miss shore add dive ocean; dewy her holly dis-
solve daddies dad shell nut heft tiding feign; end it grubby men,
other pimple, brother pimple, father pimple, shell nut pair rich fern
dirt.

—*Jim Anderson, Jeffrey Brown, John Spencer*

APE OWE 'EM

When fur stews can this sill leer I'm
    Toot rye tomb ache theme e'en ink Lear,
Youth inked wood butt bee weigh sting thyme
    Use eh, "It's imp lean on scents shear!"
Gnome attar; Anna lies align!
    Nation mice lender verse says knot—
    Fork rip tick poet real Ike mine,
How Aaron weal demesnes allot.

—*Leonard Switzer*

# 13 FEBRUARY

## Odets, Where Is Thy Sting?

A Congressman, I am told, has proposed a constitutional amendment to ban
puns; but Prohibition should have taught him that such evils as drinking, gambling, whoring, and punning cannot be eliminated by edict. When New York
seemed on the verge of losing a prestigious brewery, how did a shocked citi-
zenry respond? With puns, as in this deplorable letter from Edward E. Brown
to *The New York Times*:

A. Sock's suggestion [letter Jan. 22] that the Mayor plant an An-
heuser Busch in memory of a departing brewery, and A. H. Green's
riposte [letter Jan. 30] to the effect that the failure of the brewer
Busch to realize profits from such an act would leave him sadder
Budweiser provoked in me a sudden Piel of laughter.

Should I ever have the good fortune to meet either or both of
these gentlemen, I would certainly invite them over for a cold beer
or two, and perhaps ask them to Schaefer dinner.

Even commerce pays credit to the clout of the pun. A New York fish store is called "Wholly Mackerel."

Addison worried lest the British "degenerate into a race of punsters." Eachard wondered "Whether or no Punning, Quibbling, and that which they call Joquing, and such other delicacies of Wit, highly admired in some Academick Exercises, might not be very conveniently omitted."

Charles Lamb, on the other hand, worshiped puns the way unregenerate Hebrews worshiped the golden calf. "The puns which are most entertaining," he said, "are those which will least bear an analysis. Of this kind is the following recorded with a sort of stigma in one of Swift's *Miscellanies:*

> An Oxford scholar, meeting a porter who was carrying a hare through the streets, accosts him with this extraordinary question: 'Prithee, friend, is that thy own hare, or a wig?'

"There is no excusing this," Lamb concluded, "and no resisting it."

One man's Mede, as punsters have reported *ad nauseam,* is another man's Persian. Individuals trying to remove spilled oil from seagulls reported that they "left no tern unstoned." William Safire thought this among the best of recent puns; yet it does not touch my funnybone* at all. Were those people throwing rocks at the seagulls? Or feeding them LSD? The wordplay is over my head.

"Edna St. Vincent Malaise," muttered a jealous poet. "Housman's knee," sneered another. "Puberty is a hair-raising experience," reflected John Wildman. "Armageddon sick of it," cried Robert A. Heinlein. Norman Corwin, permitting Joe Julian to answer a call of nature during rehearsal, said, "I always want my actors to mind their pees and cues."

# 14 FEBRUARY

## *"There Are Numerous Locutions to Express the Idea of Never"*

When all the world grows honest;
When the Yellow River's clear;
When Calais meets with Dover,
Do you suppose, my dear,

I shall forget I've lost you? . . .
Not until St. Tib's Eve,
Not for a year of Sundays
Shall I forbear to grieve—

---

* *Humerus* is Latin for the upper armbone.

Till noon strikes Narrowdale; till
Latter Lammas dawns;
Till Queen Dick reigns; till Fridays
Arrive in pairs like swans;

Till the Greek calends, and the
Conversion of the Jews.
I'll mourn you till the coming
Of the Cocqcigrues.

—*W.R.E.*

# 15 FEBRUARY

## *Mary Had a Lipogram**

A. Ross Eckler re-created "Mary Had a Little Lamb" six times, excluding in turn the letters s, h, t, e, and a. In the final verse he used just half of the alphabet: e, t, a, y, n, c, l, d, m, r, h, i, and p.

*The original verse*

Mary had a little lamb,
  Its fleece was white as snow,
And everywhere that Mary went
  The lamb was sure to go;
He followed her to school one day,
  That was against the rule;
It made the children laugh and play
  To see a lamb in school.

*The verse without s*

Mary had a little lamb,
  With fleece a pale white hue,
And everywhere that Mary went
  The lamb kept her in view;
To academe he went with her,
  Illegal, and quite rare;
It made the children laugh and play
  To view a lamb in there.

*The verse without a*

Polly owned one little sheep,
  Its fleece shone white like snow,
Every region where Polly went,

---

* Michael Gartner says he always thought a lipogram was a nasty rejoinder sent via Western Union.

The sheep did surely go;
He followed her to school one time,
    Which broke the rigid rule;
The children frolicked in their room
    To see the sheep in school.

*The verse without h*

Mary owned a little lamb,
    Its fleece was pale as snow,
And every place its mistress went
    It certainly would go;
It followed Mary to class one day
    It broke a rigid law;
It made some students giggle aloud,
    A lamb in class all saw.

*The verse without t*

Mary had a pygmy lamb,
    His fleece was pale as snow,
And every place where Mary walked
    Her lamb did also go;
He came inside her classroom once,
    Which broke a rigid rule;
How children all did laugh and play
    On seeing a lamb in school!

*The verse without e*

Mary had a tiny lamb,
    Its wool was pallid as snow,
And any spot that Mary did walk
    This lamb would always go;
This lamb did follow Mary to school,
    Although against a law;
How girls and boys did laugh and play,
    That lamb in class all saw.

*Finally, the verse without half the letters of the alphabet*

Maria had a little sheep,
    As pale as rime its hair,
And all the places Maria came
    The sheep did tail her there;
In Maria's class it came at last,
    A sheep can't enter there;
It made the children clap their hands,
    A sheep in class, that's rare.
                              —*A. Ross Eckler*

# 16 FEBRUARY

### *Impossible Rhymes*

Silver is a hard word to rhyme. Here is the way Stephen Sondheim managed it:

> To find a rhyme for silver
> Or any "rhymeless" rhyme
> Requires only will, ver-
> bosity and time.

Mr. Sondheim's rhyme, in the correspondence column of *Time*, prompted this from Ira Levin:

> A woman asked me to rhyme a penguin.
> I said, "Does the erstwhile Emperor Eng win?
>
> If not, I'll send a brand-new tractor
> To "Big Boy" Williams, cinemactor;
> On the card attached, a smiling penguin
> Will say, "You're truly a man among men, Guinn."
>
> "All right," she said, "so now rhyme silver."
> But I left, because I'd had my filver.

Speonk, a town on Long Island, offers a minor challenge:

> WEE-ONKS ARE EXPECTED SOON
>
> If a masculine porker's a he-onk,
> The feminine must be a she-onk;
> When the gal meets the guy
> In a Long Island sty,
> They're a he-onk and she-onk in Speonk.
> —W.R.E.

Victorian writers did some ingenious rhyming:

> VELOCITY
>
> Having once gained the summit, and managed to cross it, he
> Rolls down the side with uncommon velocity.
> —R. H. Barham

## INTELLECTUAL

Ye lords of ladies intellectual,
Come tell me, have they not hen-pecked you all?
—*Lord Byron*

## CARPET

Sweet maid of the inn,
'Tis surely no sin
To toast such a beautiful bar pet;
Believe me, my dear,
Your feet would appear
At home on a nobleman's carpet.
—*Author Unknown.*

## MONTH

How many weeks in a month?
Four, as the swift moon runn'th.
—*Christina Rossetti*

If I were a cassaway
  On the plains of Timbuctoo,
I would eat a missionary,
  Cassock, band, and hymn-book too.
—*Samuel Wilberforce*

In the 1920s, F. P. A. rhymed Massachusetts this way:

Of tennis I played one or two sets
On a court at Richmond, Massachusetts.

Nigel Nicolson says Vita Sackville-West's grandfather, "Old Lionel," composed a saying about a girl named Rosamond Grosvenor: Rosamond Grosvenor / got nearly run ovner. This bothered Vita, then in her teens, "because she could not see how he got it to rhyme properly."

My report closes, as it began, with a rhyme for silver:

## TO VERONA

If Pegasus
  Were but a bus
That any man could board,
  I might distil Ver-
ona's silver
  Beauty in a word.
—*W.R.E.*

# 17 FEBRUARY

## *Shipwreck*

I refer in the following verse to the shipwreck that ultimately accounts for us all. One three-letter combination, dropped into the blanks, makes the meaning all too clear.

> \*\*\*, \*\*\*, \*\*\* your boat
>   Till the p\*\*\* go down;
> Fie on him who bor\*\*\*s sor\*\*\*:
> All must sink and d\*\*\*n tomorrow;
>   All must sink and d\*\*\*n.
>
> Let no wailing c\*\*\*d your throat;
>   Bar your b\*\*\* from f\*\*\*n;
> Bare your breast to Cupid's ar\*\*\*,
> Gnaw the bone and suck the mar\*\*\*,
>   Ere you sink and d\*\*\*n.
>
> Pluck the blossoms life has g\*\*\*n,
>   Wear them as a c\*\*\*n;
> Many a c\*\*\* shall fly from spar\*\*\*,
> Many a lad his \*\*\* shall har\*\*\*
>   Ere you sink and d\*\*\*n.
>                                   —W.R.E.

# 18 FEBRUARY

## *Clerihews by Bentley*

A clerihew is the ideal put-down—gentle, compassionate, unanswerable. These are by Mr. Clerihew himself, Edmund Clerihew Bentley:

> 1. Geoffrey Chaucer
>    Took a bath (in a saucer)
>    In consequence of certain hints
>    Dropped by the Black Prince.
>
> 2. The only occasion when Comte
>    Is known to have romped
>    Was when the multitude roared *"Vive
>    La Philosophie Positive!"*

3. "Susaddah!" exclaimed Ibsen,
   "By dose is turdig cribson!
   I'd better dot kiss you.
   Atishoo! Atishoo!"

4. The digestion of Milton
   Was unequal to Stilton.
   He was only feeling so-so
   When he wrote Il Penseroso.

5. What I like about Clive
   Is that he is no longer alive.
   There is a great deal to be said
   For being dead.

6. When Alexander Pope
   Accidentally trod on the soap,
   And came down on the back of his
       head—
   Never mind what he said.

7. The people of Spain think Cervantes
   Equal to half-a-dozen Dantes:
   An opinion resented most bitterly
   By the people of Italy.
                              —E. C. Bentley

# 19 FEBRUARY

## Self Service

Shakespeare called down a curse on anyone who might disturb his grave:

> Good frend, for Jesus' sake forbeare
> To digg the dust enclosed heare;
> Blest be y$^e$ man y$^t$ spares thes stones,
> And curst be he y$^t$ moves my bones.

Wrote John Gay:

> The world's a joke, and all things show it.
> I thought so once, and now I know it.

Benjamin Franklin's self-written epitaph was gentler:

> The body of
> Benjamin Franklin, printer,

> Like the cover of an old book,
>     Its contents worn out
> And stript of its lettering and gilding,
>     Lies here food for the worms.
> Yet the work itself shall not be lost,
>     For it shall, as he believes,
> Appear once more,
>                 In a new
>             And more beautiful edition,
> Corrected and amended
>                 By the Author.

Thomas Fuller said: "Here lies Fuller's earth."

Gossip columnist Walter Winchell wrote: "If only when my epitaph is readied, they will say, 'Here is Walter Winchell with his ear to the ground—as usual.'"

# 20 FEBRUARY

## *Who Says I Transpire?*

By the nature of things, the dictionary lags behind current usage—sometimes, in fact, hundreds of years behind.

Take the word *transpire*. Derived from the Latin for "breathe through," it first meant "to give off through the skin" (the body *transpires* sweat); "to exhale" (the flower *transpires* fragrance); "to breathe forth" (the dragon *transpires* fire). In a 1647 hymn Crashaw exulted:

> With wider pores . . .
> More freely to transpire
> That impatient fire.

It was natural for a word meaning "to breathe forth" to develop the more abstract sense of "to leak out," "to become known." "Yesterday's quarrel must not transpire" sounds odd today, but it was correct in 1641 and is technically correct now. Thomas Jefferson wrote, "What happened between them did not transpire," a seeming contradiction in terms, but as right as rain. Said a letter of Lord Chesterfield's: "This goes to you in confidence; you will not let one word transpire."

By 1802 the word had added a third meaning: "to occur, take place," as in "He did not know what had transpired during his absence." Noah Webster accepted "take place" as a correct definition of *transpire* in 1828. Yet more than 150 years later, the *Oxford English Dictionary* still calls this third—and most common—meaning a misusage; *Webster's Second* says it is "disapproved by

most authorities"; and the *American Heritage Dictionary* lists it as "disputed
. . . not acceptable to 62 percent of the Usage Panel."

You are speaking correct, if redundant, English if you say, "It transpired that
it transpired that the horse transpired"—"It became evident that the fact was
the horse was sweating."

# 21 FEBRUARY

## To My Greek Mistress

All you need to read off this verse as if it were English is a vague recollection of
the Greek alphabet.

> With many a Ψ I ate a Π
>   That you had baked, my dear;
> This torpor N I you—
>   I'm feeling very queer.
> O Φ O Φ upon your Π!—
>   You Δ cruel blow!
> Your dreadful Π has made me X;
>   My tears fall in a P.
> I would have Λnother lass
>   Who baked that Π, I vow;
> But still I M and M for you,
>   As sick as any cow.
>                        —W.R.E.

# 22 FEBRUARY

## Washington Crisscrossing the Delaware

Not only is each line that follows an anagram of "Washington Crossing the
Delaware," but the poem originally contained at least eight more lines, which
have not come down to us, or at least not to me. This is a tour de force, though
imperfect in some lines. It appeared November 10, 1890, in a New York magazine called *The Boys' Champion.*

> A hard, howling, tossing winter scene;
> Strong tide was washing hero clean.
> "How cold!" Weather stings as in anger.
> O silent night shows war ace danger!
> The cold waters swashing on in rage,
> Redcoats warn slow his hint engage.

When across General wish'd train t'go,
He saw his ragged continentals row.
He stands while crew sit, an oar going
And so this general watches rowing.
He hastens—winter again grows cold;
A wet crew gain Hessian stronghold.
George can't lose war with 's hands in;
He goes astern—Alight, O crew, and win!
　　　　　　　　　　—*Skeezix*

# 23 FEBRUARY

## *Squdgy Fez, Blank Jimp Crwth Vox*

The quality of existing pangrams is unsatisfactory.* Augustus Morgan's nineteenth-century "I, quartz pyx, who fling muck beds," ignored v and j, recent arrivals on the alphabetical scene. "Cwm fjord-bank glyphs vext quiz" makes room for the v and j, but is not likely to become a common remark even among geologists. Claude E. Shannon wrote, "Squdgy fez, blank jimp crwth vox," which has something to do with wearing a squashed Turkish hat and muting a Welsh violin.

　　If you are willing to fudge by repeating a few letters, the problem of including all twenty-six letters in a single passage becomes more manageable. For instance:

> "The five boxing wizards jump quickly." (31)
> "Pack my box with five dozen liquor jugs." (32)
> "Jim just quit and packed extra heavy bags for Liz Owen." (44)

　　If you wish to use each letter twice, your goal is a sentence of fifty-two letters. The nearest to this I have run into is Mary Youngquist's "Sylvan plight: five jinxed wizards jump, weigh quartz, mock quick baby fox." (60)

　　Darryl Francis found in *Webster's New International Dictionary,* second edition, three words totaling thirty-nine letters and including all the twenty-six letters of the alphabet. The words are *quick-flowing, semibolshevized,* and *juxtapyloric.* The following verse is a *lipogram,* since it lacks the letter e, and also a *pangram,* since it contains all the other letters of the alphabet:

> Quixotic boys who look for joys
> Quixotic hazards run.

---

* But see 9 April for some notable successes.—*Ed.*

A lass annoys with trivial toys
Opposing man for fun.
—*Author unknown*

# 24 FEBRUARY

## *The Girl I Never Saw*

The frustration I recall most bitterly occurred during a period when I was theoretically studying philosophy at the Sorbonne. Since I had no marketable skills, my principal source of income was my reddish, curly beard, which appealed to Left Bank artists. One of these paid me a few francs to pose for a painting of a seedy-looking fellow—me—sitting across what I took to be a parlor table from a comely nude. Between us stood an almost empty bottle of wine and an almost burned-out candle.

There was one drawback to the assignment: the artist never posed the girl and me together. Each time I arrived, I would see her there on the canvas, still pinker and more Renoirish than the time before. She looked at me with a speculative expression that never changed, but mine did; with each sitting it grew more ravenous. I pleaded with the artist, I embraced his knees, I offered to waive my pittance of a fee if only he would permit me to sit with that girl once in the flesh. Before the final sitting he agreed. But men are deceivers ever. When I arrived that last day, on the run, he announced that he considered the painting finished. I never did see that girl. I still don't know whether the small brown mole on the underslope of her left breast was real. Some day, in some gallery . . . in some attic . . . perhaps overpainted with an oil of a cow grazing beside a pond . . . a collector will find me still sitting, staring in hopeless longing at a girl I never saw. . . .

What parlor games she and I might have played! They are too numerous for a full listing, but I give you two:*

1. Choose a letter to be the first letter of a noun. Then make a list of adjective-noun combinations, each noun starting with the key letter, while the adjective linked to the first noun starts with a, the adjective for the second noun with b, and so on through the alphabet. (Skip x and z.) The first person to finish wins. For instance: Aged sweetheart, bitter sea, curious spaniel, drugged swan, enticing siren, frozen stream, golden silence, hideous sight, idle striker, juicy salad, etc.

2. The first player gives two commonly associated words. His opponent makes the second word the first word of another familiar combination, and so

---

* William and Mary Morris told me about these.

back and forth until one or the other gives up. A sampler: Gang saw, saw horse, horse fly, fly guy, guy rope, rope ladder, ladder truck, etc.

In parlor games of this sort there are forfeits. I am afraid that when I wake at night to consider the games that that girl and I might have played, I spend more time working out the forfeits than working out the games.

# 25 FEBRUARY

## Bless the Shepherd

This sestet uses only the vowel e:

> Bless the shepherd,
>   Bless the sheep,
> Bless the shepherdess.
> Ewe, Bellwether,
> Sheltered keep:
>   Send them blessedness.
>         —W.R.E.

By inserting i at appropriate intervals, you can complete the nineteenth-century quatrain below:

### APPROACH OF EVENING

> dling,   st n ths mld twlght dm,
> Whlst brds, n wld, swft vgls, crclng skm.
> Lght wnds n sghng snk, tll, rsng brght,
> Nght's Vrgn Plgrm swms n vvd lght!
>         —*Author Unknown*

Decide for yourself the vowel to be inserted (thirty-nine times) in the quatrain below:

### INCONTROVERTIBLE FACTS

> Dll hmdrm mrmrs lll, bt hbbb stns.
> Lclls snffs p msk, mndngs shns.
> Pss prrs, bds brst, bcks btt, lck trns p trmps;
> Bt fll cps, hrtfl, spr p njst thmps.
>         —*Author Unknown*

# 26 FEBRUARY

## *Who's Me?*

*Who's Who* has a new gimmick, irresistible to egomaniacs: The chosen people are asked to provide summaries of their views on life. I sent this, but it did not appear:

> Who's me?
> Who's you?
> Who's he?
> Who's who?
> —W.R.E.

Nor did my suggested postscript to the biographical sketch of a friend, the late language stylist Theodore Bernstein:

> Ted Bernstein, damner
> Of bad grammer,
> Takes up considerable room
> In Whom's Whom.
> —W.R.E.

# 27 FEBRUARY

## *Cats, Cats, Cats, Cats!*

These two monosyllabic acrostics* are verbally identical; yet they present two separate rhyme schemes. Acrostically speaking, they separate cat lovers from dog lovers.

### CATS, CATS, CATS, CATS!

> Cats come with mews,
> All have sharp claws,
> They air their views,
> Stray soon from laws,
> Climb wall. Each tom
> And each mog†—grand
> Thieves—munch meal from
> Scamp's‡ lunch. Scamp planned . . .

---

* See also 25 December.
† In English slang, pussy cat.
‡ One assumes Scamp to be the house dog.

Chain off, he might
Aim at a rout,
Touch mogs and bite
Such prime bits out!
Chance came. Grey dawn.
At once left mat.
The deuce! On lawn—
Scamp loose—no cat!


CHASE 'EM, SCAMP, GO ON!

Cats come with mews, all
Have sharp claws, they
Air their views, stray
Soon from laws, climb wall.

Each tom and
Each mog—grand thieves—munch
Meal from Scamp's lunch.
Scamp planned . . .

Chain off, he might aim
At a rout, touch
Mogs and bite such
Prime bits out. Chance came.

Grey dawn. At
Once left mat. The deuce!
On lawn—Scamp loose—
No cat!
—*J. A. Lindon*


Mr. Lindon's tour de force reminds me that I have seen no verses that use whole words instead of letters for acrostic purposes. This omission is repaired herewith:


FORECAST: CHILLY

Time befriends
For brief space—
Warm days sends;
Clothes in grace

Man and maid.
*This I wot:*

*Looks must fade,*
*Like or not.*

One is not here
Long, my chums;
Cold from hot, here
Winter comes.
—*W.R.E.*

# 28 FEBRUARY

## *The Canary, the Stallion, and the Partridge*

A *canard*, said someone who did not mind reaching, is something one canardly believe. I canardly believe that a word meaning female duck could turn into one meaning false, unfounded story, but that is what happened. From the meaningless quacking of a duck, do you suppose?

Duck itself comes from the place you would expect—old English *duce*, to duck or dive. The origins of some animal names are more surprising. For instance:

> *Canary* comes from *dog*,* as *stallion* from
> The *stall* where he is daily combed and brushed.
> And *partridge* comes from *fart*—because its thrum
> When it is flushed sounds just like . . . being
> flushed.[†]
> —*W.R.E.*

The goose laid a much prettier word than the duck. I get pleasurable goose pimples when I reflect that gossamer was once *goose summer.*

# 29 FEBRUARY

## *Twisted Proverbs*

- Perversity makes strange bedfellows.  —*R. Cecil Owen*
- The parrot does not believe all he says.  —*F. G. Messervy*

---

[*] Canaries once abounded in the Canary Islands, so called for the wild dogs (canus, dog (L.)) found there by the first settlers.
[†] It was a joy to discover this presumably inadvertent pun in the Appendix of *The American Heritage Dictionary*, under *Perd-*, to fart.

- The cock crows, but the hen lays the eggs. —*Olric*
- The fortunate always believe in a just providence. —*Irene Williams*
- Don't join a queue unless you know what's at the end of it.
  —*Gerald Challis*
- The fighter calls the bomber slow. —*N.B.*
- Second thoughts in the train are better than impulse in the taxi.
  —*Miss D. N. Daglish*
- A butterfly lives long enough. —*Lucifer*
- The crunching of a man's own toast is louder than God's own thunder.
  —*F.C.C.*
- The fire that melts lead tempers steel. —*Phiz*
- A patriot is known by his income-tax returns. —*Pibwob*

Here are some bastardized proverbs:

> A rolling pin gathers no moss.
>
> Footsore and fancy free.
>
> Many hands make housework.
>
> A penny saved is a Penny Dreadful.
>
> Faint heart never won fair weather.
>
> Don't look a saw horse in the mouth.
>
> Let sleeping bags lie.
>
> Half a wit is better than none.
>
> Cleanliness is next to impossible.
>
> Fools fall in where angels fear to tread.
>
> You can't teach an old dog card tricks.
>
> Don't kill the goose that laid the deviled egg.
>
> One picture is worth a thousand dollars.
>
> There's no fool like an old maid.
>
> Out of sight, out of order.
>
> A healthy dog has a cold beer.
>
> Politics makes strange bedbugs.
>
> Don't cross your eyes before you come to them.
>
> Don't cross your blessings before they hatch.
>
> People who live in glass houses shouldn't throw parties.
>
> Don't burn your bridges at both ends.
>
> Procrastination is the nick of time.
>
> Penny wise, pound cake.
>
> Into each cellar some rain must fall.
>
> —*Mary J. Youngquist*

Identify the proverbs below by the single word given:

        1. X dog X X X.
        2. X X X X eggs X X X.
        3. X X X mended.
        4. X X X X pudding X X X X.
        5. X X X X X X Romans X.
        6. X X X feather X X.
        7. X X X X kettle X.

# MARCH

## 1 MARCH

### *The English Is Coming*

"When I was little," says Jean Cocteau, "I believed that foreigners could not really talk at all, but were only pretending."

Yet even in M. Cocteau's childhood a strong west wind was blowing English words across the channel into France. Today he must be as familiar as any Englishman with "management," "le weekend," "le grand rush," "le beesness," "le whisky," "le leadership," "blugines" (with the spelling Frenchified), "le cocktail," and "le golf." (Says one confused Parisian: "Les Français aiment les gadgets—en anglais, les gizmos.")

The French government tries to blow the English words back home. Recently 350 of them were exiled at a stroke. "Flashback" was ordered to yield to "retrospectif"; "hovercraft" to "aeroglisseur"; "ferry boat" to "transbordeur"; "tanker" to "nàvire citerne"; "hit parade" to "palmarès."

But it is doubtful whether English will fall back for long, in France or anywhere else. In Germany, for instance—where fashion advertisements ask "Was ist IN, was ist OUT?"—English words are IN. The Germans have adopted "appeasement," "escalation," "rollback," "comeback," and "no comment." A German official who had resigned his post insisted that "Mein Walkout was richtig!" German members of "das Establishment" are served on airplanes by "Stewardesses" and "Purserettes." They may call for "a long drink." And if a business deal goes sour, they feel "frustriert."

Of course, the thing sometimes works the other way. Marshall Davidson once sat on a New York grand jury, which was hearing a French witness. The District Attorney asked, "Were you at such a place at such a time?" The translator turned the sentence into French, and the witness replied, "Yes, zat ees true." Said the translator to the jury: "Elle dit, 'Oui, c'est vrai.'"

There is no telling how far this homogenizing of languages will go. With Britain and Germany now bundling in the Common Market, says a London paper, both countries may be using these automotive terms by 1984:

- Bonnet (Hood): Der Fingerpinsher.
- Exhaust Pipe: Das Spitzenpopper Bangentuben.
- Speedometer: Der Egobooster und Lineschootinbackeruppen.
- Air Horns (Klaxons): Die Vhatderhellvosdat Klaxenfanfaren.
- Puncture (Flat tire): Das Pflatt mit Dammundblasten.
- Learner Driver: Dumkopf Elplatt.

- Estate Car (Station Wagon): Der Schnoginwagon mit Bagzeroomfurrompin inderback.
- Mini (Compact): Der Buzzboxen mit Traffiksveerinfistshaker underfinger raisen.
- Petrol (Gasoline): Das Koslijozze fur Geddinsegreezeoffendentrousen.
- T Junction: Das dontgostraitonnenkorner.
- Power Brakes: Die Shtoppinworks mit edbangenon der vindscreen.
- Juggernaut (Outsized truck): Das Damgreatvagen mit das Hausenshaken.

# 2 MARCH

## *Burma Shave*

During my college years, the Espys drove every September from Oysterville, Washington, to Redlands, California, fifteen hundred miles away, returning every June. These were not uneventful journeys. Roads and automobiles were equally unreliable. Flat tires were as common as detours. Engines overheated; so did brakes. I remember that on one side trip to Crater Lake, Oregon, we parked, like everyone else, on the rim of the crater. As we came to a halt, a mother returned to the sedan next to us and removed her sleeping infant. She had scarcely picked up the child and slammed the door behind her when the brakes of her sedan let go; it rolled over the rim and plummeted two hundred and fifty feet into the lake. On another occasion I remember seeing a horse's head poke from the side window of a passing car; how the great beast had been compressed into the tiny aft-space of a passenger car remains a total mystery to me.

Advertisers frequently painted their messages on barns by the road. One common message, the slogan of a flour company, was "Pure as drifted snow." I found this message particularly thought-provoking because it was often half-concealed by a hill of manure shoveled from the barn window.

The one assured and unalloyed pleasure on those trips was the Burma Shave signs. In the late 1920s these shaving-cream advertisements speckled the highways of the entire west coast and, I suppose, of the nation. Burma Shave signs, spaced a hundred feet apart, were designed to be read from cars traveling thirty or forty miles an hour; if you drove faster, you lost the continuity. Hence: SLOW DOWN, PA / SAKES ALIVE / MA MISSED SIGNS / FOUR AND FIVE.

There was often a drama compressed into a series of signs: BEN / MET ANNA / MADE A HIT / NEGLECTED BEARD / BEN-ANNA SPLIT. Or philosophy: IF HARMONY / IS WHAT YOU CRAVE / THEN GET / A TUBA / BURMA SHAVE. At times there was the sorrow of the ages: MY JOB IS KEEPING / FACES CLEAN / AND NOBODY KNOWS / DE STUBBLE I'VE SEEN.*

---

*If you would like to read all the Burma Shave verses, look up *The Verse by the Side of the Road*, by Frank Rowsome. Stephen Greene Press published it in 1965.

# 3 MARCH

### *Pig Latin, Columbus and a Polka*

Pig Latin, a juvenile version of macaronics, may add Latin suffixes to English words:

#### PIG LATIN LOVE LYRIC

Lightibus outibus in a parlorum,
Boyibus kissibus sweeti girlorum;
Daddibus hearibus loudi smackorum,
Comibus quickibus with a cluborum.
Boyibus gettibus hardi spankorum,
Landibus nextibus outside a doorum;
Gettibus uppibus with a limporum,
Swearibus kissibus girli nomorum.
—*Anonymous*

This is a true macaronic:

#### COLUMBUS SAILED THE OCEAN BLUE

Columbus sailed the ocean blue
Nelle mille quattro cento novanta e due
But when he got there he had to stay
Fion al mille quattra cento novante e tre.
—*Anonymous*

This macaronic translates itself:

#### A POLKA LYRIC

Qui nunc dancere vult modo
Wants to dance in the fashion, oh!
Discere debet—ought to know,
Kickere floor cum heel and toe,
   One, two, three,
   Hop with me,
Whirligig, twirligig, rapide.

Polkam jungere, Virgo, vis,
Will you join the polka, miss?
Liberius—most willingly,
Sic agimus—then let us try:
   Nunc vide,
   Skip with me,
Whirlabout, roundabout, celere.

Tum laevo cito, tum dextra,
First to the left, and then t'other way;

Aspice retro in vultu,
You look at her, and she looks at you.
  Das palmam
  Change hands, ma'am;
Celere—run away, just in sham.
  *—Barclay Philips*

# 4 MARCH

## *Clerihews*

### 1. CLERIHEWS ON ENGLISH HISTORY

One of Henry's peeves
Was that Anne of Cleves
Was cold
To hold.
  *—J. C. Walker*

The venerable Bede
Could read.
It's a pity he couldn't spel
As wel.
  *—Lakon*

When Charles II
Beckoned
Nell
  Fell.
*—Ruth Silcock*

Edward the Confessor
Was not in any way an Aggressor;
Some who were afterwards King
Were much more that sort of thing.
  *—Silvia Tatham*

### 2. CLERIHEWS BY THE SCORE

Poor old Wagner
Was not a good bargainer.
He once sold an opera four hours long
For a song.
  *—R.L.O.*

Mozart
Could never resist a tart.
In the ordinary way
He ate seven or eight a day.
  *—Stanley J. Sharpless*

# 5 MARCH

### That Wrinkled and Golden Apricot

Many a serious poet could have risen to be a fine light rhymester if he had
worked at it. Swinburne and Housman were comic poets manqués. Samuel Butler, Samuel Taylor Coleridge, William Cowper—yes, and e. e. cummings, Walter de la Mare, and T. S. Eliot too—wrote some of the funniest lines in English.

It is too bad that we remember Oliver Goldsmith for

> When lovely woman stoops to folly

but not for

> The needy seldom pass'd her door,
> And always found her kind;
> She freely lent to all the poor—
> Who left a pledge behind.

One grows in fondness for Edith Sitwell on reading

> "Tra la la—
>     See me dance the polka,"
> Said Mr. Wagg like a bear,
> "With my top hat
> And my whiskers that
> (Tra la la) trap the Fair."

I had always liked her brother Sir Osbert, but I liked him even better after
reading "Elegy for Mr. Goodbeare," which ends:

> Do you remember Mr. Goodbeare,
> Mr. Goodbeare who never forgot?
> Do you remember Mr. Goodbeare,
> That wrinkled and golden apricot,
> Dear, bearded, godfearing Mr. Goodbeare
> Who remembered remembering such a lot?
>
> Oh, do you remember, do you remember,
> As I remember and deplore
> That day in drear and far-away December
> When dear, godfearing, bearded Mr. Goodbeare
> Could remember
> No more!

(Sir Osbert once recalled that while he was attending Eton a classmate com-
mitted suicide. At the memorial service, the headmaster asked the boys whether

they could give any hint as to why so well-liked and highly regarded a lad should have done away with himself. A moment of silence. Then the proverbial boy in the back timidly waved his hand: "Do you suppose, sir, it might have been the food?")  ·

# 6 MARCH

## *Inflation*

Our forebears too worried about inflation. This commentary was written before 1905:

### AVOIRDUPOIS

The length of this line indicates the ton of coal as dug by the miner.
This one indicates the ton shipped to the dealer.
The small dealer gets a ton like this.
This is the one you pay for.
This is what you get.
The residue is:
Cinders and
Ashes.
And this line will give you some conception of the size of the bill.

—*Anonymous*

A ninety-seven-year-old bulldozer operator in Kilmoganny, Ireland, traced the inflation spiral this way:

> The price of admission to the coronation of Henry I was one cro-card. But Henry II's went up to a pollard. At any of King John's frequent coronations, it soared to a suskin, and by Henry III's time it cost a dodkin.

A crocard was a coin of base metal, circulating at two to the penny in England during the thirteenth century.
A pollard was a "clipped coin"; I do not know what that means.
A suskin, or seskin, was a small coin current in the fifteenth century, passing for a penny.
A dodkin, or doit, was a minor Dutch coin, equal to one-eighth of a stiver or about one-half of a farthing; hence, a whit; a bit. A bit is the equivalent of a real, or one-eighth of a Spanish peso, once worth 12½ cents. It is usually referred to in multiples, as two, or four, bits.

### A CROQUARD, A DOLLARD, A SUSKIN, A DODKIN

In days of Harry One, long lost,
*A croquard would pay for a look at a king.*

A glimpse of Harry Two, though, cost
*A dollard—a far more extravagant thing.*

John One robbed realm of bread and buskin;
*A peek at the monarch went up to a suskin.*
When Harry Three came on, odds bodkins!—
*The croquard and dollard had doubled to dodkins!*

I hear from a respected scholar
*A President once could be seen for a dollar.*
—W.R.E.

# 7 MARCH

## *But Honey—Are You Making Any Money?*

*There are few sorrows, however poignant,*
*in which a good income is of no avail.*
—Logan Pearsall Smith

I mentioned at lunch today that I had never had money, never expected to have money, and assumed I would always go on living as if I had money. Someone, probably Octave Romaine, asked how this was possible, and I replied that it is all a matter of practice; the Espys have been doing it for generations. But I have to say that my two brothers-in-law, both investment bankers, are of very little help. On my sixtieth birthday one of them gave me a child's brass bank shaped like a nineteenth-century mail drop box. "You have had to listen to us talk about banking so much," said the accompanying note, "that I thought you might like to have a bank of your own." Unfortunately, he made no deposit; I shook the bank hard, but there was nothing inside, not even a nickel.*

My views on money accord with those below.

As I sat in the café I said to myself,
They may talk as they please about what they call pelf,
They may sneer as they like about eating and drinking,
But help it I cannot, I cannot help thinking
  How pleasant it is to have money, heigh-ho!
  How pleasant it is to have money . . .
—Arthur Hugh Clough

I'm tired of love, I'm still more tired of rhyme,
But money gives me pleasure all the time.
—Hilaire Belloc

---

*The song I remember best from the Depression had as its refrain, "But, honey—are you making any money? That's all I want to know."

"A feast is made for laughter, and wine maketh merry; but money answereth all things."

*—Ecclesiastes*

# 8 MARCH

## *An Explosion of Drummers*

Two *San Francisco Chronicle* columns by Ralph J. Gleason list multitudinous nouns—also called venereal nouns and collectives—that might be used in the world of entertainment. (*Venereal*, from "Venus," is commonly limited today to sexual matters but relates also to hunting, the goddess being patroness of both; indeed, there are analogies between them. Young noblemen in the Middle Ages had to memorize such venereal terms as *a pride of lions, a gaggle of geese,* and *a trip of dottrel*.)

To start the game, Mr. Gleason offered *an explosion of drummers, a honk of tenors, a hipness of fans, an ego of soloists, a stride of pianos, a slush of trombones,* and the like. My favorite was *a pox of critics.*

In the next column it was the reader's turn. Charles F. Dery suggested a *clique of castanets.* Other inspirations, not all connected with the business of entertainment, were *a fuzz of policemen, a titter of thrushes, a quest of stags, a palm of hatcheck girls, a trance of jazz fans, a pomade of washroom attendants, a stack of chorus girls,* and *a drag of squares.*

Ethel Lanselt wrote:

"Dear Sir: As one who doesn't like jazz—doesn't understand it—I say don't forget an *exasperation of listeners.*"

Other collectives:

- A corruption of courts • An indignation of litigants • An arrogance of attorneys • A corpulence of bailiffs • A petulance of judges • A somnolence of jurors.
  *—Jack Bailey*

- A parley of diplomats.
  *—Ronald F. Kennedy*

- A swarm of people is called a crowd. A crowd of clouds is called an overcast. An overcast of a Broadway play is caused by too many understudies.
- A convention of surgeons is called a flotilla of cutters.
  *—Gerald Pocock*

- A clutch of straws • A fleet of foot • A litter of picnickers • A peel of strippers • A cast of fishermen • A crew of interest • A brood of tea • A s'warm of summer greetings • A s'cool of winter greetings.
  *—Alan F. G. Lewis*

- A pall of mourners.
- A strike of workers.
- A chowder of clams.
- A conversion of sinners.
    —*Roy Wilder, Jr.*

From *Reader's Digest:*

- A brace of orthodontists.
    —*Don Tewksbury*

- A quibbling of siblings.
    —*Ann Menconi*

- A scoop of reporters.
    —*Christine Heffner*

# 9 MARCH

## E Pluribus Unum

I abhor the smell of uncooked fish. There is an excellent fish store in the next block, and between one step and the next as I pass by—the exact place varies from day to day, so it is no use holding my breath—a nauseous whiff, for just one instant, invades my nostrils. Erasmus had a worse problem; he could not stand fish raw or cooked; the Lenten season was torture to him. "My heart is Catholic," he mourned, "but my stomach is Lutheran."

Which has nothing to do with the following verse, except that one of the creatures mentioned in it is an eel. The point is that the words species, congeries, shambles, and kudos, all ending in *s*, are identical in their singular and plural spellings:*

> The drunken Species homeward reels,
> Or reel; it sets the mind ajar
> That Species is and Species are.
>
> A Congeries of conger eels
> Is either are or is a bunch;
> Are either is or are for lunch.
>
> A Shambles of new-slaughtered seals
> Is either are or is deplorable;
> Are either is or are abhorrable.

---

* Ralph Beaman has written a verse featuring words of French origin—gardebras, corps, précis, faux pas, rendezvous—which, besides being identical in singular and plural spellings, share another oddity: the final s, mute in the singular, is pronounced in the plural.

No Kudos for this verse, one feels,
Is either are or is in view;
Nor is, are, it, he, she, they, due.
—W.R.E.

# 10 MARCH

### What Acts! They Ap-Paul!

Half of the entries in a book I wrote recently on word origins have vanished from my mind. With a memory that bad, how can I be expected to learn from experience? How, on my deathbed, can I repent a life ill-spent?

By the time I have fixed the name of a fellow club member in my mind—say it takes about twenty-five years—he dies. The result is that some of my best friends avoid telling me who they are.

Mnemonics is a system that seeks to counteract such faulty memory through word associations. Thus:

*For avoiding hangover:*
  Beer on whiskey very risky.
  Whiskey on beer never fear.

*For remembering the excretory organs:*
  SKILL is an anagram of *Skin, Kidneys, Intestines, Liver, Lungs.*

*For the rule of division of fractions:*
  The number you are dividing by
  Turn upside down and multiply.

  (But if I turn 75 upside down it becomes $\angle S$. How can I multiply by *that?*)

*For the successive fates of the wives of Henry VIII (Catherine of Aragon, Anne Boleyn, Jane Seymour, Anne of Cleves, Catherine Howard, Catherine Parr):*
  Divorced, beheaded, died;
  Divorced, beheaded, survived.

*For the Great Lakes, west to east:*
  Sergeant-Major *h*ates *e*ating onions (Superior, Michigan, Huron, Erie, Ontario)

*For the Seven Hills of Rome:*
  Can Queen Victoria *e*at *c*old *a*pple *p*ie? (Capitoline, Quirinal, Viminal, Esquiline, Caelian, Aventine, Palatine)

*For the planets in their order from the sun:*
  Men *v*ery *e*asily *m*ake *j*ugs *s*erve *u*seful *n*octurnal *p*urposes. (Mercury, Venus, Earth, Mars, Jupiter, Saturn, Uranus, Neptune, Pluto)

*A mnemonic on the British royal line:*

> Willie, Willie, Harry, Stee
> Harry, Dick, Harry Three
> One, Two, Three Neds, Richard Two
> Harry Four, Five, Six. Then who?
> Edward Four, Five, Dick the Bad,
> Harrys twain and Ned the Lad,
> Mary, Bessie, James the Vain,
> Charlie, Charlie, James again,
> William and Mary, Anna Gloria,
> Four Georges, William, and Victoria.
> Edward the Seventh next, and then
> George the Fifth in 1910.
> Edward the Eighth soon abdicated,
> And so a George was reinstated.
>                          (I add:)
> Then Bessie Two was coronated.

I started to write a mnemonic passage that would fix in mind the order of the books of the New Testament:

O Matthew—Mark Luke in the John! What Acts; They Ap-Paul!

But the next book was Romans, and since I could not imagine a devout Christian sharing his bathroom with a Roman heathen, I gave up.

# 11 MARCH

## A Mrs. Kr. Mr.

In my sixteen years at *Reader's Digest,* a continuing assignment was to prepare the cover essay—a brief article, approved and signed by some person of note, which by coincidence always wound up with a kind word for the *Digest.* (When I sent Groucho Marx his essay with the agreed-upon payment, he replied, "I hope your check is better than your copy.")

My usual procedure was to visit the prospective signator, come to an agreement on the thrust of the article, study his speech mannerisms, and then try to make the piece sound the way *he* sounded to me.

I particularly enjoyed this assignment, because it gave me a chance to talk on an unusually personal basis with celebrities ranging from popes to presidents and from poets to polar explorers—people whom otherwise I would never have met at all. (Albert Einstein was my favorite, first because he was a saint, and second because he wore no socks.)

All this comes to mind because today I lunched with a man who was in my department at the *Digest*. He says that when I was writing those cover essays I *became* the person in whose name I was writing. He says when I was General Marshall I walked like the General and snapped at my associate if he did not salute. When I was Winston Churchill, I took brandy before lunch and frequently mumbled, "This is an impertinence up with which I will not put." And when I was Richard Nixon, I began every second sentence with "Let me make one thing perfectly clear."

By way of thanks, I gave my friend a piece of excellent advice. I told him the *Digest* editors have not taken the concept of condensation nearly far enough. They should condense the individual words as well as the articles. I gave him this poem—inspired by a limerick I read somewhere—as a style guide, and you may expect to see the *Digest* written in abbreviations any month now:*

> The Mrs. kr. Mr.
> Then how her Mr. kr.!
> He kr. kr. kr.
> Until he raised a blr.
> The blr. killed his Mrs.
> Then how he mr. krs.!
> He mr. mr. mr.
> Until he kr. sr.
> He covered her with krs.
> Till she became his Mrs.
> The Mrs. kr. Mr.
> (and so on and on)
> —W.R.E.

# 12 March

## *Single-Rhymed Verse*

### SONNET WITH A DIFFERENT LETTER AT THE END OF EVERY LINE†

O for a muse of fire, a sack of dough,
Or both! O promissory notes of woe!
One time in Santa Fe, N.M.,
Ol' Winfield Townley Scott and I . . . but whoa.

One can exert oneself, *ff,*
Or architect a heaven like Rimbaud,
Or if that seems, how shall I say, *de trop,*
One can at least write sonnets, apropos

---

* See 26 September for a similar suggestion to *The New York Times.*
† And just one rhyme.

Of nothing save the do-re-mi-fa-sol
Of poetry itself. Is not the row
Of perfect rhymes, the terminal bon mot,
Abeisance enough to the Great O?

"Observe," said Chairman Mao to Premier Chou,
*"On voyage à Parnasse pour prendre les eaux.*
*On voyage comme poisson,* incog."
—*George Starbuck*

# 13 MARCH

## *A Croaking of Frogs*

OYSTERVILLE—The frogs are making loud communal love in the marshes today. May all their troubles be tadpoles! The time has come for two of my favorite frog verses:

### THE FROG

What a wonderful bird the frog are—
When he stand he sit almost;
When he hop, he fly almost.
He ain't got no sense hardly;
He ain't got no tail hardly either.
When he sit, he sit on what he ain't got almost.
—*Anonymous*

Come to think of it, that is not exactly a verse. But this is:

### THE FROG

Be kind and tender to the Frog,
    And do not call him names,
As "slimy-skin" or "Polly-wog,"
    Or likewise, "Ugly James,"
Or "Gape-a-grin," or "Toad-gone-wrong,"
    Or "Billy Bandy-knees,"
The frog is justly sensitive
    To epithets like these.
No animal will more repay
    A treatment kind and fair.
At least, so lonely people say
Who keep a frog (and, by the way,
    They are extremely rare).
—*Hilaire Belloc*

# 14 MARCH

### I'd Like to Be a Corsican*

*Every male Corsican thinks he is Napoleon Bonaparte.*
*—Travel article.*

I'd like to be a Corsican,
A coarsey, horsy Corsican,
And do the deeds a Corsican,
Or even those his horsican,
　　His horsican, his horsican.

When weary grows the Corsican
Of wedded intercoursican
Arrange a quick divorcican
And trot off on his horsican,
　　His horsican, his horsican.

With oaths and curses coarsican
Take courtesans by forcican
And if his throat grows hoarsican
Tap out his oaths in Morsican,
　　In Morsican, in Morsican.

The Corsican, of Corsican
Take any course, that Corsican,
Of Corsican, of Corsican,
Of course, of course, of Corsican . . .
　　*I'd like to be a Corsican . . .*
　　　　　　　　—W.R.E.

# 15 MARCH

### Amo, Amas, Felis-itous

AMO, AMAS

Amo, amas,
I love a lass,
As cedar tall and slender;
　Sweet cowslip's grace
　Is her nominative case,
And she's of the feminine gender.

* To be read loud—the louder the better.

Rorum, corum, sunt di-vorum,
  Harum, scarum, divo;
Tag-rag, merry-derry, periwig and
  hatband,
  Hic, hoc, horum genitivo.

Can I decline a numph so divine?
  Her voice like a flute is dulcis;
Her oculus bright, her manus white
  And soft, when I tacto, her pulse is.

  *Chorus* (Rorum, corum, etc.)

O how bella, my puella
  I'll kiss in secula seculorum;
If I've luck, sir, she's my uxor,
  O dies benedictorum.

  *Chorus* (Rorum, corum, etc.)
  —*O'Keefe*


## VERY FELIS-ITOUS

Felis sedit by a hole,
Intente she, cum omni soul,
  Predere rats.
Mice cucurrerunt trans the floor,
In numero duo tres or more,
  Obliti cats.

Felis saw them oculis,
"I'll have them," inquit she, "I guess,
  Dum ludunt."
Tunc illa crepit toward the group,
"Habeam," dixit, "good rat soup—
  Pingues sunt."

Mice continued all ludere,
Intent they in ludum vere,
  Gaudenter.
Tunc rushed the felis into them,
Et tore them omnes limb from limb,
  Violenter.

MORAL
Mures omnes, nunc be shy,
Et aurem praebe mihi—

Bensigne:
Sic hoc satis—"verbum sat,"
Avoid a whopping Thomas cat
Studiose.
                              —*Green Kendrick*

This is not macaronics, but it does stem from Latin:

### A CLASSICAL EDUCATION

The Latin teacher's explicating
    *Amo, amas*
To Latin students conjugating
    Right in class.
                              —*W.R.E.*

Now, back to macaronics:

### THE ELDERLY GENTLEMAN

Prope ripam fluvii solus
    A senex silently sat
Super capitum ecce his wig
    Et wig super, ecce his hat.

Blew Zephyrus alte, acerbus,
    Dum elderly gentleman sat;
Et a capite took up quite torve
    Et in rivum projecit his hat.
                              —*J. A. Morgan*

# 16 March

### *Presidents in Prime Rhyme*

This is the birthday of President James Madison, born March 16, 1751. President Madison shares with several thousand other people, alive and dead, the distinction of being my second cousin four times removed. Two other presidents similarly distinguished are James Monroe and Andrew Jackson. When I was too young to know better I spent an inordinate amount of time calculating my relationship to various presidents (anyone whose people came over before the middle of the eighteenth century can find a few in his line), but these three were the closest kin I could find. Second cousins four times removed, even presidents, count for little on a credit application at the bank; but at least a man can write verses about them.

## JAMES MADISON

James Madison was puny;
　　James Madison was small.
He built a Constitution
　　Ten Constellations tall.

We wake the better mornings,
　　We sleep the better nights,
For Jimmy's Constitution,
　　And Jimmy's Bill of Rights.

## JAMES MONROE

When the most allowed to lovers
Was to snuggle through the covers,
James Monroe arranged a deal
Called the Era of Good Feel.
Slap and tickle, touch and go!
Hail the Doctrine of Monroe!

## ANDREW JACKSON

Andy Jackson started school,
　　Ding, dang, and tallyho;
First durned day he fought a duel,
　　Ding, dang, and tallyho.

Andy warn't so good at writing,
　　Ding, dang, and tallyho;
But he got straight A's at fighting,
　　Ding, dang, and tallyho.

Licked the British in his teens,
　　Ding, dang, and tallyho;
Won the Battle of New Orleans,
　　Ding, dang, and tallyho.

Got his presidential innings,
　　Ding, dang, and tallyho;
Said, "The victor takes the winnings,"
　　Ding, dang, and tallyho.

Whopped the banks and whopped the Court,
　　Ding, dang, and tallyho.
Don't sell Andy Jackson short,
　　Ding, dang, and tallyho.

　　　　　　　　　　　　—W.R.E.

# 17 MARCH

### *Iorz Feixfuli*

Robert Ripley, from whom most of my erudition derives, said there are ten ways to spell the sound *r* in English, thirty-three ways to spell *e*, seventeen ways to spell *v*, thirty-six ways to spell *i*, and seventeen ways to spell *s*. Even if he is a bit off on one side or the other, that is a lot of spellings to memorize.

Among many savants to urge spelling reform was George Bernard Shaw, who proposed that one letter of the alphabet be altered or deleted each year, thus giving the populace time to absorb the change. Here, according to one critic, is how his suggestion would work:

> In Year 1 that useless letter "c" would be dropped to be replased by either "k" or "s," and likewise "x" would no longer be part of the alphabet. The only kase in which "c" would be retained would be the "ch" formation, which will be dealt with later. Year 2 might well reform "w" spelling, so that "which" and "one" would take the same konsonant, wile Year 3 might well abolish "y" replasing it with "i," and Iear 4 might fiks the "g-j" anomali wonse and for all.
>
> Jenerally, then, the improvement would kontinue iear bai iear, with Iear 5 doing awai with useles double konsonants, and Iears 6-12 or so modifaiing vowlz and the rimeining voist and unvoist konsonants. Bai Ier 15 or sou, it wud fainali bi posibl tu meik ius ov the ridandant letez "c," "y," and "x"—bai now jast a memori in the maindz ov ould doderez—tu riplais "ch," "sh," and "th" rispektivli.
>
> Fainali, xen, aafte sam 20 iers ov orxogrefkl riform, wi wud hev a lojikl, kohirnt speling in ius xrewawt xe Ingliy-spiking werld. Haweve, sins xe Wely, xe Airiy, and xe Skots du not spik Ingliy, xei wud hev to hev a speling siutd tu xer oun lengwij. Xei kud, haweve, orlweiz lern Ingliy as a sekond lengwij et skuul.
>
> Iorz feixfuli,
>
> M. J. Yilz.
> —*M. J. Shields*

If you cannot spell, take comfort; neither could Shakespeare.

### AMPLIFIED SPELLING

> A little buoy said "Mother deer,
> May eye go out two play?
> The son is bright, the heir is clear;
> Owe mother, don't say neigh."

"Go forth, my sun," the mother said;
   His ant said, "Take ewer slay,
Ewer gneiss knew sled awl painted read,
   But do not lose ewer weigh."

"Owe, know!" he cried, and sawt the street
   With hart sew full of glee.
The weather changed, and snow and sleet
   And reign fell fierce and free.

Threw snowdrifts grate, threw water pool,
   He flue with mite and mane.
Said he, "Tho eye wood walk by rule,
   Eye may not ride, 'tis plane.

"I'de like two meat some kindly sole,
   For hear gnu dangers weight,
And yonder stairs a treacherous whole;
   Two sloe has bin my gate.

"A peace of bred, a bneiss hot stake,
   Eye'd chew if eye were home;
This crewl fair my hart will brake;
   I love knot thus two Rome.

"I'm week and pail; I've mist my rode,"
   But here a carte came passed.
Buoy and his slay were safely toad
   Back to his home at last.
            —*Anonymous*

# 18 MARCH

### *Slicing Cooper in Twain*

OYSTERVILLE—It has been raining for a week. In the words of Edward Lear:

> O pumpkins! O periwinkles!
> O pobblesquattles! how him rain!

Since it is too wet to stick my nose outdoors, and since I have no interest in exercising my mind, I am drifting through Mark Twain's comments on J. Fenimore Cooper's early-nineteenth-century "Leatherstocking Tales." How lucky I feel that Mark Twain is not around to review any book of mine!

## "THE BROKEN TWIG SERIES"

In his little box of stage properties Cooper kept six or eight cunning devices, tricks, artifices for his savages and woodsmen to deceive and circumvent each other with, and he was never so happy as when he was working these innocent things and seeing them go. A favorite one was to make a moccasined person tread in the tracks of the moccasined enemy, and thus hide his own trail. Cooper wore out barrels and barrels of moccasins in working that trick. Another stage property that he pulled out of his box pretty frequently was his broken twig. He prized his broken twig above all the rest of his effects, and worked it the hardest. It is a restful chapter in any book of his when somebody doesn't step on a dry twig and alarm all the reds and whites for two hundred yards around. Every time a Cooper person is in peril, and absolute silence is worth four dollars a minute, he is sure to step on a dry twig. There may be a hundred handier things to step on, but that wouldn't satisfy Cooper. Cooper requires him to turn out and find a dry twig; and if he can't do it, go and borrow one. In fact, the Leatherstocking Series ought to have been called the Broken Twig Series.

—*Mark Twain*

# 19 MARCH

### *If You Lithp, Thay "He Grunth"*

In John Barth's *The Sotweed Factor,* a pupil of Poet Laureate Ebenezer Cooke rhymes several difficult words for his master by, well, cheating—pronouncing *imPORTunacy,* for instance, importunACy and *procrUStean* procrusteAN. Even by cheating, though, he cannot rhyme *month.* Ebenezer comforts him; there is no such thing as a rhyme for month, he says; it "hath not its like."

But, as noted earlier,* Christina Rossetti once wrote:

> How many weeks in a month?
> Four, as the swift moon run'th

—surely a correct, if tortured rhyme. And should a man willing to mispronounce *importunate* object to breaking a word in two for the sake of a rhyme?

> It is unth-
> inkable to find
> A rhyme for month,
> Except this special kind.
> —W.R.E.

*See 16 February.

See how easy it is?

Etymologically, the very word *rhyme* is an accident. It was introduced around 1550 through a mistaken correspondence with *rhythm*. *Rime,* the older and correct spelling, is from the Anglo-Saxon *rim*—"number, computation."

Rhyme is only one aspect of the science of versification. The two subdivisions defined below are as essential, if less familiar:

### ARSIS AND THESIS

Two antonyms to you I put:
The *arsis* tiptoes through the foot;
The *thesis*, on the other hand,
Calls out in clamorous command
(Unless, of course, they're turned around,
And each assumes the other's sound.
Then loud is arsis, thesis low,
As all you arses ought to know.)
—*W.R.E.*

# 20 MARCH

### *I Sawyer Saw. Does That Make Me a Sawyer?*

*If you grant that:*

A man sawing wood in the woods is a sawyer
While a second man, following law, is a lawyer

*It follows that:*

A crab has a claw, so a crab is a clawyer;
The rodent that gnaws at my cheese is a gnawyer;
A crow, since it caws, is correctly a cawyer.

*I now apply this reasoning to your own situation:*

If your gem has a flaw, then your gem is a flawyer;
If your yawl tends to yaw, then your yawl is a yawyer;
If your baby Charles baws, he will be a Charles Boyer;
If you suck up your tea with a straw, you're a strawyer.

*Which leads irresistibly to this doleful conclusion:*

Do these helpful lines stick in your craw?—You're a crawyer.
Do I hear you say pshaw?—Pshaw to you too, you pshawyer.
—*W.R.E.*

# 21 MARCH

*SOUVENIR**

Louisa Bonner sent me a blurred copy of this typeface tarradiddle, and John Speziali, who has printer's ink in his veins, went from shop to shop to find the faces required to re-create the poem.

A **Spartan Bookman** in his **Cloister**

Thought the **Antique** world his oyster.

*Times Roman* were his great delight,

**Italian Old Style** girls the height

Of **Radiant** beauty. What a shame

No 𝕸𝖊𝖉𝖉𝖎𝖓𝖌 𝕿𝖊𝖝𝖙 will he declaim.

Instead he's **Stymied** in his **Tower**

SHADOW like and wondering how or

When he'll find a **Lydian** pal.

A *Cursive Legend* of a gal.

He yearns to be befriended

By **Venus Bold Extended**

—*Christopher Reed,* in *The Browser,*
Harvard University Press

# 22 MARCH

*Re: Rebuses*

My thanks to Paul E. Manheim for this rebus:

Inscription on an envelope which was delivered by the Post Office to the right recipient:

WOOD
JOHN
MASS

*The title type is "Souvenir." See also 28 November.

Mary J. Youngquist prepared these word rebuses:

1.
```
        ADO
ADO            ADO
        O
ADO            ADO
        ADO
```

3.
```
E
M
A
R
F
```

5.
```
ONE ANOTHER
ONE ANOTHER
ONE ANOTHER
ONE ANOTHER
ONE ANOTHER
ONE ANOTHER
```

2.
WORLAMEN

4.
ONALLE

6.
```
M E
A L
```

# 23 MARCH

## *Chain States*

Wyoming is in Kent County, Delaware;
Delaware is in Southampton County, Virginia;
Virginia is in Kitsap County, Washington;
Washington is in Knox County, Maine;
Maine is in Coconino County, Arizona;
Arizona is in Burt County, Nebraska;
Nebraska is in Jennings County, Indiana;
Indiana is in Indiana County, Pennsylvania;
Pennsylvania is in Mobile County, Alabama;
Alabama is in Genesee County, New York;
New York is in Santa Rosa County, Florida;
Florida is in Houghton County, Michigan;
Michigan is in Osage County, Kansas;
Kansas is in Seneca County, Ohio;
Ohio is in Gunnison County, Colorado;
Colorado is in South Central District, Alaska;
Alaska is in Mineral County, West Virginia;
West Virginia is in St. Louis County, Minnesota;
Minnesota is in Colquitt County, Georgia;
Georgia is in Lamar County, Texas;
Texas is in Baltimore County, Maryland;
Maryland is in East Baton Rouge County, Louisiana;

Louisiana is in Pike County, Missouri;
Missouri is in Brown County, Illinois;
Illinois is in Sequoyah County, Oklahoma;
Oklahoma is in Daviess County, Kentucky.
—*Darryl Francis*

# 24 MARCH

*Ah, Zelda!*

Amoral angel,
Bifurcate bawd;
Coyly capricious
Duopod . . .

Eyelids embellished;
Flirtily frocked;
Glittering gewgaws
(Handily hocked) . . .

Impishly innocent,
Jaunty, jejune,
Kissably kittenish,
Loveable loon:

Marry me! Make me
Notably nowed—
Overjoyed . . . osculant . . .
Peacockish proud!

Quinquagenarian
Randily roused;
Skippetyskippeting,
Tenderly toused.

\* \* \*

*Unsanctified*
*Venus vied*
*With wanton wick*
*Xenogenic;\**

---

\*Xenogenous, really; but I needed the rhyme.

*Yielding ye,*
*Zestfully,*
Zelda Z.:

Amoral angel . . . (repeat)
—W.R.E.

# 25 MARCH

## *Up and Down Counting Song*

1. Dear ewe, dear lamb, I've 1 thee: we
2. Will 2tle through the fields together;
3. With 3d and pipe we'll jubilee;
4. We'll gambol back and 4th in glee;
5. If 5 your heart, who gives a D.
6. How raw and 6 the weather?
7. In 7th heaven me and thee
8. Will 8 and soon find ecstasy—
9. My ewe be9 is tied to me,
10. And 10der is the tether!

10. Yet there may be a 10dency
9. (Someday when 9 no more know whether
8. You 8 for me still longingly
7. Or find our love less 7ly)
6. For you in class6 sulk to flee—
5. Off 5 no doubt to new bellwether
4. And fresher 4age. . . . It may be
3. We'll both 3quire a style more free,
2. And find the Bird of Love 2 be
1. Reduced to 1 Pinfeather.

—W.R.E.

### ILL DONE

Of all the ill deeds you have done,
Which would you undo now? Name one.

Of all ill deeds you hoped to do,
Which still remain undone? Name two.

Of ill deeds in your memory,
Which would you do again? Name three.

Of ill deeds you should most abhor,
Which do you treasure most? Name four.
—W.R.E.

# 26 MARCH

### Jovanovich

Sandy Choron says this takeoff on Lewis Carroll's "Jabberwocky" has been circulating for a quarter of a century or more in New York publishing offices, with changes from time to time in the names of publishers listed.

'Twas potter, and the little brown
Did simon and schuster in the shaw;
All mosby were the ballantines,
And the womraths mcgraw.

Beware Jovanovich, my son!
The knopfs that crown, the platts that munk!
Beware the doubleday, and shun
The grolier wagnallfunk!

He took his putnam sword in hand,
Long time the harcourt brace he sought;
So rested he by the crowell tree
And stood awhile in thought.

And as in harper thought he stood,
Jovanovich, with eyes of flame,
Came houghton mifflin through the wood
And bowkered as it came!

Dodd mead! dodd mead! and from his steed
His dutton sword went kennicatt!
He left it dead, and with its head
He went quadrangling back.

"And hast thou slain Jovanovich?
Come to my arms, my bantam boy!
Oh, stein and day! Giroux! McKay!"
He scribnered in his joy.

'Twas potter, and the little brown
Did simon and schuster in the shaw;
All mosby were the ballantines,
And the womraths mcgraw.
—*Author unknown*

# 27 MARCH

### Stroke, Strike, and Other Epigrams

*To stroke,* meaning "to butter up," was used hundreds of years before Watergate:

### TO FOOL, OR KNAVE

Thy praise, or dispraise is to me alike,
One does not stroke me, or the other strike.
—*Anonymous*

Other epigrams:

### A SENSIBLE GIRL'S REPLY TO MOORE'S

*"Our couch shall be roses all spangled with dew."*
It would give me rheumatics, and so it would you.
—*Walter Savage Landor*

### THE GEORGES

George the First was always reckoned
Vile, but viler George the Second;
And what mortal ever heard
Any good of George the Third?
When from earth the Fourth descended
(God be praised!) the Georges ended.
—*Walter Savage Landor*

In fairness, I add this couplet:

Nay! The Fifth was much improved;
George the Sixth was even loved.
—*W.R.E.*

### ON QUEEN CAROLINE

Most Gracious Queen, we thee implore
To go away and sin no more,

But if that effort be too great,
To go away at any rate.
—*Anonymous*

### LE JEUNE HOMME DE DIJON

Il y avait un jeune homme de Dijon,
Qui n'avait que peu de religion.
Il dit: "Quant à moi,
Je déteste tous les trois,
Le Père, et le Fils, et le Pigeon."
—*Norman Douglas*

### LINES FOR AN EMINENT POET AND CRITIC

He has come to such a pitch
Of self-consciousness that he
Dares not scratch, if he has the itch,
For fear he is the flea.
—*Patric Dickinson*

A man said to the universe:
"Sir, I exist!"
"However," replied the universe,
"The fact has not created in me
A sense of obligation."
—*Stephen Crane*

# 28 March

## *Schizophrenic Words*

In Hebrew, says Harvey Minkoff in *Verbatim*, the root consonants *ZBL* led to both *ZrBuL*, meaning "exalted," and *ZeBeL*, meaning "manure"; *KDS* diverged to *KoDeS*, "holy," and *KeDeSah*, "prostitute." In Chinese, *kungfu* translates, on the one hand, as "task, accomplishment," and, on the other, as "leisure."

Each word in the following list has at least one definition which runs contrary to normal usage or two or more definitions which seem to contradict each other. The authority is *Webster's Second*.

- *Acidity* means "alkalinity." *Affection* means "animosity."
- *Bent* means "leveled." *Bleach* means "blacking." *Bless* means "curse." *Bluefish* means "greenfish." *Bosom* means "depression." *Bride* means "a spouse of either sex."
- *Emancipate* means "to enslave."

- *Fill* means "to pour out."
- *General* means "Admiral."
- *Harlot* means "male menial." *Help* means "hinder." *Host* means "guest."
  —*Tom Pulliam*

Additional examples appear in Answers and Solutions.

# 29 MARCH

## Hello, Honey, Everything Is Mighty Nice Up Here

A woman willed her estate to her husband but cautioned him in a videotaped message:

> Don't go to Vegas, or play with stock,
> Or drink much after six o'clock,
> Or party far into the night,
> You'll join me if you don't live right.
> And sports cars and funny hats,
> You're really much too old for that.
> And please, when all my songs are sung,
> Don't fall for someone sweet and young.

Here is mortality abbreviated:

ALPHA AND OMEGA

> From ABC to Ph.D.
> Takes 30 years or so,
> Then FHA and PTA
> May be the route to go.
> So PDQ the years go by,
> From IOUs we're free,
> And in the end we can expect
> A well-earned R.I.P.!
> —*Jean B. Boyce*

# 30 MARCH

## The Most Unkindest Cut of All

I mentioned Mark Antony's "the most unkindest cut of all" in a manuscript. The copy editor penciled in the margin, "Poor grammar. Cut 'most' or 'est.'" In fact, the double comparative and double superlative have long and honorable histories in English. These examples are cited by the *Oxford English Dictionary:*

- I should be glad . . . to see a more equaller Balance among Sea-men, and their Imployers (1669).
- I have heard, good Sir, that every Body has a more betterer and a more worserer Side of the Face than the other (1752).
- But Paris was to me / More lovelier than all the world beside (Tennyson, 1832).
- I was always first in the most gallantest scrapes in my younger days (Hardy, 1878).
- My most extremest time of misery (1881).

Improper usages today, certainly; yet they come trippingly, and add emphasis. Why not revive them?

# 31 MARCH

## *Witty Word Square*

Word squares generally bore me; I am reminded of Samuel Johnson's comparison of a woman preacher with a dog that has learned to stand on its hind legs: "It is not done well; yet you are surprised to find it done at all." Any word square created by Mary Youngquist, however, tickles brain cells and risibilities alike. This one contains twelve lines, most consisting of doubled words. The lines are sometimes repeated, and the whole reads the same from left to right or top to bottom.

```
G O R G E S G O R G E S
O M O O V E O M O O V E
R O B B E R R O B B E R
G O B B L E G O B B L E
E V E L Y N E V E L Y N
S E R E N E S E R E N E
G O R G E S G O R G E S
O M O O V E O M O O V E
R O B B E R R O B B E R
G O B B L E G O B B L E
E V E L Y N E V E L Y N
S E R E N E S E R E N E
```

Miss Youngquist (now Mrs. Hazard) explains her creative process as follows:

- GORGES! GORGES! was the enthusiastic cry of the first explorers to view the expanse of the Grand Canyon; it is recorded in the *Journal of Unusual Nature Kingdom* (*JUNK*), February 30, 1818.
- O M-O-OVE! O M-O-OVE! is the anguished utterance of a camel driver whose beast is clumsily standing on his master's foot (see *Handbook of Camel Drivers,* page xiv).
- ROBBER, ROBBER! (heard often in New York City) is an expression common to persons discovering a thief on the premises (so common, indeed, that no source need be given).
- GOBBLE, GOBBLE is from "Old MacDonald Had a Farm," a standard study of husbandry. The section on turkeys (*Meleagris gallopavo*) is frequently cited: "Here a gobble, there a gobble, everywhere a gobble, gobble."
- EVELYN, EVELYN! The impassioned outburst to his leading lady of the star of the classic silent movie *The Ecstasies of Evelyn* (see the Late, Late, Late Show).
- SERENE, SERENE. The reply of a one-hundred-year-old guru when asked the state of his mind (quoted in *Gurus I Have Known and Loved*).

# APRIL

## 1 APRIL

### April Fool

There are days when life seems like an elaborate April Fool's joke:

#### I THOUGHT AND I THOUGHT

I thought and I thought, till I thought
The thought that the ages had sought.
Unfortunately
It turned out to be
Not the thought that I ought to have thought.
—*W.R.E.*

#### WORMS

Worms aren't witty;
Worms aren't pretty;
Worms just
    squirm.
This, I think,
Serves to link
Man and
    worm.
—*W.R.E.*

## 2 APRIL

### A Hundred Words Once

Challenged to write a composition of 100 words without repeating a single word, a high school English class put their heads together and came up with this:

Let's go! The challenge is to write a composition without using any word more than once. Do you think that it can be done? If not, give one reason for doing this. While we are sitting here in English class at Pompton Lakes High School, Lakeside Avenue, New Jersey, all of us figure out something which makes sense. Mrs. Feldman helps her pupils because another teacher said they couldn't accomplish such tasks. Nobody has fresh ideas right now. Goal—100! How far did students get? Eighty-five done already; fifteen left. "Pretty soon none!" says Dennis O'Neill. Gary Putnam and Debra Petsu agree. So there!

Congratulations to the students of Pompton Lakes High School—and to Pearl L. Feldman, their teacher. Now how about you?

# 3 APRIL

## As I Lay Dying

The last words of James Croll, the teetotalling Scots physicist, were, "I'll take a wee drop o' that. I don't think there's much fear o' me learning to drink now."*

Dr. Croll's farewell fittingly rounded off his life; and I treasure several other death-bed statements for the same reason. Thus Dr. Joseph Green, a surgeon, said to his physician, "Congestion." He then took his own pulse, murmured, "Stopped," and died. As professional to the last was the Swiss physiologist Albrecht, who checked his pulse and said, "Now I am dying. The artery ceases to beat."

Dominique Bonhours, the grammarian, commented, "I am about to—or I am going to—die; either expression is used."

Wilhelm Hegel, the philosopher, also stayed in character. "Only one man understood me," he sighed . . . "and he didn't understand me."

Less admirable, but equally apt, were the last words of Dylan Thomas: "I've had eighteen straight whiskies. I think that is the record."

Asked whether he would prefer to have his niece or his nurse spend the night by his bedside, the playwright Sir Henry Arthur Jones replied: "The prettier. Now fight for it!"

I like Arthur Roth's list of apocryphal last words:

> A judge: "I have no precedent for this."
> A believer in reincarnation: "Intermission time already?"
> A lawyer: "My final brief."
> A mortician: "I'm off on a busman's holiday."
> A childless railroad conductor: "End of the line."
> A philosopher: "No cogito, ergo no sum."
> An atheist: "I was kidding all along."
> A student: "I fail."

---

*He was more flexible than my father, who told me: "At twenty-one I took my first swallow of whiskey. I had heard whiskey was an acquired taste, but I liked that first drink so much I thought it best never to take another." And he never did.

A bridge player: "I pass."
A gossip: "I'm just dying to tell someone."
An elevator operator: "Going up?"
My wife: "I'm not ready yet, give me another five minutes."

# 4 APRIL

### Anagrams from Punch

For a while I wrote a weekly anagram verse for *Punch*. Then a new editor took over. I am told that he started to hang up his hat, paused, and said to his secretary, "No—first, get rid of Espy."

I still don't see what he could have against verses like these:

### ANIMAL FARE

Each beast that in this ****** moos
(Or ******, or quacks, or honks, or coos),
Must grace our ******, cleaned and dressed.
This shows which beast is ******.

### PRE-PARENTAL PLAINT

When I ******* to be a father,
You ******* my willingness to bother.
Now I ******* , for I foresee
You'll leave the ******* to me.

### A CLERIC OF ANTIC ******

On a diet to cure him of gripes,
A ****** ate the ****** of ******,
Which altered him oddly;
He was no longer godly,
But a ****** who danced playing the pipes.

### GASTRONOMICALLY, CRANES ACT COMICALLY

A crane inside a ***** is mewed
To see how cranes ***** to food.
Cooks ***** to his every wish.
The meals are a la *****; each dish
Is flavored* with a ***** of fish.

---

* *Punch* of course wrote "flavoured."

### MAKE THAT GHOST STOP PEEKING, HONEY!

"***** tonnere!" bold François cried,
"No ghost shall ***** me from my bride!
Who ***** if we make am'rous moans
In ***** haunted by dry bones,
And love where ancient ***** died?"

### ROYAL PICK-ME-UP

One ***** *****, swiftly drained,
May make a monarch addle-brained.
But if his queen is feeling grim,
Her ***** ***** will sober him.
—*W.R.E.*

# 5 APRIL

## *Macaronic Mother Goose*

In February Mother Goose was talking fractured French, and she will again in
November. Let us see how she does in April with macaronics:

### JACK AND JILL

Jack cum amica Jill,
    Ascendit super montem;
Johannes cecedit down the hill,
    Ex forte fregit frontem.

### LITTLE BO-PEEP

Parvula Bo-Peep
Amisit her sheep,
Et nescit where to find 'em;
Desere alone,
Et venient home,
Cum omnibus caudis behind 'em.

### LITTLE JACK HORNER

Parvus Jacobus Horner
Sedebat in corner,
Edens a Christmas pie;
Inferit thumb,
Extreherit plum—
Clamans, "Quid sharp puer am I!"
—*Anonymous*

SHE LOST HER SHEEP

*Arcuconspicilla* looks for *perditas*,
"They'll come home, *trahantes caudas*!" What
   *absurditas!*
                                          —*Anonymous*

FOUR AND TWENTY MERULAE

*Nummum et saeculis saeculorum cantate!*
Four and twenty *merulae* in a pie *paratae*;
*Pieum* when *apertum est, cecinere crapulae*
*Regi quae monstrendae, ecce* pretty *epulae!*
                                          —*J. Moyr Smith*

# 6 APRIL

## *Biblical Fruitcake*

Loretta Harold phoned this recipe for fruitcake to Ellen Kimball's talk show in Boston and Ellen kindly passed it on to me:

1. 4½ cups I Kings 4:22
2. 1½ cups Judges 5:25
3. 2 cups Jeremiah 6:20
4. 2 cups I Samuel 30:12
5. 2 cups Nahum 3:12
6. 1 cup Numbers 17:8
7. 2 tbs I Samuel 14:25
8. 6 articles Jeremiah 17:11
9. Pinch of Leviticus 2:13
10. 1 tsp Amos 4:5
11. Season to taste with II Chronicles 9:9
12. Add citron, and follow Solomon's advice for making a good boy (Proverbs 23:13, 14)
    Bake in 300 oven temperature for 2-2½ hours

According to my Concordance, by the way, the Bible makes no mention whatever of lemons. This surprises me. I had always assumed that the fruit offered Eve was really a lemon, not an apple at all.

Returning to the ingredients in the recipe: I count six Bible verses referring to flour; ten to butter; two to sugar (cane); four to raisins; forty-nine to figs, fig leaves, and fig trees; five to almonds; twenty-nine to honey (and nine to honeycomb); seven to eggs (including cockatrice eggs, which might not help the fruitcake); twenty-four to salt; seventeen to baking soda (leaven); and twenty-nine to spices (not counting "spice beds," "spiced wine," and so on).

Use the recipe at your own risk.

# 7 APRIL

## *Hymn to the Spring and Villon Too*

The initial letters of the following verse, written for Queen Elizabeth I, spell "Elisabetha Regina":

### HYMN TO THE SPRING

E arth now is green, and heauen is blew,
L iuely Spring which makes all new,
I olly Spring doth enter.
S weet young sun-beams doe subdue
   A ngry, aged Winter.

B lasts are mild, and seas are calme,
E uery medow flowes with balme,
   T he earth weares all her riches,
H armonious birds sing such a psalm
   A s eare and heart bewitches.

R eserve (sweet Spring) this nymph of ours,
E ternall garlands of thy flowers,
   G reene garlands never wasting:
I n her shall last our state's faire spring,
N ow and for euer flourishing,
A s long as heauen is lasting.
               —*Sir John Davies*

François Villon's "Ballade des Contrevérités" has this acrostic conclusion:

V oulez vous que verte vous die?
I l n'est jouer qu'en maladie,
L ettre vraie qu'en tragédie,
   L ache homme que chevalereux,
O rrible son que melodie,
   N e bien conseille qu'amoureux.

An English approximation of the sentiment:

V illon! never (else I lie),
I s there joy, except to die;
   L ife is sung in tragic runes,
L ofty knights are louts disguised,
   O dious sounds dress up as tunes,
N aught but love is well advised.
               —*W.R.E.*

# 8 APRIL

## *A Fragrance of Flowers*

The morning glory opens at five or six in the morning; the African daisy at eight or nine; the tulip at ten or eleven; the goatsbeard, noonish. The four o'clock retires at around four, and the day lily at around eight.

These horological data came to mind as I considered the verse that follows, listing flowers advertised in a Boston newspaper of March 3, 1760. Exaggerate the beat if you read the verse aloud:

> LAV-en-der; HON-ey-wort (loved by BEES);
> TREE Mal-low; PAINT-ed Dame Top-knot PEAS;
> HON-es-ty (SOLD in bites, so that EACH
> HAS a bit); CATCH-fly; Flower-ing PEACH;
> SNAP-drag-on; COL-chi-cum; Lark-spur SHOOTS;
> FIF-ty-five IN-ter-mixed Tu-lip ROOTS;
> HORN Pop-py; MAR-i-gold; Hol-ly-HOCK;
> EV-er-more; SNUFF Flower; Pur-ple STOCK;
> HYS-sop; Red LAV-a-ter; Wall-eyed PINK;
> ICE-plant; Sweet MAR-jor-am; Bil-ly STINK;*
> SWEET Rock-et; WHITE Lu-pin; Col-ored BOWER;
> YEL-low Chrys-AN-the-mum; Red Wall-FLOWER;
> STRAW-ber-ry SPIN-age; Dear Love Lies BLEED-ing;
> CAR-na-tion POP-py (read-y for SEED-ing).
> —W.R.E.

# 9 APRIL

## *Words of Wood*

Pangrams are brief, more or less intelligible passages using every letter of the alphabet: "The quick brown fox jumps over the lazy dog." The goal is to use each of the twenty-six letters as infrequently as possible.

From Spetsai, an island off southern Greece, Clement Wood has sent me three pangrams of his own creation.

Clement Wood is a poet, born in 1888. He wrote *The Complete Rhyming Dictionary*, first published in 1936 and still a standard reference work.

Since I have in mind to write a rhyming dictionary myself, I am replying instantly to Mr. Wood, thanking him for his pangrams and inviting myself to visit him. Who knows—he may write a splendid introduction to my dictionary!

---

*The Scottish name. The English say Sweet William.

"I have been reading your *Game of Words*," he wrote, "and lingered over the section 'All Twenty-six Letters of the Alphabet.' Now, several sleepless nights and feverish days later, I'm happy to report to you that

MR. JOCK, TV QUIZ PH.D., BAGS FEW LYNX."

That, reader, is the ideal pangram—each of the twenty-six letters used just once. Moreover, it is intelligible without reference to a dictionary. Purists may complain that Mr. Wood has cheated by using initials; I approve of initials if they further the message.

He appended a commentary: "Serves Jock right. An academic who sells out to the mass media can expect his marksmanship to suffer."

He also sent the two following pangrams with accompanying reflections:

FEW MOCK QUARTZ GLYPH'S BVD JINX.

("I daresay the handful of union-suit buffs who choose to jeer at the caveat hewn in rocks by the ancients will have cause for regret.")

COX, JFK GRAB LEWD TV QUIZ NYMPHS*

("Scandalous—and to think I voted for JFK!")

# 10 APRIL

## *What Is the Word for #?*

Occasionally I am asked whether there is one inclusive word for the symbol #. There is not. It has different meanings under different circumstances:

> Many offices encumber
> My diurnal rounds;
> 1. Before a digit, I'm a #;
> 2. After digits, #;
> 3. In a printer's proof, a #;
> While, if at the harp
> You should pluck me from my place,
> 4. I would be a #.
> 5. In one game, I'm #;
> 6. An # on 'phones;
> 7. In business, I'm #, although
> 8. A # when in bones.
> —W.R.E.

*This is a slightly cleaned up, but just as pangrammic version of Mr. Wood's original.—*Ed.*

# 11 APRIL

## *The Subjunctive Rides Again*

The subjunctive will soon be as dead as the dodo, the carrier pigeon, and yesterday's newspaper. This has been an article of faith among grammarians for years. "The subjunctive has almost disappeared from English speech," wrote Wilson Follett, "and is retreating, though more slowly, from written prose." Ernest Gowers said, "The subjunctive is dying." H. W. Fowler went further: "The subjunctive," he announced, "is, except in isolated uses, no longer alive."

Well, these distinguished gentlemen forgot to tell the subjunctive. It is as indestructible as dandelions. In almost any magazine or newspaper you will come across subjunctives like these:

"He insisted that Hanoi agree . . ."

"The judge recommended that the convicted man serve fifteen years of his life sentence."

"My doctors' advice is that I not involve myself in any extensive campaigning."

"I advised Senator Eagleton that I have been under intense pressure that he withdraw from the ticket."

"Mr. Mitchell resigned as President Nixon's campaign manager after his wife had issued a public ultimatum that he leave politics or she would leave him."

If the deaths of the dodo and the carrier pigeon are as exaggerated as that of the subjunctive, I might look out my window right now and see those extinct beasts cavorting there.

But yesterday's newspaper is dead, all right.

# 12 APRIL

## *A Birthday Song for Medora,*
## *of the Sixth Generation*
## *to Bear That Name*

> Medora bore a-
> nother Medora
> (This story, Medora,
>     Is true);
> Who bore encore a-
> nother Medora,
> Who opted for a-
> nother Medora,
> Who raised the score a-
> *nother* Medora.

Now who's once more a-
nother Medora?
It's *you*, Medora,
It's you!

—*W.R.E.*

# 13 APRIL

## *Eve's Legend*

In the following, no vowel is used but *e:*

Men were never perfect; yet the three brethren Veres were ever esteemed, respected, revered, even when the rest, whether the select few, whether the mere herd, were left neglected.

The eldest's vessels seek the deep, stem the element, get pence; the keen Peter when free, wedded Hester Green—the slender, stern, severe, erect Hester Green. The next, clever Ned, less dependent, wedded sweet Ellen Heber. Stephen, ere he met the gentle Eve, never felt tenderness: he kept kennels, bred steeds, rested where the deer fed, went where green trees, where fresh breezes greeted sleep. There he met the meek, the gentle Eve; she tended her sheep, she never neglected self; she never needed pelf, yet she heeded the shepherds even less. Nevertheless, her cheek reddened when she met Stephen; yet decent reserve, meek respect, tempered her speech, even when she shewed tenderness. Stephen felt the sweet effect; he felt he erred when he fled the sex, yet felt he defenseless when Eve seemed tender. She, he reflected, never deserved neglect; she never vented spleen; he esteems her gentleness, her endless deserts; he reverences her steps; he greets her:

"Tell me whence these meek, these gentle sheep,—whence the yet meeker, the gentler shepherdess?"

"Well bred, we were eke better fed, ere we went where reckless men seek fleeces. There we were fleeced. Need then rendered me shepherdess, need renders me sempstress. See me tend the sheep, see me sew the wretched shreds. Eve's need preserves the steers, preserves the sheep; Eve's needle mends her dresses, hems her sheets; Eve feeds the geese; Eve preserves the cheese."

Her speech melted Stephen, yet he nevertheless esteems, reveres her. He bent the knee where her feet pressed the green; he blessed, he begged, he pressed her.

"Sweet, sweet Eve, let me wed thee; be led where Hester Green, where Ellen Heber, where the brethren Vere dwell. Free cheer greets thee there; Ellen's glees sweeten the refreshments; there severer Hester's decent reserve checks heedless jests. Be led there, sweet Eve."

"Never! We well remember the Seer. We went where he dwells—
we entered the cell—we begged the decree—

> 'Where, whenever, when, 'twere well
> Eve be wedded? Eld Seer, tell!'

"He rendered the decree; see here the sentence decreed!" Then
she presented Stephen the Seer's decree. The verses were these:

> 'Ere the green be red,
> Sweet Eve, be never wed;
> Ere be green the red cheek,
> Never wed thee, Eve meek.'

The terms perplexed Stephen, yet he jeered them. He resented
the senseless credence, "Seers never err." Then he repented, knelt,
wheedled, wept. Eve sees Stephen kneel, she relents, yet frets when
she remembers the Seer's decree. Her dress redeems her. These
were the events:
Her well-kempt tresses fell: sedges, reeds bedecked them. The
reeds fell, the edges met her cheeks; her cheeks bled. She presses
the green sedge where her cheeks bleed. Red then bedewed the
green reed, the green reed then speckled her red cheek. The red
cheek seems green, the green reed seems red. These were the terms
the Eld Seer decreed Stephen Vere.

HERE ENDETH THE LEGEND.

*—Lord Holland*

# 14 APRIL

## *Up Here in the (9)*

For each number below, substitute a word with that number of letters. By
adding the clue letters provided, supply new words until you end with a nine-
letter monster.

A. Once upon (1) time a little boy's (2) gave him an unusual
pet—a trained baby (3), whose favorite food was not bananas but
green (4), cooked in tomato juice to give them a reddish brown, or
(5) color. Although the pet, as he grew older, got nothing but (6)
for his many accomplishments, nevertheless at times he was sad-
dened almost to the point of (7) by the thought that his present,
comfortable little (8) might someday (9).
Clues: 2, p. 3, e. 4, s. 5, i. 6, r. 7, d. 8, a. 9, p.

B. (1) How nice it would be to lie (2) the sand on any (3) of the
many Florida beaches, protecting my (4) from the hot sun, far

away from this cold city built of (5)! Happy not to have done an (6) day's work, ready to settle into one of those luxurious chairs that look like (7), I would surely feel like a king and would not wish to change my kingdom for (8). (Warning! There's an apostrophe in word (8).) What a delightful way to forget all about the snow and ice up here in the (9).

Clues: 2, n. 3, e. 4, s. 5, t. 6, h. 7, r. 8, a. 9, t.

—*Maxwell Nurnberg*

# 15 APRIL

## *Snallygaster I*

As if it wasn't bad enough to have to pay my income tax today, I also received this letter:

*United States Senate*
WASHINGTON, D.C. 20510

*April 15*

Mr. Willard R. Espy
Contributing Editor
Harvard Magazine

Dear Mr. Espy:

I noted with interest on page 64 of the current issue of Harvard Magazine that you quote President Truman as having used the word "snollygoster." I am further dismayed to see that you are under the misapprehension that the word passed out of the language in the mid-Nineteenth Century, and that President Truman thought it meant "a man born out of wedlock." All of this is *wrong!*

The correct way to spell it is "snallygaster." The word probably derives from the German "schnelle Geischter" or "flying ghost." They frequently were reported in rural Maryland, about the time of an election. Voters planning to vote the wrong way would probably find it prudent to stay at home when the snallygaster was on the prowl. Far from having disappeared in the Nineteenth Century, it has been a subject of much newspaper attention in Maryland in the Twentieth Century. One of the papers to most accurately report the appearance of the snallygaster was the Valley Register, published at 123 West Main Street, Middletown, Maryland 21769.

The question of the snallygaster has also been a matter of vital interest to William Safire, distinguished columnist of the New York Times, who unfortunately fell into the same error in misspelling the word.

Knowing your high regard for accuracy, I take the liberty of calling these matters to your attention. Perhaps together we can put this straight and keep coming generations from the ignorance that might have them prey to a snallygaster's claws.

Sincerely,

Charles McC. Mathias, Jr.
United States Senator

cc: Mr. William Safire
The New York Times
Mr. George C. Rhoderick, Jr.
The Valley Register

I suspect that the letter is a fraud and that there is no such person as a Senator Mathias. Should further information transpire, I'll let you know.

MORE TO COME ON 22 APRIL.

# 16 APRIL

## Madam, I'm Adam

The briefer the palindrome, the clearer the message: "Madam, I'm Adam"; "A man, a plan, a canal—Panama"; "Able was I ere I saw Elba." Palindromes of as many as sixty letters may retain a certain cogency:

- Straw? No, too stupid a fad. I put soot on warts.
- Eros? Sidney, my end is sore!
- Are we not drawn onward, we few, drawn onward to new era?
- Now, Ned, I am a maiden nun; Ned, I am a maiden won.

As palindromes grow longer—the French wordgame book *Oulippo* has a palindromic passage that I count at around 5,000 letters—the sense diminishes and finally vanishes quite away. If, however, the components of the palindromes are entire words instead of letters, a palindromic poem may be extended indefinitely and quite sensibly. David L. Stephens sent me the following examples. The first, inspired by a German folk song, has been recorded in different translations by Burl Ives and Richard Dyer-Bennett:

Returning exquisite desire,
Burning, then ashes and smoke.
Glowing ember or flaming oak—
Unknowing, unknown secret fire!

Fire, secret, unknown, unknowing,
Oak flaming or ember glowing.
Smoke and ashes; then burning
Desire, exquisite, returning.
*—Author unknown*

## HANNIBAL, MISSOURI

Glimmering, gone—springtime stream
Lapping . . . road winding down
The shimmering hill. Hometown
Napping . . . sweet, solemn dream!
Dream solemn, sweet . . . napping
Hometown . . . hill shimmering . . . the
Down-winding road . . . lapping
Stream . . . springtime . . . gone, glimmering.
*—Author unknown*

As far as Anders R. Sterner knows, the oldest surviving graffito is this palindrome found on the wall of a lately excavated tavern of ancient Rome: "ROMA SUMMUS AMOR." Decide for yourself whether the theme is patriotism or a less lofty form of love. Another foreign-language palindrome contributed by Mr. Sterner is the Finnish word for soap salesman: "SAIPPUAKAUPPIAS."

## FOUR PALINDROMES

Draw pupil's lip upward.
Swen nixes sex in news.
Do nine men interpret? Nine men, I nod.
Rise to vote, sir.

*—Author unknown*

Toward the end of 1959, Alastair Reid, uttering the huge hoots that pass for laughter among the Scots, composed a palindrome. He then forced his friends to listen to it willy-nilly. The line became an instant classic. W. H. Auden enjoyed it so, and repeated it so often, that he has sometimes been credited as the author. He is not; the writer of that palindrome is the man to whom it is attributed here:

T. Eliot, top bard, notes putrid tang emanating, is sad. I'd assign
it a name: gnat dirt upset on drab pot-toilet.
*—Alastair Reid*

# 17 APRIL

## *Private? No!*

Punctuation can make a difference.

Private
No swimming
Allowed

does not mean the same as

Private?
No. Swimming
Allowed.

Other examples:

The escaping convict dropped a bullet in his leg.
The escaping convict dropped, a bullet in his leg.

The butler stood by the door and called the guests' names as they arrived.
The butler stood by the door and called the guests names as they arrived.

Go slow, children.
Go slow—children.

I'm sorry you can't come with us.
I'm sorry. You can't come with us.

A punctuation mark omitted or misplaced has upset the intent of many a legal document. Punctuate these sentences for clarity:

1. Said I I said you said I said said said he who said I said you said said I said said is said said said is not said said like said.
2. That that is is that that is not is not is not that it it is.
3. The murderer protested his innocence an hour after he was put to death.
4. He said that that that that that man said was correct.

See what mispunctuation can do:

A clever dog knows its master.
A clever dog knows it's master.

Do not break your bread, or roll in your soup.
Do not break your bread or roll in your soup.

For more of this kind of thing, read *Fun with Words*, by Maxwell Nurnberg.

## A PAEAN OF PUNCTUATION

Thine eyes, dear one, dot dot, are like, dash, what?
   They, pure as sacred oils, bless and anoint
My sin-swamped soul which at thy feet sobs out,
   O exclamation point, O point, O point!

Ah, had I words, blank blank, which, dot, I've not,
   I'd swoon in songs which should'st illume the dark
With light of thee. Ah, God (it's *strong* to swear)
   Why, why, interrogation mark, why, mark?

Dot dot dot dot. And so, dash, yet, but nay!
   My tongue takes pause; some words must not be said,
For fear the world, cold, hyphen-eyed, austere,
   Should'st shake thee by the throat till reason fled.

One hour of love we've had. Dost thou recall
   Dot dot dash blank interrogation mark?
The night was ours, blue heaven over all
   Dash, God! Dot stars, keep thou our secret dark!
                       —*Marion Hill*

# 18 APRIL

### *Metaphysics*

Why and Wherefore set out one day
   To hunt for a wild Negation.
They agreed to meet at a cool retreat
   On the Point of Interrogation.

But the night was dark and they missed their mark,
   And driven well-nigh to distraction,
They lost their ways in a murky maze
   Of utter abstruse abstraction.

So they took a boat and were soon afloat
   On a sea of Speculation,
But the sea grew rough, and their boat, though tough,
   Was split into an Equation.

As they floundered about in the waves of doubt
   Rose a fearful Hypothesis,
Who gibbered with glee as they sank in the sea,
   And the last they saw was this:

On a rock-bound reef of Unbelief
   There sat a wild Negation;
Then they sank once more and were washed ashore
   At the Point of Interpretation.

                *—Gelett Burgess*

# 19 APRIL

## *Old Doc*

Each word of the following passages begins with the last letter of the preceding word:

> Old Doc came even nearer, revealing gold dentures, smiling grimly. "You understand, Delbert, that the extra assistance each hour requires seven, not two, operators," said Doc. "Can't this stop permanently?" "Yes," said Delbert, taking great time enlightening good Doc Carey, "Yes, surely."

                *—A. Ross Eckler*

# 20 APRIL

## *How Mortal These Fools Be*

### LET US WONDER, WHILE WE LOITER

Let us wonder, while we loiter,
Which of us will die of goiter;
Which of stone or dysentery;
Which of rheum or beriberi;
Which of grippe or diarrhea,
Nettlerash, or pyorrhea;
Which of us turn turvy topsy,
Victim of paretic dropsy.
Be it pox or whooping cough,
Something's bound to bear us off.
All we know is, we're in trouble:
Barman, make my next one double.
           *—W.R.E.*

### NO INTRAVENOUS FOR ME

When faced with terminal disease,
No intravenous feeding, please.
No pumps imparting partial life;

No last-ditch doings with the knife.
When coma comes, please let me slide
Unhindered to the other side:
I want no plastic tubes to mar
My meeting with The Registrar.
—*W. H. Von Dreele*

### ACTUARIAL REFLECTION

Very, very, very few
People die at ninety-two.
I suppose that I shall be
Safer still at ninety-three.
—*W.R.E.*

### EARTH DOTH TWIRL

Earth doth twirl—
Furl, unfurl
    The sun . . .
And so will too
After you
    Are done.
—*W.R.E.*

A change of subject, but not of mood:

### DON'T RUB IT IN

Misericordia,
Lordia!
Take it easy,
Jeesy!
We're born in sin—
Don't rub it in!
—*W.R.E.*

# 21 APRIL

### *If Longfellow's "The Midnight Ride of Paul Revere" Were Written by Ernest Lawrence Thayer*

It looked extremely rocky for the Colonists that night;
The British were attacking with no hope of help in sight;
So, with villages in danger from the enemy so near,
They had to send a warning, and they called on Paul Revere.

There was ease in Paul's demeanor as he climbed upon his mare;
There was pride in Paul's expression as he sat so tall and fair;
And then the horse grew skittish, and she gave a sudden jump,
And Paul fell from his saddle, landing smack upon his rump.

With a smile of Yankee courage, Paul rose smartly to his feet,
And once again upon the saddled mare he took his seat;
But as he gripped the reins, she made a sudden turn around,
And once again Paul plummeted onto the dusty ground.

The smile has vanished from Paul's face, his eyes burn with a glare;
He grips the bridle fiercely as again he mounts the mare;
And now he tells the horse to gallop, in an urgent tone,
And now the air is shattered as the horse takes off—alone;

Oh, somewhere in this war-torn land the people safely know
That Redcoats are invading, taking captives as they go;
And somewhere people are prepared to flee the British force,
But there's no hope for New England—
    Paul Revere can't ride a horse!

—Frank Jacobs

# 22 APRIL

## *Snallygaster II*

A letter (see 15 April) to George C. Rhoderick, Jr., with copies to William Safire and the putative Senator Mathias:

22 April

Dear Mr. Rhoderick:

My recent mail contained a letter, of which a copy apparently went to you, by someone who signs himself Charles McC. Mathias, Jr. This writer tried to persuade me that there really is a Charles McC. Mathias, Jr.; that the writer is he; that he is a United States senator; and, by implication, that there is a United States Senate. He also expects me to believe that there exists a place called "rural Maryland."

These are dubious propositions. Fortunately I am able to test them by sending you this letter. If it is returned to me with "No Such Person" stamped on the envelope, I can dismiss the matter. If it is not returned, I can assume that you are real and that Senator Charles McC. Mathias, Jr., probably is, too.

I had mentioned in an article the word *snollygoster*, defined by

President Truman as a man born out of wedlock. The self-styled senator declares that the word is correctly *snallygaster*, probably deriving from German *schnelle Geischter*, "flying ghost." The snallygaster, he goes on, prowls around election time to intimidate possibly dissident voters.

After listing my statements about the snollygoster, he declares, "All of this is *wrong!*"

To *underline* the word *wrong* adds insult to injury.

It appears to me that the descriptions of the snollygoster given by the President and the soi-disant senator are much of a piece. The President used the word to describe a cheap and venal politician— nine times out of ten a shyster lawyer. A shyster lawyer is a bastard, and no doubt your monster is, too. QED.

Still, I should like to know more about snollygosters (snallygasters?), and you appear to be the authority in the field. What do they feed on? Are they social or solitary? Do they lie with humans? Is the bite, or sting, poisonous?

And *is* there a Charles McC. Mathias? Is he a United States senator? For that matter, is there actually a United States Senate? I am willing to concede that there really is a Commonwealth of Maryland.

If you are not out chasing snollygosters, do tell me what you can. I shall be grateful.

Sincerely,

Willard R. Espy

MORE TO COME ON 6 MAY.

# 23 APRIL

### *How I Lost the Race With Willy*

This is probably Shakespeare's birthday, but nobody knows for sure. Indeed, nobody knows for sure how he spelled his surname; family records show forty-four different versions.

Similarly, no one knows why in my undergraduate days I took for granted that I was to become a second Shakespeare. The only certainty is that I did. I even fell deeply in love with* a girl named Ann Hathaway. The sole flaw in her perfection was that she did not spell the Ann with an e.

Disillusion set in one year when I was studying at—well, attending courses at—the Sorbonne. A young Parisienne of my acquaintance worked for the Sûreté, the Paris police department, as a handwriting expert. At a critical point

---

*It did not last. She knew from the start that I was no Shakespeare.

in our relationship she decided that before matters went farther she should analyze my handwriting. She did, and found that it revealed many excellent qualities. But nowhere in my fist, she declared, was there a sign of creative imagination.

In a race with Shakespeare, a man without imagination would be carrying too much weight, it seemed to me; so I decided to abandon creative writing for journalism and advertising. They are two fields where you need no imagination. You only need to know how to lie.

One Shakespearean reference—just because this *is* probably his birthday. Scholars have long puzzled over a line in Hamlet describing the Dane as "fat and short of breath." Surely no actor has ever played him as a fat man! Comes now Patricia R. Welch and deposes roughly as follows:

> The mystery was solved by a Shakespearean scholar who stopped for a drink of water in a remote area of southern England where something akin to Elizabethan English is still spoken. A farm woman said: "You are fat," meaning: "You are perspiring." "Aha!" said the scholar (who was far from fat): "*that's* what Shakespeare meant, and *that's* why the Queen said, 'Take my napkin, rub thy brows.' Hamlet was sweating!"

# 24 April

## The Snail's on the Thorn

Entranced by a tour of English gardens, I resolved to create my own rhododendron-banked croquet lawn at Oysterville. Since I am not there often, the garden has emerged slowly. In the first year I uprooted the gorse and the evergreen blackberry bushes that held squatters' rights on the plot I had selected.* In the second year I uprooted the squatters again. In the third year, as I was about to begin planting, I was reminded that winter tides regularly inundate the plot, and would drown rhododendrons and lawn alike. So I trucked in loam from the marsh to raise the ground level, muttering all the while J. A. Lindon's burlesque:

MY GARDEN

*With a Stern Look at T. E. Brown*

A garden is a *lovesome* thing? What rot!
Weed plot,
Scum pool,
Old pot,
Snail-shiny stool

---

* "I" is misleading. J. Harold Clarke, an authority on rhododendrons, designed the garden and selected the plants. Johnny Morehead, with assists from Bob Meadows and Ollie Oman, did the work.

In pieces; yet the fool
Contends that snails are not—
Not snails! in gardens! when the eve is cool?
Nay, but I see their trails!
'Tis very sure *my* garden's full of snails!

The fourth year came around, and I plowed, disked, harrowed, rolled, dragged, fertilized, and sowed. In the fifth, I found the lawn still to be a concatenation of bumps and hollows, so I scraped off the grass and started all over. In the sixth year—only a few weeks ago—I tipped in the rhododendrons. And this morning I looked out my north window to behold—rhododendrons in white bloom! The sun itself is blooming, albeit in a watery sort of way! I shall stride the countryside today, face to the sky, bellowing this hymn of praise from "Pippa Passes":

> The year's at the spring,
> And day's at the morn;
> Morning's at seven;
> The hill-side's dew pearl'd;
> The lark's on the wing
> The snail's on the thorn;
> God's in His heaven—
> All's right with the world!
> —*Robert Browning*

One language is not enough on a day like this. I'll bellow in French too:

> L'année est au printemps;
> Le jour est au matin,
> Le matin à l'aurore;
> Le flanc de la colline est imperlé de rosée,
> L'alouette a pris son essor;
> L'escargot rampe sur l'aubépine;
> Dieu est au ciel . . .
> Tout est bien en ce monde!
> —*Translated by Jules Guiraud*

And in German:

> Das Jahr, wenns fruhlingt,
> und der Tag wird geborn
> morgens um sieben,
> der Hang, taubeperlt [sic]
> die Lerche beschwingt,
> die Schecke am Dorn:
> Gott in Seinem Himmel—
> Gut stehts um die Welt!
> —*Translated by*
> *Alexander von Bernus*

# 25 April

## *Let Stalk Strine*

A dictionary of Strine (Australian English), may be out by the time this book is published. It contains 1,800 pages and 100,000 dinkum Aussie words.

The new dictionary is not really needed, though. All the phrases that might confuse you or me are already defined in *Let Stalk Strine*, a definitive study by Professor Afferbeck Lauder, head of the Department of Strine Studies at the University of Sinny. Take a dekko:

A. **Air Fridge.** A mean sum, or quantity; also, ordinary, not extreme. As in: The air fridge person; the air fridge man in the street.

B. **Baked Necks.** A popular breakfast dish. Others include emma necks; scremblex; and fright shops.

C. **Cheque Etcher.** Did you obtain. As in: "Where cheque etcher hat?" or "Where cheque etcher dim pull, son? Where cheque etcher big blue wise?"

D. **Doan Lemmyaf.** I do not want to have to. As in: "Arn jew kids in bare jet? Emeny times die affter tellyer. Now doan lemmyaf to speak dear Ken."

E. **Egg Jelly.** In fact; really. As in: "Well, there's nothing egg jelly the matter with her. It's jess psychological."

F. **Flares.** Blooms, blossoms; e.g., corn flares, wile flares, etc., as in: Q. Wet cheque etta flares? A. Glaria sarnthay. I gom airtat Sairf Nils.

G. **Garbler Mince.** Within the next half hour. Also Greetings. As in: "I'll be with you in a garbler mince," or "With the garbler mince of the Gem of Directors."

H. **Harps.** Thirty minutes past the hour. As: Harps two; harps four; harps tait; etc. Related words are: Fipes; temps; corpse. As: Fipes one; temps two; corpse four.

J. **Jess Tefter; Lefter.** It is necessary to. As in: "She'll jess tefter get chews twit," or "You lefter filner form."

L. **Letty Mare Fit.** Let him have it. As in: "Letty mare fit tiffy wonsit. Zarf trawly zonier kid."

M. **Mare chick.** Effects produced by the assistance of supernatural powers. As: Black mare chick; mare chick momence; "Laugh, your mare chick spell is airfree ware."

N. **Numb Butter; Jessa** (Synonyms). Only. As in: "They're numb butter buncher drongoes," or "He's jessa no-hoper."

O. **Orpheus Rocker.** Psychopathic; neurotic; psychotic; slow; quick; eccentric; absentminded; unstable; excitable; imaginative; introspective; creative; or in any way different.

P. **Puck, Charlie Charm.** A whimsical character in Strine folklore, about whom many amusing anecdotes are told. Charlie Puck is famous for having introduced the popular sport of sheep-stealing. Mentioned in the national anthem ("Where sat Charlie Charm Puck you've got in your tucker bag?")

R. **Retrine.** Making an effort. As in: How to speak Strine without retrine.

S. **Sex.** Large cloth bags used as containers for such things as potatoes, cement, etc. As: sex of manure, corn sex, etc.

T. **Tiger.** Imperative mood of the verb to take. As in: "Tiger look at this, Reg, you wooden reader battit," or "Tiger perrer spargly guys."
U. **Uppendan.** To and fro; backward and forward. As in: "She walked uppendan Flinner Street farairs an then she finey got a cabbome to Cannerbry."
W. **Would Never.** Do not have. As in: "You would never light woodgermite?" or "Ar would never glue."
Z. **Zarf Trawl.** Because, after all. As in: "Zarf trawl Leica nony doomy Bess," or "Zarf trawl wee rony flesh and blood wennit Saul boiled down."

# 26 APRIL

### A Tired Song of Tired Similes

As mute as a mackerel, darling, I am;
Yet fit as a fiddle, dear, gay as a lamb;
As clean as a whistle, as ugly as sin;
As fat as a hog and as neat as a pin;
As brave as a lion, but deaf as an adder;
As brown as a berry, as mad as a hatter.

While you, my own darling, the love of my life,
Are free as the wind, and as sharp as a knife;
As blind as a bat and as sly as a fox,
As pert as a sparrow, as dumb as an ox;
As plump as a partridge, as red as a rose,
As flat as a flounder, as plain as my nose.

So come, let us marry!—and we shall be twain
As merry as crickets, and righter than rain!
Our days will be brighter than rainbows are bright;
Our hearts will be lighter than feathers are light.
Our love will be surer than shooting is sure,
*And poorer we'll be, dear, than churchmice are poor.*
—W.R.E.

# 27 APRIL

### Bad Bab

Imagine (I wrote to my friend Dick Hyman, the jazz pianist and composer) an agitated young man shouting into the ear of a dozing ancient, while pointing at a taxicab fleeing around a corner on two wheels. The driver is a young woman, and a great cabbage is about to roll off the roof.

Now place beneath your mental picture a musical score consisting of the following notes:

G A D D A D D E A F A G E D D A D A B A D A D A G
E B A D E B A B A B A B E F A C E D B A G G A G E
C A D G E A C A B B A G E A B A D A D A G E B A D
E B A B C A D G E A C A B G A D D A D B A B A C C
E D E D B A D G A F F E D A D B A D D E E D B A B
B A D B A B B A D

A moment's examination reveals a tense drama of temptation and fall:

Gad, dad
(Deaf, agèd dad)!—
A bad adage
Bade Bab
(a babe-faced baggage)
Cadge a cabbage!

A bad adage
Bade Bab
Cadge a cab!

Gad, dad,
Bab acceded!
Bad gaffe, dad!—
Bad deed, Bab!—
Bad, Bab, Bad!
—W.R.E.

The score below arrived from Dick this morning. "It makes a pleasantly quirky tune," he writes, "which I have also elaborated into a little piano piece." If you would like the elaborated piano tune, just ask me.

DISHARMONY

She would keep
Harping on about tidiness
Blowing her own trumpet
And drumming it into me

That I mustn't fiddle
With my hair.
I think she was instrumental
In our divorce.
                                        —*Alan E. G. Lewis*

# 28 APRIL

## *Don't Quote Me*

Frequently one's memory of a familiar quotation is off the mark by as little as a single trifling letter or punctuation mark. In the 1930s, columnist-wit F.P.A. devised the following quiz to put people like you and me in the dunce's corner. If you don't miss at least one of these questions, I have no wish to meet you; you are insufferable.

1. Complete the first line of "Rock Me to Sleep" beginning "Backward, turn backward . . ."
2. What is the first line of "The Old Oaken Bucket"?
3. From "The Rime of the Ancient Mariner," complete the line "Water, water everywhere . . ."

4. What words follow "Alas, poor Yorick"?
5. What grow "from little acorns"?
6. Finish the line "Breathes there . . ."
7. Finish the line "'Twas the night before Christmas . . ."

# 29 APRIL

### Funnels and Salmon

Christian Morgenstern, surrealist German poet of the early twentieth century, was as ingenious as Ogden Nash in his puns and alliterations:

#### A PAIR OF FUNNELS

A pair of funnels stroll by night. They both
collect inside themselves the white moon-
light, so clear, so calm, so bright,
which then runs down the runnels
of these funnels, making
their woodland way
much brighter,
*und so*
*weit-*
*er.*
—*Christian Morgenstern*
*(translated by Geoffrey Grigson)*


#### THE SALMON

To Switzerland, right up the Rhine,
A salmon swam.

He managed one by one each
Salmon-dam.

Up, up he went, to God knows where,
And there,

Twelve feet or more above him, rose
A weir.

Ten feet he jumped, so well, and fell,
Dismayed.

Below that Alp three
Weeks he stayed.

And then turned round at last
And swam,

In silence, back to Amst-
erdam.
          —*Christian Morgenstern*
          *(translated by Geoffrey Grigson)*

# 30 APRIL

## *Assault and Battery*

        —*Bruce McMillan*

# MAY

## 1 MAY

### Acronyms of Ailment

Profanity, obscenity, and violence are slipping into medical terminology and phraseology unobtrusively through the back door of the acronymal abbreviation. When quoted as an acronym, *coronary artery disease* becomes an insulting "CAD," *secondary carcinoma of the upper mediastinum* turns into "SCUM," *thyroid uptake gradient* transforms into "THUG," and *right atrial pressure elevation* transmutes into "RAPE." Medical papers abound in such vulgarisms as "GIP" (*gonorrheal invasive peritonitis*), "HOG" (*hepatic output of glucose*), "IMP" (*idiopathic myeloid proliferation*) and "HOOD" (*hyperbaric oxygen ongoing delivery*).

Even if not downright offensive, some acronyms can provoke depression by unpleasant association. "TAX" (*tubular ascending xanthomatosis*), "POX" (*peri-orbital xanthelasma*), "DUMP" (*diffuse uncontrolled monotonal peristalsis*) and other abbreviations of similar ilk are hardly conducive to good cheer. Nor do politically tainted acronyms such as "RED" (*rapid erythrocyte disintegration*) and "PINKO" (*papillomatous invasive keratosis oculi*) inspire confidence.

Not all, of course, is in bad taste in the acronymic ambit. There are sweet words like "PIE" which stands for *pulmonary infiltration with eosiniophils*, friendly words like "AMI" which represents *acute myordical infarction*, or "PAL" which epitomizes *pyogenic abscess of the liver*. "ALAS" (*amino levulos acid synthetase*), they are the exception rather than the rule.

—*S.V.*

## 2 MAY

### When Fishermen Meet

Bill Brougher submitted the following colloquy to *Inport,* the in-house publication of the Port of Seattle. Read it, and you will know a fisherman the next time you hear one:

"Hiyamac"
"Lobuddy"
"Binearlong?"
"Cuplours"
"Cetchanenny?"
"Goddafew"
"Kindarthay?"
"Bassencarp"
"Ennysizetoom?"
"Cuplapowns"
"Hittinhard?"

"Sordalike"
"Wahchoozin?"
"Gobbawurms"
"Fishanonaboddum?"
"Rydononaboddum"
"Whatchadrinkin?"
"Jugajimbeam"
"Igoddago"
"Seeyaroun"
"Yeahtakideezy"
"Gudluk"

—*Author unknown*

# 3 MAY

## *I Start My Week with Wednesday*

There is only one day of the week I dislike, and that is Tuesday, for the good reason given here:

I start my week with Wednesday, for it is easy to find words beginning with WED—
Well, three: Wed, itself; Wedding, and Wedge. The next day, THUR,
Gives Thurber, as well as two incense-words: Thurible, and Thurify. FRI
Is no problem either—Fricassee and Frizzle are good ones that day—and as for SAT,
Why, there are dozens of SAT words, some rather ugly: Satan, Saturnine, Satyriasis, for instance. SUN
Yields Sunder, Sundry, and Sunk, while MON
Is as rich in words as Sat; of these, Money is my favorite. But TUE
Is a stopper; I know no words beginning with TUE but Tuebor, "I will defend," the motto of Michigan, and Tueiron, a pair of blacksmith tongs.
. . . Which is why I start my week with Wednesday.

—*W.R.E.*

# 4 MAY

## *Odd Ends*

- *Sanka* brings five cups of coffee in French Canada. *Dry martini* brings three servings in Germany. (*Words Ways* does not mention that the natural response to "sanka" in the United States is "You're welcome.")
- Logophiles call a word that remains a word after dropping any one letter a *charitable* word. The charitable word *seat* can shrink to *sea, set, sat,* or *eat.*

- A word that becomes a different word through the addition of an appropriate letter is a *hospitable* word. The hospitable word *rap* welcomes *trap, reap, rasp,* and *rapt.*
- The longest common word having only two vowels is *latchstrings.*
- *Strengthlessness* is not only a common three-syllable word of staggering length, but also a univocalic; it employs only the vowel *e.*
- A laxative manufacturer coined the name *Serutan* for its product, and reminded customers that Serutan is "nature's" spelled backward. Such a reversal would be less winsome in the case of the acid neutralizer Tums or the liqueur Bols. And would Embargo be an acceptable name for a brassiere?
- James Rambo devised a sentence that uses the vowels in order, one to a word: "Schmaltz's strength thrills throngs, sculpts rhymes." Somehow, though, an extra *e* slipped into that last word. How about "Ann's bed is old but dry"?
- Fill in the seven missing initials of the words below to spell out a proper noun. Then try again; you may find another:

-umble

-mpire

-atter

-onics

-rinal

-aster

-arely

*—Word Ways*

# 5 MAY

## *Era Uoy a Diamrab?*

In back slang, man is pronounced nam and curious turns to suoiruc. A backward boy is a yob, which inspired the first of the two back-slang verses here.

1. A DIAMRAB fell in love,
   and wed her TSEUG.
   Of all Earth's NERDLIHC
   Theirs were the TSE.

2. Era uoy sa gnuoy saw I nehw
   Etihw metsys eht delb I
   Slevon dna esrev gnidaer nehw
   Thgir eht morf gnitrats yb

   Ma I sa dlo era uoy nehw
   Tfereb yllauqe dna
   Od I sa neht trofmoc ekat . . .
   *By reading right from left.*
   *—W.R.E.*

# 6 MAY

## *Snallygaster III*

CHARLES McC. MATHIAS, JR.
MARYLAND

REPLY TO:
358 RUSSELL SENATE OFFICE BUILDING
WASHINGTON, D.C. 20510

## United States Senate
WASHINGTON, D.C. 20510

May 2, 1978

Mr. Willard R. Espy
30 Beekman Place
New York, New York 10022

Dear Mr. Espy:

Your letter to Mr. Rhoderick contains only one positive statement, and that, alas, is also <u>wrong</u>! You said, "I am willing to concede that there really is a Commonwealth of Maryland." There may be a Commonwealth of Massachusetts and a Commonwealth of Virginia, but there is no "Commonwealth of Maryland."

Maryland is, in fact, the Free State of Maryland. It is so called because of highly vocal opposition to the Volstead Act. Some of us might prefer that we had earned the title "Free State" by our early practice of religious tolerance or by the early assertion of the right of women's suffrage.

The ancient liberties of Maryland are so firmly rooted that it was not until the Federal Government turned off the tap on Congressman John Boynton Philip Clayton Hill that our yelps for freedom established for all the time our right to the title, the "Free State."

Be that as it may, we are the Free State of Maryland, the only one in the Union, and proud of it.

As for further word on the snallygaster-snollygoster controversy, I enclose Mr. William Safire's latest comment.

Sincerely,

Charles McC. Mathias, Jr.

CM:lrs

cc: Mr. Safire
    Mr. Rhoderick

**The New York Times**
WASHINGTON BUREAU
1920 L STREET, N.W.
WASHINGTON, D.C. 20036
(202) 293-3100

WILLIAM SAFIRE

Dear Mac —

A snally gute flies
with its left wing,
while a snolly gute
flies with its right
wing. that's the
difference.         Best

Bill

The Senator may be real, after all.

MORE ON 9 MAY.

# 7 MAY

### Exception to the Rule

David L. Silverman got to brooding awhile back, and dredged from his mind a paragraph of profundities about rules and exceptions. This is the way it goes:

Is the old maxim true about there being an exception to every rule? Well, no doubt we can all think of rules that appear to have no exceptions, but since appearances can be deceiving, perhaps the old maxim is true. On the other hand, the maxim itself is a rule, so if we assume that it's true, it has an exception, which would be tantamount to saying that there is some rule that has no exception. So if the maxim is true, it's false. That makes it false. Thus we know at least one rule that definitely has an exception, viz. "There's an exception to every rule," and, although we haven't identified it, we know that there is at least one rule that has no exceptions.

I sometimes wish my mind could attain the abstraction of David's. I tend to feel rather than think. This is particularly true in human relations, and most particularly true in my relations with the female of the species. Here I have one special female in mind:

### EXCEPTIONS PROVE THE RULE? THEY DO

Exceptions prove the rule? They do;
   But *no* exceptions prove it too;
Though maids have oft held men in thrall,
   Your rule o'er me's exceptional.
There's no exception to the rule
   Of you, the queen, o'er me, the fool.
Yet I the rule's exception prove:
   You cannot rule, except I love.

(There's something Shakespearean about those last two lines, don't you think?)

# 8 MAY

### *Where Did That Poisoned Pawn Come from, Mr. Fischer?*

Bobby Fischer, the bad boy of chess, was sued by his lawyer for alleged non-payment of legal fees. The New York *Post*'s headline on the story:

### NEXT MOVE IS FISCHER'S
#### *His Lawyer Quits & Seeks Check*

Mr. Fischer would not think the chess moves below make sense, but if you translate the symbols into their standard English equivalents you will find that the verse rhymes, and even scans.*

---

*A. Ross Eckler says, "I doubt that even a chess expert can reconstruct some of the lines you give." Feel free to consult the answers.

The match begins; the breaths are bated.
Will Black resign? Will White be mated?
White's Ruy Lopez circumvents
Black's Nimzo-Indian defense.
Now White (intent) and Black (intenter)
Maneuver to control the center.

White moves. Too bold? Perhaps from whisky?
NxB!?
Now Black, to plaudits from the ringside,
Correctly O-O.
QxQ (White's ranks are thinning)
!!

The mating net is drawing tight:
PxP, RxN.
White, backed against his R wall
In vain seeks check perpetual.
Of Q, R, B, P bereft,
He—to right, he—to left.

*Poor White in Zugzwang sealed his fate;*
*His Fianchetto came too late.*
*He pondered a Maroczy Bind,*
*Could see no future, and resigned.*

—W.R.E.

# 9 MAY

## *Snallygaster IV*

O me of little faith! There truly is a George Rhoderick, and therefore a Senator Mathias, and therefore a United States Senate, and, therefore, perhaps, even a United States of America. How good it is to know these things!

Here are extracts from a letter which arrived today:

Dear Mr. Espy:

I assure you that I am very much alive, and have been since the year 1895, and thus can offer some first-hand information concerning the animal (or bird, or beast) which has generated the present exchange of letters.

First, let me assure you that Senator Charles McC. Mathias is indeed the legislative solon he claims to be. He is a native of our own Frederick County, which is delightfully referred to by its many residents as "rural Maryland."

President Harry S. Truman's "Snollygoster" must not have been an ancestor of Maryland's famed "Snallygaster," for according to your own research this nineteenth-century phenomenon was a member of the human race—albeit a "bastard." This "Snolly-goster," which was called into being in the 1860s, according to your own report, and which is affirmed by William Safire, of the *New York Times,* in his *The Language of Politics,* apparently did "fall asleep" after the "pressing need for it no longer existed," and was only revived by President Truman as one of his many familiar and cogent expletives with which he blasted his political antagonists.

But it was in the year 1909 that the monstrous and reason-defying "Snallygaster" appeared over the reaches of the beautiful and historic Middletown Valley of western Maryland.

Its introduction to the people of the Middletown Valley was made by my father, the late George Carlton Rhoderick, who was in the year 1909 the editor and proprietor of the *Valley Register.* I am sending you a copy of the article which introduced the creature to the paper's readers. Later I will send you copies of the following two articles.

> Sincerely yours,
> Geo. C. Rhoderick, Jr.
> President, *The Valley Register, Inc.*

Perhaps Senator Mathias and I have been talking at cross-purposes. There is a snollygoster, and there is a snallygaster, two distinct breeds, both still extant.

MORE ON 16 MAY.

# 10 MAY

## *More Words of Wood*

Arthur Miller, sitting alone in a bar, was approached by a well-tailored, slightly tiddly fellow who addressed him thus:

"Aren't you Arthur Miller?"

"Why, yes, I am."

"Don't you remember me?"

"Well . . . your face seems familiar."

"Why, Art, I'm your old buddy Sam! We went to high school together! We went out on double dates!"

"I'm afraid I—"

"I guess you can see I've done all right. Department stores. What do *you* do, Art?"

"Well, I . . . write."

"Whaddya write?"

"Plays, mostly."

"Ever get any produced?"

"Yes, some."

"Would I know any?"

"Well . . . perhaps you've heard of *Death of a Salesman?*"

Sam's jaw dropped; his face went white. For a moment he was speechless. Then he cried out, "Why, you're ARTHUR MILLER!"

I was reminded of this story when I heard this morning from Clement Wood, whose earlier letter is recorded on 9 April.

Alas, my Wood is after all not, it appears, the man who wrote *The Complete Rhyming Dictionary* nearly fifty years ago. My Wood writes: "I revere that master of rhymes. I consult him. I admire his impromptu verses. But I believe he is indeed dead. God rest his soul."

I still plan to call on my Mr. Wood in Greece. I would travel a long way to meet the man whose latest letter encloses this beguiling tribute to the game of Scrabble®:

### DEATH OF A SCRABBLE MASTER

This was the greatest of the game's great players:
If you played BRAS, he'd make it HUDIBRASTIC.
He ruled a world 15 by 15 squares,
Peopled by 100 letters, wood or plastic.

He unearthed XEBEC, HAJI, useful QAID,
Found QUOS (see pl. of QUID PRO QUO) and QUOTHA,
Discovered AU, DE, DA all unitalicized
(AU JUS, DA CAPO, ALMANACH DE GOTHA).

Two-letter words went marching through his brain,
Spondaic-footed, singing their slow litany:
AL (Indian mulberry), AI (a sloth), EM, EN,
BY, MY, AX, EX, OX, LO, IT, AN, HE . . .

PE (Hebrew letter), LI (a Chinese mile), KA, RE,
SH (like NTH, spectacularly vowelless),
AY, OY (a cry of grief, pain or dismay);
HAI, HI, HO—leaving opponents powerless.

He, if the tiles before him said DOC TIME,
Would promptly play the elegant DEMOTIC,
And none but he fulfilled the scrabbler's dream,
When, through two triple words, he hung QUIXOTIC.

The day his adversary put down GNASHED,
He laid—a virtuoso feat—beneath it GOUTIER,
So placed that six more tiny words were hatched:
GO, NU, AT, SI, then (as you've seen, no doubt) HE, ER.

Plagued by a glut of U's, he racked up TUMULUS,
Produced ILLICIT when he had a boom in I's.
When once he couldn't hang his pretty AZIMUTH,
He found a dangling E, created HUMANIZE!*

Receive him, EARTH (HEART's anagram is there);
His memory all players BLEES (var., BLESS, Scot.).
Inscribe his CENOTAPH (CAT PHONE) "I ACTS QUEER,"
for which he would of course read "REQUIESCAT."
　　　　　　　　　　　　　　　—*Clement Biddle Wood*

# 11 MAY

## *Philander Is a Wallaby?*

Which of the following definitions (per *Webster's New International Dictionary*, second edition) is correct?

1. bole—*a.* a crumbly clay; *b.* a dose; *c.* the momentum of one gram moving with a velocity of one centimeter per second; *d.* a recess or cupboard in a wall.
2. breve—*a.* a letter of authorization; *b.* a double whole note; *c.* to post accounts; *d.* one of a family of Asian and Australian birds.
3. brock—*a.* a male red deer two years old; *b.* a horse; *c.* the European badger; *d.* a cow.
4. cade—*a.* a European juniper; *b.* a barrel, cask, or keg; *c.* a measure of herrings, orig. 720; *d.* a spoiled child.
5. cope—*a.* to muzzle a ferret by sewing up its mouth; *b.* the tongue or pole of an oxcart; *c.* the duty paid to the lord of a manor on the ore raised; *d.* the top part of a set of flasks.
6. crap—*a.* buckwheat; *b.* residue from rendered fat; *c.* money; *d.* the gallows.
7. drag—*a.* a planker; *b.* a fox's trail; *c.* a drogue; *d.* a kind of coach.
8. dun—*a.* to cure codfish; *b.* a fortified residence surrounded by a moat; *c.* a May fly; *d.* to resound.
9. flag—*a.* a slice cut in plowing; *b.* a partition between grate rooms; *c.* a groat, fourpence; *d.* a woman.
10. frith—*a.* a narrow arm of the sea; *b.* a hedge esp. a wattled hedge; *c.* to preserve in peace; *d.* unused pasture land.
11. gib—*a.* to act like a cat; *b.* a removable plate to hold other parts in place; *c.* a male salmon; *d.* a prison.
12. hob—*a.* the male ferret; *b.* a quoits pin; *c.* to clear of tufts; *d.* a cutting tool consisting of a fluted steel worm.

---

*An examination of tournament records confirms that the T in AZIMUTH was a blank.—*CBW*

13. kip—*a.* a piece of wood used in playing two-up; *b.* 1,000 pounds; *c.* 40.68 pounds; *d.* the common tern.
14. moil—*a.* a steel bar sharpened to a point; *b.* a hornless ox; *c.* to moisten or wet; *d.* to burrow.

—*Girard Orway*

# 12 MAY

## *Redundance*

French wits play a word game called Redundance. The idea is to strip a poem of all except the last few words of each line, and still retain, or even enhance, its original sense. I have never seen this game played in English. Here is what might happen with Hamlet's famous soliloquy:

> The question:
> To suffer
> Fortune,
> Troubles? . . .
> To sleep,
> End shocks?
>
> Consummation: . . .
> To sleep?
> *The rub*
> *May come*
> *Off this mortal coil.*
>
> Respect
> Long life,
> Contumely,
> Delay,
> The spurns
> The unworthy takes.
> Make,
> Bear
> Weary life.
>
> Of something after death,
> Whose bourn
> Will have
> Of
> Us all
> Resolution,

Thought,
Moment . . .
Turn awry.

—*W.R.E.*

I am not sure this game works very well in English. Too bad.


# 13 MAY

## *Morituri Te Salutamus*

A verse to impress on my readers the correct spelling of *minuscule*:

### MORITURI TE SALUTAMUS

(When publishers war, says a book column, marginal writers perish.)

About to die, we hail you as we goosestep to the field;
We'll be back a little later, either with or on our shield.
We're a thin red line o' 'eroes, yet you look at us askance
If we but hint you might increase our minuscule advance—
*Minu, minu, minuscule Advance, VANCE, V A N C E.*

For you, O Caesar, we expand our cannonades of prose;
We slash, we stab, we lop a limb, we bloody up a nose.
Like bayonets our vowels rage, like swords our conson*ants;*
O, can't you add a tittle to our minuscule advance—
*Minu, minu, minuscule Advance, VANCE, V A N C E?*

While you stick pins in battle maps, we to the death contend
With someone not our enemy, who might have been our friend.
For you we draw and quarter him with verbal ele*gance,*
And you come up, dear Caesar, with a minuscule advance—
*Minu, minu, minuscule Advance, VANCE, V A N C E.*

Though *Roots* he raise against us—yea, though *Jaws* against us raise he—
We'll sweep the field with *Scruples,* and repeat with *Princess Daisy,*
About to die, we hail you. But, O Caesar, do enhance . . .
Enlarge . . . augment . . . aye, multiply our minuscule advance—
*Minu, minu, minuscule Advance, VANCE, V A N C E.*

(A muttering as of distant thunder, with heat lightning on the horizon:)

*You haven't got a minu-, minu-, minusculish chance.*

—*W.R.E.*

# 14 MAY

## Bird and Behemoth

That some words have more than one correct pronunciation is a nuisance when one has to make a choice, but it is a boon for wordplayers. Without that eccentricity of the language, Lord Kennet could not have written:

### A BIRD IN THE BUSH

I live in hope some day to see
The crimson-necked phalarope;
(Or do I, rather, live in hope
To see the red-necked phalarope?)

"Behemoth" has not two but three accepted pronunciations, an oddity considered here:

### BEHOLD NOW BĒHĒMŎTH (BĒHEMŎTH? BĒHEMŌTH?)

Behold now! By the Jordan dreameth
That beast by scholars called bē-hē´-moth;

Though scholars of another cloth
I understand say bē´-he-mŏth;
While others still, rejecting both,
Refer to him as bē-he-mōth´.

The beast is one, the sound trichotomous;
The fact is, he's a hip-pō-pot´-a-mus.
—W.R.E.

# 15 MAY

## Harpin' Boont in Boonville

Boontling, one of the oldest invented languages in the United States, is a creation of the isolated Northern California hamlet of Boonville, pop. (1969) 1,003. A *Time* report on Boontling is abbreviated here:

One day in '92, sitting around the Anytime saloon, Reg and Tom Burger and the Duff brothers started putting some of their old Scotch-Irish dialect words together with some on-the-spot code words into a language that the enemies—be they womenfolk, their rivals, their elders, their children—could not possibly understand. It caught on rapidly, losing its value as a code; soon "boontlingers" and their friends were eagerly trying to shark (con) each other with new inventions.

It was more fun to call coffee *zeese* instead of coffee, because it recalled old J.C., a cook who made coffee so strong you could float an egg in it. Or to call working *ottin'*, after an industrious logger named Otto. To call a big fire in the grate a *jeffer*, because old Jeff Vestal always had a big fire going. To say *charlie ball* for embarrass, because old Charlie Ball, an Indian, was so shy he never said a word. To say *forbes*, short for four bits, and *tubes*, for two bits. To call a phone a *buckywalter* after Walter Levi, known back then for having a phone at home. To say *ball* for good, because the old standard of quality was the Ball-band shoe, with the red ball on the box.

Other words came right out of old Scotch-Irish dialect—*wee* for small, *kimmie* for man, *tweed* for young man, *deek* for look at. Still other words were borrowed from the Pomo Indians, who moved off to a reservation after an early settler set up his general store in the middle of their camping ground. A few words are corruptions of French, like *gorm* (gourmand) for eat.

Then there were the code names for *nonch* (not-nice) subjects. To go to bed with a girl was to *burlap* her, because one day in the 1890s someone walked into the general store, found no clerk, checked the storeroom and found him making love to a young lady on a pile of sacks. The word caught on, although it got competition from *ricky-chow*, an onomatopoeic description of the twanging bedsprings in the Boonville Hotel's honeymoon suite.

Some of the language was developed to cushion tragedy; everybody feared having their sheep frozen or starved by a sudden change in the weather. That was too big a disaster just to report baldly, so they would say "That frigid perel [cold rain, which resembles little pearls] made many white spots [dead lambs]. There'll be nemer croppies [no more sheep, which crop the grass] come boche season [*boche*, meaning deer, is derived from a Pomo word]."

Now Boontling is spoken by only a minority of Boontners. They have a club that meets every other week in one of the members' houses to *harp* (speak). There are twenty members, though more like two hundred harp and understand. Mack Miller, in his sixties, drives down from Ukiah, a larger town on the coast, "because I'm tonguecuppy [sick] when there's nemer to harp Boont with."

But *codgiehood*, their word for old age, is overtaking most of the Boontlingers. The oldtimers—Wee Ite and Buzzard, and Fuzz and Deekin', Wee Tumps and High Pockets, and Iron Mountain, Skeeter, and Sany—are dwindling. They are saying their last sayings in Boont: "A dom in the dukes is baller than dubs in the sham

[bush]." A couple of dude ranches have sprung up in the valley, and just a year ago, for the first time ever, a bank dared open a branch in once-woolly Boonville. The end is near.

—*Timothy Tyler*

# 16 MAY

## *Snallygaster V*

From the *Valley Register,* Middletown, Maryland, February 12, 1909:

### MONSTER GO-DEVIL, OR WINGED BOVALUPUS, IN THIS SECTION OF MARYLAND

IT KILLED BILL GIFFERSON IN NEW JERSEY—NEARLY CAUGHT A WOMAN AT WILLIAMSPORT—SHOT AT NEAR HAGERSTOWN—SEEN AT SHEPHERDSTOWN—LAID EGG NEAR BURKITTSVILLE—GOVERNMENT TO SEND TROOPS AFTER IT.

The terrible beast that has been causing so much alarm in New Jersey is undoubtedly headed this way. The creature was first heard from in New Jersey about a month ago, when its tracks in the snow were observed. They could be seen in a field, and then they would entirely disappear. This was the source of much mystery until it was discovered that the fearful beast could fly as well as it could walk. James Harding was the first man to see it, and he described it as a sort of cross between a vampire, a tiger, and a bovalupus. It has enormous wings, a long pointed bill, four legs armed with claws like steel hooks, one eye in the center of its forehead, and it screeches like a locomotive whistle. . . . Bill Gifferson was the first victim of the Go-Devil, or whatever it may be called. He was walking along a country road when it swooped down upon him, carried him to the top of a high hill and, perching there, pierced his jugular vein with its needle-like bill and slowly sucked his blood while it gently fanned him with its wings.

The beast was seen near Hagerstown last week. George Jacobs was out hunting when he saw a strange-looking thing flying over his head. He thoughtlessly fired at it, but the shot rattled from its tough hide as if he had shot against an iron plate. The enraged Go-Devil took after him and he barely escaped by dodging into a stable and slamming the door. Its yawps were fearful.

The *Shepherdstown Register* reports that the great beast was seen along the cliffs about a half-mile above that town last week and that the government was notified of its presence there.

MORE TO COME ON 10 JUNE.

# 17 MAY

## *Schizophrenic Words*

Depending on their context, some words change their meanings, even turn them inside out. *Sanction,* for instance, may be either authoritative approval or penalty for noncompliance. If you say I am *imposing,* you may mean either that I am impressive or that I am taking unfair advantage of you. To *stem* from is to develop from, but to *stem* is also to block—that is, to stop the stemming. To *cleave* is either to adhere or to split in two. If you are *fast* you may be quick, loose-living, or tied up; and in the last case you will have to *fast* unless someone comes along to feed you.

Some words have reversed meaning over the years. *Bully\** is a bully example. To *ban* once meant to summon. *Let,* meaning to permit, meant to hinder in the old law term "without let or hindrance."

When you dress a chicken you are removing its feathers, but when you dress yourself you are putting yours on; you trim a Christmas tree to embellish it, but a fat cut of meat to disembellish it; when you trip you may be either moving nimbly or stumbling; "weather" means both to wear well and to wear out; "overlook," both to inspect and to neglect; "cavalier" to be either gallant and gentlemanly, or haughty and ungentlemanly; "to think better of," to like a person better or to like his suggestion less. And both "best" and "worst" mean "to defeat."

"Deduction" as noun form of the verb "deduct" means "subtraction," while as noun form of the verb "deduce" it means "a logical inference." Similarly, "revolution" as noun form of "revolt" means "total change"; as noun form of "revolve," it means "orbital motion about a point."

What does *mean* mean? Well, it means *mean:* "I mean it." It means *mean:* "I mean you're a *mean* man." It means *mean:* "I mean you're a mean man of *mean* estate." And it means *mean:* "I mean you're a mean man of mean estate who hews to the golden *mean.*"

# 18 MAY

## *Bowwow, Dingdong, and Pooh-pooh*

*bowwow theory n :* a theory that language originated in imitations of natural sounds (as those of birds, dogs, or thunder).

*dingdong theory n :* a theory that language originated out of a natural correspondence between objects of sense perception and the vocal noises which were a part of early man's reaction to them.

*pooh-pooh theory n :* a theory that language originated in interjections that gradually acquired meaning.
> —*Webster's Third New International Dictionary*

---

\*See 24 January.

Apple-biting Adam spied
  Lovely Eve anew.
Did he imitate a dove?
  Did he bill and coo?
Or did sense perceptions speed
  To his brain and through,
Causing him to voice a noise
  Meaning "I love you"?

Which are right and which are wrong,
Bowwow theorists or dingdong?

Other scholars base their claim
  On another clue:
They say Adam blurted, "Ah!
  "Wow!" "Oho!" or "Ooh!"—
Interjections which would all
  More than likely do,
So that their conjecture seems
  Sound as the other two.

Which one's got it, anyhow—
Pooh-pooh, dingdong, or bowwow?

Happy breed whose chase has such
  Cheerful beasts in view!
We, the others, wonder, as
  Thunderclouds accrue,
What new sound will signify
  Human speech is through—
Whimper? Bang? Old Gabriel's
  Final view halloo?

Cataclysm, which are you:
Bowwow, dingdong, or pooh-pooh?
      —*Ormonde de Kay*

# 19 MAY
### *The Food of Love*

R. M. Walsh built a verse in the *Saturday Evening Post* around metaphors of food—"She takes the cake," "some tomato," "full of baloney," and so on. I thank him for these conceits, some of which I have borrowed here:

Johnny boy was top banana,
  Johnny boy was full of beans;
Johnny boy brought home the bacon—
  Plenty lettuce in his jeans.

Johnny boy fell hard for Anna,
   Thought her sweet as apple pie,
Yet could not her love awaken—
   She had other fish to fry.

Johnny boy grows soft as custard,
   In a pretty pickle he;
Milk of human kindness stumbles—
   He's not Anna's cup of tea.

Johnny boy can't cut the mustard,
   Anna keeps him in a stew.
That's the way the cookie crumbles;
   I say fudge, and so should you.
          —W.R.E.

# 20 MAY

## I Do Not Love Thee

Certain epigrammatic verses recur, written in different languages and attributed to different authors. The first-century Latin poet Martial wrote: *"Non amo te, Sabidi, nec possum dicere quare; / Hoc tanto possum dicere, non amo te."* ("I do not love thee, Sabidus, nor can I say why; but this much I can say, I do not love thee.") In the seventeenth century an Oxford student named Tom Brown, told to translate this passage, produced the famous quatrain:

I do not love thee, Dr. Fell;
The reason why I cannot tell;
But this alone I know full well:
I do not love thee, Dr. Fell.

An even earlier rendition:

### ANTIPATHY

I love him not; but shew no reason can
Wherefore, but this: *I do not love the man.*
          —*Author unknown*

This French version was contemporaneous with Tom Brown's:

Je ne vous aime pas, Hylas;
Je n'en saurois dire la cause,
Je sais seulement une chose:
C'est que je ne vous aime pas.
          —*Comte de Bussy-Rabutin*

# 21 MAY

*Measure for Measure*

### THE I-DON'T-CARE SCALE

| | | |
|---|---|---|
| 2 jots | = | 1 tittle |
| 3 tittles | = | 1 continental |
| 2 continentals | = | 1 tinker's dam |
| 4 tinker's dams | = | 1 damn |

### LINEAR MEASURE

| | | |
|---|---|---|
| 2 hops | = | 1 skip |
| 2 skips | = | 1 jump |
| 24 jumps | = | 1 stone's throw |
| 3 stone's throws | = | 1 piece |
| 12 pieces | = | 1 way-the-hell-and-gone |

### APPLAUSE SCALE

| | | |
|---|---|---|
| 2 salvos | = | 1 accolade |
| 2 accolades | = | 1 triumph |
| 3 triumphs | = | 1 ovation (sitting) |
| 4 ovations | = | 1 lionization |
| 2 lionizations | = | 1 outtasight |

### PAPRIKA MEASURE

| | | |
|---|---|---|
| 2 dashes | = | 1 smidgen |
| 2 smidgens | = | 1 pinch |
| 3 pinches | = | 1 soupçon |
| 2 soupçons | = | too much paprika |

### POLITICAL OPPONENT'S MEASURE

| | | |
|---|---|---|
| 2 nincompoops | = | 1 fathead |
| 2 fatheads | = | 1 incompetent |
| 3 incompetents | = | 1 opportunist |
| 2 opportunists | = | 1 machiavelli |

### ALCOHOLIC BEVERAGE MEASURE

| | | |
|---|---|---|
| 2 fingers | = | 1 tot |
| 2 tots | = | 1 shot |
| 2 shots | = | 1 slug |
| 4 slugs | = | 1 snootful |
| 2 snootfuls | = | 1 night in jail |

ALTERCATION SCALE

| 2 tussles | = | 1 fray |
|---|---|---|
| 3 frays | = | 1 fracas |
| 2 fracases | = | 1 skirmish |
| 2 skirmishes | = | 1 fight |

HISTORICAL INVECTIVE SCALE

| 2 scamps | = | 1 rascal |
|---|---|---|
| 3 rascals | = | 1 knave |
| 2 knaves | = | 1 varlet |
| 4 varlets | = | 1 scoundrel |
| 2 scoundrels | = | 1 charlatan |

—*Joe Ecclesine*

# 22 MAY

## *Maudit Soit Ton Père*

Francis H. Wilson believes, and I have no reason to dispute him, that the longest curse word is German: *Himmelherrgottkreuzmillionendonnerwetter!* We cannot touch it. We are backward in anathema; our vocabulary of invective centers on tired obscenities. A magazine named *Maledicta* is trying to reform us, but it has a downhill road to travel.

The Spaniards, ceremonious in polite conversation, convey the ultimate insult with a gesture of the head and a curt, contemptuous phrase: *tu madre,* "your mother." "Not saying the operative word," asserts Robert M. Adams, "seems a particularly devious and deadly form of obscenity, since it forces the victim to contaminate his own mind, to call up the expression that the speaker does not even deign to voice."

The French are more given to Rabelaisian profusion in their obscenity. Herewith some French cursing:

### LA COLOMBE DE L'ARCHE

Maudit
soit le père de l'épouse
du forgeron qui forgea le fer de la cognée
avec laquelle le bûcheron abattit le chêne
dans lequel on sculpta le lit
où fut engendré l'arrière-grand-père
de l'homme qui conduisit la voiture
dans laquelle ta mère
rencontra ton père!

—*Robert Desnos*

A rough translation:

### FROM THE ARK, A DOVE

Cursèd
be the father of the wife
of the blacksmith who beat out the iron for the ax
with which the woodsman cut down the oak
from whose wood was framed the bed
in which was conceived the great-grandfather
of the man who drove the carriage
in which your mother
met your father!

—W.R.E.


# 23 MAY

### *Four Kate, Won Eye a Door*

You may wonder whether the verses below are composed of homophones or homonyms, but don't ask me. I can't tell the difference.

### ANT SONG

Necks tweak coffer mere Rome ants
Holed mead ants and ants and ants
Ants sir ants sir ants Urdu
Lettuce turnip pay sore too.

### ANN DREW

Ann drew ann drew ann drew drew ann
Ann drew drew ann ann drew ann drew

### A CYST ME TWO

A cyst me two purse you ewe Kate;
My cent tea meant four yew is grate.
My heart is melon colic, Kate;
Ah, wood that eye mite German eight
In ewe all so this can't sir, Kate!
Ah, wood that eye mite in cull Kate
Eye doll a tree of me in Kate!
When icey yew my I's die late.
Yet ewe a peer in viol eight;
Two know a veil do eye play Kate
Ewe Kate.
My purr puss four yew eye reel late

And men shun how eye dale lea weight
Four ewe bee four yore man shun gait;
But this a noise ewe, four yew hate
Roam ants, deer Kate.
In cents eight oh pals chorus Kate
And sin till late
Know more than ewe, in hew man Kate.
Die earn a lee eye sup lick Kate
Ewe Kate,
My car is mat tick Kate.
O Kate, a bait
My sore did state!
Deep lore my fate!
Come Munich Kate
Affect shun, Kate!
Bee knot can tanker us, deer Kate—
Cap it you late!
Say yew will bee my candy date
For mat tree moan knee all estate.
Prey, ant sir, Kate!

### KNOT TWO KNOT FOUR WON EYE A DOOR

'Tis not a miss a miss two fined
With prom miss sinner glance, sir;
If miss with miss stir bee come bind,
Then miss chief is the ant, sir.

Alas two idle eyes ice ought
In sum seek lewd dead sex shun;
The no bull ass a lass wood knot
Axe seed too my affect shun.

If few sum made den wood a choir
She may a void dew wall so;
All ads are freak went lea a fire,
All asses soft tar fall so.

—W.R.E.

# 24 MAY

## *Words with One Syllable Work*

I propose shortly to put in a few long words for long words. Now, however, I present the case for words of one syllable:

When you come right down to it, there is no law that says you have to use big words when you write or talk.

There are lots of small words, and good ones, that can be made to say all the things you want to say, quite as well as the big ones. It may take a bit more time to find them at first. But it can be well worth it, for all of us know what they mean. Some small words, more than you might think, are rich with just the right feel, the right taste, as if made to help you say a thing the way it should be said.

Small words can be crisp, brief, terse—go to the point, like a knife. They have a charm all their own. They dance, twist, turn, sing. Like sparks in the night they light the way for the eyes of those who read. They are the grace notes of prose. You know what they say the way you know a day is bright and fair—at first sight. And you find, as you read, that you like the way they say it. Small words are gay. And they can catch large thoughts and hold them up for all to see, like rare stones in rings of gold, or joy in the eyes of a child. Some make you feel, as well as see: the cold deep dark of night, the hot salt sting of tears.

Small words move with ease where big words stand still—or worse, bog down and get in the way of what you want to say. There is not much, in all truth, that small words will not say—and say quite well.

—*Joseph Ecclesine*

# 25 MAY

## *Recovered Charades*

Will Shortz sent these charades:

> A thing whereon all Princes lie,
> And as we all express a sigh,
> What man into the world brings in,
> An Indian weed whose leaf is thin,
> A wood by kings esteemed much,
> The part of speech when naming such:
> These Initials join'd declare
> A town where friendly people are.
> —*Country Magazine, May 1784*

> An insect of the smallest kind
> If you transpose, you soon will find
> That from all mortals I do quickly fly;
> When gone, my loss in vain they'll mourn,
> In vain will wish for my return,
> Tho' now to kill me, ev'ry art they try.
> —*Matilda,*
> *(Weekly Museum, July 16, 1796)*

# 26 MAY

## *Time on Your Feet*

Russell Baker once entered a bill of particulars against clichés connected with time. Why, he asked, should time not hang light on one's feet, instead of heavy on one's hands? Try one's body, instead of one's soul? Run long, instead of short, and in, instead of out? Jump up and down noisily instead of standing still? Bus or drive, instead of flying? Why is time money, but never credit? Ripe, but never green? Why does one have the time of one's life, but never of one's day or week? Why does one arrive in the nick of time, but never in the slash? And is not time not just the great healer but the great sickener of all things?

# 27 MAY

## *Do Not Mispell or . . .*

Two reflections on grammar:

### ONCE UPON A TIME I USED

Once upon a time I used
To mispell
To sometimes split infinitives
To get words of out order
To punctuate, -badly
To confused my tenses
to ignore capitals
To employ common or garden clichés
To indulge in tautological repetitive statements
To exaggerate hundreds of times a day
And to repeat puns quite by chants.
But worst of all I used
To forget to finish what I
　　　　　　　　　—*Alan F. G. Lewis*

### SPELLING REFORM

With tragic air the love-lorn heir
　　Once chased the chaste Louise;
She quickly guessed her guest was there
　　To please her with his pleas.

Now at her side he kneeling sighed,
　　His sighs of woeful size:
"Oh, hear me here, for lo, most low
　　I rise before your eyes.

"This soul is sole thine own, Louise—
   'Twill never wean, I ween,
The love that I for aye shall feel,
   Though mean may be its mien!"

"You know I cannot tell you no,"
   The maid made answer true;
"I love you aught, as sure I ought—
   To you 'tis due I do!"

"Since you are won, O fairest one,
   The marriage rite is right—
The chapel aisle I'll lead you up
   This night!" exclaimed the knight.
                          —*Anonymous*

# 28 MAY

## *Kind of Four of a Kind*

I suppose it is too much to expect day-and-night adulation. There must be some brief moment when somebody says to himself that even Richard Nixon was not perfect; can Willard Espy be? I hear overtones of such criticism:

### THEY SAY

They say though I'm
A rhyming man,
From time to time
My verse don't scan;

And what is worse,
From time to time
They say my verse
Don't even rhyme.

I can reply to these cynics only that when I was seven or eight years old, a verse of mine opposing bolshevism was printed in the county paper. I even remember that it rhymed "stitches" with "ditches." And surely I have improved since then. I must admit, though, in the doggerel hereunder the improvement is not striking:

### 1. FOR THE GRAVESTONE OF THE LATE JOHN SHALLOW, ESQ.

When young, preferring books to sleep,
   I read by midnight tallow;
My teachers said that I was deep,
   But I knew I was Shallow.

When old, I lay till sunrise cheep
   Awaiting Death's low hallow.
The grave that holds me now is deep,
   And I no longer Shallow.

### 2. WHEN HOMER SMOTE THE STRINGS

When Homer smote the strings, and told
   Of men and gods on fire,
The stable boys yelled, "Hear that old
   Blind liar beat that lyre!"

### 3. A VERY CLEVER COMMENT

How very clever you would be
   If you were cleverer than me!
And I'd be very clever too
   If I were cleverer than you.

### 4. WILLIAM'S DECLINE

At twenty-one or such
   Of William Little, lover,
No girl could ask too much,
   For he was stuffed with clover.

Now, sixty winters through him
   And snow along his jaw,
Their first wink would undo him,
   For William's stuffed with straw.
            —W.R.E.

# 29 MAY

### *Echoing Sentence, Echoing Rhymes*

One can play on the echoing quality of words in a number of ways. In this sentence from *Word Ways*, the first syllable of each word repeats the last syllable of the word preceding it:

   Jackson's sons are Arthur (thirsty!), Steven (vender), Dermot (motors), Orson (on air), Errol, Roland and Andrew.

Other echoes:

### GO WEST, YOUNG MAN!

Go west, go west! And when thou goest,
Take west my low esteem—my lowest!
Owe west of here the bills thou owest!

Throw west of here the bull thou throwest!
No estimable man thou knowest
But joins me in, "Go west, pest! *Go* west!"
—*W.R.E.*

### DYNASTIC TIFF

Oh I am the King of Siam, I am!
   With cunning I rule from Bangkok!
The King of Bagdad is a sham, a sham,
While *I* am the King of Siam. (I am.)
All others I gladly goddam, Goddam
   The worthless contemptible flock!
Oh, I am the King of Siam, I am!
   With cunning I rule from Bangkok.

Oh I am the King of Bagdad, egad!
   To Hell with the King of Siam!
His ruling is merely a fad, a fad,
While *I* am the King of Bagdad, egad!
His manners, moreover, are bad, quite bad,
   What can you expect from a ham?
Oh I am the King of Bagdad, egad!
   To Hell with the King of Siam!
         —*Geoffrey Hellman*

### JUST DROPPED IN

*Secretary of State John Foster Dulles conferred today with Burmese Premier U Nu. He said later he had come here neither to woo neutral Burma nor to be wooed. . . . His reception was studiously polite.*—The New York Times.

He did not come to woo U Nu,
And there wasn't much of a state to-do,
And they sat around and talked, those two,
And there isn't a doubt that they mentioned Chou.

When reporters asked, "A political coup?"
He waved them aside with a light "Pooh-pooh."
But he didn't just come to admire the view,
Which he certainly knew *you* knew, U Nu.
         —*William Cole*

# 30 MAY

## *Eletelephony*

I reached my apogee at the age of six. Nothing was beyond my power then, though I did have a little difficulty tying my shoe laces in a double bow. I was delighted to be no longer five, and had no desire to become seven. I knew that once seven I'd wish to be eight, and so on until the tide turned, so that at thirty I'd prefer to be only twenty-nine.

There is no age to match six, and there is no verse to match a six-year-old-oriented verse like this one:

Once there was an elephant,
Who tried to use the telephant—
No! No! I mean an elephone
Who tried to use the telephone—
(Dear me! I'm never certain quite
That even now I've got it right.)

Howe'er it is, he got his trunk
Entangled in the telephunk;
The more he tried to get it free,
The louder buzzed the telephee—
(I fear I'd better drop the song
of elephop and telephong!)
—*Laura Elizabeth Richards*

# 31 May

## *Curtailed Words*

We tend to shorten some words as they become old chums, just as William, once we know him better, becomes Bill. Some of these curtailed words, says Fowler, "establish themselves so fully as to take the place of their originals or to make them seem pedantic; others remain slangy or adapted only to particular audiences." The jingle below contains several of each sort.

### DEAR PERAMBULATOR, HOW THIN YOU'VE GROWN!

Do you recall, as I do,
When words before anointment
Were weighed upon a hay-scale
To prove their embonpointment?

When words, like Gibson girls, were
Strategically plump,
And won their beauty contests
By girth of bust or rump?

Ah, how I loved to watch them
Come waddling down the lane:
*Quadrangle! Mobile Vulgus!*
*Fanatic! Aeroplane!*

And *Zoologic Garden!*
   *Stenographer! Raccoon!*
*Stool Pigeon! Schizophrenic!*
   *Detective! Pantaloon!*

*Vice President!* and *Doctor!*
   *Biopsy! Autobus!*
*Professional!* And *Mamma!*
   And *Stradivarius!*

*Tricycle* and *Bicycle,*
   *Perambulator* too,
And even *Spatterdashes*
   Hove grandly into view.

        \*    \*    \*

But now the style's to diet;
   The pounds fall one by one;
Lo! yesterday's Fat Lady's
   Today's Live Skeleton:

The gaunt high-fashion model,
   The wraith of a gazelle;
What's in is see-through costumes
   And see-through words as well.

*Fan, Mob, Quad, Dick,* and *Stooly;*
   *Plane, Steno, Zoo,* and *Bike;*
*Coon, Pants, Pro, Bus,* and *Bio;*
   *Zoo, Doc, Ma, Strad,* and *Trike.*

Dear, plump *Perambulator*
   Has shrunk to *Pram,* and what
Remains of *Spatterdashes?*
   For me, one lonely *Spat.*
                 —W.R.E.

# JUNE

## 1 JUNE

### To a Cow in June

June is, among other things: Fight the Filthy Fly Month, National Ventilation Month, and June Dairy Month. You can honor all three, according to the Providence *Journal*, by swishing a cow's tail:

> Swish, Month of Ventilation Nash-
> onal! Swish, Month of Dairy, too!
> Swish, Month to fight the Filthy Fly!
> Thy caudate member swish, dear Moo!
> —*W.R.E.*

June is also a month for idle reflections:

### ALL HAIL!

> Hail to thee, blithe spirit!—
> Answer me, I beg!
> Bird thou never wert, but
> Wert thou ever egg?
> —*W.R.E.*

### MY DENTAL FLOSS

> My Dental Floss,
>   Come Smiles, come Tears,
> Has served my Teeth
>   For Years and Years;
> And that is Very
>   Nice, my Dears.
>
> And yet I know
>   Without a Doubt,
> Some day that Floss
>   Will Quite Run Out.
> This gives me Much
>   To Think About.
> —*W.R.E.*

## CHARLES DICKENS AND THE DEVIL

Charles Dickens found the Devil
  Stealing Charles Dickens's chickens.
"What the Dickens!" said the Devil.
  "What the Devil!" said Charles Dickens.
                      —W.R.E.

# 2 JUNE

### S *ay* I *t* L *oud*—L *augh,* Y *ell*

"A re you deaf, Father William?" the young man said,
"D id you hear what I told you just now?
E xcuse me for shouting! Don't waggle your head
L ike a blundering, sleepy old cow!
A little maid dwelling in Wallington Town
I s my friend, so I beg to remark;
D o you think she'd be pleased if a book were sent down
E ntitled 'The Hunt of the Snark'?"

"P ack it up in brown paper!" the old man cried,
"A nd seal it with olive-and-dove.
I command you to do it!" he added with pride,
"N or forget, my good fellow, to send her beside
E aster Greetings, and give her my love."
                      —*Lewis Carroll*

### HE SQUANDERS RECKLESSLY HIS CASH

The acrostic below appeared in *Golden Days* on October 10, 1885. Two twelve-letter words, formed one from the fourth and the other from the final letters of the lines—remarkable!

He squanders recklessly his cash
In cultivating a mustache;
A shameless fop is Mr. Dude,
Vain, shallow, fond of being viewed.
'Tis true that he is quite a swell—
A smile he has for every belle;
What time he has to spare from dress
Is taken up with foolishness—
A witless youth, whose feeble brain
Incites him oft to chew his cane.
Leave dudes alone, nor ape their ways,
Male readers of these Golden Days.
                      —*Mrs. Harris*

The next acrostic may be read three ways—from left to right; vertically; or from right to left and from left to right in alternate lines, a form the ancient Greeks called *boustrophedon,* "as the ox turns in plowing." It uses words instead of letters.

### YOUR FACE YOUR TONGUE YOUR WIT

| Your face | Your tongue | Your wit |
|-----------|-------------|----------|
| so faire | so smooth | so sharp |
| first drew | then mov'd | then knit |
| Mine eye | Mine eare | My heart |
| thus drawn | thus mov'd | thus knit |
| affects | hangs on | yeelds to |
| Your face | Your tongue | your wit |

—*Anonymous*

A despairing, not to say sacrilegious, acrostic:

### IN GOD WE TRUST

I nsane titterings heard on the stair,
N ightmarish shadows thrown on the wall,
G rim windless blasts felt in the old hall,
O dd ghosts invade my sick mind and soul.
D aily I ail with a strange malaise;
W ild with terror, my lovely Gervaise
E ntreats we leave while my mind is whole. . .
T aut with fear I search this haunted pile,
R oaring her name, but Gervaise has fled.
U nless . . . Why is my hand stained this red?
S adly I recall her tortured smile
T hat now fills my heart with dark despair.
—*Walter Shedlofsky*

# 3 JUNE

## *Haiku Prove I.Q.*

The Japanese haiku is a verse-form consisting of seventeen syllables—five each in the first and third lines, seven in the second—to which the reader adds his own associations and imagery. Here is one:

Oh! I ate them all
And oh! What a stomachache—
Green stolen apples!
—*Shiki*

I have few associations to add to haikus (you will see in a moment my reason for spelling the plural variantly), so I am not particularly fond of them. Or I was not until I discovered this splendid American example:

### THE TRADITIONAL GRAMMARIAN AS POET

Haiku, you ku, he,
She, or it kus, we ku, you
Ku, they ku. Thang ku.
—*Ted Hipple*

Now, there, I said to myself, is a haiku that is worthwhile. And if Ted Hipple can do it, so can I:

Haikus show I.Q.'s
High I.Q.'s like haikus. Low
I.Q.'s—no haikus.*
—*W.R.E.*

# 4 June

## *When Baby Gurgles Guam and Georgia*

Two-letter abbreviations for all states of the United States were introduced only in 1963, and I am not used to them yet. So I quickly lost the thread this morning when I heard the Oysterville postmistress singing, as she popped the letters of the day into their boxes, something that sounded like this:

When baby gurgles GUAM and GEORGIA,
Then how I NEVADA baby's PENNSYLVANIA,
ARIZONA slapping NEBRASKA with loud huzzah
He sings INDIANA KENTUCKY OREGON cries, "Hurrah!
MICHIGAN tad's OKLAHOMA OHIO tra LOUISIANA LOUISIANA!"
But when the sound is WASHINGTON WASHINGTON WASHINGTON
He loudly shouts, "Where ARKANSAS you MASSACHUSETTS?
Our ALABAMA is ILLINOIS OHIO pish OHIO bah!
The MARYLAND's off at baccarat!
OHIO MASSACHUSETTS go HAWAII you INDIANA our cah
And fetch him to MAINE, near OREGON fah!"
Then I don't NEVADA PENNSYLVANIA at a'.

"But that makes neither meter nor sense," said I.
"It certainly does," said the postmistress; "here, I'll write it out for you."
This is what she wrote:

---

*William Cole says it's the other way around.

When baby gurgles GU and GA,
Then how I NV baby's PA,
AZ slapping NE with loud huzzah
He sings IN KY OR cries, "Hurrah!
MI tad's OK OH tra LA LA!"
But when the sound is WA WA WA
He loudly shouts, "Where AR you MA,
Our AL is IL, OH pish, OH bah!
The MD's off at baccarat!
Oh MA go HI you IN our cah
And fetch him to ME, near OR fah!"
Then I don't NV PA at a'.

       —W.R.E.

# 5 JUNE

### *Out of Sight, Out of Mind*

The oft'ner seen, the more I lust,
 The more I lust, the more I smart,
The more I smart, the more I trust,
 The more I trust, the heavier heart.
The heavy heart breeds my unrest,
 Thy absence therefore I like best.

The rarer seen, the less in mind,
 The less in mind, the lesser pain,
The lesser pain, less grief I find,
 The lesser grief, the greater gain,
The greater gain, the merrier I,
Therefore I wish thy sight to fly.

The further off, the more I joy,
 The more I joy, the happier life,
The happier life, less hurts annoy,
 The lesser hurts, pleasure more rife.
Such pleasures rife shall I obtain
When distance doth depart us twain.

      —*Barnaby Googe*

# 6 JUNE

### *It Stands to? Reason*

*(With a bow to Frank Sullivan, cliché-killer)*

To everything its what? *Its season.*
This statement stands to what? *To reason.*

What is crushing? *Cost.*
What is temper? *Lost.*

What is commentary? *Wry.*
And wit? *Dry.*

What are pathways? *Winding.*
And snowstorms? *Blinding.*

What does absence render us?
*Conspicuous.*

A miss is good as what? *A mile.*
What is durance? *Vile.*

What's the street of writers? *Grub.*
There is what? *The rub.*

If you have a life, you *Bet it.*
If an appetite, you *Whet it.*

Conscientious to a? *Fault.*
I am grinding to a? *Halt.*
—W.R.E.

# 7 JUNE

### *The British Crossword Labyrinth*

Several of my friends have taken up residence in London, saying nasty things over their shoulders about the deteriorating quality of life back in the States. Their return to the womb carries with it a curious self-abasement before all things British. This reverses the attitude of fifty years ago, when Britishers existed for Americans principally as a subject for bad jokes.

One thing that Londoners do better than New Yorkers is to verbalize. The conversation of what was once called the upper classes is frequently civilized and even elegant.

This preoccupation with words is reflected in their crossword puzzles. Turn to the crossword puzzle in the *Times* of London, and you will find what Anthony Lewis describes as "a mass of maddening puns and in-jokes":

"Far from benign in a saint of citrus associations" is the clue: the word turns out to be "inclement." Why? You have to know the old nursery rhyme about St. Clement Dane's Church: "Oranges and lemons says the bells of St. Clement's."

Or try "distraught intent air of Melmoth, for instance." The answer is "itinerant." Why? "Intent air" is an anagram of the answer. And there was a gothic novel by Charles Maturin called Melmoth the Wanderer.

But even the *Times* cannot match the clues that Shipwinkle used to put out in the *New Chronicle*. Take this one: "In church, in short; short measure, at your pleasure; that twisted chin provokes the solver's grin." All that, and the answer is "inch."

Neither at home nor in school do Americans live in such heady companionship with words. An Englishman named Roy Dean solved before millions of television viewers, in three and three-fourths minutes, a London *Times* puzzle that I could not have solved in three and three-fourths days.

My guess is that before long these expatriated Americans will come slinking back home. The crossword puzzles here are easier.

# 8 JUNE

### *The Frolicsome Flea*

When Tom Buckley was writing a *New York Times* column called "About New York," he occasionally asked me to turn a macaronic verse into clear English for his readers. This one came from B. F. Skinner, the behavioral psychologist, who does not know its origin. Each stanza uses successively English, French, German, Latin, and Italian:

> There once was a frolicsome flea
> Son chien lui dépluit comme abri
>     Er wollt' lui einen Kater
>     Sed observat mater
> Non lasci i parenti cosi.
>
> But he listened not to their prayer
> Il quitta son père et sa mère,
>     Er spring t' auf 'ne Katze
>     Sed haec rasitat se
> Lo mangi, orribile a veder.
>
> Around and about the gore flew
> Aie pitié du petit fou
>     Mit lautem Geschrei
>     Vae mihi, o vae,
> Il povero acese in giu.
>
> The moral of this little tale:
> Ne tentez la force de vos ailes;
>     Bleib', ruhig zu Haus
>     Sit domui laus
> Alla casa dimora fedel.
>                                 —*Anonymous*

My approximation of "The Frolicsome Flea":

A Flea, bored with Dog as a diet,
Heard of Cat, and decided to try it.
He cried, "I must go!"
But his parents said, "No!
Stay at home on our Dog and keep quiet."

The Flea didn't heed them a mite;
He jumped on a Cat for a bite.
This maddened the Puss,
Who scratched the Flea loose
And ate him—a horrible sight!

The dying Flea popped with a splat—
Oh, pity the poor little brat,
Crying, "Ma, take me back!"
As, alas and alack,
He slid down the throat of the Cat.

My Moral, dear friends, is a hot one;
What seems like a snack may be not one;
If you live on a pup,
Stay at home and shut up;
Be glad of a home if you've got one.
                                    —W.R.E.

# 9 JUNE

### Fame

Except for Zoltan Zandar, everyone listed in this tour de force was or is a living person.

Alfred Adler, analyzing,
    Probed the psyche, saw obsessions;
Béla Bartók, improvising,
    Blended chords in odd progressions;
Calvin Coolidge, silent, solemn,
    Thought of running, didn't choose to;
Dorothy Dix inscribed a column,
    Lulled the lovelorn, made them news, too;
Edward Elgar, mad for marches,
    Wrote five *Pomp and Circumstances*;
Fannie Farmer knew her starches,
    Turned out cookbooks, saved romances;
Greta Garbo, hibernating,
    Fled from films with little laughter;

Henry Hudson, navigating,
  Edged the Arctic, died soon after;
Ilya Ilf, pooh-poohing purges,
  Razzed Red Russians with wry stories;
Jesse James, obeying urges,
  Stole from banks, gained outlaw glories;
Kublai Khan found home-life dreary,
  Conquered Asia, met the Polos;
Lotte Lehmann sang *Valkyrie*,
  Filled up halls for *Lieder* solos;
Margaret Mitchell, done with Scarlett,
  Wrote no more, abandoned Tara;
Nita Naldi, sultry starlet,
  Played the siren, echoed Bara;
Oliver Optic fed the hopper,
  Dashed off books for fledgling readers;
Pontius Pilate came a cropper,
  Proved the least of lesser leaders;
Quisling, quisling, tried for treason,
  Lost his life with few men grieving;
Robert Ripley, straining reason,
  Dug up facts beyond believing;
Sarah Siddons lit up stages,
  Woke the critics from their slumbers;
Thomas Telford earned his wages,
  Threw up bridges in great numbers;
Ugolino, unaesthetic,
  Sold out Pisa, drew damnation;
Vladimir Vasek waxed poetic,
  Mourned in meter Czech privation;
William Wallace sought no respite,
  Rallied clans, was hanged in London;
Xerxes, xenophobic despot,
  Lost a navy, wound up undone;
Yen Yang-chu attained his wishes,
  Streamlined Chinese ways of learning;
Zoltan Zandar, quite fictitious,
  Ends this piece, his fame thus earning.
                                    —*Frank Jacobs*

# 10 June

## *Snallygaster VI*

The *Hagerstown Mail* says that the monster was seen on the railroad bridge at Shepherdstown last Monday night by the engineer of No. 83, who described it as having an elastic neck and a very long, sharp beak. From descriptions sent to the Smithsonian Institution at Washington, they write back that it is either a winged bovalupus or a Snallygaster, as it has some of the characteristics of both. These animals are exceedingly rare and the hide of a Snallygaster is said to be worth a hundred thousand dollars a square foot, as it is the only thing known that will properly polish punkle shells used by the people of Umbopeland, in Africa, as ornaments. Telegrams and letters are pouring in from scientists and naturalists, and a strict watch is being kept to try to locate its den or roost.

A gentleman from the southern part of the Valley says that the Go-Devil was seen in the mountains between Gapland and Burkittsville last Tuesday night, where it laid an egg—an egg almost as large as a barrel, covered with a tough, parchmentlike shell of a yellowish color.

What alarms us now is that this terrible beast has been seen in the southern part of the Middletown Valley. This vampire-devil is seldom seen during the day, feeding at night only, and the strange part is that it seems to prefer men to women, though it attacks the latter at times. It never gets after children, unless very hungry, as they do not have sufficient blood to satisfy it.

It is said that President Roosevelt is so anxious to see the monster that he may postpone his African safari until it can be captured.

MORE ON 16 JULY.

# 11 JUNE

## Cynarae, Hot Woe!

Once you start spoonerizing well-known verses, you can go on forever, but the joke grows stale after the first few lines. So I manfully refrain from entering here more than the first stanza of my spoonerized Cynarae:

> Mast light, ah, nesterbight, letwixt her yips and nine
> There shell thy fadow, Cynara! thy sheath was bred
> Umon sy pole wetween the bisses and the kine;
> And I was pesolate and dick of a gold assion.
> Yea, I was hesolate and dowed my bed;
> I have thin baithful to fee, Cynara! in fy mashion.
> —W.R.E., *after Ernest Dowson*

The best spoonerisms are those in which the altered words make an eerie sort of sense:

> A: Hot woe, Barley Chinks!
> B: Hot woe, Chilly Bass!

A: Blocking showy, Miss Thorning.
B: Glowing a bale.
A: Porter on the willows? Tut-tut!
B: Mad for the bite. Cuddles on the pot.
A: A very washy splinter.
B: All blood and mowing.
A: Here's to spray in the Ming!
B: Sadsome glummer! 'Ware fell!
A: Low song!

—*J. A. Lindon*

# 12 JUNE

## *We Canal Praise*
## *the Streets of New Orleans*

The cartoonist John Chase wrote a book about New Orleans streets, listing three of them in his title: "Frenchmen, Desire, Good Children." Other New Orleans streets are capitalized in the quartet of quatrains below:

Streets! where all ABUNDANCE win
   Through eager INDUSTRY!
Streets! aSWAMP in PEACE and
   LOVE,
In LAW and PIETY!

Where LAFITTE are not of clay!
   Where no mouth need pucker!
(If you CHEW a LEMON, pray
   OUR LADY OF PROMPT
   SUCCOR!)

Where e'en MADMAN lives in HOPE,
   And NUNS in CHURCH shoot
   CRAPS;
Where CROSSMAN yields to
   HARMONY,
   And VIRTUE sighs, "Perhaps . . ."

Streets! where GREATMEN praise
   DELORD,
   And PIRATES dread the PITT!
Where the POETS' final word
   Is, "AMEN, boys! That's it!"

—*W.R.E.*

# 13 JUNE

## *Praisegod Barebone—I Begin with E!*

Among the Christian names in my family register, my favorite is Seaborne, given to a girl born in the middle of the Atlantic Ocean in the middle of the seventeenth century. If my home were in Texas I would surely cast my vote for a politician there, Barefoot Sanders, on account of his first name alone. If Jeff Nightbyrd and Tom Turnipseed were in my district, I would vote for them too.

*The Dictionary of National Biography* told *Webster's Biographical Dictionary*, which told Anna Peirce, who in turn told me, that Praisegod Barebone (after whom the 1653 "Barebone's Parliament" was named) reportedly had two brothers christened (1) Christ-came-into-the-world-to-save Barebone, and (2) If-Christ-had-not-died-thou-hadst-been-damned Barebone, the latter shortening to Damned Barebone.*

Flie-fornication is among the names in English parish registers. A Texas farmer born as recently as 1883 was christened Daniel's-wisdom-may-I-know, Stephen's-faith-and-spirit-choose, John's-divine-communion-seal, Moses's-meekness, Joshua's-zeal, Win-the-day-and-conquer-all Murphy—Dan, for short.

Anna Peirce also mentioned that a number of her colonial forebears were christened Freelove, the name presumably referring to Agape rather than Eros.

Some generations back, kinfolk of Louisa Bonner named their first boy Walter. He died, and they named their next Walter Restored. He too passed away, and they named their third Walter Restored Twice—Walter R. T. Jones.

More recently, an oil man—and a successful one—named his son Carbon Petroleum Dubbs. Since names represent us to the outside world, it is not surprising that we should be sensitive about them. "To think," mourned my Great-aunt Shae, "that I should have lived to address a daughter 'Mrs. Jones, Hayfork!'" My own family briefly modified its surname. In the 1880s my grandfather had accumulated what appeared to be enough money to start a dynasty. His children (my father alone dissenting) feared that E-s-p-y looked too much like the name of pig farmers (which indeed the seventeenth-century Ulster Espys probably were). So they persuaded grandpa to change the spelling to "Espey," which they thought had a rather Norman shine to it. Unfortunately, my grandfather later lost in gold most of what he had made from oysters, whereupon the family reverted to the old spelling. If you ever find me spelling my name Espey, you will know there has been an oil strike in our oyster beds.

"As his name is, so is he," says I Samuel, and there is something to that. I am lucky to have a surname beginning with E. If my name began with M, says the Council for Alcoholism,† I should be eight times more prone to alcoholism than the average drunk. If my name began with any letter from S through Z (this according to the British Medical Association), I should have twice the usual sus-

---

*The Greek word for name is *onoma*, and an onomasticon is a collection of names. Members of the Sunday department of *The New York Times* once suggested such cognates as *onomasticate*, to chew over funny names; *onomaster*, one who onomasticates superbly; and *autonomast*, one who enjoys his own funny name. But in what way does *onoma* connote anything funny?

† Glasgow, Scotland.

ceptibility to ulcers, and be three times as subject to heart attacks. The frequency of neuroses in us A-R types is half that of you S-Z people, and our life expectancy is twelve years greater.

But I don't feel too well, at that.

# 14 JUNE

### Jack Be Nimble

"There probably is no commoner name in nursery rhymes and tales than Jack," says *Games*. "We have Jack and Jill, Jack Sprat, Little Jack Horner, Jack in the Beanstalk, Jack the Giantkiller, and, of course, our favorite candlestick hurdler. The name is common in words and phrases as well."

Each clue below leads to an answer containing the name Jack. For example, "Halloween fixture" would be *Jack-o'-lantern*.

1. Handyman
2. Hard cider
3. Classic dive
4. Win big
5. "21"
6. Toy
7. Paul Bunyan, e.g.
8. British emblem
9. Exceptionally adept
10. Singing family
11. Game of dexterity
12. Autumn "visitor"
13. Fast-starting hare
14. Tight garment
15. Hand-held rock drill
16. Warm-up exercise
17. Religious plant
18. Pancake

—*Gene Traub*

# 15 JUNE

### He Beat You to That One, Too

Some slang terms remain just that, neither disappearing nor yet becoming acceptable English. Expressions used by Shakespeare, yet still borderline after three hundred years, include "dead as a doornail," "done me wrong," "a hell of a time," "not so hot," "go hang yourself," "she fell for it," and "how you do talk." Do you know in which of Shakespeare's plays the following locutions appear?

> The game is up
> I have yet room for six scotches more
> I have been in such a pickle
> I cannot tell what the dickens his name is
> I'll not budge an inch
> Not so hot
> The first thing we do, let's kill all the lawyers
> I'll tell the world
> There is something in the wind
> I will tell you my drift
> Spread yourselves
> With bag and baggage
> It's Greek to me

Not Shakespeare but Sir Walter Scott—in *Redgauntlet*—introduced the expression "Tell that to the Marines."

# 16 JUNE

### *Balamer Is in Murlin*

Some odd pronunciations are localisms; like certain wines, they do not travel well. Howard K. Smith twitted Baltimoreans for their local twang:

"They call their city Balamer, Murlin. They call garbage gobbidge, legal liggle. Paramour is their word for power mower. And if you ever ask directions there, remember that Droodle Avenue means Druid Hill Avenue. Clays means clothes. Doll means dial—the phone. Cancil means council, as in town council. Council means cancel, as with a check." Replied Baltimore officials, male-chauvinistically: "What's so funny about a paramour to cut the grass?"

A correspondent wrote Cleveland Amory: "For real hair-tearing mispronunciations, nothing could top the new car dealers on Phoenix TV. All their noo cores have par steering, diss brakes, tinn-ed winshills, and the used cores are in lock-noo condition."

Even my home state of Washington, in most respects impeccable, has its oddities of pronunciation. Sequim, a village where, by a freak of nature, no more than two or three inches of rain falls in a year, though the rainfall roundabout is never less than a hundred, is called *Squim*. John F. Kennedy lost Washington's electoral vote in 1960, say some, because he pronounced Spokane (Spoke-Ann to natives)* *Spokayne*. A Washingtonian calls Wahkiakum County Wah-KEYE-a-kum, and next door an Oregonian says Wil-lam´-ette River; visiting easterners will say Wah-ki-ak´-um and Wil-la-mette´ every time.

*See 8 July.

# 17 JUNE

## *Collegiate Quiz*

It is commencement time; across the country, speakers on campus daises explain to students what has gone wrong. Here are the meanings of the names of some well-known colleges and universities. How many can you identify?

1. By God. 2. A dove. 3. Famous spearman. 4. Big hill. 5. New town. 6. Bold friend. 7. Army guard. 8. Sacred oak on a hill. 9. A leader. 10. Fertile upland. 11. A servant. 12. Elm wood. 13. Upper linden tree. 14. Chief guardian. 15. A place to sit. 16. Brave as a bear. 17. Birch meadow. 18. Dark wasteland. 19. From the mound. 20. Springs in the meadow.

—*Thomas L. Bernard*

# 18 JUNE

## *Kipling Rudyards*

J. K. Stephen wrote a complaint about poor writing which ended:

> When the Rudyards cease from Kipling
> And the Haggards ride no more.

To which David McCord added:

> Still for us where Cottons mather
> In the spring the Willas cather
> As of yore.

Perhaps with such precedents in mind, Arthur Berger wrote as follows:

> John
> Was Gay
> But Gerard Hopkins
> Manley
>
> Dame May
> Was Witty
> But John Greenleaf
> Was Whittier

Oscar
Was Wilde
But Thornton
Was Wilder

# 19 JUNE

### Y Is X a Y of Y?

David W. Silverman suggested selecting some word or expression—say, arbitrarily, *land pollution*—calling it X, and then solving the equation "X is a Y of Y": X (land pollution) = Y (soil) of Y (soil). Land pollution is soil of soil. A pun. Mary Youngquist promptly forwarded the following X's to *Word Ways*; you will find the matching Y's in back.

1. Ilk
2. House construction
3. Greta's clothes
4. Ale steward
5. Paying the check
6. Bunches of partly eaten apples
7. Policemen hiding in the woods
8. Silver-colored dish
9. Clothing storage for undergarments
10. Put mother's sister up for a gambling stake.

# 20 JUNE

### I Gave Her Simple Flowers

OYSTERVILLE—Twelve years have passed since the afternoon when a caterpillar tractor ripped the gorse from a plot of land alongside the family house to start my croquet garden, but the lawn has not yet sprouted a wicket. Yet at least rhododendrons are in glorious bloom around the borders; indeed, Louise has just carried an enormous armful into the cottage and is arranging them in tall vases.

I wonder if I would like flowers so much if they were not such convenient sources of verbal imagery: rose-pink, tulip-pure, and so on. Their names have a resonance of loveliness; words reminiscent of flowers retain the resonance even when their actual meaning is ghastly.* Miss Pym, Josephine Tey's fictional detective, noticed how many horrid diseases sounded like the names of flowers:

> *Emphysema* [she reflected] might be the gardener's name for a sort of columbine. And *kyphosis* she could picture as something in the dahlia line. *Myelitis* would be a small creeping plant, very blue,

---

*See 17 November.

with a tendency to turn pink if not watched. And *tabes dorsalis* was obviously an exotic affair of the tiger lily persuasion, expensive and very faintly obscene.

A pleasant example of words used for sound rather than sense:

I gave her simple flowers: hegemony,
Miasma, scrofula. She bent her knee
To stroke the palliasses gambolling
About her feet. We heard the fichu sing.
Cool limousine we drank; smooth summary
Was all our meal . . . A litmus scuttled by;
Two millimeters fluttered overhead;
Our path lush serials festooned . . . then said
My love, my Calomel, "I must go home,"
And, sighing, sought her father's palindrome.
—*Ruth Collins*

# 21 JUNE

## Petersonese

One of the fringe benefits of playing for the Houston Oilers is listening to Coach Bill Peterson, who does things with the language that have not been heard since Casey Stengel was in his prime.* After Miami's Jim Kiick and Larry Csonka ran all over his team, Peterson explained, "We just weren't compared for their backfield." Discussing strategy, he said, "We're changing our floormat this week." Of a limping player, "He has a chronicle knee injury." Of the Oakland Raiders: "That Oakland is tough. They timidate your offense, they timidate your defense, they even timidate the officials."

He has said, "This is the crutch of the problem," and "Things are going bad, but we've got to keep our cools." In training camp, he told his squad, "We're all in this together, and don't you remember it." He also spoke of the team's goal for the year: "Men, I want you thinking of just one word all season. One word and only one word: Super Bowl!" And in the waning minutes of a game with Denver, he proclaimed, "Don't you guys think for a minute that I'm going to take this loss standing down."

One day, reflecting on all the problems a coach has in handling the various personalities among his players, Peterson confessed, "Sometimes I feel like that psychiatrist, Frood."

—*Robert W. Creamer*

* See 14 August and 18 November.

# 22 JUNE

### Midsummer Madness

Before starting the business of the day, I remind you of what the day is:

MIDSUMMER DAY

Midsummer Day no other than
Indeed this is, although

It's odd, since summer just began
A day or two ago.
—W.R.E.

I am a longtime collector of Uncommon, Improper Nouns—words that once were proper names, but have become part of the vernacular. A sub-order of these eponyms consists of words that still represent a person's name, but have become code for some characteristic with which that person is identified. Thus a hero-worshiping biographer is a *Boswell;* a man of vast wealth, a *Croesus;* an irresistible lover, a *Casanova.* Such code names are included in the following sonnet:

WHEN CHARON FERRIES ME ACROSS THE STYX

When Charon ferries me across the Styx,
And Cerberus acknowledges I'm dead,
Pray, Boswell, carve some legend at my head!
Say that I sharpened Machiavelli's tricks;
Out-Croesused Croesus and his golden bricks;
Loved on when Casanova wearièd;
Pushed back Canute's rude ocean in its bed;
Was funnier than Chaplin in the flicks.

Dear Boswell, will you carve in stone how I
Awhile to Joan was Darby, and awhile
To Damon, Pythias? Will you descry
Jack Ripper's rictus underneath my smile?

More likely, Boswell, you will not recall
A blessed thing worth writing down at all.
—W.R.E.

# 23 JUNE

### Love, Plants, and Corn

Some verses attain a risible immortality simply because they are so badly written. This horrid example is by the grandfather of Charles Darwin:

### THE LOVES OF THE PLANTS

So the lone Truffle, lodged beneath the earth,
Shoots from paternal roots the tuberous birth.
No stamen-males ascend, and breathe above,
No seed-born offspring lives by female love.
So the male Polypus parental swims,
And branching infants bristle all his limbs.
So the lone Taenia, as he grows, prolongs
His flatten'd form with young adherent throngs;
Unknown to sex the pregnant Oyster swells,
And coral-insects build their radiate shells.
                                        —*Erasmus Darwin*

The following epitome of good bad verse was written in Salem, Massachusetts, in the nineteenth century:

Corn, corn, sweet Indian corn,
Greenly you grew long ago,
Indian fields well to adorn,
And to parch or grind hah-ho!
                                        —*Reverend William Cook*

# 24 JUNE

## *Bull and Bossy Created He Them*

OYSTERVILLE—Fifty years ago Oysterville was a scattering of truck farms and hayfields along the edge of the bay. The pervasive sounds of every day were the barking of dogs, the grunting of pigs, the mooing of cows, the cackling of hens, and the neighing of horses.

I puzzled, and still do, over some of the names indicating which of these beasts were male, and which female. Both bull and cow, for instance, are of the genus *Bos* (whence beef), but only the cow is a bossy. Why were the castrated bulls we raised for the market steers, while the castrated bulls that hauled my grandfather west along the Oregon trail were oxen? Why, moreover, were oxen in other parts of the world happily potent (indeed, the word *ox* means "besprinkler, begetter")? Would a gelded ox in India be an ox-ox?

I had no difficulty with the idea of a male deer as a buck, or the female as a doe; the male sheep as a ram, or the female as a ewe.

Why, since a goose might be of either sex, could the male be a gander as well, while the female had to remain a goose?

I found it faintly offensive, though I had no idea why, that while a female dog was called, neutrally, a bitch, to call a woman a bitch was a vulgar insult. The expression "to tomcat around," on the other hand, did not bother me—perhaps because I did not know what it meant.

# 25 June

## *Point of View*

Bertrand Russell is credited with inventing the self-centered game of which David L. Silverman here gives examples:

I am thrifty. You're a bit of a tightwad. He's a real skinflint.
I'm cautious. You're timid. He's chicken-hearted.
I'm human. You're prone to err. He's a blundering idiot.
I have hepatitis. You drink too much. He's an alcoholic.
I'm human. You've got an eye for the girls, haven't you? He's lecherous.
I'm diplomatic. You take a pragmatic approach to the truth. He's a hypocrite.

# 26 June

## *Confound Your Words, Your Looks, Your Handwriting!*

Ambiguity takes many forms.

"I counted girls going barefoot to classes; about one in every four." Does that mean, asks *Word Ways*, that one of every four girls goes barefoot to class? Or that barefoot girls go to one out of four classes? Or that girls choose to go to one out of every four classes barefoot? Or that one of every four students is a barefoot girl? Or, perhaps, that the girls have four legs?

Another form of ambiguity:

### AFFAIRE DE COEUR MANQUÉE

Like hammered gold the tresses shone that crowned
   That fragile head.
     My heart more bravely stepped.
Then passing by, I dared to look around,
   And saw the beard.
   And wept.
               —W.R.E.

Here a poet tackles the ambiguity of illegibility:

### ANSWERING YOURS OF (DATE ILLEGIBLE)

The morning mail is here; I have your
    charming letter;
   I kiss each word you penned, with
    ecstasy devout;
I love each little word; I'd love them
    even better
   If I could make them out.

Your writing is as strange and dark as
    modern art is;
  A rippling, trembling line, with curls
    and whirls between;
—Alas, what news is this! "Flinty," you
    say my heart is?
  Or "flirty," do you mean?

Inscrutable, the page yields not to my
    entreaty,
  You speak in covered words of Delphic
    mystery;
It looks as though you think that I am
    "such a sweety";
  (Or "sweaty," can it be?)

Can "deary" be the word? I trust it is
    not "beery,"
  My whispers, not my whiskers, that
    linger in your ear;
And do you find my verse so cheesy or so
    cheery?
  And am I deaf or dear?

Your writing swoops and swirls, with no
    suggestion whether
  I am an Awful Slob or only Awful
    Slow;
Did you perhaps suggest that we should
    "roam" together?
  Or is it double o?

My brain resembles now the Battle of
    Manila,
  Even your signature I study with
    dismay;
Lola or Lena, Lisa, or Lina, Laura,
    Lilla—
  Who are you, anyway?
              —*Morris Bishop*

Finally, I offer for your consideration what might be called an ambiguity of morals:

### FOR ADULTS ONLY

Adult, her eighteen-year-old form;
Adult, her hazel eyes . . . and warm.

Adulter, he who pens these lies;
He deems adulterers . . . unwise.

No, no! let never such as he
Adulterate virginity!
He knows adultery is naughty.
He really oughtn't do it . . . ought he?
—W.R.E.

# 27 JUNE

### Broken-Hearted Pieces

OYSTERVILLE—Doug Todd, public relations director of the Dallas Cowboys, once heard a country song containing the line, "If you want to keep the beer real cold, put it next to my ex-wife's heart." He has been collecting such ululations ever since. Dr. Leslie L. Nunn, who lives down the road a piece, brought me some examples from the Todd collection this morning. A few are adapted here, with thanks and apologies to the original lyricists:

Forever wasn't quite as long as I had counted on;
I've been a long time leaving, but I'll be a long time gone.

You ask me what it was went wrong, but you already know:
I was too busy hanging on, as you were letting go.

She's just a name dropper, and she's dropping mine;
If today was a fish, I would cut off the line.

She'll love you to pieces. The question is whether
She'll be there to put all the pieces together.

Our marriage was a failure, sure; and yet I might point out
That our divorce ain't really such a much to brag about.

We swore, "For better or for worse," and we were not far wrong;
We swore for better or for worse, but not for very long.

Do you think my bed's a bus stop, you pop in and out so free?
When your phone's no longer ringing, you will know that it is me.

If you could fake it we might make it, but I swear that this is true:
If you keep checking up on me, I'm checking out on you.
—W.R.E.

# 28 JUNE

## *Dangler and Ellipsis*

Danglers make a sentence say what you don't mean:

- The bride wore a long white lace dress which fell to the floor.
- The women included their husbands and children in their potluck suppers.
- In Germany a person cannot slaughter any animal unless rendered unconscious first.
- Even more astonishing was our saving the lives of little babies who formerly died from sheer ignorance.
- For those of you who have small children and don't know it we have a nursery downstairs.

—*Naomi Russell*

The foregoing collection is from *Verbatim*. The editor, Laurence Urdang, added two danglers he particularly liked:

- Plunging 1,000 feet into the gorge, we saw Yosemite Falls.
- When a small boy, a girl is of little interest.

### ELLIPSIS

Ellipsis is the dropping of words in a sentence on the assumption that the recipient's mind will fill them in for sense, as in "I'll light my [tobacco and smoke my] pipe." A poorly considered ellipsis can cause trouble:

- When properly stewed, I really enjoy apricots.
- I plan to mow the lawn with my wife.
- Mommy will put your pajamas on.
- Alice can eat herself.
- Wash your face in the morning and neck at night.
- A gentleman never crumbles his bread or rolls in his soup.

—*G. A. Cevasco, Verbatim*

An ellipsis between lovers:

> With nary care
> He sipses
> The dripses
> From her lipses,
>
> Dismissing
> From that kissing
> The ellipses.
> —*W.R.E.*

# 29 June

### Birds and Bees

Birds and bees
Are black and blue
They hem and haw
They p and q
They're fast and loose
And back and forth
They're cut and dried
And south and north
They're fair and square
They're cat and mouse
They're in and out
Of home and house
They're true and false
They're bones and skin
They're fuss and bother
Kith and kin
They're fine and dandy
Square and round

Bits and pieces
Safe and sound
Free and easy
Hearty, hale
Pins and needles
Head and tail
They drib and drab
Take and give
In fits and starts
They die and live
They're 'tween and 'twixt
They're now or never
And each and all
And good, not clever
I'd tit for tat
Could I but be
From stem to stern
A bird and bee.

—W.R.E.

# 30 June

### Trojan 'orses Inside

Ernest Bevin, foreign secretary in Britain's postwar Labor government, chopped bloody hunks from the cultured Oxbridge syntax of the Foreign Office. Said he of Molotov, his opposite number in the Soviet Union: "The words was scarcely dry on the words out of me mouth when he tore the 'ole thing up." And again, rejecting a Foreign Office recommendation: "I ain't 'avin' it. If you open up that Pandora's box you'll find a lot of Trojan 'orses inside."

- Warren Austin, our ambassador to the United Nations, suggested to warring Jews and Arabs that they sit down and try to settle their differences "like good Christians."
- Samuel Goldwyn was neither malapropping nor mixing metaphors when he said: "A verbal contract isn't worth the paper it's written on." This is a lapsus comicus, a simple verbal confusion.
- My mother specialized in the lapsus comicus. "I haven't been to South Bend," she remarked, "since the last time I was there." And: "He looks so much older than he did when he was young."
- A supporter of Morris Udall, a onetime aspirant for the Democratic nomination for the presidency, described him as "the splitting image of Abe Lincoln."

- A governor fighting for reelection spoke of "traveling incarnito," "being pacific on the issues," and having "intentional fortitude." He also decried his critics' "unmeditated gall."
- Max Ascoli, editor of the *Reporter*, explaining why he need not reduce the number of his staff: "Thanks goodness; we are already underhanded."
- In 1923, when Theodore S. Abbott was Cambridge correspondent for the *Boston Post*, he asked the sergeant on duty at the East Cambridge police station what was new. "Nothing but a couple arrested for lewd and luscious conduct," said the sergeant.

# JULY

## 1 JULY

### A Troop of Tropes

You are even cleverer than you realized. If you doubt it, look up the formidable Greek appellations of rhetorical devices you use unconsciously every day. You trope, trope, trope—that is, you use words figuratively. When you intensify a compound word or phrase by inserting one or more words in the midst of it ("abso-goddamn-lutely," "what place soever," "South by God Carolina"), you are employing tmesis—Greek for "to cut." Each of the numbered expressions in the story below is a rhetorical device with an impressive name. You will find the names in the Answers and Solutions.

Tom and Mary, sharing a small apartment (without benefit of clergy) (1), had dreamed for years of a Caribbean holiday, and finally felt justified in going to the bank to withdraw Mary's favorite necklace (a family curio) (2) and their life-savings which they converted into travelers' checks. They then contracted for two two-way tickets to and from the southern island of their dreams (which still, incidentally, was under the Crown) (3).

"It will be a good change from the Borscht Circuit (4). It usually rains up there, anyway," remarked Tom, meteorologically (5).

They were carried away by elation and a large airplane (6). Food and drinks were served, and he called her Ducky (7) just like in the old days. We need not elaborate on their arrival at the island, the long trip through the boondocks (8) to the hotel; the unpacking, the small, warm room, how pleasant so ever (9) (for they had thought air conditioning an unnecessary expense).

Their "threads" (10) (as Tom put it) hung up, and their travelers' checks discreetly hidden, the happy couple changed into bathing attire which naïvely (11) covered the whiteness of their limbs (12). They rushed to the beach. Everything seemed to live up to the superlatives of the travel brochure: "It's a beautiful world (13), and this is one of its loveliest countries."

"Not bad, eh?" (14) said Tom.

"I'll be forever grateful (15) for this!" said Mary. Then she exclaimed: "Oh, my! I forgot to take off Mother's necklace!"

"Never mind—it has a strong clasp. The old bag (16) saw to that."

"She'd turn over in her grave if she were alive today (17), to see how careless I am!"

Then it happened. A wave like a watery giant (18), spawned 'way (19) out in the gulls' territory (20), hissed (21) and thundered into shore. It was the Sunday punch of an expert (22). Mary's necklace was gone.

Sadly, they straggled up the beach to the hotel and rode the elevator to their floor.

"Well, I never!" (23)

A horrible premonition sent them dashing to the secret place where their money had been hidden. Nothing remained.

—*John McClellan*

# 2 July

## *Crush vs. Whip*

Once upon a time there was a baseball team in New York called the Giants. When it removed to San Francisco, a *New Yorker* writer penned the following advice to the sports writers of the latter city:

Apparently, the St. Louis Cardinals are much more friable than they used to be, for a paper in San Francisco recently ran the headline; "GIANTS CRUSH CARDINALS, 3-1." Now, we don't want to suggest that our city's eldest franchise has got in with a group of orange squeezers who don't know real pulverization when they see it. There's been too much of such carping already. When a boy leaves home, a mother's duty is to hold her tongue, we always say. While voices around us cried that the West Coast was, variously, a vile limbo, an obscure religious sect, a figment of Walter O'Malley's fevered imagination, and a tar pit of busherism certain to fossilize whatever it enveloped, we kept mum. As a reward to ourself for restraint, therefore, we *will* offer some advice about the science or art of baseball-headline verbs. These we have seen evolve from a simple matter of "WIN" and "LOSE" into a structure of periphrasis as complex as heraldry in feudalism's decadence. New York City, now a quaint port known principally for her historical monuments, once boasted three—we swear it, *three*—baseball teams, and a dozen daily newspapers. The lore accumulated here should be passed on to headline writers in all the fresh, brash towns likely to be visited as the major leagues, driven by a dark fatality, continue their migration toward Asia.

The correct verb, San Francisco, is "WHIP." Notice the vigour, force, and scorn obtained, quite without hyperbole. This table may prove helpful:

3-1—WHIP
3-2—SHADE
2-1—EDGE
1-0—(Pitcher's name) BLANKS*

Turning back and working upward, we come to 4-2, known professionally as "the golden mean," or "absolute zero." The score is uniquely characterless. The bland terms "BEAT" and "DEFEAT" are called in from the bullpen (meaning an area in which pitchers not actually in the game may "warm up"). However, 4-1 gets the coveted verb "VANQUISH." Rule: Any three-run margin, *provided the winning total does not exceed ten,* may be described as a vanquishing. If, however, the margin is a mere two runs and the losing total is five or more, "OUTSLUG" is considered very tasty. You will notice, S.F., the trend called Mounting Polysyllabism, which culminates, at the altitude of double digits, in that trio of Latin-root rhymers, "ANNIHILATE," "OBLITERATE," and "HUMILIATE." E.g., "A's ANNIHILATE O'S, 13-2."

Special cases:

1. If the home team is on the short end of the score, certain laws of mutation apply. "SHADE" becomes "SQUEAK BY." For "OUTSLUG," put "WIN IN SLOPPY CONTEST." By a judicious exploitation of "BOW," the home team, while losing, can be given the active position in the sentence and an appearance of graciousness as well.

2. Many novice banner writers, elevated from the 2-col. obscurity of Class A ball to the black-cap. screamers of the big leagues, fumble the concept of "SWEEP." It always takes a *plural* object. Doubleheaders and series can be swept, but not regulation single games. (The minimal "WIN STREAK" is three games long; five makes a "SURGE.") A team that neither sweeps nor is swept splits. A headline familiar to New Englanders is "SOX SPLIT."

3. Which brings up the delicate matter of punning, or paronomasia. Each Baltimore journal is restricted by secret covenant to one "BIRDS SOAR" every two weeks. Milwaukee, with a stronger team, is permitted twelve instances of "BRAVES SCALP" before the All-Star game. "TIGERS CLAW" and "CUBS LICK" tend to take care of themselves. As for you, San Francisco, the lack of synonyms for "giant" briefer than "behemoth" and "Brobdignagian," together with the long-standing failure of New York's own writers to figure out exactly what giants *do* (intimidate? stomp?), rather lets you out of the fun. In view of this, and in view of the team's present surprising record, you may therefore write "GIANTS A-MAYS."[†] But don't do it more than once a month; moderation in all things, S.F.

*—John Updike*

---

[*] Below, in smaller type, you may have "Twirls 3- (4-, 5-) Hitter." Two-hitters are "spun." For a one-hitter, write "Robbed of No-hitter."
[†] Mr. Updike is punning on the name of Willie Mays.

# 3 July

## Cockney Alphabet

This form of wordplay was first called to my attention by Barbara Huston, who lives more than six thousand miles from the Bow Bells of London. I have since received examples from as far away as Melbourne, Australia, and Rome, Italy. Eric Partridge and Rufus Segar are two who have written books of comic Cockney alphabets. R. L. Denyer tells me that the Western brothers, Kenneth and George, played the game on BBC before World War II. So did Clapham and Dwyer.

The number of expressions that can be fitted into the Cockney alphabet is limited only by one's willingness to force unnatural pronunciations onto words—and by one's sense of shame.

Some common variants:

A for 'orses, A for ism
B for lamb, B for mutton
C for sailors, C for yourself
D for ential, D for dumb, D for mitty
E for Adam, E for brick, E for Peron, E for lution
F for vescent, F for so nice, F for been had, F for cacious
G for police
H for mellowness
I for looting, I for an eye, I for nated, I for L tower
J for oranges, J for hear about . . . ?, J for nile delinquent, J for see a dream walking
K nanabel, K for ancis, K for teria
L for leather
M for sis, M for size
N for a cockerel, N for sir, N for lope
O for the garden wall, O for populated, O for my dead body, O for sexed, O for coat
P for relief, P for idious Albion, P forming fleas
Q for the pictures, Q for tickets, Q tea pie
R for mo, R for crown
S for as I'm concerned
T for two, T formation
U for got, U for ia, U for mism
V for la France, V for section, V for la différence
W money, W for a match, W for a Siamese ram
X for breakfast
Y for mistress, Y for heaven's sake
Z for breezes

We associate Cockneys with the inaspirate h. C. W. V. Meares, who grew up in London but not within sound of the Bow Bells, reports that he and his schoolmates delighted in the following A for ism: "It ain't the 'opping over the 'igh 'edges that 'urts the 'orses 'ooves; it's the 'ammer, 'ammer, 'ammer on the 'ard 'ighway."

# 4 JULY

### Beef, Lemons, and Cheese

Our victory in the War of Independence owes a good deal to outsiders, including the Poles and the French. Poland gave us Kosciusko; France gave us Lafayette. There are indications that in their hearts the Poles still prefer the Americans to the Soviets. The *New York Times* reports that a Polish admiral, entertaining Russian naval dignitaries, ended an effusively sycophantic speech with a hearty "Comrades! A toast to your glorious Navy! Bottoms up!"

During one of the breathing spells of the Napoleonic Wars, Bonaparte arranged for an international flotilla to line up for review by the empress. As her barge passed each vessel, sailors clinging to the shrouds were supposed to wave their hats and shout three times, "*Vive l'Impératrice!*" The frigate representing the United States received a special commendation, though the crew had not learned the French words. Instead, the captain had them shout lustily, "Beef, lemons, and cheese!"

# 5 JULY

### Remember Cyclamates?
### Maybe They Weren't So Harmful after All

The headline is from the *Wall Street Journal.* A subhead continues, "New Studies Said to Contradict Cancer Evidence That Led to FDA's Ban on Sweeteners."

The *Journal* story inspired me to write the following verse, which I dedicate to Dr. Milton Helpern, retired chief medical examiner of New York City, a scientist who steadfastly refuses to concede that two and two make more than four, even in ecology.

#### A MOUSE OF MY ACQUAINTANCE

A mouse of my acquaintance in seven days was fed
    Twice twenty thousand swordfish; and THAT MOUSE IS DEAD.
The mercury in swordfish is an enemy to dread;
    He ate twice twenty thousand, and THAT MOUSE IS DEAD.

His sister gnawed through pizzas (I am told one million four);
    There's talk of botulism, and THAT SISTER IS NO MORE.
Their brother downed ten thousand turkeys lined with pesticide;
    It took a week to kill him, but THAT POOR MOUSE DIED.

So stay away from hormones, and from salmonella too;
    Be impolite to cyclamates, and DDT eschew;
For additives and chemicals can kill you just like *that*,
    Though (confidentially) those mice were done in by the cat.
                    —W.R.E.

# 6 July

### Sea, Alter Onto!

These nursery rhymes are drawn from the names in the Toronto telephone book:

Ryder Cocke Hosse
Turban Berry Crosse
Tuzzi Affan Leddy
Oppinga Wye Torres
Rings Anna Fynn Gersh
Annabelle Sanna Towes
Furr Shi Shallouf Music
Ware Evert Shi Ghosh.

Barr Barre Black Shipp
Haff Yew Anney Wool
Yetts Herr, Yetts Herr
Three Baggs Voll
Wan Farr Durr Master
Won Forder Dame
An Wun Varder Littleboys
Watt Lief Sinne Allain.

Jack Spratt Codd Ita Knowe Fatte
Hitz Wyver Codd Ita Noll Ean
Anso Bett Wynn Ditto Offen
Thayer Lick Turr Platte Kleane.

Merrie Merry Quaint Caunt Ririe
Howe Dussiaulme Garden Groh
Witt Silver Belson Cockell Schells
And Pretty Mayes Allin Arro.

Jaques Aingell
Wenn Opper Hill
Topicha Paylor Watter
Jaques Fell Down
Ann Brooke Hiss Crown
Angell Kamm Tumber Linne Affe Tarr.

Little Jack Horner
Hee Sattin Acorn Knerr
Eaton Niece Christmas Pye
When Heap Putt Innis Thumm
Anto Kautz Appel Lum
Ens Hedd Watte Good Boye Amm Ei.

Liddle Mees Muffitt
Saa Tonner Tufford
Eaton Herr Corzon Waye
Winn Alongo Kammer Spyra
Unda Sathe Down Beese Eidher
Ann Frydmann Mies Muffitt Taw Way.

(Just to show how easy the trick is, the author constructs one verse in two different ways:)

Singer Songer Sikka Spence
A Puckett Fuller Wry
Forrin Twinney Black Birze
Beckett Inner Pye
Wenner Pye Wass Opal
The Beers Spick Annis Singh
Nowe Wasson Datta Dainty Dische
Toussaint Bee Forder King?

Zinga Zunka Garson Spenst
Pock Effs Fowler Aye
Farrand Wenn Ablack Burss
Becki Tinney Pye
Wenther Pyne Watts Appin
Tee Busby Gann Tosh Ing
Noh Wax Sindall Adeney Ting
Tuzex Bee Ford Durkin?
—*Jay Ames*

# 7 JULY

### *He Goddam Mad Dog, Eh?*

Good palindromes almost make sense: "Madam, I'm Adam"; "Able was I ere I saw Elba"; "A man, a plan, a canal, Panama." "Yreka Bakery" almost makes sense if you live in Yreka, California (though there is no longer a Yreka bakery there). "Sex at noon taxes" makes increasing sense as the years pile up. (Michael Gartner combined this with "I moan, Naomi," to create "'Naomi, sex at noon taxes,' I moan.") Dmitri Borgmann's "Was it a bar or a bat I saw?" may be a pretty silly question, but it is a reasonable sentence, as is Martin Gardner's "Norma is as selfless as I am, Ron."

J. A. Lindon makes poems of one-line palindromes:

### HA! ON, ON, O NOAH!

> Eel-fodder, stack-cats red do flee,
> Unglad, I tar a tidal gnu,
> I tip away a wapiti,
> Ewer of miry rim for ewe.

My favorite among lateblooming palindromes is James Thurber's "He goddam mad dog, eh?" A pedant might scratch this entry because of the spelling of goddam. But foreigners call Englishmen goddams, don't they? Thurber probably ran into his mad dog while it was out with Englishmen in Noel Coward's midday sun.

It is my impression that nobody with a palindromic name ever died in the sanctity of his countrymen's love. Where is Premier Lon Nol of Cambodia now? U Nu, erstwhile premier of Burma, had a palindromic name. So did Laval, the quisling premier of France.

There are few rational palindromes of more than fifty or sixty letters. (Penelope Gilliatt made a better try than most in this 51-letter oddity: "Doc, note, I dissent. A fast never prevents a fatness. I diet on cod.") But if you waive rationality, there is no limit to the length a palindrome can reach. The author of the following 450-letter phenomenon has written other palindromic verses more than 1,000 letters long:

### THE FADED BLOOMERS' RHAPSODY

> Flee to me, remote elf—Sal a dewan desired;
> Now is a Late-Petal Era.
> We fade: lucid Iris, red Rose of Sharon;
> Goldenrod a silly ram ate.
> Wan olives teem (ah, Satan lives!);
> A star eyes pale Roses.
>
> Revel, big elf on a mayonnaise man—
> A tinsel baton-dragging nice elf too.
> Lisp, oh sibyl, dragging Nola along;
> Niggardly bishops I loot.
> Fleecing niggard notables Nita names,
> I annoy a Man of Legible Verse.
>
> So relapse, ye rats,
> As evil Natasha meets Evil
> On a wet, amaryllis-adorned log.

Norah's foes' orders (I ridiculed a few) are late, Pet.
Alas, I wonder! Is Edna wed?
Alas—flee to me, remote elf.
                              —*Howard W. Bergerson*

# 8 JULY

## *Omak Me Yours Tonight*

### (Or, Ilwaco Million Miles for One of Your Smiles)

The bulk of the Washington State place names abused in this verse derive from
Indian words that sound as if they should mean something in English. They
don't. They are explained, though, in the Answers at the back of the book.

> Chet suffered sore from Acme;
> Yet (so I'm Tolt), all day
> Upon his Fife he'd Toutle
> Dabob Spee-Bi-Dah-ay
> . . . And brush the girls away.
>
> He loved to Walla Walla
> In breakers warm and wet.
> In all Duwamish waters
> Would splash and Wollochet.
>
> And was he brave? Wenatchee!
> Also Elochoman—
> Till Latah he fell in with
> A Lilliwaup named Ann.
>
> Olalla Palouse was Annie.
> Lor' Lummi, wasn't she, though!
> She had Asotin something
> That should have laid Chetlo.
>
> But it was hair of Auburn
> That Chester loved in maids,
> While ne'er was raven's Quilcene
> More black than Annie's braids.
>
> Chesaw him in Dewatto,
> A-floating on his back,
> With Tatoosh on his Tumtum
> That made her lips go smack.
>
> Now Whatcom over Annie?
> 'Twas love, Attalia that.

Her heart went Hamma Hamma,
And her teeth went Klickitat.

She cried, "You are Malott, dear!
Wynoochee kiss me, pet?"
The Mattewa, such ardor
Did not Startup in Chet.

So Anacortes Chester,
Thurston to Havermale.
But he replies, "Tonasket!
Ohop off! Hit the trail!"

"Naselle me your embraces,"
She begs him with sweet moan;
"My family's Algona;
I sleep and dream Malone."

With Methow in her madness,
Once more the girl began:
"I Sekiu and you only;
Alava you," Spokane.

"Though man and maiden Canby
Olequa in God's view,
You're free to Sauk and kick me.
Go on—Satsop to you.

"My itch Tacoma to you is
Mowich than e'er I've had.
Draw closer!—Touchet!—Scatchet!—
Or else I shall go mad."

"Come Offut," quoth Chet Coulee;
"Pysht Pysht! You plead in vain.
Shoo! Skagit! Having walked here,
Newaukum home again!"

Then Ann began to Yellepit,
And soon she Yelm some more;
Then she began Taholah;
Then she began to roar:

"Tahuyah think you're talking,
Yacolt and frigid fella?"
In Sucia angry Vashon
All this and Moran yella.

She Vader in, and gave him
Back to Leland La Push;
She Twisp his nose, and Chucka-
nut pie in his mush.

*Lebam! ** Bangor! ** Kapowsin!***
"Oh, Memaloos!" begged he;
"You've just knocked out a Mohler!
Dosewallips broke my knee!"

She Kickit him. He hollered:
"Wawawai! Let's cry Queets!"
Klipsan Moclips she gave him;
He grovelled at her feets.

"Elwha-cha doing? Stop it!
Become Ione instead!
I Wauna you!" Chet pleaded.—
In a Semiahmoo they were wed.

Thus did our Doughty hero
To his dear Anatone:
No more does Chester Toutle,
Or Annie dream Malone.

The Colfax is, Snohomish
More Happy, Neah or fah:
Soon Chester Willapa be,
And Annie be a ma.

*Moral*
Utsalady who knew a fat Liplip
Often Kachess the cockiest male.
You must Coweman—jostle him—Ruff him—
If Flattery doesn't a-Vail!

I offer this word Towal spinsters:
Don't Blaine yourself—just beat your man.
You'll Seattle work out for you just
Azwell as for Lilliwaup Ann.
                                                —W.R.E.


# 9 July

## *"I Never Nurs'd a Dear Gazelle"*

A verse in *Lalla Rookh,* by Thomas Moore, ends:

> I never nurs'd a dear gazelle,
>     To glad me with its soft black eye,
> But when it came to know me well,
>     And love me, it was sure to die!

Parodists found this irresistible. Charles Dickens wrote, "I never nursed a dear gazelle, to glad me with its soft black eye, but when it came to know me well, and love me, it was sure to marry a market-gardener."

One poet was so taken with Moore's verse that he parodied it twice:

> I've never had a piece of toast
> Particularly long and wide,
> But fell upon the sanded floor,
> And always on the buttered side.
> —*H. S. Leigh*

### 'TWAS EVER THUS

> I never rear'd a young gazelle
> (Because, you see, I never tried);
> But had it known and loved me well,
> No doubt the creature would have died.
>
> My rich and aged Uncle John
> Has known me long and loves me well,
> But still persists in living on—
> I wish he were a young gazelle.
> —*H. S. Leigh*

Lewis Carroll tried his hand:

> I never loved a dear Gazelle—
> Nor anything that cost me much;
> High prices profit those who sell,
> But why should I be fond of such?
>
> To glad me with his soft black eye
> My son comes trotting home from school:
> He's had a fight but can't tell why—
> He always was a little fool!
>
> But, when he came to know me well,
> He kicked me out, her testy Sire;
> And when I stained my hair, that Belle
> Might note the change, and thus admire
>
> And love me, it was sure to dye
> A muddy green, or staring blue:
> Whilst one might trace, with half an eye,
> The still triumphant carrot through.
> —*Lewis Carroll*

# 10 JULY

## *The French Don't Talk like You and Me*

The French cat leads a varied life, says Israel Shenker. Where you and I buy a pig in a poke, the Frenchman buys a cat in a pocket. He has a cat in his throat where we have a frog. The worm turns for you and me, but the cat turns for a Frenchman.

Cows bemuse the Frenchman, too. You may be hungry enough to eat a horse; the Frenchman would eat a cow. It may rain cats and dogs in America, but it rains cows in France. To insult a Frenchman you not only call him a dirty pig; you also say "dirty cow."

Because the French Academy frowns on evolution of the language, says Mr. Shenker, "some things will probably still move at the pace of an escargot. 'Insérer une pièce d'un franc dans la fente supérieure' may forever remain 'Insert a one-franc piece in the superior slot.' And heaven forbid that the French railroads give up their translation of 'Pour avoir de l'eau, tournez le robinet indifféremment à gauche ou à droite'—'To obtain water turn the tap indifferently to the right or to the left.' "

The French, for their part, are convinced that it is English that does not make sense, and—in a sense—they may be right. Take the plight of the Frenchman who came to London and one morning called on an English friend. "Mr. Marlborough is not down yet," said the maid. In an hour the Frenchman called again. "My husband is not up yet," said the wife. Flinging his arms wide, the exasperated Frenchman cried, "Pliss, when will he be in ze middle?"

# 11 JULY

## *Far (Out) from the Madden Crowd*

Mary Ann Madden is den mother to a waggle of wild wags, Madden as hatters, who pepper her column in *New York* magazine with verbal conceits.

> I find
> Mary Ann Madden
> My kind.
> Long may she gladden
> —With mis'able,
>     Quizzable
>     Risible
> Tricks of the mind—
> My inner man!
> Long may Mary Ann
>     Madden!
>         —W.R.E.

Reader responses to Maddening challenges:

## REPUNCTUATED AND REDEFINED NAMES

- WALT W. HITMAN—dispenser of poetic justice
- BENJA MIND (ISRAELI)—mideastern hallucinogenic
- SAMMY D. AVIS, JR.—second-best U.S. entertainer

## NEAR MISSES

- I feel rotten, Egypt, rotten.
- A man, a plan, a canal—Suez!

## SILLY DEFINITIONS

- CARBUNCLE—(1) a nearly identical nephew, (2) brothers of your mother's carburetor

## INVENTED NAMES FOR OCCUPATIONS

- HEINZ ZEIT—German historian (follower of Forsyte)

## ONE-WORD INSERTS

- Into the valley of death rode the six hundred dumbbells.
- He who hesitates is, uh, lost.
- Mene, Mene, Tekel, Upharsin, Inc.
- Love is just $5 around the corner.

# 12 JULY

### *A Pest Iamb, Anapest Rick Ballad Was*

#### (Or a Ballad in a Sad Café)

I lunched with Rick Ballad. *I* lunched; Rick did not. He is on a medically supervised diet which has cut his weight from 250 pounds to 225 pounds in a fortnight; he still has 25 pounds to go. Each day he takes only water, at least six glasses, plus black coffee, with an admixture of a devilish powder that provides him with a total intake of exactly 400 calories. It is a sad sight to see him sipping his Perrier while I sip my scotch, but it is for his own good. I would like to think this villanelle on poetic meter, composed in his honor, contributed to his reform:

> Rick Ballad (God him pity)
> Set out last night to dine.
> His menu was a Ditty
> In Galliambic line.

His soup was Virelaic;
    His cocktail, Dipodee;
His Spondee was Alcaic;
    His Distych, Ditrochee.

He took a pinch of Rhythm,
    Of Ode and Choriamb,
And mixing Rondeaux with 'em
    He seasoned his Iamb.

He ordered baked Sestinas
    And half-baked Doggerel;
He licked his Lyric clean as
    A Sapphic Kyrielle.

He flavored Terza Rima
    With Pastoral and Thesis;
Had Chant Royal with cream—a
    Bucolic Diaeresis.

His Tercet was a salad
    Of Sonnet and Cinquain.
"Ballade too," ordered Ballad,
    "And Double the Refrain."

Verse Onomatopoeian,
    Szysigium to taste,
Enlarged unendingly an
    Enjambement of waist.

Then Ballad gorged on Dactyl,
    While Trochee and Molossus
Still down his maw were packed till
    He outcolossed Colossus.

(Colossus fell, and wallowed.
    So, too, poor Ballad fell;
And, dying, left unswallowed
    His final Villanelle.)
                                —W.R.E.

# 13 July

*Punctuation (Parenthetical)*

### THE LESSON

Of all the fleas that ever flew
    (And flying fleas are rather few

((Because for proper flying you
(((Whether you are a flea or not)))
Need wings and things fleas have not got)) )—

(I make the further point that fleas
Are thick as these parentheses
((An illustration (((you'll agree)))
Both apt and pleasing to a flea)) )—

Now then where were we? Let me see—
Ah, yes—We said to fly you ought
(Whether you are a flea or not)
To have some wings (yes, at least two
((At least no less than two will do
(((And fleas have something less than one
((((One less, in fact (((((or, frankly, none
((((((Which, as once more you will agree ))))))
Limits the flying of a flea))))) )))) ))) )) ).

And let me add that fleas that fly
Are known as Flears. (You can see why.)
All I have said thus far is true
(If it's not clear, that's up to you.
((You'll have to learn sometime, my dear,
That what is true may not be clear
(((While what is clear may not be true
((((And you'll be wiser when you do.)))) ))) )) ).

—*John Ciardi*

# 14 JULY

### *Unwind My Jaw, Untie My Tongue*

In French a tongue twister is a passage *à décrocher la mâchoire*—"to unwind the jaw"—or *pour délier la langue*—"to untie the tongue." I give you these tongue twisters to commemorate Bastille Day:

Ton thé t'a-t-il ôté ta toux?
(Has your tea got rid of your cough?)

Si six scies scient six cigares
Six cents scies scient six cents cigares
(If six saws saw six cigars, six hundred saws saw six hundred cigars.)

Les chemises de l'archiduchesse
Sont sèches et archisèches.
(The archduchess's shirtwaists are dry and more than dry.)

Un chasseur sachant chasser chassait un chat.
(A hunter, knowing how to hunt, hunted a cat.)

Didon dîna, dit-on, du dos d'un dodu dindon.
(Dido dined, they say, off the back of a plump turkey.)

La pipe au papa du Pape Pie pue.
(Pope Pius's father's pipe stinks.)

Ces six saucissons-ci sont six sous les six.
(These six sausages are six cents for six.)

A Rocquevaire, la rivière se verse vers les verres du ver vert.
(At Rocquevaire, the river flows toward the glasses of the green worm.)

I'm not sure what you would call the next one. It's not really a tongue twister; it's a group of French words which become incomprehensible when pronounced rapidly. Try it out on a Frenchman. He will swear that it is in some Oriental tongue:

Pie a haut nid, caille a bas nid:
Verre n'a pas d'eau: rat en a, chat en a.

This means, more or less:

The magpie's nest is high,
The grouse's nest is low;
The water glass is dry;
    The cat and rat
    Have water, though—
The mole, also.
            —W.R.E.

Quel bruit a nui à l'huître? Le bruit que j'ai ouï hier nuit a nui à l'huître.
(What noise annoyed the oyster?
The noise I heard last night annoyed the oyster.)

# 15 July

### Last Request

I'll die, my DVS sins 2 XP8,
    Where K9, snake and AVN
    'Mid murmurs APN
        XUV8;

While U, by 4N springs RTZN,
AKN DETs SML8,
And 4 the water in the cooking pan
   2 S28
      Wait.

*Dear NTT, from whom doth MN8*
*The S¢ of U4EA 4 me;*
*U OPM B9, U OP8 . . .*
*IDL HNC of XTC . . .*

These D¢CC pray grant: no LEGG,
No $S PNN 2 X-10-U8
  My sins; no O my sad state.
Nay—raise T DMM; cheer for my DCC;
  Then help some new FMRL mate
     EE
  His TDm, and all his ¢S sate
    And TT.
      Please.

              —W.R.E.

### ON MorAA AND MorLET

The vs my hurrAA R 4
R vs of a TDS mor-
L D¢C, EE us chaps
Who OKZNLE lapse.
          —W.R.E.

# 16 July

## Snallygaster VII

From the *Valley Register,* Middletown, Maryland, February 19, 1909:

### THE GREAT GO-DEVIL
### WAS SEEN IN OHIO

#### T. C. Harbaugh Saw It Sailing Toward Maryland

The great Go-Devil must have passed over Ohio before it reached Maryland, as will be seen from the following letter from T. C. Harbaugh, of Casstown, Ohio, which was received too late for last week's issue.

Casstown, Ohio, February 9, 1909

Editors of *The Register:*

A gigantic monster passed over this place last night about 6 o'clock. It was plainly visible, had two immense bronze wings, an enormous head from which horn-like objects protruded, and a tail 20 feet long. It emitted a noise like the screech of an octtollopus. Some who saw it declared it to be a Snallygaster. The monster was moving toward Maryland. From the brief view I had of it, I think it was either an octtollopus, a gigantillocutus or a Snallygaster. . . . I sincerely hope that this monster will not visit your beautiful Valley.

T. C. Harbaugh

MORE ON 12 AUGUST.

# 17 JULY

## *Tax That Fellow Under the Tree*

Senator Russell Long said, "Tax reform means don't tax you, don't tax me, tax that fellow under the tree." Albert Jay Nock said, "Virtue is more to be feared than vice, because its excesses are not subject to the regulations of conscience." These aphorisms are funny because they prick human foibles.

Samuel Butler, a master aphorist, commented that life is one long process of getting tired. Butler also remarked that the fight between theists and atheists is about whether God shall be called God or shall have another name.

Some of Butler's finest aphorisms deal with the art of lying:

- If a man is not a good, sound, honest, capable liar there is no truth in him.
- Any fool can tell the truth, but it requires a man of some sense to know how to lie well.
- I do not mind lying, but I hate inaccuracy.
- Lying has a kind of respect and reverence with it. We pay a person the compliment of acknowledging his superiority whenever we lie to him.

# 18 JULY

## *Alcoholic Disarray*

Don't mix anagrams and alcohol. When the label on your scotch turns from TEACHERS to CHEATERS, forgo the next drink. Take leave of rye when SEAGRAMS becomes MASSAGER. If your weakness is brandy, think hard when you read PER-

NOD as PONDER. And though you may not be seeing pink elephants, you are coming close when you reach for a DRAMBUIE and see a RAPID EMU.

A WHISKY drinker may ask, "WHY SKI?" Indeed, I ask that question when I have had nothing to drink at all. Similarly it is understandable that a man brooding over his BELLOWS on ice should SOB WELL.

*Enigma*, publication of the National Puzzlers' League, is the source of the forgoing anagrammatic observations on alcohol. Some further Enigmatic thoughts on the subject:

1. SOUR MASH. SO RUM HAS?
2. AN ALCOHOLIC BEVERAGE. GAL, CAN I HAVE COOL BEER?
3. A BOTTLE OF WHISKEY. IT BE THY FLASK O' WOE.
4. DEMON ALE. LEMONADE.

On entering the National Puzzlers' League the new member adopts a special name, or *nom*. (Mine is Wede.) The four anagrams above are credited to the following noms: (1) Hap. (2) Amaranth. (3) Amaranth. (4) Merlin.

# 19 JULY

## *How Do I Love Thee? Let Me Count the Fuel Stops*

### *(with apologies to Elizabeth Barrett Browning)*

Effective July 17 Pacific Western Airlines flies Seattle to Vancouver non-stop; and on to Yellowknife, Fort Chipewyan, Grand Forks, Inuvik, Tofino, Bella Coola, Cambridge Bay, Peace River, Norman Wells, Dawson Creek, Hay, Bella Bella, Penticton, Tahsis, Castlegar, Trail, and Fort McMurray.—*Advertisement*

In your time, Liz, lips meeting lips in surrey
    Swore love eterne, swore faithfulness for life.
Now love's more like a flight to Fort McMurray,
    With pauses to refuel at Yellowknife,
Fort Chipewyan, Grand Forks, and Inuvik;
    Tofina, Bella Coola, Cambridge Bay;
Peace River, Norman Wells, and Dawson Crick.
    Our love's eterne—with pauses on the way.

I buckle seat belt, tamp out cigarette
    When coming down at Hay or Bella Bella,
And hope that Fort McMurray will not fret
    If Penticton awhile delay a fella,
Or Tahsis please, or Castlegar regale.
    *I shall but love thee better after Trail.*
                         —W.R.E.

Elizabeth Barrett Browning was not the first nor the last to ask, "How do I love thee?" Some answers suggested in *Word Ways:*

- The cardiologist: with all my heart
- The marathon runner: all the way
- The contortionist: head over heels
- The psychoanalyst: unshrinkingly
- The dieter: through thick and thin
- The wheelwright: tirelessly
- The elephant trainer: roguishly
- The mink farmer: furtively
- The farmer: whole hog
- The couturier: in my fashion

# 20 JULY

## *Singular Plurals, Obliging Objects*

### SINGULAR PLURALS

Now if mouse in the plural should be, and is, mice,
Then house in the plural, of course, should be hice,
And grouse should be grice and spouse should be spice
And by the same token should blouse become blice.

And consider the goose with its plural of geese;
Then a double caboose should be called a cabeese,
And noose should be neese and moose should be meese
And if mama's papoose should be twins, it's papeese.

Then if one thing is that, while some more is called those,
Then more than one hat, I assume, would be hose,
And gnat would be gnose and pat would be pose
And likewise the plural of rat would be rose.
                          —*Author unknown*

### OBLIGING OBJECTS

I steal the keel
I stole the coal
I have stolen the colon.
    —*A. M. Zwicky*

I smite the kite / I smote the coat / I have smitten
    the kitten
I bite the mite / I bit the mitt / I have bitten
    the mitten

I break the take / I broke the toque / I have broken
  the token
I take the bake / I took the book / I have taken
  the bacon.

—*Martha Awdziewic*

They choose the hues.
They chose the hose.
They have chosen the hosen.

They mow the banks of the row.
They mowed the banks of the road.
They have mown the banks of the Rhone.

I do it with the buoys.
I did it with the biddies.
I have done it with the bunnies.

—*A. M. Zwicky*

# 21 JULY

## Two for Cassin

I will let you guess how long ago this verse to my fourth daughter was written:

In a rush the years are passin'—
One and one makes two for Cassin.
Lucky Years, to coexist
With Miss Eyes-of-Amethyst!
Not-so-Lucky Years, to know
She will stay, while they must go!

Soon, perhaps, some lovesick Year
Will refuse to leave you, dear—
What if 19 blankty 7
Opts for Cass instead of heaven?
Oh, what fun if we could wait
Evermore for blankty 8!

—*W.R.E.*

# 22 JULY

## Newspeak and Nadsat

Whenever a politician utters an équivoque, we begin running, flapping our wings like Chicken Little, to tell the king that the sky of freedom is falling; Newspeak has arrived. In Newspeak, the language George Orwell dreamed up for *1984*, *goodsex* means chastity, *joycamp* a forced labor camp, the *Ministry of Love* a prison for the torture of dissenters. And so on.

Yet if you reread *1984*, you will find that nobody in the book speaks Newspeak. Nobody. To be sure, one character is writing a Newspeak dictionary, and another is translating Oldspeak into Newspeak, but when they converse, they use English. Or Cockney.

"If you want a stronger version of 'good,' " says the dictionary maker, "what sense is there in having a whole string of vague useless words like 'excellent' and 'splendid' and all the rest of them? 'Plusgood' covers the meaning, or 'double-plusgood' if you want something stronger still."

But does he use "plusgood" himself? No, he says "better," as if Newspeak had never been invented.

Newspeak is just not a language one can speak, and if it has to catch on before we become a tyranny, we are still safe.

Nadsat, now, is a donkey with a different bray. Nadsat, Anthony Burgess's *Clockwork Orange* language, is spoken in a social disorder where teen-age gangs plunder, murder, and rape at will. It is current counterculture slang hyperbolized, and under certain circumstances could even happen. (Mr. Burgess, by the way, has drawn much of his Nadsat vocabulary from Russian; one wonders how London teen-agers became familiar with Russian words.)

Nadsat, as Stanley Edgar Hyman points out, also employs gypsy talk ("O my brothers"); rhyming slang ("luscious glory" for hair, rhyming perhaps with "upper story"); association ("cancer" for cigarette); amputation ("pee and em" for pop and mom); schoolboy transformations ("baddiwad" for bad), and portmanteau words ("chumble" for, Mr. Hyman guesses, "chatter-mumble").

A dictatorship might make Newspeak the official language, but no one would use it. Alienated groups, from pickpockets to Weathermen, have always used some equivalent of Nadsat. But it will never become official.

# 23 JULY

## *A Windy Love Song, Annotated*

The wind that blew down the Methodist Church at Oysterville was a dawdler compared to some of the winds in the following sonnet.

| | |
|---|---|
| Doldrumed, with sail a-sag and rudder free, | *Doldrums:* The calm often met with at sea near the Equator. |
| To squalls and calms and baffling gusts a prey, | Changeable weather is characteristic of the doldrums. |
| I drift. At length a zephyr breathes my way. | *Zephyr.* A west breeze almost too light to measure. |
| With moist chinook behind. Then burns at me. | *Chinook.* A warm, moist, southwest wind of the Washington and Oregon coast. |

| | |
|---|---|
| Sirocco!—desert sand storm in the sea! | *Sirocco.* A south wind beginning dustily in the Sahara but moistening as it crosses the Mediterranean. |
| North veers the wind; a mistral chills the day; | *Mistral.* A dry, cold norther that blows through the Rhone Valley toward the Mediterranean. |
| Behind howls bora, puffing frozen spray; | *Bora.* A cold and violent nor'easter blowing on the Dalmatian coast of Yugoslavia in the winter. |
| The gale's now storm. I run; I scud; I flee, | *Gale:* 25–63 mph. *Storm:* 64–75 mph. |
| Pursued by whirlwind, baguio and monsoon; | *Whirlwind.* A rotating, forward-moving column of air. *Baguio.* A tropical cyclone. *Monsoon.* A wind system in S.E. Asia blowing from opposite directions at different times of year. |
| Cyclones to lar and star in ambuscado; | *Cyclone.* A rotating wind of up to 150 mph. |
| Above me, jet stream, hurricane, typhoon; | *Jet stream.* A tropospheric wind, moving from the west at upwards of 250 mph. *Hurricane.* A cyclone of more than 75 mph, usually accompanied by heavy rain. *Typhoon.* A tropical hurricane in the western Pacific or China Sea. |
| Beneath me, vortex; and before, tornado. | *Vortex.* Whirlpool. *Tornado.* A rotating column of air whirling at speeds of up to 300 mph. |
| They rush upon me. Then, their task complete, | |
| They cease, and drop me, winded, at your feet. | |

—*W.R.E.*

# 24 July

## *Larva, Pupa, Imago*

OYSTERVILLE—We arrived last night; I made my first summer inspection of the croquet garden* this morning. The gaps have vanished from the laurel hedge; the rhododendron bushes are rubbing shoulders; the new cypress tree has grown so fast that I'll have to transplant it; and everywhere insects are

* See 20 June.

buzzing, crawling, burrowing, flying, stridulating, supremely indifferent to the presence of their landlord.

There are parallels between etymology, the study of words, and entomology, the study of bugs.

Some 4 million insects are busy insecting at this moment on any moist acre (if you don't believe me, go count them for yourself). The figure is roughly comparable to the number of words in the English language. Some insects, like some words, evolve substantially in structure and activity:

### LARVA, PUPA, IMAGO

When I was a larva,
Brashly I would chortle,
"You will see me carve a
Monument immortal."

Growing to a pupa,
Older now and wary,
Still I hoped to scoop a
Brief obituary.

Now, a worn imago,
I don't bother to
Mention my lumbago:
What is that to you?
　　　　　—W.R.E.

One insect, *Phylloxera quercus,* has twenty-one forms, every one of which appears unrelated to the rest. On the other hand, insects of different species may look and act so much alike that the least wary entomologist will hedge on which is which. To confuse them would be entomological malapropping.

Words are equally deceitful. Take *logistics.* Everybody knows what it means—the transport, quartering, and supply of troops and, by extension, comparable arrangements in other activities. Yet there is an entirely different logistics, meaning "calculation by arithmetic." The first word comes from *lodge*—French *loger*—and the second from Greek *logos,* "word or number."

Words are similar to insects, too, in the variety of their life spans. A May fly will die in twenty minutes. A queen ant, if permitted to mature, has a life expectancy of sixteen years. Similarly, in language, the word *Edsel,* for a failed automobile, is lucky to last a generation; the word for *wheel,* in variant forms, has been with us for ten millennia.

# 25 JULY

### *Palindromes of Number*

The *Times* of London printed a letter sent by a reader on 27 July 1972, of which the sole point was the date. 27 July 1972, written numerically, goes the same backward as forward—27/7/72. Said the letter:

Apart from the three rather less pleasing palindromes arising on the 27th of the 8th, 9th, and 11th months of this year, today's is the last palindromic date until 18-1-81, when I shall of course write to you again, unless I wait until the even more pleasing 18-8-81 and unless I am by then no longer in a position to be

Your obedient servant,

MATTHEW NORGATE

If Mr. Norgate's calendric palindromes confuse you, it may be because most Americans write the month before the day, while our English cousins generally, but by no means always, put the day before the month. If you stipulate that the palindrome must consist of two digits, one digit, and a final two digits, as he does, there will be no palindromic dates in this country until the next century, when there will be 10/1/01, 11/1/11 (!), 12/1/21—and that is all. But Mr. Norgate is wrong in that stipulation, because though 27/7/72 may be more symmetrical than 2/7/72, the latter is equally palindromic. Both Englishmen and Americans can look forward to a palindromic date in every year that does not end in 0: 5/7/75, 6/7/76, 7/7/77 (!), 8/7/78, 9/7/79, 1/8/81, etc. Each of these of course will fall on a different day in England than in America.

# 26 JULY

## No Wonder There Are Keel Marks on Her Lips

When your houseguests grow weary of television, bridge, and Perrier water, pass around slips bearing a familiar line of poetry and ask each player to add a rhyming line. Victorian wordplayers called these efforts "bouts rimés." Richard Armour calls them "punctured poems." Under any name, they are fun.

Some risible examples:

MARLOWE:        Was this the face that launched a thousand ships?
*No wonder there are keel marks on her lips.*

SHAKESPEARE:    Full fathom five thy father lies.
*I pushed him. I apologize.*

CONGREVE:      Music hath charms to soothe the savage breast.
*That's why I keep a flute tucked in my vest.*

THOMAS BROWN:  I do not like thee, Doctor Fell.
*The reason is you charge like hell.*

BROWNING:      I sprang to the stirrup, and Joris and he;
*I sat upon Joris, the third guy on me.*

| | |
|---|---|
| MILTON: | When I consider how my light is spent. |
| | *I'm glad utilities come with the rent.* |
| | —*Richard Armour* |
| | |
| WORDSWORTH: | My heart leaps up when I behold |
| | *My pumpernickel green with mold.* |
| | |
| ROSSETTI: | Who has seen the wind: Neither you nor I, |
| | *But California smog will surely catch your eye.* |
| | |
| KILMER: | I think that I shall never see— |
| | *My contact lens fell in my tea.* |
| | |
| POE: | Once upon a midnight dreary, |
| | *Late-late show starred Wallace Beery.* |
| | —*Mary Youngquist and Harry Hazard* |

I'll take you home again, Kathleen;
*That last martini turned you green.*
              —*Bill Balance*

# 27 JULY

## *Hitchcock Steers a Bull*

Alfred Hitchcock, reflecting that it takes only a simple excision to turn a bull into a steer, castrated a number of well-known entertainers by dropping a single letter from their first names:

Ickey Rooney • Orgie Jessel • Rank Sinatra • Lark Gable • Reer Garson • Helley Winters • Ick Cavett • Ill Cosby • Irk Douglas • Lip Wilson • Uke Ellington • Ex Harrison

Leonhard Dowty points out that marriage can produce memorable name twists:

If Tuesday Weld married Frederic March II, she would be Tuesday March II. If Carole Lombard married Isaac Singer, she would be Carole Singer. If Ginger Rogers married Theodore Mann, she would be Ginger Mann. If April Stevens married Monty Love, she would be April Love.

A number of celebrities in and out of show business are known by other names than they received at birth. The adopted names of the people listed here became household words:

Nicholas Bronstein • Lev Bronstein • Gladys Smith • Mary Ann Evans • Israel Baline • Benjamin Kubelski • Albert of Saxe-Coburg • Michael Goldbogen • Archie Leach • Domenico Teotocopulo

A book called *Hundreds of Things to Do on a Rainy Day* suggests names for young people who plan a career in the public eye:

Luke Warm • Kitty Litter • Ella Vater • May O'Naise • Sal Hepatica • Ben O'Fishal

# 28 JULY

## *More John Hancocks*

Ever since John Hancock writ his name large on the Declaration of Independence, *John Hancock* and *signature* have been synonymous. Here are the John Hancocks of ten well-known people, all dead. How many can you identify?

1. Composer

4. Dictator

7. President

2. Novelist

5. Queen

8. Poet

3. Emperor

6. Conductor

9. Madman

# 29 July

### *Young Johnny and Ugly Sal*

Young Johnny, chancing to discover
That everybody loves a ——,
Concluded it would be his pleasure
To wed in ——, repent at ——.
He said to ugly Sal, "I'm bound,
My dear, love makes the world go '——.
Your looks, that make an angel weep,
Are only epidermis ——.
Who says men seldom —— make
At girls with ——? a mistake!
Appearances ——, 'tis true;
Yet better *they* deceive, than *you*.
It's not immortal beauties that
Make mortal hearts go pitty-pat;
You're wealthy, Sal, per my research:
A rich bride goeth —— to church."


Sal felt her laggard pulses start:
——, —— her hands; ——, —— her heart.
She thought: "Each day it truer gets:
Men wink at blondes, but wed ——!
Though gray my hair beneath the dye,
No older than I —— am I;
This hand shall soon the —— rock,
And —— the world (per Doctor Spock)!"
Who takes a wife, he takes a ——;
For John, the marriage was disaster.
Love makes —— pass away, I guess.
But t'other way around no less.
Who weds for love, his —— are great,
But daytime is the normal state;
And marriages, in —— made,
On dusty Earth are soon decayed.
The lewdest bride may pass for ——
Unless too soon she goes to waist.
And when such fruits begin to show,
The cuckold is the last to know.


*Now one last, sad reminder to end John's dreary tale:*
*The —— of the species is more deadly than the ——.*
                                        —W.R.E.

# 30 July

## The Nicknaming of States

Nations are often personified. France is Marianne, England John Bull, the United States Uncle Sam. The fifty American states, however, have taken another tack: they adopted nicknames, sometimes several nicknames to a state. Most of these nicknames are assembled, capitalized, in the stanzas below.

1. SHOW ME the LAND OF OPPORTUNITY!
2. LAND OF ENCHANTMENT! EMPIRE of the FREE!
3. The INLAND EMPIRE! EMPIRE OF THE SOUTH!
4. Show me a PELICAN, and in its mouth

5. A NUTMEG, which no SOONER doth it eat
6. Than it a pit of GRANITE must excrete!
7. Here OLD NORTH, NORTH STAR, HEART OF DIXIE stay
8. With OLD LINE, LONE STAR, DIAMOND, and BAY.

9. Here CONSTITUTION holds CENTENNIAL
10. In SILVER SUNSHINE by a KEYSTONE wall.
11. Here OLD DOMINION and OLD COLONY
12. Split GOLDEN TREASURE in EQUALITY.

13. HOOSIER, ALOHA! Welcome, VOLUNTEER!
14. CORNHUSKER, LITTLE RHODY—glad you're here!
15. You also, HAWKEYE, TAR HEEL, wily SIOUX—
16. Let me be FIRST to walk BLUE GRASS with you!

17. To climb, in BIG SKY COUNTRY, MOUNTAIN GREEN;
18. MOUNTAIN of PINE TREE and of WOLVERINE.
19. GRAND CANYON we'll explore, and BUCKEYE breach;
20. We'll sniff MAGNOLIA, and eat GARDEN PEACH.

21. In JAYHAWK, SAGEBRUSH, EVERGREEN we'll tarry;
22. Grow BLUE HEN, BEEF, and COTTON in the PRAIRIE;
23. Plant yellow SUNFLOWER, of all blooms the GEM.
24. To grace our BEEHIVE with its diadem.

25. PALMETTO leaves will yield their cooling shade
26. When BADGER, BEAVER, COYOTE promenade
27. With FLICKERTAIL and GOPHER, to the yammer
28. (GREAT LAND above!) of YELLOWHAMMER.

—W.R.E.

# 31 July

### *I'm Afraid Mr. Arch Will Recline*

More malapropisms.

Arch Winters has a friend named Miss Rosemary. Miss Rosemary has a cook named Beatrice. One day Beatrice served Arch an unsatisfactory dish of grits. "If you invite Mr. Arch again, Miss Rosemary," she mourned, "I'm afraid he will recline." Beatrice also told her employer, "Miss Rosemary, you don't understand men. You got to have a neat house to depress them." And she complained to Arch about Miss Rosemary's absentmindedness: "She just can't seem to get accumulated."

Bob Knille found these malapropisms in Smollett's *Humphrey Clinker:*

- Methinks you mought employ your talons better, than to encourage servants to pillage their masters.
- What is life but a veil of affliction? O Mary! the whole family have been in such a constipation.
- The 'squire did all in his power, but could not prevent his being put in chains, and confined among common manufacturers.
- I was going into a fit of asterisks.
- Yours with true infection, Win. Jenkins.

Malapropping becomes an art form here:

- Be it ever so hovel, there's no place like home.
- I was down on the lower East side today and saw those old Testament houses.
- I got up at the crank of dawn.
- We are all cremated equal.
- I refused to tell him who I was—I used a facetious name.
- The food in that restaurant is abdominal.
- Explain it to me in words of one cylinder.
- Congress is still in season.
- In all my bored days.
- All of Abe Lincoln's pictures make him look so thin and emancipated.

*—Goodman Ace*

A young woman I know, complaining about a shockingly small raise she had received, said three times with emphatic sarcasm, that the raise had come to a "whooping" $5 a week. She meant "whopping."

# AUGUST

## 1 AUGUST

### Fifty English Emigrants

You will readily identify most of these words. It may be more difficult, however, to identify the languages that have naturalized them.

1) stiff-ticket; 2) biftek; 3) colcream; 4) strajkar; 5) blajnpigg; 6) aperashen; 7) lof-letter; 8) te lu fong; 9) telewizja; 10) njeuspapier; 11) peda; 12) salang; 13) pikunikku; 14) bara i minne; 15) blaekbor; 16) atomi pommi; 17) smoking; 18) bondes; 19) puddi gud; 20) engin; 21) dipoidh; 22) Geancach; 23) racchettiere; 24) fanfurria; 25) mpasketmpall; 26) cora; 27) gemlingshus; 28) makinchprc; 29) redingote; 30) guafay; 31) herkot; 32) nailon; 33) ajskrym; 34) peipi; 35) o kontri; 36) kawboju filmas; 37) kaddam; 38) sityholly; 39) k'a fei; 40) vilda vastern; 41) muvingpikceris; 42) p'u-lo-lieh-t'a-li-ya; 43) saiduak; 44) guachiman; 45) gescreent; 46) risurin; 47) schiacchenze; 48) calamazo; 49) vacuomme-clineaur; 50) enugkh.

—*Leonard R. N. Ashley*

## 2 AUGUST

### Word Ways' *Ways with Words*

*Word Ways* is a quarterly publication whose editors, contributors, and readers are maniacs—logomaniacs.

Who but *Word Ways* would serve drinks on the house because "unoriental" (not to mention "suoidea," the name of the superfamily of pigs and peccaries) has all the vowels in reverse order? Who but *Word Ways* would display, with the pride of a cat bringing home an eviscerated frog, a collection of three-syllable, four-letter words—aero, aery, Aida, area, aria, idea, iota, Iowa, Ohio, oleo, olio, and urea? Or demonstrate that by adding a single letter you can turn certain one-syllable words into three-syllable words—smile into simile, lien into alien, came into cameo? Or reduce two-syllable words to one-syllable words by adding letters—rugged to shrugged, ague to plague, aged (the adjective) to staged or raged?

Words of two or more identical parts—cancan, Sing Sing, dodo, papa, tartar, wogga wogga, cha-cha-cha—are called tautonyms or reduplications. It took *Word Ways* to teach me that there are words with *four* identical parts: Kukukuku (a people inhabiting parts of eastern New Guinea); Fofo Fofo (a town in Papua); angangangang (a kind of Javanese gong).

It was not enough for *Word Ways* to point out that there are as many as nine letters in some common one-syllable words: scratched, screeched, scrounged, squelched, strengths, stretched. It went on to list unisyllabic words of *ten* letters—words I shall not repeat here, since I can think of no use for them.

Offhand, how many words would you say have just one letter? Twenty-six, notes *Word Ways:* every one of the letters in the alphabet.

Or take the matter of miscegenation among states. Alaska, says *Word Ways,* blends Alabama and Nebraska; Arkansas is a cross between Arizona and Kansas; North Dakota mixes North Carolina and South Dakota; South Dakota is part South Carolina and part North Dakota; South Carolina is part South Dakota and part North Carolina. The entire United States is summed up within the bounds of one state: LoUiSiAna.

It would never have occurred to me that "indivisibility" and "niminypiminyism" have each, phonetically speaking, seven i's and no other vowels; or that you can say, but not write, "There are three ways to spell (to, two, too?)," while you can write, but not say, "There are three ways to pronounce 'slough.'"

A quick check reveals dozens of excerpts from the pages of *Word Ways* in this book, and there may be some I have forgotten to credit.

You might do a little checking of your own. Send a $25 check to Faith W. Eckler, Spring Valley Road, Morristown, New Jersey 07960, and she will send you *Word Ways* every three months for a year.*

# 3 AUGUST

## *Drinking Song of a Hard-Hearted Landlord*†

Though my ant-ant-ant-ant-ant-ant-ant-ant-ant-ant a lass who's a
    loner,
So many con-der-der-der-der-der-der-der-der-der-der are milling
About with pre-tion-tion-tion-tion-tion-tion-tion-tion-tion-tion to
    own her,
They'd be dear at ha'penny-ha'penny-ha'penny-ha'penny-ha'penny-
    ha'penny-ha'penny-ha'penny-ha'penny-ha'penny the shilling.

CHORUS: They'd be dear at, *etc.*

The dril-dril-dril-dril-dril-dril-dril-dril-dril-dril that frame her
    sweet forehead

---

* The price information has been updated for this book—*Ed.*
† See also 29 January.

Would merit niel-niel-niel-niel-niel-niel-niel-niel-niel-niel at-tion-
tion-tion-tion-tion-tion-tion-tion-tion-tion;
But her ement-ement-ement-ement-ement-ement-ement-ement-
ement-ement mine—and *I*'m horrid:
I jeer at romantic in-tion-tion-tion-tion-tion-tion-tion-tion-tion-
tion.

CHORUS: I jeer at, *etc.*

If she der-der-der-der-der-der-der-der-der-der her payments I
heed not
How der-der-der-der-der-der-der-der-der-der this lass when unbent
Treat ant-ant-ant-ant-ant-ant-ant-ant-ant-ant as humans? Indeed
not:
Their dency-dency-dency-dency-dency-dency-dency-dency-dency-
dency not to pay rent.

CHORUS: Their dency-, *etc.*

—W.R.E.

# 4 AUGUST

## *The Sword Is Mightier Than the Pen*

Dear Grandson Taylor:

How excited you must be to realize that at the age of only one day you are
already named Taylor—and after both sides of your family, at that! The Taylors on your mother's side, which is mine, lived in Virginia, and fought the Indians and British a lot. The Taylors on your father's side lived in New England,
and learned to read books. One was a very famous Poet whose works no one
understands.

If you should decide to model yourself after the Taylor line, I suggest that you
look to my side. Poets are all very well, but everyone knows that the Sword is
Mightier than the Pen. This hortatory verse is written especially for you, and I
hope you will engrave it on your heart:

> Bulwer Lytton (long gone to his final reward)
> Proclaimed the Pen mightier, sir, than the Sword.
> Ever since then, whenever a Poet drops by,
> We hear him reiterate Lytton's old lie.
>
> Democritus, long before Lytton, averred
> That any old action beats any old word;
> So Poets say quickly they spoke but in jest
> When challenged to put Lytton's *mot* to the test.

With, alas, one exception. A Poet I knew
Was silly enough to think Lytton spoke true.
Of *eau de vie forte* he drank down quite a store,
Then challenged a Swordsman to *combat à mort*.

While the Swordsman was yet in a daze from surprise,
The Poet fired gallons of ink in his eyes,
Backed up by barrages of sonnets; rondels;
Ballades; chants royals; triolets; villanelles.

The trochees and dactyls about him exploded
So fast that the Swordsman was quite incommoded.
He was epigrammed, similed, punned, metaphored,
Until with reluctance he unsheathed his sword

And lopped off the head of that Rhymer of Rhymes,
Then returned to perusing the sports in the *Times*.
The dying head sighed, "It may be now and then
That the edge of the sword has an edge on the pen."

*Dear Poets, when Swordsmen drop over to play,*
*It's wise to say, "Sorry—I'm out for the day."*
*(And will be, till foxes lie down with the hens;*
*And will be, till smiths hammer swords into pens.)*
—W.R.E.

# 5 AUGUST

## To a Chorus of Hallelujahs

OYSTERVILLE—A tourist once knocked at the door of our home here and asked my father, "Do you belong to that church across the street?"

"No," said Papa. "That church across the street belongs to me."

And it did. Grandpa had built it for the local Baptists in 1892. When eventually the Baptists died or moved away, ownership reverted to the Espys. We recently deeded it to the Oysterville Historical Society. Maybe this time the gift will stick.

Before 1892, baptizing took place in Shoalwater Bay, to a chorus of hallelujahs; the hour of the ceremony depended on the schedule of the tides. The new church, though, was designed for modern baptisms, boasting a capacious zinc-lined font under a trapdoor behind the pulpit. When the time came for the first indoor baptism, the deacons carried water up the aisle in buckets to fill the font. Not until the baptism was over did they realize that they would have to empty the font the same way they had filled it—by hand; there was no drain.

From then on baptisms again took place in the bay, with as many hallelujahs as before. The first indoor baptism since 1892 was that of a Welsh baby. My brother Edwin, whose job is religion, performed the ceremony. But Ed did not dunk the baby; he just sprinkled him.

### Reflections During the Sermon

President Truman attended the First Baptist Church in Washington. One Sunday a tourist breathlessly demanded of an usher, "Will the President be attending the service?"

"I don't know about that," replied the usher, "but we expect the Lord to be here as usual."

# 6 AUGUST

## The Sounds of Oysterville

HANDSAWWWWWWWWWWWWWWWWW
—*Richard Lebovitz*

The sound reproduced by Mr. Lebovitz in that one-line, one-word, onomatopoeic poem was a regular refrain in my home village of Oysterville half a century ago. Today it is replaced by a snarl:

CHAINSAWWWWWWWWWWWWWWWWW

Another sound inseparable from Oysterville in my mind has been missing since August 7, 1959. That is the voice of my father not-swearing. His most common not-swearing expletives were "Son of a sea cook!", "Consarn it!", "Dad durn it!", "Dad dum it!", "Dad cuss it!", "Ding bust it!", and "Souwegian!" The ultimate in rage came out as "Devil!" or, more commonly, "Devilation!" Since my father was by nature a cheerful man, and by self-discipline a controlled one, he seldom uttered even these harmless-appearing epithets; but when they came, they came like thunderbolts. It was when he said "Dad cuss it!" in the midst of a hurricane that the Methodist church fell down.

> In Oysterville,
> Mosquitoes whine, and mating frogs are shrill;
> While bumblebees, bluebottle flies, and uzzers
>     Are buzzers.
>
> In Oysterville,
> The chipmunks scold, the yellowhammers drill;
> While certain clicks one hears in Oysterville
>     Are misadventures
>     Of dentures.
>                                    —*W.R.E.*

# 7 AUGUST

## *The Thermostat Is Set Too High*

Today, for the first time in fifty years, I heard from Richard Stalker, who in his boyhood was a summer visitor to Oysterville. He sent me these three Tom Swifties:

"The thermostat is set too high," said Tom heatedly.
"The chimney is clogged," said Tom fluently.
"Golly, that old man is bent over," said Tom stupidly.

Winners of a Tom Swifty contest in the *Minneapolis Tribune*:

"Let's gather up the rope," Tom said coyly.
"I just ran over my father," Tom said transparently.
"Don't you love sleeping outdoors?" Tom said intently.
"Let's invite Greg and Gary," Tom proposed gregariously.
"I've been stung," Tom said waspishly.
"Here are my Tom Swifty entries," Deb wrote submissively.
"I'm circulating a petition," Anita Bryant said gaily.
"Let's trap that sick bird," Tom said illegally.
"This boat leaks," Tom said balefully.
"Welcome to my tomb," Tom said cryptically.
"I just returned from Japan," Tom said disorientedly.
"I lost my trousers," Tom said expansively.
"I'll never stick my fist into the lion's cage again," Tom said
 offhandedly.
"I can't find the oranges," Tom said fruitlessly.
"Are you fond of venison?" Tom said fawningly.

* * *

"Your meat, madam!" announced the two butcher boys jointly.
"Sacked for cheek, madam, but I'm reformed," said the maid expertly.
"Sold out of lobsters," said the fishmonger crabbily.
"I see Ararat," said Noah dryly.
"They did it while camping," said the aggrieved husband intently.
"You're a fool to say 'Can do' when it's already been done," she told him
 candidly.
"Dinner is over," announced the cannibal houseboy masterfully.
"The dam is back to front," said the builder madly.

—*J. A. Lindon*

"Have some Canary wine," she trilled.
"I will correct your math," he added.

—*P.F.*

# 8 AUGUST

## *Salisbury, Colquhoun, and Cuchulain*

Christine Magriel asked a London coster how to reach her hotel. He replied, "It's beside Mahblahtch." "Mahblahtch?" asked Christine in confusion. "Yes, Miss, *Mahblahtch*," said the coster, sketching a wicket with his hands. The light dawned. "Oh!" said Christine, "Marble Arch!"

The British laugh a lot at the way they pronounce their proper names, and I suppose that is better than crying. Louisa Bonner, who called today's unattributed limericks to my attention, justifies the first one on the grounds that the Latin name of Salisbury was Sarum, while the abbreviation of Hampshire is Hants. But since nobody says Sarum any more, or pronounces Hants the way it is spelled, I see no way of making the verse innerly consistent either in scanning or in rhyme.

### THE YOUNG CURATE OF SALISBURY

There was a young curate of Salisbury
Whose manners were quite halisbury-skalisbury.
   He ran around Hampshire
    Without any pampshire,
Till the vicar compelled him to walisbury.

### A YOUNG MAN CALLED CHOLMONDELEY COLQUHOUN

A young man called Cholmondeley Colquhoun
Kept as a pet a babolquhoun.
   His mother said, "Cholmondeley,
    Do you think it quite colmondeley
To feed your babolquhoun with a spolquhoun?"

Erse, or Scottish Gaelic, has its own pitfalls of pronunciation, as is demonstrated here:

### CUCHULAIN

The pronunciation of Erse
Gets worse and worse.
They spell it Cuchulain—
No fuchulain!
       —A. D. Hope

# 9 AUGUST

## *For the Common Market*

It's easy to be witty in French.
You don't have to know French well.
Think of those expressions (this is the secret) . . .

Goût du néant, esprit de l'escalier,
Dégoût de la vie, nostalgie de la boue,
Adieu suprême des mouchoirs.
All you have to do is take two nouns,
Any old nouns, the iller-assorted the better,
And couple them with a genitive,
Shrug, throw your hands out (not too far),
In a French sort of way,
And give the casual knowing look of someone
Who knows the girl at the bar.
Try it and see . . .
With faint disdain . . . c'est un sentiment de vestiaire,
Goût de Londres, tendresse des wagons-lits
Or sighing
Les au revoir de vendredi.
Everyone will say how well you know French.
I've tried it on Frenchmen, and I know.

In German just couple the words together,
Like any old strangers meeting in any old street . . .
Himmelschnabel Apfelpudel Heldenbegeisterun Weltkrebs . . .
No one will know any better.

In Italian, it will be helpful to know the first line of Dante,
And also, brushing away a tear,
"Italia, Italia, terra di morti."
And go straight on to business.

I will advise later about the Scandinavian countries.

*—Michael Burn*

# 10 AUGUST

## *Shame on Uncle Allie*

OYSTERVILLE—Our home here is a red frame cottage, built in 1863 and measuring thirty-three by twenty-three feet. It is the oldest, smallest house in the village. According to the authoritative biography *The Life and Works of Mr. Anonymous*, copyright 1977 by Willard R. Espy, the prior occupant was my Great-uncle Allie, who at the age of one hundred sixteen died quietly in the chair I am now sitting in.

It is a shame that so many bookstores classify that biography as fiction. Every word of it, except for the passing references to Uncle Allie, is true. I did not lie, though sometimes Uncle Allie did. He was proud to be known as Mr. Anonymous, and failing overwhelming proof would claim authorship under that pseudonym of any verse ever published. He was particularly proud of a limerick about the common cormorant or shag, who laid eggs inside a paper bag; it turns out that Christopher Isherwood wrote that. Uncle Allie also claimed title to "On Benjamin Jowett," by H. C. Beeching, and "On the Hon. George Nathaniel Curzon, Commoner of Balliol," by J. W. Mackail and Cecil Spring-Rice. I fear that Eugene Field, not Uncle Allie, wrote "The Little Peach," or at least one version of it. Uncle Allie took credit for "I Cannot Eat But Little Meat," but William Stevenson beat him to it by 300 years. Why, Uncle Allie even appropriated an anatomical limerick by Don Marquis.

He stole in most ungentlemanly fashion a quatrain that runs:

> Hogamous higamous
> Men are polygamous
> Higamous hogamous
> Women monogamous.

According to Carolyn Foote, a dear friend by correspondence, it was Ann Pinchot who originated *Hogamous higamous*. She started awake in the night with the immortal words somersaulting over each other in her head and scribbled them on the back of an envelope by the light of a candle.

Uncle Allie was a disgrace to the family.

Even I am not perfect. Though I idolized the late trumpeter Satchmo Armstrong, I once referred to him as a saxophonist. I have credited Longfellow with Holmes's *Wonderful One-Hoss Shay*, shifted the North Star into the Big Dipper, and switched the Kentucky Derby from Louisville to Lexington.

Chief Justice Vinçon used to spit tobacco juice regularly and accurately into a spittoon. Bob Bendiner once asked him why, in view of his invariable accuracy, he bothered with a mat under the spittoon. "Just to remind me, son," said the Chief Justice, "that nobody is perfect."

My excuse for knuckleheaded errors is that I type fast.

# 11 AUGUST

## *Can We Write This Wrong?*

We're on speaking terms with the phrase "on the double,"
But say "on the single," and, boy, you're in trouble.

Take "nevertheless"—we hear it galore,
Yet nary a murmur of "nevermore."

Note this: "in the long run"—unless it's a race;
Why not "in the long walk" to slacken the pace?

Of course "notwithstanding," but no, it's unfitting
Wherever you're standing to say "notwithsitting."

The list of "well-heeled" is often unrolled,
Yet never unrolled is a list of "well-soled."

If facts are "forthcoming," we'd feel better knowing
That sooner or later they will be "forthgoing."

In brief, if "the odds are good," tell me, my lad,
Why we don't allow that "the evens are bad"?
                                    —*A. S. Flaumenhaft*

# 12 AUGUST

## *Snallygaster VIII*

More on the Snallygaster from a 1908 issue of the *Valley Register*, Middletown, Maryland:

> The Jersey Go-Devil, or bovelipus, or bovelipus, or whatever you choose to call it, about which the *Register* told last week, has not yet harmed anyone in this section, though it is said to have nearly caught a woman near Scrabble a few nights ago. It is reported that the creature roosted Friday night in Alex Crow's barn, halfway between Shepherdstown and Sharpsburg, where it laid another egg. The egg was taken possession of by some Sharpsburg men, who have rigged up a big incubator, and will endeavor to hatch it out. We think the law should interfere in this matter. It is bad enough to have one flying Devil in the neighborhood, let alone hatching out new ones.
>
> Last Tuesday night a gentleman from Hansonville, this county, called the *Register* by phone and informed us that we should notify President Roosevelt that the Snallygaster had passed over that section about 6:30 o'clock that evening. After sucking up and eating all the goldfish from Ramsburg's pond, it flew away with a noise like a mighty cataract and was reported to have nearly killed three men who were crossing a field.
>
> Saturday morning Mr. Wm. E. Moore, of Yellow Springs, called the *Register* by phone and requested us to secure for him a setting of eggs from the Snallygaster, if possible. He said there was a good deal of chicken stealing going on over there and a few young Snallygasters turned loose in the community could put an end to it.

MORE ON 17 SEPTEMBER.

# 13 AUGUST

## *Coleridge on Cologne*

I once calculated that there would be no carbon monoxide cluttering up the air of New York today if only the city had had sense enough to ban gasoline-powered vehicles back in 1903. The same calculation showed, though, that horse manure would now be up to the ninety-second floor of the Empire State Building.

These conclusions were passed along to my limited public as a pleasantry; but pleasantries are suspect these days. My ensuing mail was divided between correspondents who felt I was being disrespectful toward ecology, and correspondents who felt I was being disrespectful toward horses. The reactions bothered me: how, I wonder, can one solve any serious problem except by way of a joke?

A hundred and fifty years before ecology became a parlor, bedroom, and bath game, a poet made a joke of the miasma investing the city of Cologne:

> In Köln, a town of monks and bones,
> And pavements fanged with murderous stones,
> And rags, and hags, and hideous wenches,
> I counted two-and-seventy stenches,
> All well defined and separate stinks!
>
> Ye nymphs that reign o'er sewers and sinks,
> The river Rhine, it is well known
> Doth wash your city of Cologne;
> But tell me, nymphs, what power divine
> Shall henceforth wash the river Rhine?
> —*Samuel Taylor Coleridge*

How about *eau de cologne*, Sam?

# 14 AUGUST

## *Sentences Askew*

Red Smith, the sportswriter, recalls that Grantland Rice once interviewed Babe Ruth on radio. Because the Babe sometimes struck out in conversation, Rice typed out the questions and answers in advance. "Well, you know, Granny," Ruth read in answer to a question, "Duke Ellington said the Battle of Waterloo was won on the playing fields of Elkton." "Babe," Granny said after the show, "Duke Ellington for the Duke of Wellington I can understand. But how did you ever read Eton as Elkton? That's in Maryland, isn't it?" "I married my first wife there," Babe said, "and I hate the gawdarn place."

Skewed sentences are among life's unalloyed pleasures; they do not embarrass the skewer, since he is unaware that anything has gone amiss, and they are a source of innocent merriment for the hearer.*

Well, once in a while they do embarrass the skewer. Warren Austin, the United States ambassador to the United Nations, was not allowed to forget his suggestion to the quarreling Israelis and Arabs that they should "sit down and settle their differences like good Christians."

---

*See 21 June and 18 November.

The mayors of New York have a noble tradition of skewing. Jimmy Walker announced, "We're launching this innovation for the first time." Robert Wagner said, "I have reiterated over and over again what I have said before."

No one has exceeded Casey Stengel for sheer incomprehensibility: "I would be batting the big feller if they wasn't ready with the other one, but a left-hander would be the thing if they wouldn't have knowed it already because there is more things involved than could come up on the road, even after we've been home a long while." Mr. Stengel remarked that "Gil Hodges is so strong he could snap your eyebrows off," and said of another player, "He's so lucky he could fall in a hole and come up with a silver spoon." A cogent bit of Stengelese advice: "Don't cut off your nose yourself."

Then there was Sam Goldwyn. He denied originating "Include me out," but admitted to "It's a dog-eat-dog world, and nobody's gonna eat me." "No, thanks," he told his hostess, "coffee isn't my cup of tea." Other Goldwynisms: "Most directors bite the hand that lays the golden egg." "When I want your opinion, I'll give it to you." "I had a monumental idea last night, but I didn't like it." "I never put on a pair of shoes until I've worn them five years."

Either Goldwyn or Gregory Ratoff said of television, then in its infancy, "I won't believe it until I see it in black and white." It was certainly Ratoff who told John Huston, "John, if you weren't the son of my beloved friend Walter, and if you weren't a brilliant writer and a magnificent director, you'd be nothing but a common drunk."

# 15 AUGUST

## Verse Aid

How to pronounce the difficult names of certain authors:

*Woiwode:*
He went into the store and bought some plywood, he
Was going to build a little boat, was Woiwode.

*Anthony Powell:*
He's as English as a Dover sole—
He's An'tony—believe me—Powell.

*The creator of Jeeves:*
Leave at once, it's not a good house:
I see no books by P. G. Wodehouse.

*Donald Barthelme:*
Begob! His stories starthle me—
That divil of a fella, Barthelme!

*Nabokov:*
Who could get every joke of
Vladimir Nabokov?

*Synge:*
>Authenticity's the thing
>With John Millington Synge.

*A twosome:*
>Say "pooch."
>Then A. Quiller-Couch.
>Then Joseph Wood Krutch.

*A couple of contemporaries:*
>Who's that in the purple dhoti?
>Why bless my soul, it's T. Capote!

>Father, looking in the cradle,
>Said, "Let's name him Leon Edel;
>I think that suits him rather well—
>Better than Leon Edel."
>>—*William Cole*

# 16 AUGUST

## *A Country Summer Pastoral*

I would flee from the city's rule and law,
  From its fashion and form cut loose,
And go where the strawberry grows on its straw,
  And the gooseberry on its goose;
Where the catnip tree is climbed by the cat
  As she crouches for her prey—
The guileless and unsuspecting rat
  On the rattan bush at play.

I will watch at ease for the saffron cow
  And the cowlet in their glee,
As they leap in joy from bough to bough
  On the top of the cowslip tree;
Where the musical partridge drums on his drum,
  And the woodchuck chucks his wood,
And the dog devours the dogwood plum
  In the primitive solitude.

And then to the whitewashed dairy I'll turn,
  Where the dairymaid hastening hies,
Her ruddy and golden-haired butter to churn
  From the milk of the butterflies;

And I'll rise at morn with the early bird,
  To the fragrant farmyard pass,
When the farmer turns his beautiful herd
  Of grasshoppers out to grass.
                              —*Anonymous*

# 17 AUGUST

## *She Wallowed in the Zuyder Zee*

I was drinking cider in a Seattle saloon today with a chance acquaintance named Captain Michael Benett, who explained the origins of the nautical terms port and starboard to me as follows:

> The starboard side of the ship was the side on which the steering oar was put out and was therefore called the steer-board side. With the steering oar out over the starboard side, it was natural to berth the ship on the other side so as not to damage the oar. The left side of the ship therefore became the side over which the loading took place, and became known as the loadboard side, later changed to larboard side.
>
> In the larger ships a door was cut in the larboard side for loading and it was called a port (from the French word for door). Later, in order not to confuse the two similarly sounding words, larboard and starboard, it was decided to call the left side of the ship the port side and the right side the starboard side.

Captain Benett and I then sang the following song:

> She wallowed in the Zuyder Zee,
> The breeze had ceased to spank;
> The crew of her was him and me,
> A Dutchman and a Yank.
>
> Inside her there was cider, there was cider in the sea,
> And cider on the starboard side, the larboard side, the lee,
> And much of such inside the Dutch, and much of such in me.
>
> From starboard spake the Dutchman, and full merrily spake he:
> "The starboard is the steer-board side, so steer me two or three;
> And when we've sipped the cider, we will sip the cider sea."
>
> From larboard then the Yankee spake, the Yankee being me.
> "The larboard is the loading side, so load in two or three."
> We'll sip up all the cider, see, and then the Zuyder Zee."
>                                         —*W.R.E.*

# 18 AUGUST

### *Let's Be Frank about This, Frank*

Emperor Francis Joseph Otto of Austria-Hungary was born on this day, and so, a great many years later, was an infant boy who eventually reached life's pinnacle by becoming my brother-in-law. His parents named him in honor of the emperor, but he was smart enough to cut out the other sobriquets at an early age and become simply Frank. My morning reading would be easier if such figures in the news as Abolhassan Bani-Sadr, President of Iran as I write, had followed Frank's example. The problem presented by Bani-Sadr's name led to this limerick, which appeared in Emmett Watson's column in the *Seattle Post-Intelligencer*:

> What a very strange name, Bani-Sadr!
> Than most other names, it seems hadr.
> It must be the same
> As the old family name
> That he got from his madr and fadr.
> —*Clarence Murton*

While on the subject of Middle Eastern presidents, and before returning to the matter of Frank's birthday, I give you this uncomplimentary but clever palindrome by Michael Miller about the President of Egypt:

### DRAT SADAT, A DASTARD

I have no reason to think that the passage of years is of particular concern to Frank, but if it ever bothers him I hasten to remind him that his situation is scarcely unique:

> A mid-life crisis
> Once or twice is
> Not the rarest
> Of men's vices.
> Men in fear of
> Ebbing id-life
> Often have a
> Mid-life mid-wife.
> —*W.R.E.*

Another view of the problem:

> To know one's Age requires, I guess,
> A superficial Cleverness,
> As when, at Twenty-one, I knew
> That right ahead lay Twenty-two.

Although Transitions have occurred
Since then, I find the sequence blurred:

At present I am Nip and Tuck
'Twixt Skeleton and Babe at Suck.

I may be Old, but I can say
That I was Older, yesterday.
                              —W.R.E.

# 19 August

## A Conservatory of Republicans

At about this time, every fourth year, representatives of the Republican and Democratic parties forgather to choose their presidential nominees. If names define, these delegates and alternates to the 1976 Republican National Convention were a varied lot:

- Lawrence Sweet and Arthur Sour, Harold Savage and Kerry Noble, Jimmie Angel and Arthur Outlaw, Elain Lust and William Love, David Forward and Charles Coy.
- Vivienne Raven, Harvey Drake, Alfred Snipes, Henry Lark, Grace Crow, Louis Bird, and Roland Byrd.
- Sharon Carr, Mary Alice Ford, Debbie Lincoln, Francisco Vega, and Ada Nash.
- Charles Soda, Earl Coke, Orvas Beers, Patt Ginn, Sue Ice, and Peggy Bender.
- Evan Lips, Beth Arms, Howard Face, and Douglas Head.
- Henry Hatter, Robert Hunter, Howard Baker, Velma Farmer, Gordon Miner, Ivy Shoemaker, Margaret Haymaker, Austin Stonebreaker, and Augusta Hornblower.
- Sandra Rich, Robert Poor, Ivy Banks, Irene Cash, Jacquelyn Till, Ruby Price, and Money Cummins.
- Marshall Cain and Peggy Abel.
- Gaynelle Waters, Van Poole, John Marsh, Edward Brooke, Evelyn Rivers, and Dwight Dam.
- Charles England, Richard Israel, Joseph Canada, Marshall French, Jeanie Turk.
- Charles Currier and William Ives.
- Frances Garland, Evans Rose, George Bloom, and Ellie Flowers.
- Dort Bigg and Walt Little, Patricia Short and William Long, Donald Large and Mildred Small.
- John Rushing and James Speed.
- Wendell Harms, Thomas Hury, Bernadine Burns, and Bryce Payne.
- Selma Steele, Dorothy Wood, Ellis Ivory, Mitch Silver, Norris Cotton, and Frank Whetstone.

- Claire Bass, Charles Trout, Will Gill, and Ody Fish.
- Margaret Black, Hubert White, Fred Gray, Carol Browne, Harry Redd, and Paul Green.
- Jared Scripture, Bill Church, and John Nave.
- Monroe Knight, Mary Bishop, Martha King, and Arthur Pope.
- Jane Fox, Stephen Wolfe, Harold Coons, Richard Badger, James Lyon, Ruth Hare, and Robert Pigg.
- Eliza Sprinkle and Walter Wrinkle.
- Lawrence Barley, George Rice, James Cherry, Sylvia Berry, Wanda Roe, Jane Ham, Jerry Lamb, and Harold Bean.
- Phyllis Barbee and Ken Doll.

—*James T. Wooten*

# 20 AUGUST

## *Word Belt*

We played this word game last night. I was not very good at it. Try it, though; it's fun, and you will doubtless do better than I did:

> The first player defines a word. The next identifies it, then gives the third player a definition of another word whose first three letters are the last three of the original word. And so on and on: opaque—querulous; ouster—terrain (some players may drop out on that last one, but there are words beginning with ain). A player who fails to identify a word defined, or whose own word has the wrong letter arrangement, is eliminated, and the play continues until only one contestant remains.

If you correctly name the words defined below, you will have a word belt:

> Lithe • Abundant • Salesman • Courageous • Excessive • Greek letter • Mild oath • Ingenious contrivance • Scene of Christ's betrayal • Old age • Instrumentality • Whole • Peaceful

Another game to talk about, if not to play, on a rainy evening, is "Firing the Fireman." It is based on the assumption that holders of different jobs are discharged in different ways. An orchestra leader, says John Fuller, is disbanded; an electrician, discharged; a postman, unzipped.

Herb Caen developed an analogous game, "I Could Have Been," for his column in the *San Francisco Chronicle*. Readers submitted such entries as these:

> I could have been a
>
> - proctologist, but I could never get to the bottom of things.
> - dermatologist, but I was too thin-skinned.

- nun, but I had sworn to kick the habit.
- railroad builder, but I couldn't make tracks fast enough.
- baker, but there was no dough in it.
- Bill Buckley's assistant, but I wasn't right for the job.

# 21 AUGUST

### Spel It Rite

When the witch said
Abradacabra
Nothing happened.
She's a hopeless speller.
—*Alan F. G. Lewis*

The American Philological Society, saying the arbitrary nature of spelling hinders education, wastes millions, and loses two years' time for each schoolchild, proposed that Congress do away with unsounded letters and use soft *g* for *j*. This was one reform that Congress had sense enough to reject. To strip words of their etymological accretions would send language back to the Neanderthals.

Besides, the oddities of spelling can provide considerable amusement. Melville Dewey, inventor of the library classification system, spelled one word G H E A U G H T E I G H P T O U G H. Thus:

GH is P, as in hiccough;
EAU is O, as in beau;
GHT is T, as in naught;
EIGH is A, as in NEIGH;
PT is T, as in pterodactyl,
OUGH is O, as in though.

That is, potato.

### THE HARBOR OF FOWEY

Yes, I have my own views
    But the teachers I follow
Are the lyrical Miews
    And the Delphic Apollow
Unto them I am debtor
    For spelling and rhyme
And I'm doing it bebtor
    And bebtor each time.
—*Sir Arthur Quiller-Couch*

THUMB FUN

Milkmaids, butchers,
Carpenters, they say,
Always get their thumbs
In the whey, weigh, way.
—*William E. Engel*

Some authorities blame television for the declining standards of spelling in classrooms. A class of third graders in Connecticut was asked to spell *relief*. Quicker than a thirty-second spot, says the *New York Times*, more than half spelled out "R O L A I D S."

# 22 AUGUST

## *The Web Retangled*

Sir Walter Scott said:

Oh, what a tangled web we weave
When first we practice to deceive!

To which Phyllis McGinley rejoined:

Which leads me to suppose the fact is
We really ought to get more practice.

J. R. Pope agreed:

But when we've practiced quite a while
How vastly we improve our style!

The two latter couplets betray a deplorable abdication of moral responsibility. Let the authors heed this warning from one of the few completely frank and honest men I know:

Forget, dear friends, that practice angle!
You'll only tangle up the tangle.
—*W.R.E.*

# 23 AUGUST

## *Swiftly Speaking*

A month or so ago I told you that American crossword puzzles are no match for their British counterparts in verbal ingenuity. But I must acknowledge that

Will Weng, who edits *The New York Times* crossword puzzles, is catching up. His selections are a steaming, seething, stinking, odious mudpot of puns, anagrams, and hidden words. One puzzle by Edward J. O'Brien is built around thirty-four Tom Swifties—puns of the sort that you figure out only to discover you have to figure out what you have figured out.

I list here a few examples from Mr. O'Brien's opus. They may make you a *Times* puzzle addict for life. Or you may treat them as a warning to avoid the *Times* puzzle page as you would avoid quicksand.

"Who, what?" said Tom warily. "Young M.D.," said Tom internally. "Gold leaf," said Tom guiltily. "John," said Tom wanly. "Elec. unit," said Tom amply. "Go easy, Mr. Roper," said Tom politely. "Coda," said Tom finally. "Shirtwaist," said Tom blowsily. "Maid's night off," said Tom helplessly. "K-," said Tom rationally. "Pass the cards," said Tom ideally. "Quiet meadow," said Tom silently. "Zero," said Tom naughtily. ". . . and lose a few," said Tom winsomely. "Drei . . . fünf," said Tom fearlessly. "Brothers," said Tom grimly. "Oriental gift," said Tom pleasantly. "One pair," said Tom abrasively. "X's and," said Tom wisely. "I bequeath," said Tom willingly. "Just Newsweek," said Tom timelessly. "Tripod," said Tom easily. "Pope," said Tom piously. "Furn.," said Tom aptly.

# 24 AUGUST

## *Charades Again*

Charades from *The Enigma*, monthly magazine of The National Puzzlers' League:

*Homonym* (\*9 \*8, \*1 4 3 3 4)
They asked the ONE, "How many men should we arrest today?"
"Shah supporters? TWO!" he said. "Now please go on your way."
—*Ralf P. Olio*

(The digits within parentheses indicate the number of letters in each word of the solution. The asterisks signal capital letters. The comma separates ONE from TWO. ONE thus consists of two capitalized words, the first of nine and the second of eight letters. TWO consists of five words, the first having one letter, capitalized. The others have four, three, three and four letters respectively.)

ONE, since both words are capitalized, is probably a name. The words "Shah" and "arrest" give the name away; it has to be the Ayatollah Khomeini, the leading figure in the Islamic revolution that overthrew the Shah.

### 1. SPOONERGRAM (4 '1' 4, *6 4)

It was raining ONE today,
  And that is nothing new.
My little car exploded, though,
  And it started raining TWO.

### 2. HOMONYM (*8 5, 5 6)

The romeo had met his match,
  A girl who did say no.
It happened on a ONE; and since
  All gossip travels so,
It made the Sunday paper—
  "TWO" the headline read.
The lecher's rep was ruined;
  In shame he sold his bed.

### 3. SPOONERGRAM (*11, 2 4 2 3)

An upstate New Yorker (from ONE),
Asked out for a short downhill run,
  Said, "Ya hafta risk TWO,
  Which I don't wanna do;
So I'll stay off the slopes for my fun."

### 4. HOMONYM (13, 6 8)

My father drinks whiskey, thinks tea is a TWO,
As potent as ONE and as tangy as dew.
                              —Ralf P. Olio

# 25 AUGUST

## The Susurrant Schwa

A schwa, indicated in dictionaries by an ə, is a vowel so unstressed that it all
but loses its distinction of sound, thus:

The ə on his diurnəl rounds
  Is minəs all but minər sounds;
Yet may, phonetəcəsts əgree,
  Transmit a wide vəriəty
Of audəble phənomənə:
    Aə, Eə, Iə, Oə . . .
    Uə.

                              —W.R.E.

A schwa carried past the point of no return vanishes into an apostrophe. Philip Cohen relates this hyperapostrophic story:

> An old salt was telling of going through a typhoon in his sailing ship. At the top of the storm, he said, "M' jibs'l's lines snapped. And m't'g'll'nts'l's'd'a done the same if it hadn't slacked off just then."

Mr. Cohen found the eight-apostrophe "m't'g'll'nts'l's'd'a"—surely a record—in *Slaves of Sleep*, a science-fiction novel by L. Ron Hubbard. When he rechecked his source, the apostrophe between g and l had disappeared, but I prefer the story as I first received it.

# 26 AUGUST

## *Back and Forth*

How many of these palindromes can you identify from the definitions?

1. Baby's napkin     — — —
2. The first woman     — — —
3. Woman's name; former monetary unit of India     — — — —
4. Property paper     — — — —
5. Man's name; German king     — — — —
6. Twelve o'clock     — — — —
7. Blow your horn     — — — —
8. Chick vocalization     — — — —
9. Air or highway monitor     — — — — —
10. Flat; even     — — — — —
11. In Spanish, it's señora     — — — — —
12. Send a patient to a specialist     — — — — —
13. Iranian VIPs     — — — — —
14. Not duets     — — — — —
15. Eskimo watercraft     — — — — —
16. Basic doctrine     — — — — —
17. Related to government     — — — — —
18. Woman's name; the mother of Samuel     — — — — — —
19. More like a beet     — — — — — —
20. Decorate the wall a second time     — — — — — — —

*—Edward Rawder*

# 27 August

## *Professor Otto R. Osseforp*

A Harvard Bulletin interview between Professor R. Osseforp, holder of the Emor D. Nilap Chair in Palindromology at Harvard, and Solomon W. Golomb (Ph.D. '57), includes this palindromic exchange:

"And what about your new novel, could you tell me the title?"
"Dennis Sinned."
"Intriguing. What is the plot?"
"Dennis and Edna sinned."
"I see. Is there more to it than that?"
"Dennis Krats and Edna Stark sinned."
"Now it all becomes clear," I agreed. "Tell me, with all this concern about the ecology, what kind of car are you driving nowadays?"
"A Toyota."
"Naturally, and how about your colleague, Prof. Nustad?"
"Nustad? A Datsun."*

# 28 August

## *Doublets*

When Lewis Carroll was not preparing mathematical treatises, or writing *Alice in Wonderland*, or taking photographs of little girls, you might have found him working on Doublets, in which the puzzler travels from one word to another by a series of letter substitutions. Each step must consist of but one letter change, which forms a real word. *Head*, for instance, becomes *foot*, as follows: *Head, held, hold, fold, food, foot.*

Here are some of his Doublets, and the number of steps he used in the metamorphosis. Perhaps you can outdo him:

1. *Eye* to *lid* (4)
2. *Pig* to *sty* (5)
3. *Ape* to *man* (6)
4. *Army* to *navy* (8)
5. *Cain* to *Abel* (9)
6. *Wheat* to *bread* (7)
7. *River* to *shore* (11)
8. *Winter* to *summer* (14)

---

*Ralph G. Beaman adds: "and his wife May?"
"Aha! May? A Yamaha!"

# 29 AUGUST

$\mathcal{C}$ *fm*

(From the Philadelphia *Minerva*, February 13, 1796)

The enigma:

$\mathcal{C}$ **fm**

The answer:  effeminacy: f m in a C.
                —*Toby*

And that, children, is a rebus charade, which may combine pictures, equations, ABC language, or any other convenient visual device to transmit—or conceal—its message.

1. B = m ) K
2. O°
   —*Mary J. Youngquist and Harry Hazard*

Betsy Burr says this one was familiar in her childhood:

$$
\begin{array}{r}
3.\ \text{UR 2 GOOD} \\
\text{2 ME} \\
\text{2 BE} \\
\underline{4\ \text{GOT}} \\
10
\end{array}
$$

4. Here symbols used three times in a row are to be pluralized (CCC = seas or seize), while symbols repeated two times, or more than three times, are to be read directly (CCCC = foresees, CC = to seize). The conversation is between Caesar and a foreign refugee, which accounts for the accent:

M N 4 L CCCNNN

— AL, CCCR!
— PPP 2 U, O 4NR! RIII! U R?
— I M RSTTT, XLNC, N RABN XIL.
— Y R U N XIL, RSTTT?
— I UUU 2 BAAAΠ, O CCCR.
— MSE BBBNS! ½ U E-10?
— ES, QQQQQQQQQQ IR, I 8 H EEE N VL Π—XLN, 2. O CCCR, I ½ 1 DDDIR. I 444E EZ AAAA UUUU IR, F I M AAAΠ 4 U. I ½ N IPPP UU 222Π . . .

— N IPPP! ½ U CN N NME RME?
— ES, XLNC, N A CQR CT, AJ¢ 2 A 4S, 2 RMEEE.
— I ½ CN UR CT, N III A UR CT S MT! R U AAAΠ 4 NE1 LLL? CCCM, N!
— O CCCR, U R YY UU 444! I M NO¢! I C 2 CTTT: 1 S MT, N 1 2 RMEEE OQΠ. I M UR LI, N I ½ A WWW UU IR. U C, I M AAAΠ N I M A CR, 2.
— F U R A CR, I SQ, R U 8 L R O 4 NN?
— ES, CCCR, I 4C 9 CCCNNN F EZ SSSSSS 4 U B4 U XΠR.
— 9 CCCNNN! N M I 2 XΠR N 9 CCCNNN? Y? LI B 6, Π?
— O CCCR, U L XΠR B4 UR L F A DZZZ, 2MIIIRO. ½ U NE NMEEE?
— FU, FU.
— I 4C U L ½ 2 ULOGGG, O CCCR: 1 R8R 2 AQQQ UR NMEEE N 1 2 XQQQ M; 1 2 XP8 N 1 2 X-10-U8; 1 222A "PPP, PPP" N 1 2 RQ 4 "N I 4 N I"; 1 2 8S 2 UR TRNE N 1 2 8S 2 UR NRG N XLNNN: A 4M 4 NNNN6, CCCR, B4 UR NMEEE' DMIII. ES, 7TULE UR NMEEE L XΠR, 2—XLNC, R U OK? XQQQ RSTTT, CCCR, F 5 4CN 2 FR!
— O L, IIIA 2 RMMM! A C F NMEEE 0888, RSTTT! 2 RMMM!

—*Betsy Burr*

# 30 AUGUST

## *Cat Words*

Everyone knows that words ending in –*cat* (particularly *scat*, but also such resonant, reverent words as *magnificat* and *requiescat*) are cat words. But you may not know that words ending in –*cate* or –*cated* are also cat words. The final –*e* (–*ed*) was added by cat haters, just to deny cats their due. Read this verse as carefully as a cat licks its fur. Thereafter spell all cat words in proper cat fashion.

1. Let us arise now to invocat
   The CAT;
   No less the raffish Allocat
   Than the elegant Domesticat.

2. Let us arise now and pat
   The intricat
   Complicat
   Delicat
   Indelicat
   Sophisticat
   Unsophisticat
   CAT!

3. The wicked *hat*
   The CAT.

They defecat
Upon the CAT.
They deprecat
And imprecat
The CAT.
They'd send a Syndicat
To eradicat
The CAT.

4. The wicked even *altercat*.
   (Oh no! not that!)

5. Got to, CAT!
   Fornicat!—
   Propagat!—
   CAT!
   Duplicat!
   Triplicat!
   Quadruplicat!
   Quintuplicat!

6. The wicked shall not dislocat
   Confiscat
   Suffocat
   Your kittens, CAT—
   We'll see to *that!*—
   You Silicat!

7. Let us arise now, and excommunicat
   The damn'd souls who fabricat . . .
   Prevaricat . . .
   About the CAT.
   Let us arise, and stat:
   SCAT!

8. Let us now dedicat
   Mouse and rat
   To the CAT.
   Masticat,
   CAT!
   Extricat
   Lean and fat!

9. Our senses you intoxicat,
   Our mental joints you lubricat,
   CAT!

10. One caveat:
    Do you reciprocat
    Our passion, CAT?
    CAT?
    *CAT!*
    We supplicat
    You, CAT:
    *Com M E W nicat*
    With us, CAT!
                    —W.R.E.

(A number of cat words—educat, indicat, inculcat, advocat, abdicat, locat, placat, coruscat, and so on—are not included. Enough is enough of anything, even cats.)

# 31 AUGUST

## *Garbled Geography*

HOW MUCH DID PHILADELPHIA PA?

How much did Philadelphia Pa?
    Whose grass did K.C. Mo?
How many eggs could New Orleans La?
    How much does Cleveland O?

When Hartford and New Haven Conn
    What sucker do they soak?
Could Noah build a Little Rock Ark
    If he had not Guthrie Ok?

We call Minneapolis Minn,
    Why not Annapolis Ann?
If you can't tell the reason why
    I'll bet Topeka Kan.

But now we speak of ladies, what
    A Butte Montana is!
If I could borrow Memphis' Tenn
    I'd treat that Jackson Miss.

Would Denver Cola cop because
    Ottumwa Ia dore?
Ah, though my Portland Me doth love,
    I threw my Portland Ore.
                    —*Anonymous*

Name these:

| | |
|---|---|
| 1. The cleanest state. | 7. The most unmarried. |
| 2. The most seaworthy. | 8. The most Catholic. |
| 3. The most fatherly. | 9. The highest numbered. |
| 4. The most personal. | 10. The most Islamic. |
| 5. The most surprised. | 11. The best writer. |
| 6. The most professional. | 12. The most shady. |

## GEOGRAPHICAL LOVE SONG

In the State of Mass.
There lives a lass
   I love to go N.C.;
No other Miss.
Can e'er, I Wis.,
   Be half so dear to Me.

R.I. is blue
And her cheeks the hue
   Of shells where waters swash;
On her pink-white phiz
There has Nev. Ariz.
   The least complexion Wash.

La.! could I win
The heart of Minn.,
   I'd ask for nothing more;
But I only dream
Upon the theme,
   And Conn. it o'er and Ore.

Hawaii, pray,
Can't I Ala.
   This love that makes me Ill.?
N.Y., O., Wy.
Kan. Nev. Ver. I
   Propose to her my will?

I shun the task
'Twould be to ask
   This gentle maid to wed.
And so, to press
My suit, I guess
   Alaska Pa. instead.
               —*Anonymous*

# SEPTEMBER

## 1 SEPTEMBER

### *Tomorrow the Rain Will Be Only a Drizzle*

OYSTERVILLE—We are in the midst of our annual equinoctial storm. It is not really equinoctial, but that is what we call it. It will last four days. Day before yesterday the sky, which had been as light a blue as the color of a robin's egg, darkened to blue-black. The wind swung south and lost its temper over something; it sent frightened clouds rushing across the sky like birds fleeing before a fire. In the night the downpour started. The rain is so thick now that we cannot see our picket fence, much less the bay.

Tomorrow morning, though, the wind will be resting in the north, and the rain will be only a mizzle. Silver will begin sifting through the cloud; by noon the cover will have broken into a flock of slowly cropping sheep, and after lunch I will take a nap on the sun deck.

Oysterville weather has grown gentler since I was a child; or is it only gentle for the period of my visits? Perhaps Washington has begun issuing regulations about the portions of wind, shine, and the like to be permitted each day:

THERE OUGHT TO BE A LAW

Roads are muddy?
Make a study.

Day too warm?
Vote reform.

Caught a chill?
Draw a bill.

Cold and raw?
Pass a law.

Snow and ice?
Pass it twice.

Storm and bluster?
Filibuster.

Ash and grit?
Veto it.

*If, flouting your concern,*
*The weather takes a turn,*

*Adjourn.*
                              *—W.R.E.*

This poet foresees apprehensively the day when the weatherman will not simply forecast the weather but arrange it:

Cancel that call
For a squall!

Blow
Up a snow!

A freshet—
And rush it!

Thaw
Arkansas!

Precipitate
The Bay State!

Pour it on
Oregon!
                              *—Hope E. Stoddard*

# 2 SEPTEMBER

## *The Yellow Prose of Texas*

To know the full marvel of the brand that Texas has burned into the hide of the English language, you have to spend a few days there. The next best thing is to buy a copy of Jim Everhart's *Illustrated Texas Dictionary*. In passing on the excerpts below I regret only that I cannot show you the grotesque facial distortions with which Mr. Everhart, in accompanying photographs, illustrates the definitions.

- ails—other than the person or thing implied. "Ah only done what anybody *ails* would do."
- beggar—larger in size, height, width, amount, etc. "The *beggar* they come the harder they fall."
- cheer—in this place or spot. "Yawl come riot *cheer* this minute."
- fair—a distressing emotion aroused by impending danger. "The only thing we have to *fair* is *fair* itself."

- hep—to render assistance. "Ain't nobody gonna *hep* me?"
- lacked—was on the verge of or came close to. "Ah *lacked* to died laughin'."
- main—of ugly disposition, nasty. "That there is one *main* man."
- often—so as to be no longer supported or attached. "Now stan still so ah can shoot that apple *often* yore had."
- riot—correct or proper. "That's jes as *riot* as rain."
- squire—honest and above board. "Everything is fire and *squire*."
- truss—reliance on integrity. "Don't yawl *truss* me?"

Mr. Everhart's final definition is the word thank—to have a judgment or opinion of. "Jes *thank*," he says, "of what yew must sound lack to a Texan!"

# 3 SEPTEMBER

### *Lewd Play, Sir*

Dick Cavett, a master of the offhand anagram, turned "Alec Guinness" into "genuine class," and Oscar Wilde into "O lad I screw." The letters of his own name can be arranged into "I crav'd chatter," appropriate for the host of a talk show. He says in a note that came this morning, "Is there a word for a sentence made up of anagrams of the same word? E.g., the other day I thought of, 'Go paste Gestapo postage to pages.' What's wrong with me?"

Nothing is wrong with him, except that he suffers from a virulent form of anagrammania; as far as I know there is no cure for that, nor any name for the kind of sentence he describes. How about calling it a concategram? Or a concavettgram?

Will Shortz, with a singular lack of respect, offered "Lewd play, sir," as an anagram for "Willard Espy." Other, more elegant transmutations:

| | |
|---|---|
| Arguments | Must anger |
| Armageddon | Mad god near |
| Christianity | 'Tis in charity |
| Democratic | Rated comic |
| Diplomacy | Mad policy |
| HMS *Pinafore* | Name for ship |
| Moonlight | Thin gloom |
| Ms. Steinem | Smites men |
| Prayeth | Therapy |
| Sexual intercourse | Relax, insure coitus |
| Weird nightmares | Withering dreams |
| Eddie Cantor | Actor, indeed |
| Victoria, England's Queen | Governs a nice quiet land |
| Twenty Thousand Leagues Under the Sea | Huge water tale stuns; end had you tense |
| The Lay of the Last Minstrel | This story that all men feel |

| | |
|---|---|
| The Morse Code | Here come dots |
| The South Sea islands | A thousand islets shine |
| Dante Gabriel Rossetti | Greatest idealist born |
| The nudist colony | No untidy clothes |
| Catherine de Medici | Her edict came in—die |

\* \* \*

LONDON (Reuters)—Nicholas Fairbairn, a Scottish Member of Parliament, says he has discovered the true meaning of Nessiteras rhombopterxy, the name given to the fabled Loch Ness monster by a leading British naturalist, Sir Peter Scott, who claims that recent photographs prove the monster's existence.

Mr. Fairbairn said the name is an anagram: "Monster hoax by Sir Peter S."

\* \* \*

Stephen Sondheim noted that "Cinerama" juggles into "American"; Lewis Carroll, that "William Ewart Gladstone" can be turned into "Wild agitator means well"; and Richard Edes Harrison, that "Beverly Sills" transforms superbly into "Silvery Bells."

# 4 SEPTEMBER

### The Conversational Reformer

When Theo: Roos: unfurled his bann:
   As Pres: of an immense Repub:
And sought to manufact: a plan
   For saving people troub:
His mode of spelling (termed phonet:)
Affec: my brain like an emet:

And I evolved a scheme (*pro-tem*)
   To simplify my mother-tongue,
That so in fame I might resem:
   Upt: Sinc:, who wrote "The Jung:,"
And rouse an interest enorm:
In conversational reform.

I grudge the time my fellows waste
   Completing words that are so comm:
Wherever peop: of cult: and taste
   Habitually predom:
'Twould surely tend to simpl: life
Could they but be curtailed a trif:

"'Tis not in mort: to comm: success,"
   As Addison remarked; but if my meth:
Does something to dimin: or less:
   The waste of public breath,
My country, overcome with grat:
Should in my hon: erect a stat:

For is not "Brev: the Soul of Wit"?
   (Inscrib the mott: upon your badge).
The sense will never suff: a bit
   If left to the imag:
Since any pers: can see what's meant
By words so simp: as "husb:" or "gent:"

When at some meal (at dinn: for inst:)
   You hand your unc: an empty plate,
Or ask your aunt (that charming spinst:)
   To pass you the potat:,
They have too much sagac:, I trust,
To give you sug: or pep: or must:.

Gent: Reader, if to me you'll list:
   And not be irritab: or peev:,
You'll find it of tremend: assist:
   This habit of abbrev:,
Which grows like some infec: disease,
Like chron: paral: or German meas:.

My bust by Rod: (what matt: the cost?)
   Shall be exhib: devoid of charge,
With (in the Public Lib: at Bost:)
   My full-length port: by Sarge:
That thous: from Pitts: or Wash: may
      swarm
To Worsh: the Found: of this Reform.

Meanwhile I seek with some avid:
The fav: of your polite consid:.
                              —*Harry Graham*


# 5 SEPTEMBER

### *Dirty Work on the Appellation Trail*

Old King Cole was a merry old soul. So is young Bill Cole, author of some of the most splendid light verse around. I hope Bill is assembling his collected works right now, so that we can gorge ourselves on conceits such as this:

### DIRTY WORK ON THE APPELLATION TRAIL
### OR: I CAN'T REMEMBER THE MNEMONIKER

At a party they cry, "Oh, here comes Carol!"
And in someone comes in a man's apparel!
It's signed on the letter, but I have to ask:
Is it Hilary *fem.* or Hilary *masc.*?

Fellows named Joyce and females named Jeremy
Cause confusion at the marriage cerem'y;
There's a Shirley he and a Shirly *female*—
How on earth can a Shirley *he* male *be* male?

Men are named Beverly, women named Frankie—
Ycleptomaniacal hanky-panky!
Women named Leslie and men named Ēvelyn—
Sometimes I don't know *what* to believe in!

Imagine a boy with a name like Florence
Hiding in corners and crying in torrence!
I knew another—they called him Jocelyn!
A situation *I'd* not be docilyn!

To be doubly sure his life will be dismal,
Name a boy Vivian at his baptismal;
It's shaking your fist at man and at nature
To label a boy with such no-manclature!

With Marian "a" and with Marion "o"
At least you have something on which to go;
When there's Frances with "e" and Francis with "i"
You can differentiate girlie and guy.

My friend has a niece of the female kidney,
But he introduced her as "Sidney," didn' he?
How far will they go with this mad vagary?
Will they name girls Sam? Will they name boys Mary?
                                        —*William Cole*

# 6 SEPTEMBER

## *A Chronology of Anagrams*

The moon circles the earth and the earth circles the sun and the anagrams go on, year after year. Some dates, some anagrams:

| 1883 | Chester Arthur: *Truth searcher.* |
| 1884 | Dante Gabriel Rossetti: *Greatest born idealist.* |
| 1894 | Court of general session: *Scenes of rogues on trial.* |
| 1899 | The death of Robert G. Ingersoll, the famous agnostic: *Goes, gathering the belief that no Lord comforts us.* |
| 1903 | The detectives: *Detect thieves.* |
| 1904 | A confirmed bachelor: *I face no bold charmer.* |
| 1906 | Charitableness: *I can bless earth.* |
| 1908 | The Dead March in Saul: *Hear deathland music.* |
| 1912 | Beer saloons: *Booser's lane.* |
| 1917 | Blandishment: *Blinds the man.* |

I do not recall where I found the dates for the foregoing anagrams (perhaps in *Word Ways?*) nor can I date the following, perhaps the earliest of them all:

Astronomical observations: *To scan a visible star or moon.*

# 7 SEPTEMBER

### *You're a Frog, I'm a Limey / You Say Merde, I Say Blimey*

Cultural differences between the French and the English are mirrored in their idioms:

| *The English* | *The French* |
|---|---|
| To wear your heart on your sleeve. | Avoir le coeur sur la main. (To have the heart in one's hand.) |
| So good he could grow wings. | Etre à encadrer. (Fit to be framed.) |
| To win in a breeze. | Arriver dans un fauteuil. (To arrive in an armchair.) |
| Nothing to sneeze at. | Ne pas crâcher dessus. (Nothing to spit on.) |
| To win hands down. | Arriver les doigts dans le nez. (To arrive with fingers in one's nose.) |
| Born with a silver spoon in the mouth. | Etre né coiffé. (Born with a hat on.) |
| To be pushing up daisies. | Manger les pissenlits par la racine. (To eat dandelions by the roots.) |
| To have bats in the belfry. | Avoir une araignée au plafond. (To have a spider on one's ceiling.) |
| Good weather for ducks. | Un temps de chien. (Dog's weather.) |
| To make a mountain out of a molehill. | Se noyer dans un verre d'eau. (To drown in a glass of water.) |

| | |
|---|---|
| To have a poker-face. | Avoir un front d'arain. |
| | (To have a brass forehead.) |
| To rule the roost. | Faire le pluie et le beau temps. |
| | (To make rain and fair weather.) |
| To be a lady-killer. | Etre la coqueluche des dames. |
| | (To be the ladies' whooping-cough.) |
| To strike it rich. | Faire son beurre. |
| | (To make one's butter.) |

—*Marcelle Dorval*

# 8 SEPTEMBER

### *A Lewdness of Limericks*

A poet unknown to me wrote:

> The limerick's an art form complex
> Whose contents run chiefly to sex;
> It's famous for virgins
> And masculine urgin's,
> And vulgar erotic effects.

Morris Bishop phrased the same indictment more elegantly:

> The limerick's furtive and mean;
> You must keep her in close quarantine;
> Or she sneaks to the slums
> And promptly becomes
> Disorderly, drunk, and obscene.

Many a literary craftsman of the second or third water, and a few of the first, have tried their hands at dirty limericks. The Norman Douglas compilation of these sits on my shelf beside a collection of 1700 edited by G. Legman. Between them, the two books may tell you more about dirty limericks than you want to know.

Wading through 1700 off-color limericks is like wading against a current of hip-deep sludge. Naughtiness without cleverness, however, makes for a depressing limerick. Indeed, the most famous limericks, certainly including Lear's, are not off-color at all. Take the senior Oliver Wendell Holmes's immortal pun on Henry Ward Beecher:

> A great Congregational preacher
> Called a hen an elegant creature.
> The hen, just for that,
> Laid an egg in his hat.
> And thus did the hen reward Beecher.

With the exception of a mild oath, there is nothing that Anthony Comstock himself could find objectionable in this, perhaps the most familiar limerick of all:

> A wonderful bird is the pelican,
> His bill will hold more than his belican.
>> He can take in his beak
>> Food enough for a week,
> And I'm damned if I see how the helican.
>> —*Dixon Lanier Merritt*

## SOME SAINTLY CITIES

> A sporty young man in St. Pierre
> Had a sweetheart and oft went to sierre.
>> She was Gladys by name,
>> And one time when he came
> Her mother said: "Gladys St. Hierre."

> A globe-trotting man from St. Paul
> Made a trip to Japan in the faul.
>> One thing he found out,
>> As he rambled about,
> Was that Japanese ladies St. Taul.

> A guy asked two jays at St. Louis
> What kind of an Indian the Souis.
>> They said: "We're no en-
>> cyclopedia, by hen!"
> Said the guy: "If you fellows St. Whouis?"

> A bright little maid in St. Thomas
> Discovered a suit of pajhomas.
>> Said the maiden "Well, well!
>> What they are I can't tell;
> But I'm sure that these garments St. Mhomas."
>> —*Ferdinand G. Christgau*

## A COUPLE OF YAKS

> A yak from the hills of Iraq
> Met a yak he had known awhile back.
>> They went out to dine,
>> And talked of lang syne—
> Yak-ety, yak-ety, yak.
>> —*W.R.E.*

## THE OLD MAN FROM DUNDOON

> There was an old man from Dundoon
> Who always ate soup with a fork,

For he said, "As I eat
Neither fish, fowl, nor flesh,
I should finish my dinner too quick."
—*Anonymous*

### THERE WAS A YOUNG FELLOW OF TRINITY

There was a young Fellow of Trinity
Who found $y^e \sqrt{\infty}$;
   But $y^e$ number of digits
   Gave him $y^e$ fidgets;
He dropped Math and took up Divinity.
—*Anonymous*

# 9 SEPTEMBER

## *The Venereal Game*

Venus pursued her prey indiscriminately in bower or bosky dell, but in the venereal game* only the bosky dell is involved. *An Exaltation of Larks,* by James Lipton, lists scores of venereal terms, relics of mediaeval times. Some—"a school of fish"; "a pride of lions"—are still in general use; others—"a skulk of foxes"; "a barren of mules"—are still used by specialists; still others have vanished from the general ken. Mr. Lipton also went on to conjure up his own collectives, such as "an unction of undertakers," "a float of dancers," "a dilation of pupils," and "a wince of dentists." This is a game open to all. It is played with gusto on Mary Ann Madden's competition page in *New York* magazine, with results like these:

> a riot of students • a peck of kisses (or bad boys) • a Buckley of Bills • a mine of egotists • a host of parasites • a complement of sycophants • a range of ovens • a furrow of brows • a nun of your business • a lot of realtors • a whack of Portnoys • a knot of Windsors • a wagon of teetotalers

# 10 SEPTEMBER

## *How Can I Know What I Think Till I See What I Say?*

The dilemma thus expressed (by W. H. Auden) is examined further here:

### HOW COULD THE POET

How could the poet
possibly know
till the very last word
in the very last row?

---

\* See also 20 January, 19 November.

For a poem's a word
plus a word, plus a word,
added, subtracted,
and thoroughly stirred.

And thought makes the word,
and the word makes thought,
and some things come
that were never sought.

At what he has said
when his say is done,
the poet's surprised
as anyone.
                              —*Richard Armour*

# 11 SEPTEMBER

## *Last Lines*

Earlier, I asked you to identify a number of books by their opening lines. Now match the last sentence with the title of some of the same books:

*The last sentence*

1. The hand of Providence brought me in my drifting to the very doors of the British Linen Company's bank.
2. It came from afar and travelled sedately on, a shrug from eternity.
3. Hot dog.
4. But over the old man's head they looked at each other and smiled.
5. The knife came down, missing him by inches, and he took off.
6. After awhile I went out and left the hospital and walked back to the hotel in the rain.
7. Come, children, let us shut the box and the puppets, for our play is played out.
8. One bird said to Billy Pilgrim, "Poo-tee-weet?"
9. I shall still lose my temper with Ivan the coachman, I shall still embark on useless discussions and express my opinions inopportunely . . . but my life, now, my whole life, independently of anything that can happen to me, every minute of it, is no longer mean-

*The book*

A. *The Naked and the Dead*, Norman Mailer
B. *The Good Earth*, Pearl Buck
C. *Slaughterhouse Five*, Kurt Vonnegut
D. *Farewell to Arms*, Ernest Hemingway
E. *Vanity Fair*, William Makepeace Thackeray
F. *Kidnapped*, Robert Louis Stevenson
G. *Darkness at Noon*, Arthur Koestler
H. *Catch-22*, Joseph Heller
I. *1984*, George Orwell

ingless as it was before, but has a positive meaning of goodness with which I have the power to invest it.

10. I loved Big Brother.

11. Small fowls flew screaming over the yet yawning gulf; a sullen surf beat against its steep sides; then all collapsed, and the great shroud of the sea rolled on as it rolled five thousand years ago.

12. So we beat on, boats against the current, borne back ceaselessly into the past.

13. For all to be accomplished, for me to feel less lonely, all that remained to hope was that on the day of my execution there should be a huge crowd of spectators and that they should greet me with howls of derision.

14. None of them was ever more than a thin slice, held between the contiguous impressions that composed our life at that time; remembrance of a particular moment; and houses, roads, avenues are as fugitive, alas, as the years.

15. And it was like a confirmation of their new dreams and excellent intentions that at the end of their journey their daughter sprang to her feet first and stretched her young body.

16. I have been there before.

17. It is a far, far better thing that I do than I have ever done; it is a far, far better rest that I go to than I have ever known.

18. I took her hand in mind, and we went out of the ruined place; and, as the morning mists had risen long ago when I first left the forge, so the evening mists were rising now, and in all the broad expanse of tranquil light they showed to me, I saw no shadow of another parting from her.

J. *Great Expectations,* Charles Dickens

K. *The Great Gatsby,* F. Scott Fitzgerald

L. *The Stranger,* Albert Camus

M. *The Metamorphosis,* Franz Kafka

N. *Anna Karenina,* Leo Tolstoy

O. *Moby Dick,* Herman Melville

P. *Swann's Way,* Marcel Proust

Q. *Tale of Two Cities,* Charles Dickens

R. *Huckleberry Finn,* Mark Twain

# 12 SEPTEMBER

## *Please, Please Keep Coming*

A puzzle we insecure types never solve is, How can I get from where I am to where I want to be? As for me, I not only doubt whether I shall ever get where

I am going, but if I do get there I doubt whether anyone will be waiting to meet me. This insecurity is reflected in the verses that follow.

### CHERCHEZ, CHERCHEZ LA FEMME

The Beauty has drawn up a guide for the Beast
To Ninety-six Fifteen Thirteenth Street Northeast.
"You can't lose your way," she declares, "if you drive:
Follow Fifth, University, Interstate Five;
For Bellevue, cross toll bridge, pay thirty-five cents;
From then on it's easy as finding the Gents':

First Eighty-four, right; and then left, Twenty-four;
Then Ninety-four, right; left on Fourteen once more.
When you hit Ninety-seven, go only a block"
(The Beast is now suffering cultural shock)
"To Ninety-six Fifteen Thirteenth Street Northeast."
("Couldn't *you* come to *my* place instead?" begs the Beast.)
                                        —*W.R.E.*

### COME ANY OLD WAY

Come any old way, dear, or come any new way;
Expressway or parkway or freeway or throughway
Or pathway or skyway or highway or tollway;
Come any old way, dear, but come, come the whole way—

By pathway or railway or roadway or stairway
By driveway or crescent or circle or airway;
By midway, arterial, or, if you wish,
By plaza or plaisance or square or Boul' Mich'.

By boulevard, avenue, alley, ascension,
By detour or thoroughfare, rut or extension.
The way doesn't matter, but dear, perservere
By lane or by trail or by street, till you're here!
                                        —*W.R.E.*


# 13 SEPTEMBER

## *English Is Unamerican*

Though the differences between English and American are shrinking fast, some English usages still bemuse an American, and vice versa. If you score 100 percent in rendering the expressions below into American, you must have spent a while in England.

(1) Advert; (2) Arterial road, or trunk road; (3) Bathe (noun); (4) Beetroot; (5) Blackleg; (6) Booking clerk; (7) Box; (8) Break (school); (9) Cab rank; (10) Calendar (school or university); (11) Car park; (12) Carrier; (13) Catmint; (14) Chips; (15) Close season (for hunting); (16) Clothespeg; (17) Compere (of a show); (18) Cornet (of ice cream); (19) Crawling (taxi); (20) Crisp (noun); (21) Deputation; (22) Doss house; (23) Flex; (24) Friendly society; (25) Full stop; (26) Gingernut; (27) Goods van; (28) Hire purchase system, or hire system; (29) Holiday maker; (30) Hooter (automobile); (31) Indian rubber; (32) Inland mails; (33) Larder; (34) Leading article, or leader; (35) Left-luggage office, or room; (36) Market gardener; (37) Match (e.g., football); (38) Meat pie; (39) Mobile police; (40) Nib; (41) Page, or buttons; (42) Passage (in a private house); (43) Perambulator, pram, or baby coach; (44) Petrol; (45) Poste restante; (46) Public prosecutor; (47) Raider; (48) Rump (of beef); (49) Running expense, or working expense; (50) Season-ticket holder; (51) Sell up; (52) Service lift; (53) Shepherd's pie; (54) Shocker; (55) Shorthand typist, or writer; (56) Single ticket; (57) Soda bar; (58) Stomach warmer; (59) Stockist; (60) Studentship; (61) Swede, or horse turnip; (62) Telly; (63) Ticket of leave; (64) Tin; (65) Timber; (66) Torch; (67) Tramp (verb); (68) Troopship, or trooper; (69) Truncheon; (70) Try (in football); (71) Turning; (72) Underdone (meat); (73) Watch glass; (74) Witness box; (75) Wood wool.

# 14 SEPTEMBER

*Place Names in England*

### 1.

Ascott-under-Wychwood,
   Wotton under Edge,
The Cokers Down Ampney
   Cold Ashton Lower Swell;
   Bewdley, Stewkley,
   Birdlip Upper Slaughter;
Leatherhead, Mow Cop
   Great Gidding Pucknowle!

### 2.

Meyese Hampton Horspath
   Ashby-de-la-Zouch,
Great Missenden Woking
   Much Wenclock Crickhope Linn;

Thrapston, Bawtry,
Fencot Murcot Firkins:
Pucklechurch, Preesgweene
St. Blazeys Owl Pen!
—*Robert A. Fowkes*

The foregoing verse deals with places where Englishmen live. This one deals with the kinds of scent they wear:

I love that woodsy mensy scent
That just for mensy men is meant—
Some open-airsey moorsey gent
Named Sidney, Claud, or Cyril;
It's advertised so whimsy well
That peatsy smell should sell like hell
To Mumsy's precious: it's a smell
Makes flimsy men seem virile!
—*Pat Bullen*

# 15 SEPTEMBER

## *The Song of Snohomish*

William S. Wallace sent me a poem consisting entirely of baseball players' nicknames.

"You might have missed it," he wrote, "when it appeared in the *New York Times Magazine*."

I had not missed it; I had saved it. It will be around as long as baseball is. See how many of the players you can identify:

Catfish, Mudcat, Ducky, Coot,
The Babe, The Barber, The Blade, The Brat.
Windy, Dummy, Gabby, Hoot.
Big Train, Big Six, Big Ed, Fat.

Greasy, Sandy, Muddy, Rocky.
Bunions, Twinkletoes, Footsie, The Hat.
Fuzzy, Dizzy, Buddy, Cocky.
The Bull, The Stork, The Weasel, The Cat.

Schoolboy, Preacher,
Rajah, Duke,
General, Major, Spaceman, Spook.

Shoeless Joe, Cobra Joe, Bullet Joe.
Bing.

Old Hoss, Mule, Country, Rube.
Smokey Joe, Fireman Joe, Jersey Joe.
Ping.
Bulldog, Squirrel, Puddin' Head, Boob.

The Georgia Peach, The Fordham Flash.
The Flying Dutchman, Cot.
The People's Cherce, The Blazer, Crash.
The Staten Island Scot.

 Skeeter, Scooter,
 Pepper, Duster,
 Ebba, Bama, Booms, Buster.

Specs, The Grey Eagle, The Toy Cannon.
Tex.
The Earl of Snohomish, The Duke of Tralee.
Art the Great, Gorgeous George.
Ox, Double X.
The Nashville Narcissus, The Phantom, The Flea.

The Little Professor, The Iron Horse, Cap.
Iron Man, Iron Mike, Iron Hands, Hutch.
Jap, The Mad Russian, Irish, Swede, Nap.
Germany, Frenchy, Big Serb, Dutch,
 Turk.
 Tuck, Tug, Twig.
 Spider, Birdie, Rabbit, Pig.

Three-Finger, No-Neck, The Knuck, The Lip.
Casey, Dazzy, Hippity, Zim.
Flit, Bad Henry, Fat Freddie, Flip.
Jolly Cholly, Sunny Jim.

 Shag, Schnozz,
 King Kong, Klu.

Boog, Buzz,
Boots, Bump, Boo.

Baby Doll, Angel Sleeves, Pep, Sliding Billy.
Buttercup, Bollicky, Boileryard, Juice,
Colby Jack, Dauntless Dave, Cheese, Gentle Willie,
Trolley Line, Wagon Tongue, Rough, What's the Use.

 Ee-yah,
 Poosh 'Em Up,
 Skoonj, Slats, Ski.

Ding Dong,
Ding-a-Ling,
Dim Dom, Dee.

Bubbles, Dimples, Cuddles, Pinky.
Poison Ivy, Vulture, Stinky.

Jigger, Jabbo
Jolting Joe
Blue Moon
Boom Boom
Bubba
Bo.

—*William S. Wallace*

# 16 SEPTEMBER

## *Time Out of Mind*

*Time* used to pun as compulsively as hayfever victims sneeze. On the world of art, for instance:

- What did the little boy with Montezuma's revenge say? "Daddy, I've got to Gauguin."
- What do you do with the barrel so we'll have a barrel of fun? Rouault.

In the 1972 primaries *Time* took a fancy to presidential aspirant Edmund Muskie, apparently on the basis of his comment in New Hampshire that "the state cannot be taken for granite." (He turned out to be a prophet.) The newsmagazine loved Adlai Stevenson for describing Barry Goldwater as "a man who thinks everything will be better in the rear future." It also hailed the common nineteenth-century epithet for Prime Minister Disraeli: "England's Jew d'esprit."

In *Time*, Dorothy Parker "was always chasing Rimbauds." Alexander Woollcott knew "a cat hospital where they charge four dollars a weak purr." Peter De Vries dreamed "a female deer was chasing a male deer. I woke up and realized it was a doe trying to make a fast buck."

The personal lives of the Ottoman sultans, to *Time*, "were mainly a matter of bed and bored." Ibrahim, who ordered his 1,001 concubines trussed, weighted, and tossed into the sea, is denominated "Harem-scare-'m Ibrahim."

From *Time*'s obituary on Oscar Levant:

Whenever opportunity knocked, Levant immediately bit its hand.
Upon greeting George Gershwin, for example, Oscar went Wilde:

"George, if you had it to do all over again, would you fall in love with yourself?"

The late humorist S. J. Perelman, visiting Taipei, found himself "surrounded by a draggle of highly painted professional ladies who obviously wanted more than his autograph. Only with some difficulty did the world traveler extricate himself from their importunities, but he emerged with wit unblunted. 'It was a case,' he mused to a friend on the way back to his hotel, 'of the tail dogging the wag.'"

# 17 September

## Snallygaster IX

From the *Valley Register*, Middletown, Maryland, March 5, 1909:

### EMMITSBURG SAW THE GREAT SNALLYGASTER

#### It Ate a Coal Bin Empty and Then Spit Fire

##### LOOKED LIKE A "COON-SCOOPER"

#### Its Snout Resembled a Silo and Its Mouth Leaked a Fluid Like Melted Brimstone— Flew Off with a Well

It was bad enough to hear that the Snallygaster was anywhere in the State, but it is worse to know that it has been right here in the Emmitsburg District. Ed Brown was sitting on the bench outside the Railroad Station, reading the "Life of E. H. Harriman" and waiting for the evening train to come in, when the monster seized him and would have flown off with him had not Bill Snider, who dashed up in his automobile, grabbed Brown by the foot, which broke his suspenders and he dropped to the ground. Ghostlike wings beat the air and fire singed the pike.

"It looked like a giraffe on roller skates," said Mr. Snider. "Its beak was serrated with great tusks and between them lay the partly consumed flesh of a man. Its snout resembled a silo and from the corners of its mouth leaked a fluid like melted brimstone."

As the Snallygaster passed over Emmitsburg, deputy game warden Capt. Norman Hoke, aware of the danger, showed his badge and backed by the full authority of the law, ordered it from the County.

John Glass, who was returning from a sale at Bridgeport, where he had purchased a well, threw the newly acquired well at the

Snallygaster with such good aim that he is now minus a few ready-made holes, for the well passed over the Snallygaster's huge snout. When last seen in the woods to the west of Taneytown, the monster wore the well like a nose-ring.

The End

# 18 SEPTEMBER

### I Dreamed the Devil's Wife Proposed a Game

A number of bodily parts, Don Davidson reminds me, show up in the language as metaphors. Dancers *heel and toe:* sails *belly* in the wind. But I really needed no reminder; this trick of the language had already undone me in the nightmare recalled below.

> I dreamed that I was kidnapped by the Devil,
> And since I couldn't raise the ransom money
> The Devil's wife proposed a game to free me.
> She said, "If you will chat a little with me,
> And never mention any fleshly member,
> I'll see that dear Nick lets you out of Hell;
> But any part you name is forfeit to me."
> "You've got a lot of cheek," I said, "to think
> That I would trust you, or believe your mouthings.
> I know what's passing through your head; I've watched you
> Go nose among the relicts of the damned
> And elbow through their innermost recesses.
> I've watched you when you kneed those fallen angels
> And fingered hapless sinners for your husband.
> If I were better heeled, I'd pay my ransom
> And hold my tongue. And even as things are,
> I'm not about to neck with you, or even
> To foot a measure with you on the dance floor.
> A woman of your kidney's hard to stomach.
> Still, when it comes to using words, I figure
> That I can stay abreast of any devil.
> If you aren't ribbing—if you'll swear by Hell
> That you will toe the line, and knuckle under
> When fairly beaten by me—then I'll shoulder
> The full responsibility if any
> Injuncted reference escapes my lips.
> But come—we've jawed and chinned enough already;
> I've met your terms. I think I'll ankle off now
> And thumb a truck-ride back to Oysterville.
> (Have I said something wrong? You eye me strangely.)"

*I woke, and found I had no cheek, or mouth;*
*No head; no nose; no elbow, knee, or finger;*
*No heel; no tongue; no neck; no foot; no kidney;*
*No stomach, breast, or rib, or toe, or knuckle;*
*No shoulder, lips, or jaw, or chin, or ankle;*
*No back; no eye.*
*I wonder why.*

—W.R.E.

# 19 September

## Reas'ning but to Err

Pope says man is ". . . born but to die, and reas'ning but to err." The author of the following essay has concluded that some of our errors are largely typographical:

FIRST, there are incomprehensible blunders:
'xbl gvtrpjklhjtrkeosixl . . .'

SECOND, some blunders, much like the first, place gibberish in a context wherein a certain sense emerges. Here, for instance, is a movie review culled from the Washington (D.C.) *Daily News:*

Sitting in the middle of the bed, being wheeled across London by three attentive young men, Nancy falls in love with the conveyance. Need I say what the outcome is? Kfln. Shrd cmfw cmfw cm.

THIRD, there are changes in the form of a word which result in the complete reversal of the writer's intention, as witness this sentence from the FBI Law Enforcement Bulletin:

We would hope that a record-breaking summer of strife and lawfulness can be averted.

FOURTH, the linotypist, we presume, gets the lines from two or more stories mixed up, as in this article, quoted in full, from the Davenport (Iowa) *Times-Democrat:*

DRINKING NOTE: For a mild and tasty appetizer, try three dog, put a drop of castor oil in each eye to protect them from soap-parts of tomato juice with one part sherry.

FIFTH, there are those messages that execute an about-face for the want of one intended letter, as we can see in this headline from the Little Rock (Ark.) *Democrat:*

### DECLINE IN MORALITY
### SAID TREAT TO U. S.

SIXTH, there are errors that carry a self-fulfilling message, like this headline from the Toronto (Ont.) *Financial Post:*

### DEFECIT BUDGETS LIKE LIQUOR:
### TOO MANY AND YOU GET STUPID

SEVENTH, we have writing from which a single letter has been dropped, as in our fifth category, only this time the effect is not to reverse the intended meaning, but rather to transform it into a wildly hilarious statement. As evidence, I give you the following article, quoted *in toto,* from the Milwaukee *Journal:*

> Southern Michigan's peasant population, now in the midst of its nesting season, is up about 25% over the spring of 1964.

EIGHTH, we have what is either an inspired solecism or an intentional twist from a bored reporter. Whatever the cause, the effect is a Spoonerism that makes sense, as in this UPI wire lead, which must go down in reportorial annals as the gayest of all attributions:

> According to informed White Horse souses . . .

NINTH, there is the situation where, because of a linotypist's peccadillo with just one letter, a crucial word shuffles off its mortal coil and the whole sense of the article reverses itself and, not content with this alone, permits the entrance of an otherwise unuttered truth. This sample is from a Reuters article, dateline Harrogate, England, May 29, 1967. The article begins by stating that the overwhelming majority of 500 headmasters at the National Association of Head Teachers meeting voted to continue the caning of their captive students. One headmaster justified his use of the cane, and with help from the linotypist it came out this way:

> But we are not living in Utopia. Creating, lying, stealing and pornographic scribbling still distresses us, and what are the remedies to be when kindness fails?

We must agree with this headmaster: if there is any certain remedy for creating, it must be a sound thrashing with a cane.

Of the same sort must be this headline from the Nyack (N.Y.) *Rockland County Journal-News:*

### GLUE FACTORIES HAVE STOPPED

### USING OLD HAGS FOR ADHESIVES

TENTH, there is writing that is not incorrect in any literal sense, but is ambiguous to the point of being ludicrous. These we cannot call typos, since, presumably, the linotypist rendered it precisely as it was given to him. For instance, an Iowa newspaper recently headlined a story about the marriage of a boy from Manly, Iowa, to a girl from a town named Fertile, in this way:

### MANLY BOY MARRIES FERTILE GIRL

An Illinois newspaper couldn't resist this headline about nuptials between a boy from Oblong, Illinois and a girl from Normal, Illinois:

### OBLONG BOY MARRIES NORMAL GIRL
*—Temple G. Porter*

I imagine Mr. Porter would put this news item from the Los Angeles *Times* in a category of "remarkably precise dating":

Engineers surveying for a railroad in Northern Turkestan have uncovered the skeleton of a massive saurian that must have passed away 3,000,000 years ago last Friday.

# 20 SEPTEMBER

## *The Naughty Preposition*

I have a friend, one of the best direct-mail copywriters in the country, whose rigid rule for his children is that they must never end a sentence with a preposition. But some sentences are ridiculous precisely because they fail to end with prepositions.

And why end a sentence with just one preposition? Why not use several? The late Mr. Bishop did—and his judgment was excellent:

> I lately lost a preposition;
>    It hid, I thought, beneath my chair.
> And angrily I cried: "Perdition!
>    Up from out of in under there!"
>
> Correctness is my vade mecum,
>    And straggling phrases I abhor;
> And yet I wondered: "What should he come
>    Up from out of in under for?"
>            *—Morris Bishop*

# 21 SEPTEMBER

### *Sight Rhymes, Slight Rhymes*

Alliance does not rhyme with dalliance, a fact known to lovers as well as poets. (This is because the Lord our God is a jealous god, who frowns on fooling around.) Alliance and dalliance are sight rhymes—words that rhyme to the eye but not the ear. The impossibility of using sight rhymes in verse is demonstrated in these two stanzas:

> I am just a humble student,
> I don't want to seem impudent;
> Poems are not what I type.
> I appreciate human glory,
> Drama, fiction, and history,
> But I cannot follow your recipe.

> Mine is not a playful nature;
> I am rational and mature,
> Working points of logic through.
> No; my verse would sound too strident,
> All its hollowness evident.
> As I clank and grind and huff and cough.
> —Hedya Pachter

# 22 SEPTEMBER

### *Much Ado About Malapropisms*

Simpletons were malapropping before the word was invented—none to better effect than Constable Dogberry, who here instructs his watch in *Much Ado About Nothing:*

> *Dogberry* (to First Watchman): You are thought here to be the most senseless and fit man for the constable of the watch, therefore bear you the lantern. This is your charge: you shall comprehend all vagrom men; you are to bid any man stand, in the prince's name.
> *Watch.* How, if a'well not stand?
> *Dogb.* Why, then, take no note of him, but let him go; and presently call the rest of the watch together, and thank God you are rid of a knave. . . . You shall also make no noise in the streets; for, for the watch to babble and to talk is most tolerable and not to be endured.
> *Sec. Watch.* We will rather sleep than talk; we know what belongs to a watch.

*Dogb*. . . . Well, you are to call at all the alehouses, and bid those that are drunk get them to bed.

*Watch*. How if they will not?

*Dogb*. Why, then, let them alone till they are sober; if they make you not then the better answer, you may say they are not the men you took them for.

*—William Shakespeare*

# 23 SEPTEMBER

## *I Saw a Peacock with a Fiery Tail*

To make sense of this exercise in punctuation, insert commas (or, as I prefer, semicolons) to taste: " . . . brimful of ale / I saw a Venice glass"; etc.

> I saw a peacock with a fiery tail
> I saw a blazing comet drop down hail
> I saw a cloud wrapped with ivy round
> I saw an oak creep on along the ground
> I saw a pismire swallow up a whale
> I saw the sea brimful of ale
> I saw a Venice glass full fathom deep
> I saw a well full of men's tears that weep
> I saw red eyes all of a flaming fire
> I saw a house bigger than the moon and higher
> I saw the sun at twelve o'clock at night
> I saw the man that saw this wondrous sight.
> *—From The Westminster Drollery, 1671.*
> *Author Unknown*

# 24 SEPTEMBER

## *Word and Line Palindromes*

Palindromes of words are easier to create than palindromes of letters, and more likely to make sense. Some pleasing specimens:*

From *Word Ways*:
• So patient a doctor to doctor a patient so.
• Girl, bathing on Bikini, eyeing boy, finds boy eyeing bikini on bathing-girl.
• You can cage a swallow, can't you, but you can't swallow a cage, can you?

---

*The *Word Ways* selections are by J. A. Lindon; the others, in order, by David Phillips, William Hodson, G. J. Blundell, Naomi Marks, and Gerard Benson.

From *The New Statesman:*
- Bores are people that say that people are bores.
- Does milk machinery milk does?
- God knows man. What is doubtful is what man knows God.
- Women understand men; few men understand women.
- "Come, shall I stroke your 'whatever' darling? I am so randy." "So am I darling. Whatever your stroke, I shall come."

Suggestive that last one may be, but it is too clever to omit.

Using not the letter of the word but the entire line as a unit, J. A. Lindon came up with a palindromic triolet:

### AS I WAS PASSING . . .

As I was passing near the jail
I met a man, but hurried by.
His face was ghastly, grimly pale.
He had a gun. I wondered why
He had. A gun? I wondered . . . why,
His face was *ghastly!* Grimly pale,
I met a man, but hurried by,
As I was passing near the jail.

# 25 September

### Address Unknown

James de Kay, like Doctor Emmanuel, has a very big head with brains inside, and what happens inside those brains is likely to be a question like this: If a Spaniard finds Los Angeles in his atlas, does he assume that an American atlas would say "The Angels"?

This verse is for James:

Sing tra la la for Red Stick LA
  And Holy Faith New Mex.;
For Earring WA sound loud huzzah;
  Cheer Body of Christ Tex.
Raise roundelay for Monks IA,
  To Yellow TX sing;
But if you send your mail that way,
  Your mail will stray,
I'll bet you anything.

—*W.R.E.*

# 26 SEPTEMBER

### Tear-O-Lear-O-Loo

These by the king of nonsense:

### ALPHABET

A  tumbled down, and hurt his Arm, against a bit of wood.
B  said, "My Boy, O do not cry; it cannot do you good!"
C  said, "A Cup of Coffee hot can't do you any harm."
D  said, "A Doctor should be fetched, and he would cure the arm."
E  said, "An Egg beat up with milk would quickly make him well."
F  said, "A Fish, if broiled, might cure, if only by the smell."
G  said, "Green Gooseberry fool, the best of cures I hold."
H  said, "His Hat should be kept on, to keep him from the cold."
I  said, "Some Ice upon his head will make him better soon."
J  said, "Some Jam, if spread on bread, or given in a spoon."
K  said, "A Kangaroo is here,—this picture let him see."
L  said, "A Lamp pray keep alight, to make some barley tea."
M  said, "A Mulberry or two might give him satisfaction."
N  said, "Some Nuts, if rolled about, might be a slight attraction."
O  said, "An Owl might make him laugh, if only it would wink."
P  said, "Some Poetry might be read aloud, to make him think."
Q  said, "A Quince I recommend,—a Quince, or else a Quail."
R  said, "Some Rats might make him move, if fastened by their tail."
S  said, "A Song should now be sung, in hopes to make him laugh."
T  said, "A Turnip might avail, if sliced or cut in half."
U  said, "An Urn, with water hot, place underneath his Chin!"
V  said, "I'll stand upon a chair, and play a Violin."
W  said, "Some Whisky-Whizzgigs fetch, some marbles and a ball."
X  said, "Some double XX ale would be the best of all."
Y  said, "Some Yeast mixed up with salt would make a perfect plaster!"
Z  said, "Here is a box of Zinc! Get in, my little master.
    We'll shut you up! We'll nail you down! We will, my little master!
    We think we've all heard quite enough of this your sad disaster!"
                                                    —Edward Lear

### COLD ARE THE CRABS (Sonnet)

Cold are the crabs that crawl on yonder hills,
Colder the cucumbers that grow beneath,
And colder still the brazen chops that wreathe
     The tedious gloom of philosophic pills!
For when the tardy film of nectar fells
The ample bowls of demons and of men,
There lurks the feeble mouse, the homely hen,

And there the porcupine with all her quills.
Yet much remains—to weave a solemn strain
That lingering sadly—slowly dies away,
Daily departing with departing day
A pea green gamut on a distant plain
When wily walruses in Congress met—
　　Such such is life—

### A LETTER TO EVELYN BARING

Thrippsy pillivinx,
　Inky tinky pobbleboskle abblesquabs?—
Flosky! beebul trimble flosky!—Okul
scratchabibblebongibo, viddle squibble tog-a-tog,
ferrymoyassity amsky flamsky ramsky damsky
　croclefether squiggs.

　　　　　　　　　　　　Flinkywisty pomm,
　　　　　　　　　　　　　　Slushypipp

# 27 SEPTEMBER

## Wacky Wordies

In a rebus, one is supposed to discern a familiar phrase, saying, cliché, or name from each arrangement of letters and/or digits. In the rebuses below, Box 1a depicts the phrase "Just between you and me," while Box 1B shows "Hitting below the belt."

|   | a | b | c | d | e | f |
|---|---|---|---|---|---|---|
| 1 | you just me | belt hitting | lo head heels ve | V I O L E T s | A B E DUMR | agb |
| 2 | cry m i l k | -c ᴣ▭-+ | Symphon | ejddeǝuıd cake | arrest you're | timing tim ing |
| 3 | O TV | night fly | s T I N K | injury + insult | r o rail d | my own heart a person |
| 4 | at the · of on | dothepe | wear long | strch groound | lu cky | the market |

# 28 SEPTEMBER

## Th Hrglphs F Th Nw Yrk Tms

Only the consonants were represented in early Egyptian script. The time may have come to revive this system.* Lt s s hw tpcl Nw Yrk Tms dtrl wld rd wtht vwls:†

### PKNG ND TWN

Th prgrss md n Mrcn rltns wth Chn snc 1971 hs bn drmtc nd t hs ld t rptd spcltn bt th pssblt f cmpltng th prcss b stblshng fll dplmtc rltns, clrl dsrbl mv. Th nl rl bstcl hs bn nblt t gr bt Twn.

Wht md th brkthrgh f 1971-72 pssbl ws Pkng's dcsn tht th Twn qstn ws nt rgnt. Th rslt, drng Prsdnt Nxn's 1972 vst, ws "splt" r prtll dsgrd cmmnq. Pkg xprssd sprt vw bt Twn, sttng tht t ws "th crcl qstn bstrctng th nrmlztn f rltns" nd mkng fv spfc cmplnts bt Mrcn plc thr. Th mplctn ws tht 11 fv wld hv t b crrctd bfr fll dplmtc rltns cld b stblshd.

The style of the foregoing may seem a trifle dense, but the message is as clear as in most editorials, and shorter, which, on balance, must be to the good.

Nd jst thnk f ll th nwsprnt tht wld b svd!

# 29 SEPTEMBER

## Profanity of Flowers and Fish

George Johnson says an eighteenth-century English scholar silenced the abuse of Billingsgate fishwives by thundering: "Parallelepipedon!" (A parallelepipedon in geometry is a regular solid bounded by six plane surfaces—a cube, for example.) The names of flowers and shellfish can be as alarming: "You false hellbore! You

| Flowers | Shellfish |
|---|---|
| You devil's-bit scabious! | You hairy mopalia! |
| You dwarf spurge! | You denticulate donax! |
| You lousewort! | You speckled tegula! |
| You henbit dead nettle! | You wentletrap! |
| You swine's cress! | You measled cowry! |
| You pignut! | You false cerith! |
| You moneywort loosestrife! | You deadman's fingers! |
| You creeping toadflax! | You bent-nose macoma! |

* Charles Kingsley made a start when he introduced Professor Ptthmllnsprts in "The Water Babies."
† See 11 March for a similar suggestion to the *Reader's Digest*.

viper's bug loss! You wart-necked piddock!" Or the names of insects: "You sandbug! Spittlebug! Stinkbug! Louse!"
Recommended curses:

# 30 SEPTEMBER

### If You Are the Doer, Am I the Doee?

Logic, in grammar, leads to trouble:

> Caudated to a verb, the suffix -er
> Denotes the agent setting things a-stir:
> Thus, *runner, almoner.* The suffix -ee
> Denotes the done-to, as in *legatee.*

> Though I have known exceptions, to be sure,
> To suffix -ee (if not to suffix -er),
> The pairing's elegant, and in my view
> Deserves extension. Hence I give to you:

> *Squander* and *squandee* and *launder* and *laundee,*
> *Thinker* and *thinkee* and *ponder* and *pondee,*
> *Worker* and *workee* and *singer* and *singee,*
> *Cougher* and *coughee* and *bringer* and *bringee.*

> A *squander*'s a wastrel; when he is bereft,
> It's fair to assume that a *squandee* is left;
> If I be the *buyer,* the *buyee* you'll be;
> If I am the *sleeper,* you'll be the *sleepee.*

> So *hearer* to *hearee* and *writer* to *writee,*
> And *winner* to *winnee,* and *fighter* to *fightee.*
> It is you I *prefer,* so you're my *prefee;*
> And when you *inter* me, I'll be your *intee.*
> —W.R.E.

### HAD I BUT NUDE

We know the meaning of *butt,* as in the butt of a joke; we know the meaning of *nude,* as in nude beaches; we know the meaning of *seed;* we know the meaning of *dude,* as in dude ranch; we know the meaning of *deed,* as in a deed to property, or an infamous deed. But combine these in a certain way and the meanings change:

> Had I butt nude,
> Had I but seed,
> Would I have dude
> The dids I deed?
> —W.R.E.

# OCTOBER

## 1 OCTOBER

*The Flying Pyramid*

I
AM
THE
WELL
KNOWN
LEGEND
HAUNTED
WANDERER
ENDLESSLY
CELEBRATED
MASTERFULLY
IMMORTALIZED
TRADITIONALLY
UNDERSTANDABLE
NOTWITHSTANDING
INCOMPREHENSIBLE
QUASIOTHERWORLDLY
MUMBOJUMBOINFESTED
CLOSETMACHIAVELLIAN
MACROCEPHALICULTURAL
PSEUDOANTHROPOLOGICAL
PSYCHOANALYTICORIENTED
ULTRAPATHOLOGICOCENTRIC
SUPERTERRESTRIALDEPENDENT
CRYPTOANTIHUMANITARIANIST
MYTHOGRAPHICOSCHOLASTICISM

—*Richard Wincor*

# 2 OCTOBER

## *Ballad of Soporific Absorption*

Told that General Grant was a whiskey drinker, Lincoln said he wished he could send that whiskey to his other generals. I don't know Sir John's favorite drink, but any light versifier could use a few cases of it.

Ho! Ho! Yes! It's very all well,
    You may drunk I am think, but I tell you I'm not,
I'm as sound as a fiddle and fit as a bell,
    And stable quite ill to see what's what.
    I under *do* stand you surprise a got
When I headed my smear with gooseberry jam:
    And I've swallowed, I grant, a beer of lot—
But I'm not so think as you drunk I am.

Can I liquor my stand? Why, yes, like hell!
    I care not how many a tossed I've pot,
I shall stralk quite weight and not yutter an ell,
    My feech will not spalter the least little jot:
    If you knownly had own!—well, I gave him a dot
And I said to him, 'Sergeant, I'll come like a lamb—'
    The floor it seems like a storm in a yacht,
But I'm not so think as you drunk I am.

For example, to prove it I'll tale you a tell—
    I once knew a fellow named Apricot—
I'm sorry, I just chair over a fell—
    A trifle—this chap, on a very day hot—
    If I hadn't consumed that last whisky of tot!—
As I said now, this fellow, called Abraham—
    Ah? One more? Since it's you! Just a do me will spot—
But I'm not so think as you drunk I am.

ENVOI

So, Prince, you suggest I've bolted my shot?
Well, like what you say, and soul your damn!
    I'm an upple litset by the talk you rot—
But I'm not so think as you drunk I am.

—*John C. Squire*

# 3 OCTOBER

## *Pinking the Politician*

How the art of political insult has decayed! I recall no memorable ad hominem hereabouts since Clare Boothe Luce explained Senator Wayne Morse's political positions as a result of his having fallen from a horse and landed on his head. Even this was more a roundhouse swing with a broadsword than a precise lunge with a rapier.

In general, the English pink more deftly than Americans. Benjamin Disraeli remarked that a traveler, learning that Lord John Russell was leader of the House of Commons, "may well begin to comprehend how the Egyptians worshiped an insect." Disraeli used his rival, William Gladstone, to illustrate the difference between a misfortune and a calamity: "If Gladstone fell into the Thames, it would be a misfortune. But if someone dragged him out again, it would be a calamity." (Gladstone, for his part, once said of bishops appointed by him who voted against him in the House of Lords: "Have they forgotten their Maker?" But he was not pinking; he was perfectly sincere.)

Pinkest and most cherubical of pinkers was Winston Churchill. He once described Clement Attlee as "a modest man with much to be modest about," and again as "a sheep in sheep's clothing." He credited Ramsay MacDonald with "the gift of compressing the largest amount of words into the smallest amount of thoughts." He said of Stanley Baldwin, "He occasionally stumbles over the truth, but he always hastily picks himself up and hurries on as if nothing had happened." And of Sir Stafford Cripps, known for arrogance, he remarked: "There, but for the grace of God, goes God."

# 4 OCTOBER

## On the Indispensability of Encyc. Brit.

Turning to the *Britannica* for a clearer understanding of SEDITION, I remarked with some surprise that the next entry was SEDUCTION. Seduction has occasioned a considerable body of law in the United Kingdom:

> Thy characters I daily scan,
> *Encyclopaedia Britan.;*
> My scanty knowledge I accrete
> At thy august Britannic feet.

> Behold! but now I read an entry
> Invaluable to the gentry:
> A sober, step-by-step instruction
> On statutes governing SEDUCTION

> (Defined here as a pleasant trade
> Between a Maker and his Maid,
> Wherein the Maker reprehens-
> ibly *suggests;* the Maid *consents*).

> If you are under twelve, my fault
> Is rude felonious assault;

Think twice, love, ere you whisper "Yes":
Consent deprives you of redress.
*Volenti non injuria fit,*
Points out *Encyclopaedy Brit.*

Belowstairs, innocent coition
May bring about indisposition.
Be warned, if awkward labor pains
Delay your cleaning out the drains,

Your master may your lover sue
For daily chores undone by you:
An action lies at law if lusting
Leaves furniture in need of dusting.

If you are hired to make my bed
And wind up made in it instead,
I'm legally immune unless
Our deal required that you undress.
But if I wait until you've teened,
Then I have only misdemeaned.

For facts like these am I addic-
ted to *Britannica Encyc.:*
Seduction scarcely is my speed;
Still, thanks, *Britan. Encyclopaed.!*
                                        —W.R.E.

# 5 OCTOBER

## Singular Plurals

Axes is the plural form of both ax and axis; bases the plural form of both base and basis. Wherefore:

### 1.

Paul Bunyan swung his ax, with view
To sundering the globe in two;
The ax that made that mighty probe
Stuck at the axis of the globe.
Pray tell, Larousse, pray tell, Bowditch,
Of those two axes, which was which?

### 2.

The base of any basis from the basis of its base
Is easy to distinguish in the ordinary case;

But give them plural number, and it's *bases* that you get;
Don't try to disentangle them; you'll only get upset.
—W.R.E.

Another point of view on plurals:

Two staffs make staves;
Two giraffes don't make giraves.
One giraffe
Makes one laugh.
—David McCord

Which reminds me: *pease* was once both singular and plural. Because it just naturally sounded plural, the singular shrank to *pea*.

# 6 OCTOBER

## Unsafe at Ant Speed

One letter is changed in each of these passages from a *New York* magazine competition—and oh, the difference to Mary Ann Madden!

- Why can't a woman be more like a mat?
- Wish you were her.
- I've got you under my ski.
- I thank whatever gods may be / For my unconquerable soup.
- Small apartment for runt.
- Don't feel the animals.
- God help those who help themselves.
- A rabbi's foot brings good luck.
- . . . and the Cabots talk only to cod.
- I hate to see a grown man dry.
- Welfare Department, Pity of New York.
- Caution: Misuse of these pills could prove fetal.
- I was the product of a dating mother.
- Rome wasn't built in a bay.
- Anyone who mates dogs and babies can't be all bad.
- Unsafe at ant speed.

# 7 OCTOBER

## Yknits Seiknip

A "Stinky Pinkies" definition elicits two words that rhyme; "Birth at the North Pole," for instance, emerges as "shivery delivery." In the variant below, the second word reverses the spelling of the first; a "buddy on your knee" is "lap pal." The parenthesized figure in each line is the number of letters in the word. Proceed:

1. a crazy female animal (3)
2. manufactured a Dutch cheese (4)
3. a gadid veterinarian (3)
4. reimbursed for a baby's fanny cover (6)
5. a stag that feeds on bamboolike grass (4)
6. spoil a male sheep (3)
7. exceptional guy in Nevada city (4)
8. hero of California town (4)
9. in the style of Esau or his descendants (4)
10. summary description of a certain horse (5)
11. criticize a golf score (3)
12. rework a German river (4)
13. a grain of the Chinese "way" (3)
14. Pythias' wandering friend (5)
15. blue jeans material taken from the earth (5)
16. bite from a small point (3)
17. love, Italian style (4)
18. a moray on the sheltered side (3)
19. hoarfrost on an Arab prince (4)
20. a platelike creature (6)

—*Boris Randolph*

# 8 OCTOBER

## *Opposite Proverbs*

1. A man's reach should exceed his grasp.
   A bird in the hand is worth two in the bush.
2. Haste makes waste.
   He who hesitates is lost.
3. Above all, to thine own self be true.
   When in Rome, do as the Romans do.
4. It is never too late to learn.
   You can't teach an old dog new tricks.
5. Good things come in small packages.
   The bigger, the better.
6. There is no point in beating a dead horse.
   If at first you don't succeed, try, try again.
7. He who hesitates is lost.
   Act in haste, repent at leisure.

8. Two is company, three is a crowd.
   The more, the merrier.
9. . . . do it well or not at all.
   Half a loaf is better than none.
10. Nothing ventured, nothing gained.
    Better safe than sorry.
11. Never judge a book by its cover.
    Clothes make the man.
12. Out of sight, out of mind.
    Absence makes the heart grow fonder.
13. Many hands make light work.
    Too many cooks spoil the broth.
14. Never send a boy to do a man's job.
    . . . and a little child shall lead them.
15. Actions speak louder than words.
    The pen is mightier than the sword.
16. Never change horses in mid-stream.
    Variety is the spice of life.
17. Silence is golden.
    The squeaky wheel gets the grease.
18. Practice makes perfect.
    All work and no play makes Jack a dull boy.
19. A penny saved is a penny earned.
    The love of money is the root of all evil.
    —*M. H. Greenblatt*

# 9 OCTOBER

## *Even Homer Nods*

I know *Schadenfreude* when I encounter solecisms by competent writers. It is comforting to know I do not err alone. For instance:

• WHO-WHOM
  "After her in his affections came Selwyn, whom he soon saw was the most intelligent of the whole litter."—*David Garnett, Lady into Fox*
  "He wanted to do a book on the Hungarian poet Petöfi, whom he had convinced himself was of a stature with Pushkin."—*George Steiner, "An Appreciation of Edmund Wilson"*
  (If the two writers had set apart their interjected clauses—in the first case "he soon saw"—and in the second "he had convinced himself"—by commas, they would not have made those mistakes.)

• DO-DOES
  "The great body of Americans do not want Detroit to suffer, does not expect the impossible, and . . ."—*Wall Street Journal editorial*

(One may argue about whether a singular verb used in a plural sense should take a plural or a singular verb, but it can't take both in succession.)

- REDUNDANCY
"Few other Western journalists know Egypt more intimately than Cairo Bureau Chief Wilton Wynn."—*Letter from the publisher,* Time
(Strike that "other," *Time.*)

- I AS OBJECT OF A PREPOSITION
"Harvard must maintain high standards that make people like Henry Rosovsky and I work twice as hard."—*from a talk by Derek Bok, president of Harvard University*
(President Bok knows that the pronoun is the object of the preposition "like" and has to be in the accusative: "People like me [not I] work twice as hard.")

- IS, ARE
"The revelations of modern biology is a remarkable human and scientific story."—*Jeremy Bernstein reviewing* The Eighth Day of Creation *in the New York Times Book Review*
(Revelations *are.* A remarkable human and scientific story *is*—but that is another remarkable human and scientific story.)

# 10 OCTOBER

## *What Is the Question?*

I am told that this game was popular at the White House during the Thousand Days of J. F. Kennedy. The answers come first:

1. Dr. Livingston, I presume.
2. Oh, about 20 drachmas a week.
3. No strings attached.
4. February 29th, for example.
5. Chromatic scales.
6. A Greek letter.
7. Strontium 90, Carbon 14.
8. Around the world in 80 days.
9. George Washington slept here.
10. From the rockbound coast of Maine.
11. Stork Club.
12. Poetic justice.

All right—what are the questions?

# 11 OCTOBER

## The MAD Poetry Round Robin

If the writers for *MAD* are not insane geniuses, at least they are genially insane. One of them likes to filter famous authors' verses through other famous authors' pens, with results like those below:*

### IF POE'S "THE RAVEN" WERE WRITTEN
### BY JOYCE KILMER

I think that I shall never hear
A raven who is more sincere
Than that one tapping at my door
Who's ever saying, "Nevermore;"
A raven who repeats his words
Until I think I'm for the birds;
A raven who, I must assume,
Will dirty up my living-room;
A raven fond of bugs and worms
With whom I'm on the best of terms;
Let other poets praise a tree—
A raven's good enough for me!

### IF KILMER'S "TREES" WERE WRITTEN
### BY JOHN MASEFIELD

*I must go up in a tree again
    and sit where the bullfinch warbles;
Where the squirrel runs up and down a limb
    and the owl has lost his marbles;
And the squawks and hoots and chirps and squeaks
    that all the birds are making
Fill the air around so I can't hear
    the branch beneath me breaking!*

*I must go up in a tree again,
    from where people look like ants,
And all I ask is a branch that's smooth
    so I won't rip my pants;
And a dozen bugs running up my leg,
    and the sap so sticky,
And the cooing doves and the screaming crows
    making messes icky;*

*See also 21 April.

## IF MASEFIELD'S "SEA FEVER" WERE WRITTEN
## BY CARL SANDBURG

*Fish Tank for the World,*
*Shark Breeder, Maker of Waves,*
*Lousy with Herring and the Nation's Saltcellar;*
*Briny, bottomless, undrinkable,*
*Home of the Big Flounder:*
*They tell me you are stormy, and I believe them;*
*    for I have crossed you on a tramp steamer*
*    and have lost my lunch at the poop rail.*
*And they tell me you are messy, and my reply is:*
*    Yes, it is true I have swum in your surf and*
*    have emerged yecchy, with seaweed.*
*And having answered, I ask myself: Why am I not*
*    writing a poem about Chicago instead of a poem*
*    about the Fish Tank for the World, Shark Breeder,*
*    Maker of Waves, Home of the Big Flounder, and*
*    Saltcellar to the Nation?*

## IF CARL SANDBURG'S "CHICAGO" WERE WRITTEN
## BY RUDYARD KIPLING

You can talk of Mandalay,
Of Calcutta or Bombay,
    Where the heat'll make a fuzzy-wuzzy fry;
But if to drink you're driven
And don't give a damn for livin'
    Then you oughta hit the road for windy Chi.

It's a town where hoods and thugs
Like to send a dozen slugs
    Right through a copper pretty as you please;
Where the breezes blow like hell,
And that awful stockyard smell
    Is enough to bring a blighter to his knees.

For it's Chi! Chi! Chi!
Guns are shootin' and I'm just a passerby!
Though your buildings may be pretty,
You can keep your bloomin' city
'Cause I'm headin' back to Injia, windy Chi!
                                    —*Frank Jacobs*

There is no room for the rest of the round robins: "If Kipling's 'Gunga Din' Were Written By Clement Clarke Moore"; "If Moore's 'The Night Before Christmas' Were Written By Robert W. Service"; "If Service's 'The Shooting of

Dan McGrew' Were Written By Henry Wadsworth Longfellow"; and "If Thayer's 'Casey At the Bat' Were Written By Edgar Allan Poe."*

# 12 OCTOBER

### *Political Economy*

What hours I spent of precious time,
　　What pints of ink I used to waste,
Attempting to secure a rhyme
　　To suit the public taste,
Until I found a simple plan
Which makes the lamest lyric scan!

When I've a syllable de trop,
　　I cut it off, without apol.;
This verbal sacrifice, I know,
　　May irritate the schol.;
But all must praise my dev'lish cunn.
Who realize that Time is Mon.

My sense remains as clear as cryst.,
　　My style as pure as any Duch.
Who does not boast a bar sinist.
　　Upon her fam. escutch.;
And I can treat with scornful pit.
The sneers of ev'ry captious crit.

I gladly publish to the pop.
　　A scheme of which I make no myst.,
And beg my fellow scribes to cop.
　　This labor-saving syst.
I offer it to the consid.
Of ev'ry thoughtful individ.

The author, working like a beav.,
　　His reader's pleasure could redoub.
Did he but now and then abbrev.
　　The work he gives his pub.
(This view I most partic. suggest
to A. C. Bens. and G. K. Chest.)

If playwrights would but thus dimin.
　　The length of time each drama takes,

---

*But see 21 April for one more link in Jacobs's chain, "If Longfellow's 'The Midnight Ride of Paul Revere' Were Written By Ernest Lawrence Thayer."

(The Second Mrs. Tanq. by Pin.
   Or even Ham., by Shakes.)
We could maintain a watchful att.
When at a Mat. on Wed. or Sat.

Have done, ye bards, with dull monot.!
   Foll. my examp., O, Stephen Phill.,
O, Owen Seam., O, William Wat.,
   O, Ella Wheeler Wil.,
And share with me the grave respons.
Of writing this amazing nons.!
             —*Harry Graham*

# 13 OCTOBER

### *"Hark to the Mewsicians of Bremen!" Mewed the Caterpillar*

"Easel" derives from the Danish word for "ass"; an easel, like an ass, being a bearer of burdens. Had an easel rather than an ass sounded the C for the Musicians of Bremen, he and his fellows might have sung like this:

The monkeywrench chattered
   The easel brayed
The firedog barked
   The sawhorse neighed
The duckpin quacked
   The weathercock crowed
The chickenpox cheeped
   The cowlick lowed.
           —*W.R.E.*

Here are a dozen adjectives that refer to specific animals. How many of the animals can you identify: 1. Cervine. 2. Colubrine. 3. Hircine. 4. Larine. 5. Lutrine. 6. Meline. 7. Mephitine. 8. Musteline. 9. Ovine. 10. Phocine. 11. Sciurine. 12. Viverrine.

# 14 OCTOBER

### *The Variety of Abel Green*

If a headline reading STICKS NIX HICK PIX means to you that films with bucolic themes flop in Bucolia, you speak on equal terms with *Variety*, the bible of show business. Abel Green, editor of *Variety* for forty years,* legalized such linguistic tender as boff, yocks, plushery, femcee, flivved, and crix. For Mr. Green, TV networks were webs; festivals, fests; film biographies, biopics; executives, exex. If he wanted to hear from you by telephone, he would say, "Gimme an Ameche"—Don Ameche having played Alexander Graham Bell in a motion picture about the invention of the telephone. A Green analysis of the demise of Toots Shor's restaurant began: "The raison d'être for el foldo . . ."

Even funerals were show biz to Abel Green. His headline for a report on the last rites for one of his best friends was "S.R.O. attendance of over 1,000 at Temple Emmanuel." He embraced the lowly pun; one of his headlines summarized the engorging career of Linda Lovelace, of the x-rated film *Deep Throat*, in four words: A STAR IS PORN.

# 15 OCTOBER

## *Rhadamanthine Sea*

When I was studying freshman composition in college, Carroll Montague, a junior, graded my weekly compositions. Once he scribbled in the margin, "Try to improve your vocabulary." The next week, in an effort at lightness, I wrote "Ah, the Rhadamanthine Sea!" Carroll graded me C−, remarking, "Wisecracks aren't vocabulary, smarthead. One more Rhadamanthus out of you and I'll Rhadamanthus your Panthus."

Like Rhadamanthus, he was an inexorable judge. Later, when we became friends, he taught me a lesson about honesty of taste that I try not to forget.

Carroll and I smoked pipes, and each had a favorite brand—mine Velvet and his Prince Albert, or perhaps the other way around. I boasted of my brand, and he of his. Now the two tobaccos came in containers of oiled paper, in tins of identical size and shape. It occurred to Carroll to exchange these containers behind my back, and for days I rhapsodized over my brand while smoking his.

When he told me how I had been foxed, I resolved never again to tell myself that I had reached a conclusion on a matter of taste, whether the subject was Velvet tobacco or Picasso paintings, when, in fact, I was simply reflecting some accepted fashion. I have tried to abide by this rule, but it is not easy. We often live by other people's convictions, lacking genuine convictions of our own. Without outside reassurance, some of us would doubt whether we are alive.

Carroll died of a heart attack this morning. He would have known instantly that the lines below hark back to our dispute over pipe tobaccos:

> I saw the universe wheel by,
> Reflected in my neighbor's eye.
> When presently my neighbor blinked,
> The universe became extinct.
> —W.R.E.

*He died in 1973.

# 16 OCTOBER

## *A Collection of Crocks*

"If crockery is a collection of crocks," writes Evan Esar, "then flattery is a collection of flats, scullery is a collection of skulls, sorcery a collection of sources, and monastery a collection of monsters." I have used Mr. Esar's collectives in the following Japery (a collection of Japes) which is based on the reasonable assumption that any word ending in –ry must be a Collection of Something or Other.

From a Sorcery
I bring you this curious Factory.
One day a Gallantry
A Jury
And a Hickory
Who included a Calory
And a Dickery
Left their Flattery
To walk on a Dockery
With a Monastery.
There they met a Gallery
Among whom were a Janissary
A Salary
And a Misery.
The Hickory
Had brought a Henry
And the Henry
Had brought a Chicory.
The Gallery
Agreed to dance a Jiggery
On the Dockery
With the Gallantry
The Jury
And the Hickory
But not the Monastery.
This enraged the Monastery
Who loosed in the Jiggery
A Battery
And made off in the confusion with the Henry
And the Chicory.
With the prodigious Cursory
The Hickory
Sic'ed a Curry
A Colliery
And a Berry
On the fleeing Monastery

But the clever Monastery
Ran into a Story
Where they sold the Henry
And the Chicory
For a Sentry.
With a quick Peccary
The Henry
And the Chicory
Ate a Pillory
And a Buggery.
When the police caught the Monastery
They rode them on a Raillery
And in a Celery
Rapped a Scullery.
The judge imposed a Finery.
But the Hickory
Never got back the Henry
Or the Chicory
For the Hickory
Were a Foolery.

—W.R.E.

# 17 OCTOBER

## Puzzle School

This elementary school teacher uses word puzzles and games of his own creation, like these, to enhance his students' vocabulary and knowledge of English.

### PARTWORDS

You are given three letters that appear consecutively anywhere in a word. Try to find a word for each partword.

| | | |
|---|---|---|
| _____ WBO _____ | _____ WBE _____ | _____ RWO _____ |
| _____ BST _____ | _____ MPH _____ | _____ FTN _____ |
| | _____ TSW _____ | |

### FILL-IN STATION

Fill in the blanks with consonants to form 14 or more different words. *All* vowels are given.

| | | |
|---|---|---|
| __ __ OU __ | __ __ OU __ | __ __ OU __ |
| __ __ OU __ | __ __ OU __ | __ __ OU __ |

```
__ __ OU __        __ __ OU __        __ __ OU __
__ __ OU __        __ __ OU __        __ __ OU __
__ __ OU __        __ __ OU __
```

## MATCH-UPS

Pair these 16 word parts to form 8 whole words.

| | | | |
|---|---|---|---|
| IMP | SET | NER | ING |
| RES | CUR | MES | SHO |
| SION | CLO | OTS | ALE |
| VES | MAN | THE | SES |

```
_____        _____
_____        _____
_____        _____
_____        _____
```

—*George Bredehorn*

# 18 OCTOBER

### *Colloquy between a Devout Man and His Wicked Echo*

An echo may convey a different meaning from the original phrase:

*A good man muttered to himself as he walked on a hill;*
*And Echo followed after him, as Echo always will.*

Good man: I bend my neck to be God's sacrifice;
           One final throe will win me Paradise.
Echo: *One final throw will win,* me pair o' dice!

Good man: I seek out God behind His shining gate,
           Where cherubims and angels scintillate.
Echo: Where cherubims and angels *sin till late.*

Good man: Flesh, fall away! I climb the spirit's heights!
           How futile now, those orgiastic nights!
Echo: *How few till now,* those orgiastic nights!

Good man: Beyond the grave, eternal life begins.
           But what is life? Forgive me, Lord, my sins!
Echo: But what is life for? Give me, Lord, my sins!

—*W.R.E.*

# 19 OCTOBER

### *Mini, Minu*

A number of years ago, when I couldn't find "miniscule" in my desk dictionary, I briskly turned to my unabridged and didn't find it there, either. How do you react upon not finding in the dictionary a word you think you know? Trembling, I managed to call the reference room of the New York Public Library and was calmly told that the word is spelled m-i-n-u-s-c-u-l-e. As it turned out, this librarian was the last person I've run across who knew how to spell the word. Everyone else spells it wrong, in the same way.

Even when the subject is a dictionary, as in the review of the two-volume Oxford English Dictionary in *Medical World News*, the reproductions are described as "sharp but miniscule."

The *Milwaukee Journal* refers to a chemical additive as being a "miniscule ingredient."

*Newsfront* tells of someone grabbing a "miniscule slice of the Democratic party pie."

The *Chicago Tribune Magazine* mentions "her cheerful, miniscule candybox of an apartment."

It's rampant in *The New York Times*. On the sports page there are terms of "Lilliputian dimensions and miniscule skills." A sub-headline in the news section reads: "Impressive or Miniscule?" And there is mention of a magazine with a "relatively miniscule 15,000 subscribers"—who, even if they were minuscule, would probably have trouble lifting the magazine.

But don't think it's solely an American failing. The *Montreal Star* tells of an amount of "alleged marijuana that was so miniscule that it was destroyed in the laboratory." It does sound American, though, from the alleged to the miniscule.

And in Philip Roth's *Goodbye, Columbus,* in both the hardcover and paperback editions, a letter is written in "an extraordinarily miniscule hand."

Is this the way language changes?

*—Sidney Harris*

# 20 OCTOBER

### *Have Angleworms Attractive Homes?*

Have Angleworms attractive homes?
Do Bumble-bees have brains?
Do Caterpillars carry combs?
Do Dodos dote on drains?

Can Eels elude elastic earls?
   Do Flatfish fish for flats?
Are Grigs agreeable to girls?
   Do Hares have hunting-hats?
Do Ices make an Ibex ill?
   Do Jackdaws jug their jam?
Do Kites kiss all the kids they kill?
   Do Llamas live on lamb?
Will Moles molest a mounted mink?
   Do Newts deny the news?
Are Oysters boisterous when they drink?
   Do Parrots prowl in pews?
Do Quakers get their quills from quails?
   Do Rabbits rob on roads?
Are Snakes supposed to sneer at snails?
   Do Tortoises tease toads?
Can Unicorns perform on horns?
   Do Vipers value veal?
Do Weasels weep when fast asleep?
   Can Xylophagans squeal?
Do Yaks in packs invite attacks?
   Are Zebras full of zeal?
             —*Charles E. Carryl*

# 21 OCTOBER

## *Forgotten Positives*

A reviewer once complained that in an article about forgotten positives I myself had "forgotten the classic text on this subject, which begins with the line: 'I know a little man who's ept and ert.'" Well, I had not forgotten it—I had never seen it. But I have seen it now, and here is the first stanza:

I know a little man both ept and ert
An intro? extro? No, he's just a vert
Sheveled and couth and kempt, pecunious, ane:
His image trudes upon the ceptive brain.
             —*David McCord*

I included in the article a quatrain of my own, "I Dreamt of Couth." I add herewith a second stanza:

I dreamt that bulating the youth would dulate
In a peccable, ferior vein.
I'm turbed that he's funct and chalant, and I'll state
I'd be poverished having his dain.
             —*W.R.E.*

(By the way, when was the last time you heard scruple used as a verb, save in the negative "does not scruple to . . ."? Yet it is a lovely word of conscience: "She scrupled," wrote Jane Austen, "to point out her own remarks to him, lest it seem like ill nature.")

# 22 OCTOBER

## *Headlines, Road Signs*

Sometimes headlines do not mean quite what they seem to say, as in this from the *New York Post:*

### JOHN WAYNE
### TURNED TO GOD
### ON HIS DEATHBED

His fans always said that man could do anything.

### VERMONT DEMOCRATS
### BACK SALMON FOR SENATE,
### WOMAN FOR GOVERNOR

Fish lib?

### ALONG 8TH AVENUE,
### WHERE LEER IS KING

Supported by his three daughters?
Two from the *Chicago Tribune:*

### MOST ON DEATH ROW
### HERE WERE APPEALING

### SERIOUSLY INJURED
### IN FATAL FIRE
### —*Robert T. Harker*

From the *Baton Rouge State-Times:*

### MAN BOOKED FOR WRECKLESS DRIVING
### —*Ashley C. Worsely*

From an old *New York Herald Tribune:*

### A GRATEFUL NATION
### BURIES SAM RAYBURN

We thought we would never be rid of him.

A caption under a photograph in the *Los Angeles Times* of Aristotle Onassis examining the home of Buster Keaton for a possible purchase:

**ARISTOTLE CONTEMPLATING THE HOME OF BUSTER**
*—Marjorie Wihtol*

A roadside sign:

WE BUY JUNK
AND
SELL ANTIQUES

*The Times Diary*, an English publication, consists of photographs of such nonplussing notices as these:

- Same day cleaners. 48 hour service.
- Drive slowly and allow cows to pass.
- P at any time.
- No overtaking for the next 200 yrs.
- Health food & kosher flowers.
- New & used antiques.
- Up steps to sunken garden.
- Buses only. Except buses.
- Raise legs before moving.
- Guests & seamen. No admittance. (In Virginia)
- No loitering without permission. (In Japan)
- Caution. Workers working. (In India)
- Please do not feed the animals, if you have any suitable food please give it to the guard on duty.
- No entry. In only. (Kenya)
- Foot wearing prohibited. Socks not allowed. (Rangoon temple)
- Don't let worry kill you off. Let the Church help.
- Site entrance. Please enter from opposite direction.
- Jet blast is dangerous. Passengers only beyond this point. (Texas)
- Special force training area. Restricted to unauthorized persons. (Uganda)
- Hallwood hospital. Strictly no admittance.

# 23 OCTOBER

*Upon October Twenty-Third*

Upon October
Twenty-third
A singular
event occurred:

I put my paper
To my pen;
I put my paper
Back again;

For though the world
Was in distress,
It always had been,
More or less

With murder, war,
And peculation,
Adultery,
Discrimination,

And princes in,
And princes out,
And not a thing
To write about.*
—W.R.E.

# 24 OCTOBER

## *Every Dog Is an Isogram*

*Word Ways* reminds me that an isogram is a word which uses each letter the same number of times. In *dog*, each of the three letters is used once. *Deeded* is an isogram in which each letter is used three times. There are not many three-pair isograms; Dmitri Borgmann, who specializes in such oddities, can name only one more—*geggee*, Scottish for "a victim of a hoax."

Two-pair isograms of ten letters include *intestines*, *arraigning*, *tool steels*, *horseshoer*, and (describing unattainable women) *superpures*. *Happenstance* and *shanghaiings* are two-pair twelve-letter isograms.

Mr. Borgmann's ears prick up at fifteen-letter isograms such as *dermatoglyphics* ("the science of the study of skin patterns"); *white gyrfalcons*; *uncopyrightable*; *prediscountably*; and *South Cambridge*, N.Y.

If anyone tells you he knows a commonly used isogram of sixteen letters or more, he is trying to make a geggee of you.

The shortest word containing all five vowels, says Jonathan Delfin, is *sequoia*, a tree named after the Cherokee Indian who put the language of his tribe into writing. It is also a nonpattern isogram; each letter occurs once only.

Similar in spirit to the isogram is the stammer—a passage in which a letter repeats itself uninterruptedly and inordinately. Some stammers:

---

*The only event worth recording that I can recall occurring on 23 October was the birth of one of my daughters.

A burg*oo o' ooze*. Five o's
You'd think *Judd'd DDT* those bugs. Five d's
The Philadelphi*a AAA a*dded two staff members. Five a's
—*Maxey Brooke*

Bi*ll'll, ll*amalike, stand staring in the distance. Six l's
—*R. Merrill Ely*

A sweet young thing named Bessie B.
Collects letters 'twixt R and T.
Perhaps the very lack of range
Makes Be*ss's s's s*eem so strange. Six s's
—*Author unknown*

A burgoo, by the way, is a porridge, or in the United States a stew served in the open air.

# 25 OCTOBER

## *Stinky Pinkies*

Stinky pinkies—nouns modified by rhyming adjectives—pall even faster than limericks, but a few, such as these, are good enough to renew one's faith.

1. Ardent employee.
2. Unimaginative surface decoration.
3. A cactus that goes out of its way to needle you.
4. A world of igneous rock.
5. Boisterous policy meeting.
6. Dismal chorus.
7. Childish wall-painting.
8. Brackish nut-confection.
9. Fanatic slave.
10. Fruitful interval of time.

—*David L. Silverman*

# 26 OCTOBER

## *Surf Bird, Shore Bird*

*"A goldfinch is sometimes called a thistletweeker, a linet a linet tweaker,*
*a curlew a whelp."*
—*The Sea Farer (early Anglo-Saxon)*

Are the shore birds around Oysterville peeps, or snipe? I know only that they belong to the Charadrii family, with cousins innumerable. I learned this from reading Peter Matthiessen's *Wind Birds**—a writing as precise and lovely as a snipe's clawprint in wet sand. A few of the subspecies Mr. Matthiessen mentions are listed here:

> Surf bird, shore bird, veering over,
> Are you Dowitcher, or Plover?
>
> You at edge of tide who sprint
> Are you Avocet, or Stint?
>
> You who Peewee, you who Pipe,
> Are you Tattler? Curlew? Snipe?
>
> Wader, sitting on your eggs,
> Are you hatching Yellowlegs?
>
> Wind bird, glinting in the sun,
> Are you Stilt? Peep? Simpleton?
>
> Turnstone? Oystercatcher? Knot?
> Ox-eye? Doughbird? Whimbrel? Spot?[†]
>
> Thick-knee? Godwit? Dotterel?
> Chickenbird? Or Rail? Ah well . . .
>
> It suffices that you be
> Of Sub-order *Charadrii.*
>
> —W.R.E.

# 27 OCTOBER

## *Books for Every Worm*

A list of recommended books for fall reading:

| TITLE | AUTHOR |
|-------|--------|
| *Playing by the Rules* | P. Knuckle |
| *Love for Sale* | I. M. Willing |
| *Bikini Exposures* | Belle E. Button |
| *Aid to a Bookworm* | Dick Shunary |
| *Feed-Lot-Tales* | Lotta Bull |
| *Under the Rock* | Liz Ard |
| *The Final Fall* | Eileen Dover |

---

*The English say waders; in this country we generally say surf birds or shore birds.
† The correct name is Spotted. Sorry, Peter.

| | |
|---|---|
| *Cotton Field Capers* | E. Z. Pickens |
| *Urban Renewal Guide* | Dinah Mite |
| *The Bovine's Complaint* | I. C. Hands |
| *The Useless Crutch* | Candy Cane |
| *Love's Labor Lost* | Ms. Carriage |
| *The Missing Sea Treasure* | Nan Tucket |
| *My Final Fling* | I. M. Dunne |

—*Virginia Hager*

# 28 OCTOBER

### *Polish Up Your Polish, Zywacki!*

Heteronyms are words identical in spelling, but different in both sound and meaning. Polish (pertaining to Poland), and polish (to make smooth or glossy) are heteronyms.

The word *os*, reports *Word Ways*, is a four-way heteronym: "Pronounced AHSS, it means a bone, also a mouth or an opening; pronounced OASS, it refers to a narrow ridge or mound of gravelly and sandy drift, deposited by a sub-glacial stream; pronounced OZE, it designates ciphers or zeroes; pronounced OWE-ESS, it is a verb defined as 'to record the time of arrival and departure of a train by telegraphing the information in a certain manner.'"

Until I read the foregoing, I would have considered OS a misspelling of Dorothy's Kingdom of OZ.

# 29 OCTOBER

### *Double Trouble*

*Score 2 points each. Maximum score: 30.*

Each seven-letter word below contains double letters. Change them to new double letters to make a new word. There are fifteen answers altogether, because three words can be changed in more than one way.

| *Example* | COTTAGE | Collage |
|---|---|---|

1. FLITTER
2. SCUFFLE
3. MILLION
4. FOOLING
5. DRIBBLE

6. BAGGAGE
7. GAZETTE
8. COLLECT
9. HAMMOCK
10. ADDRESS
11. CHANNEL
12. BALLOON
—*Will Shortz*

# 30 OCTOBER

## *Caught in the Middle*

To discover the common words hidden below, put two letters before each of the four-letter combinations capitalized, and two after.

L E C I

"L E C I," the untaught cry:
What's next, and what's before?"

"I'll not tell you that," says I,
"But give three answers more:

As E V I A is to priest,
J U T A's to major;

While R I D I's a deceased
Geographer, I'll wager."
—*W.R.E.*

# 31 OCTOBER

## *Dipping for Apples*

It is Hallowe'en, but there are no backyard privies to overturn any more, so I think I'll stay home. I might invite friends to try to seize with their teeth apples floating in a tub of water. But the teeth of some of my friends are not what they used to be, so the game might not prove popular. Instead I think I'll go back through my daybooks, dipping for verses I meant to include in this almanac but forgot.

This first one I did not exactly forget; I was advised against including it by a friend who said it showed poor taste. Perhaps poor taste is excusable on Hallowe'en.

## FOR A RESTLESS MISTRESS
*Virility has been associated with baldness.—News item*

> You have not said, but I infer
> You like your lovers lustier,
>
> And resonate at optimum
> To quickbeat of a martial drum.
>
> So you'll be pleased, I have no doubt,
> To hear my hair is falling out.
> —W.R.E.

My second selection, by an unknown author, repeats elegantly a well-known injunction:

## TEACH NOT THY PARENT'S MOTHER

> Teach not thy parent's mother to extract
>   The embryo juices of the bird by suction.
> The good old lady can that feat enact
>   Quite irrespective of thy kind instruction.

My third Hallowe'en apple, also anonymous, reflects a literary point of view that many of us share:

## AS I WAS PLAYING ON THE GREEN

> As I was playing on the green
> A little book it chanced I seen.
> Carlyle's *Essay on Burns* was the edition;
> I left it laying in the same position.

Finally, a sentimental quatrain:

## THE FLOW OF LOVE

> Flo was fond of Ebenezer—
>   "Eb," for short, she called her beau.
> Talk of Tides of Love, great Caesar!
>   You should see them—Eb and Flo.
> —T. A. Daly

# NOVEMBER

## 1 NOVEMBER

### Saints Preserve Us

All Saints' Day. The devils have been chased back to Pandemonium. The saints are in charge again. If the saint you pray to is not giving satisfaction, here are some alternatives:

| | |
|---|---|
| • For postal workers | St. Amp |
| • For alcoholics | St. Agger |
| • For musicians | St. Accato |
| • For actors | St. Age |
| • For flower children | St. Amen |
| • For thieves | St. Ealthy |
| • For football players | St. Adium |
| • For poets | St. Anza |
| • For young actresses | St. Arlet |
| • For expectant mothers | St. Ork |
| • For politicians | St. Ump |
| • For men who fail to shave | St. Ubble |
| • For foolish folk | St. Upid |
| • For butchers | St. Eak |
| • For kite flyers | St. Ring |
| • For golfers | St. Roke |
| • For beer drinkers | St. Ein |
| • For bus missers | St. Randed |
| • For jocks | St. Amina |

—*Virginia R. Hager*

## 2 NOVEMBER

### Page-flipping in a Daybook

• *A Whole Greater than the Sum of Its Parts*

Can a three-letter word have four syllables? Yes—in a manner of speaking. *Viz.* (to wit, namely) is an abbreviation that should be pronounced as if spelled out: vi-de-li-cet.

- *Four Words in One*

Take so. Take in. Take ever. Take where. Rearrange them. You have where-insoever.

Take i. Take a. Take ties. Take men. Rearrange them. You have amenities.

Take tin. Take city. Take a. Take per. Rearrange them. You have pertinacity.

- *Self-descriptive Sentence*

> In this sentence, the word "and" occurs twice, the word "eight" occurs once, the word "four" occurs twice, the word "fourteen" occurs once, the word "in" occurs twice, the word "occurs" occurs twelve times, the word "sentence" occurs twice, the word "seven" occurs once, the word "times" occurs five times, the word "twice" occurs four times, and the word "word" occurs twelve times.
> —*Howard W. Bergerson*

(Actually, "twice" occurs five times, but then the word "four" would occur only once—and *then* "twice" would occur four times. . . . You try to make it work.)

- *Cease, Qircl!*

Spell cease: c as in cue, e as in eye, a as in are, s as in sea, e as in ell. Qircl, right? Or, says Dick Anderson, spell yes: y as in you, e as in enemy, s as in see. So long, unc.*

- *Qwertyuiop*

"What," writes Christopher Reed, "is the longest word that can be made with the letters in the top row of letters on a typewriter (qwertyuiop)? In case you don't know,† it's typewriter." Actually, there are at least three longer, if less familiar, words: proprietory, proterotype, and rupturewort.

- *Count-up*

One would think that MENSA members, having high IQs, would be able to count to ten; but this advertisement in their journal stopped at nine:

"Want a Wooden Overcoat? Buy H*on*est John Whi*tw*orth's heal*th-re*-energizing sul*fo-ur*anyl-impregnated 'Com*fi-ve*st' with its unique qua*si-x*yloid fibers—obtainable only from the Paradi*se Ven*ding Company, Harpurville Hei*gh*ts, *Ni*nevah, New York."

---

* Other words from *Word Ways* that use the same device: A as in "aisle," C as in "czar," D as in "djinn," K as in "knew," P as in "psalm," W as in "wrong," X as in "xylophone."
† I did not.

# 3 NOVEMBER

## On Smouldering Nuendoes

One of my complaints about a recent long-awaited anthology of American light verse was that it failed to include examples of the splendid work of Felicia Lamport. This is the kind of magic she offers:

### HINT

There never is trouble in finding a spouse
For the ebriated man with the lapidated house.

### SOIREE

The gentle wives fillet a soul
  Eptly, while the men doze;
Or roast a reputation whole
  On smouldering nuendoes.

### SENSICAL SITUATION

Men often pursue in suitable style
The imical girl with the scrutable smile.

### SERENITY

The man who wants a quiet life
  And traught, commoded days
Should find himself an otic wife
  With sipid, centric ways.
          —Felicia Lamport


# 4 NOVEMBER

## Curious Couples

Mary Ann Madden asked readers of *New York* magazine to submit two authentic familiar quotations, "unexpectedly if appropriately coupled." A sampling of the results:

1. " 'Twas brillig, and the slithy toves / Did gyre and gimble in the wabe / All mimsy were the borogroves, / And the mome raths outgrabe."—*Lewis Carroll*

2. "If you do not itemize deductions and line 18 is under $10,000, find tax in Tables and enter on line 19. If you itemize deductions or line 18 is $10,000 or more, go to line 46 to figure tax."
          —*Michael Schreiber*

1. "We shall never understand each other until we reduce the language to seven words."—*Kahlil Gibran*

2. "Doc, Grumpy, Sleepy, Happy, Bashful, Sneezy, and Dopey."
   —*Snow White*
   —*Jack Ryan*

1. "With all my worldly goods I thee endow."—*Book of Common Prayer*

2. "A fool and his money are soon parted."—*American proverb*
   —*Jack Labow*

1. "That feller runs splendid but he needs help at the plate, which coming from the country chasing rabbits all winter give him strong legs, although he broke one falling out of a tree, which shows you can't tell . . ."—*Casey Stengel*

2. "Let me make one thing perfectly clear."—*Richard M. Nixon*
   —*John F. Keppler*

1. "For whither thou goest, I will go; and where thou lodgest I will lodge."—*Book of Ruth, 1:16*

2. "I'm Ruth. Fly me to Miami."—*Airline commercial*
   —*Celia Krapoff*

1. "Youth is wholly experimental."—*Robert Louis Stevenson*

2. "And so to bed."—*Samuel Pepys*
   —*Kathy Mansfield*

1. "In the same hour came forth fingers of a man's hand, and wrote over against the candlestick upon the plaster of the wall of the king's palace; and the king saw part of the hand that wrote."—*Daniel 5:5*

2. "Kilroy was here."—*World War II graffito*
   —*Mrs. June Beattle*

1. "Consider the lilies of the field . . . they toil not, neither do they spin."—*Matthew 6:28*

2. ". . . With a little bit of luck, / Someone else will do the bloomin' work."—*My Fair Lady*
   —*Eileen Tranford*

# 5 NOVEMBER

### *There's Nothing Funny*
### *about Falling into the 'Ay Cutter*

It was once an article of faith among Americans that the English had no bump of humor. The typical Englishman was Joseph C. Lincoln's Lord James:

> I drawed a long breath. "That fortune'll be the death of me yet, Eureka," I told her. "If I fell into the hay cutter I presume likely you wouldn't fret; you'd know I'd come out fine."
> "Oh, you silly!" says she, and laughed. Lord James had come in, and he heard the last part of this. He rubbed his chin. "Why did she laugh?" he wanted to know. "My word! There's nothing funny about falling into the 'ay cutter."
> "Don't you see?" says Eureka, trying to explain. "He means he'd come out fine—chopped fine. He's joking, as usual."
> "But—but that wouldn't be a joke; that would be 'orrible! Chopped in a 'ay cutter! My word!"

But the more I try to isolate the distinctions between the British and the American sense of humor the more elusive I find them. My guess is that these two lines would not stir an Englishman's risibilities as they stir mine:

> The cow kicked Nelly in the belly in the barn.
> Didn't do her any good; didn't do her any harm.

But for all I know that couplet might evoke hilarity throughout the United Kingdom. For that matter, most Americans may not consider it funny at all; perhaps it amuses me simply because I hail from Oysterville.

I assume that James Payn, who wrote the following in 1884, was English; but if he was really Mark Twain writing under a nom de plume, I should not be surprised:

> I never had a piece of toast
> Particularly long and wide
> But fell upon the sanded floor,
> And always on the buttered side.

It would take a library the size of the British Museum to hold all the funny things said by Englishmen, from Geoffrey Chaucer to Anthony Burgess. Since there is no room for a library here, I am going to rest my case on just one English writer—Charles Dickens. Has anyone uttered more truths, and often bitter truths, in a form that so compelled laughter?

- In came a fiddler—and tuned like fifty stomachaches. In came Mrs. Fezziwig, one vast substantial smile.

- He has gone to the demnition bow-wows.
- "If the law supposes that," said Mr. Bumble, "the law is a ass, a idiot."
- With affection beaming in one eye, and calculation shining out of the other.
- Oh Sairey, Sairey, little do we know wot lays afore us!
- Secret, and self-contained, and solitary as an oyster.
- I am a lone lorn creetur, and everythink goes contrairy with me.
- Barkis is willin'.
- Annual income twenty pounds, annual expenditures nineteen nineteen six, result happiness. Annual income twenty pounds, annual expenditure twenty pounds ought and six, result misery.
- It was as true as turnips is. It was as true as taxes is. And nothing's truer than them.

The other day Marc Connelly, no Englishman, quoted Oscar Wilde, no Englishman either, to the effect that "Only a man with a heart of stone could read Dickens's death scene of Little Nell without laughing."

# 6 November

## Extracts from 1066 and All That

Julius Caesar, having defeated the Ancient Britons by unfair means, such as battering rams, tortoises, hippocausts, centipedes, axes and bundles, set the memorable Latin sentence, "Veni, Vidi, Vici," which the Romans, who were all very well educated, construed correctly. The Britons, however, who of course still used the old pronunciation, understanding him to have called them "Weeny, Weedy and Weaky," lost heart and gave up the struggle, thinking that he had already divided them All into Three Parts.

The Scots (originally Irish, but by now Scotch) were at this time inhabiting Ireland, having driven the Irish (Picts) out of Scotland; while the Picts (originally Scots) were now Irish (living in brackets) and vice versa. It is essential to keep these distinctions clearly in mind (and versa visa).

King Alfred was the first Good King, with the exception of Good King Wenceslaus, who, though he looked forth, really came first (it is not known, however, what King Wenceslaus was King of).

The Barons compelled John to sign the Magna Charter, which said:

1. That no one was to be put to death, save for some reason—(except the Common People).
2. That everyone should be free—(except the Common People).

3. That everything should be of the same weight and measure throughout the Realm—(except the Common People).
4. That the Courts should be stationary, instead of following a very tiresome mediaeval official known as the *King's Person* all over the country.
5. That "no person should be fined to his utter ruin"—(except the King's Person).
6. That the Barons should not be tried except by a special jury of other Barons who would understand.

Magna Charter was therefore the chief cause of Democracy in England and thus a *Good Thing* for everyone (except the Common People).

After this King John hadn't a leg to stand on and was therefore known as "John Lackshanks."

The Roundheads, of course, were so called because Cromwell had all their heads made perfectly round, in order that they should present a uniform appearance when drawn up in line. Besides this, if any man lost his head in action, it could be used as a cannonball by the artillery.

When Charles I had been defeated he was brought to trial by the Rump Parliament—so-called because it had been sitting for such a long time—and found himself guilty of being defeated in a war against himself, which was, of course, a form of High Treason.

The Great War was between Germany and America and was thus fought in Belgium, one of the chief causes being the murder of the Austrian Duke of Sarajevo by a murderer in Serbia . . . The War lasted three years or the duration, the Americans being 100% victorious.

America was thus clearly top nation, and History came to a .*
—*W. C. Sellar and R. J. Yeatman*

# 7 November

## *Anagrammatical Onomastica*

If you are dissatisfied with your given name, but reluctant to abandon it altogether, juggle the letters around to see what happens:

- Abbe, Babe, Ebba
- Abe, Bea
- Abel, Albe, Bela
- Adeline, Daniele
- Aden, Dean, Edna
- Aldine, Daniel
- Alice, Celia
- Allie, Leila

---

*Our English friends render . not as "period," but as "full stop."

- Alvina, Lavina
- Amy, May
- Ancel, Lance
- Anita, Tania
- Ann, Nan
- Annette, Nanette
- Anthea, Athena
- Antoine, Antonie
- Arnoldo, Orlando
- Braden, Brenda
- Brady, Darby
- Broun, Bruno
- Carla, Clara
- Carlo, Carol, Coral
- Carmel, Marcel
- Caroline, Cornelia
- Christian, Christina
- Claus, Lucas
- Colin, Nicol
- Crispian, Crispina
- Dale, Elda, Leda
- Darleen, Leander, Learned
- Dolly, Lloyd
- Dorothea, Theodora
- Dot, Tod
- Edsel, Leeds
- Elise, Elsie
- Elmer, Merle
- Ernie, Irene
- Esther, Hester
- Fidel, Field
- Forrest, Forster
- Gale, Glea
- Gary, Gray
- Hamlet, Thelma
- Hays, Shay
- Jane, Jean
- Janos, Jason, Jonas, Sonja
- Lawton, Walton
- Leo, Ole
- Leon, Noel
- Lion, Olin
- Lona, Nola
- Maire, Marie
- Mario, Moira
- Mary, Myra
- Mat, Tam
- Norma, Ramon
- Oliva, Viola
- Rosamond, Rosmonda
- Salem, Selma
- Waldorf, Walford
- Warner, Warren

—*Word Ways*

# 8 NOVEMBER

### Just Because . . .

Kittens have paws they don't have pawses,
Lions have maws they don't have mawses,
Tigers have jaws they don't have jawses,
And crows have caws they don't have cawses.

*I make one pause, I make two pauses:*

Nine jackdaws aren't nine jackdawses,
Seven seesaws aren't seven seesawses,
Five oh pshaws aren't five oh pshawses,
Three heehaws aren't three heehawses.

*Do you give two straws? Do you give two strawses?*
—*David McCord*

# 9 NOVEMBER

### To *Stimulate Voraciousness?* To *Simulate Veraciousness?*

When Dashiell Hammett was making his living as a detective, he submitted to his superiors a report containing the word *voracious*. They changed it to *truthful*, explaining that *voracious* might be too hard for the client to understand. In another report they changed *simulate* to *quicken* for the same reason.

This hemi-demi-semi-macaronic verse warns us against such malapropping:

### MOTS JUSTES

Oh, let the *Mot* be *comme il faut*
  Or let it be *sub rosa*.
They are not fond in the *beau monde*
  Of the *mal à propos* Sir.
And (*chi lo sa?*) a small *faux pas*
  A minor *lapsus linguae*
May overthrow your *status quo*
  And brand you—not *distingué*.
So *suaviter in modo* Sir and everything *pro rata*
For they who err in *Savoir Faire* are not
  *persona grata*.

—H.J.R.

These heartwarming malapropisms are cited by *Verbatim:*

- The use of drugs is on the upcrease.
- If the circumstances were on the other foot.
- I don't pull any bones about it.
- You're talking around the bush.
- You are out of your rocker.
- You set my hair on edge.
- I think we need to get down to the brass roots (grass tacks?) of the problem.
- If he had actually broken a crime or could be accused of breaking a crime . . .
- He will lend an ear to anyone who wants to listen.
- Nixon on the death of Adlai Stevenson: "In eloquence he had no peer, and very few equals."

—James D. White

# 10 NOVEMBER

### Epigrammatic Espy

Anybody can write an epigram. The only trouble is that most of us don't write them very well. Here are some of mine:

### TO A YOUNG POETESS

You're beautiful, you're sweet,
But God!—
How your iambic feet
Plod!

### MENCKEN: A UNIVOCALIC

Mencken terse?
The reverse.

### ON SALT-SPRINKLING

The Bird of Love, which lit
  at our command,
Too briefly halted.
The moral? Keep the Shaker
  close at hand,
The Tail well salted.

### LOVE'S A GAME

Love's a game
Indeed, my pet;
I think its name
Is Russian Roulette.

### BLEST ARE THE POOR

Blest are the poor. I never guessed
I'd be elected to the blest.

# 11 NOVEMBER

## *What Can't Be Hope*

The late Brooks Hays, for twenty years a congressman from Arkansas, regarded with awe the language quiddities of his native state. Recalled Mr. Hays:

> "Hope" for helped was introduced to me by an unlettered Sunday School teacher. "The little boy Samuel hope the priest Eli in the temple." Later I understood more quickly what he meant in saying

> "What can't be hope has to be bore."

In Arkansas a metaphor may be its own opposite, as in this recollection by a man who had just purchased and subdued a mule:

"Yes, sir, Graves. I tell you that mule was a wild one—wild as a buck—just as wild as a buck! I gave him the works. Had to tame him, you know, and would you believe me, when I went out to the barn next morning, he was tame—as tame as a buck, as tame as a buck!"

# 12 NOVEMBER
## I'd Walk 1.6093 Kilometers for a Camel

"Metric System Inches Along," says a newspaper headline. True enough; the British are walking the last kilometer toward substitution of the metric system of measurements for our present inches, pints, and pounds, and bills to the same end are pending in the United States Congress. Which leads a *New York Times* man to comment:

> "A miss is as good as a kilometer." Or would you believe: "A gram of prevention is worth a kilogram of cure"? Many would be aghast at the thought of converting, "I love you, a bushel and a peck," to liters and hectoliters. Will angry men cry: "I'll beat you to within a centimeter of your life"? Or "Give him a millimeter and he'll take a kilometer"?
> It used to be said, "A pint's a pound the world around"—that is, a pint of water weighs one pound everywhere. Today, it would be more accurate to say: "Wherever in the world I am, a cubic centimeter is a gram."
>
> —*Walter Sullivan*

# 13 NOVEMBER
## Pandora Opens a Can of Worms

My sister Dale, whose birthday this is, does not regularly read the *Wall Street Journal,* but she does know something about clichés, and about congressmen, and I think she will enjoy this *Journal* account:

> Clichés and hackneyed expressions are the mortar of congressional speech. The middle-aged men who make their living with words feel the need, under the pressures of extemporaneous debate, to use combinations of words they've heard before and are comfortable with. So hoaxes are always "cruel,"* an inadequate proposition is always "woefully inadequate," and whatever a "little guy" pays, he pays "through the nose."
> Some people are collectors of Capitol Hill clichés. One such connoisseur is John Pastore of Rhode Island, who as a senator for 23

*Not a cliché, says A. Ross Eckler:  hoaxes *are* always cruel.

years has heard them all. He prides himself on being able to reel off dazzling clusters of bromides in his own speeches, as in this heroic combination on the Senate floor:

"I say today, let us not throw out the baby with the bath water, let us not lose sight of the forest for the trees, let us not trade off the orchard for an apple."

Sen. Pastore used the most common form of the baby and the bath water cliché, but others sometimes employ original variations.

Sen. Mike Gravel of Alaska: "It seems that many times when we want to change the water, we wind up throwing out the baby."

Rep. Frank Denholm of South Dakota: "I do not agree with those here or elsewhere that favor throwing out the baby because of dirty water."

Tiresome clichés can be enriched somewhat by mixing them inventively. A memorable mixture came from the late George Andrews of Alabama one day during a House debate on busing. Addressing members from the North, Mr. Andrews shouted: "Now the chickens are coming home to roost and the monkey is on your back."

Congressional prose tends toward the stuffy side, but now and then somebody will attempt comedy. Rep. Silvio Conte is a severe critic of federal compensation payments to beekeepers whose bees are killed by pesticides, and he worded an attack this way:

"This federal giveaway should really set my colleagues off buzzing, if it does not make them break out in hives.

"My waxing rhetorically would be very funny if it were not for the taxpayers who are getting stung . . . if Congress were to continue this program, it would lay itself bare to the stinging indictment of taxpayers that it has, may I say, bees in its bonnet."

A snappy saying is about all today's lawmakers ever try for. With the death of Everett Dirksen, elegant oratory isn't heard in the Senate any more. Democratic Leader Mike Mansfield of Montana thinks the reason is that Senators just don't have the time to put a high polish on their rhetoric. Whatever the reason, the result is an addiction to what's been said before, and it accounts for the sound of all those apprehensive babies sloshing around in their bath water.

—*Arlan J. Large*

# 14 NOVEMBER

## *Philologos*

The first line of this macaronic limerick is Greek; the second, Italian; the third, English; the fourth, French; and the final line, Latin.

Philologos 'onomati Louis
Parla lingue quaranta due.
When he heard tell
De la tour de Babel,
Ait, "Quorum pars magna fui."
—*Anonymous*

My rendering:

Said a polyglot teacher named Lou,
Who of languages spoke forty-two,
"Don't sneer at the fable
Of the Tower of Babel:
I was straw boss of the crew."
—*W.R.E.*

*Quorum pars magna fui* is from *The Aeneid*. It means "Of which things I was a major part."

# 15 NOVEMBER

## *Daffy Definitions*

I mentioned my sister Dale's birthday two days ago. She is eleven months my junior, so we will be the same age for the next month. Usually we can't mark the occasion together, since we live on opposite sides of the continent. This time, though, we were in the same place at the same time. The place was a restaurant that affected paper napkins, and I kept mine as a souvenir. It contains the following rubrics, listed as "Daffy Definitions":

- Moderate. A guy who makes enemies left and right.
- Sad case. A dozen empties.
- Psychologist. One who when a beautiful woman enters the room watches everyone else.
- Texas. Miles and miles of nothing but miles and miles.
- Jacks or better. What it takes to open bus windows.
- Will. A dead giveaway.
- Knapsack. Sleeping bag.
- Panhandler. An intern.
- Cannibal. A guy who goes into a restaurant and orders the waiter.
- Arch criminal. A guy who robs shoe stores.
- Stagnation. Country without women.
- Perpetual motion. A cow drinking milk.
- Operetta. A person who works for the telephone company.
- Marriage license bureau. The two dollar window where everybody loses.

- Yale. A Swedish prison.
- Smelling salts. Sailors with BO.
- Incongruous. Where they make our laws.

Herman Schauss defines an apiary as a monkey cage; a condominium as a birth-control device for tots; a lapidary as infant's nourishment; a moratorium as an undertaking establishment; a Pap test as a paternity determinant. Charlotte Laiken says necrophilia is esprit de corpse; Barbara Huff considers a noose the niece of a moose; and naughty, to J. Bickart, means "zerolike; filled with zeroes," as, "Little Orphan Annie has naughty eyes."

# 16 NOVEMBER

## Double Duty

Insert in the blank space between each of the two matched syllables below a syllable that will make one word of the first syllable, and another out of the second.

| | | | | | |
|---|---|---|---|---|---|
| 1. Back | ____ | Robe | 11. Ham | ____ | Tuce |
| 2. Bar | ____ | Der | 12. Hand | ____ | Body |
| 3. Bor | ____ | Ive | 13. House | ____ | Man |
| 4. Com | ____ | Ey | 14. Mis | ____ | Tain |
| 5. Cur | ____ | Ted | 15. Pre | ____ | Ence |
| 6. Door | ____ | Stone | 16. Prow | ____ | Ence |
| 7. Ex | ____ | Tive | 17. Pur | ____ | Able |
| 8. Fire | ____ | Ways | 18. Sun | ____ | Tee |
| 9. Foot | ____ | Son | 19. Tas | ____ | Rant |
| 10. Fret | ____ | Mill | 20. War | ____ | Well |

# 17 NOVEMBER

## Beautiful Words

*The Book of Lists* asked me for the ten words I considered most beautiful. There are as many opinions on that subject as there are people, and I tried to develop a consensus. I asked television viewers and radio listeners to send me their favorites, but few bothered to. I finally fell back on friends and acquaintances.

Alastair Reid chose *twilight*; Marya Mannes, *voluptuous*; Joan Fontaine, *affluence*; James Flexner, *wanderer*.

Mildred Luton sent me an account of a French grandmother who regretted that none of her granddaughters had been named Diarrhea. Informed of the word's unpleasant associations, the old lady sighed.

"What a pity!" she said. "So beautiful—fit for a princess!"

Most, but by no means all, of the words suggested were onomatopoeic: *liquefaction; melodious; murmuring; ululation; whirlpool; babbling.* Others frequently mentioned were the familiar *cellar door; daffodil; delight; fruitful; gloaming; lavender; meadow; rendezvous; philanderer; rhapsody; sapphire;* and *scenario.* Biology and illness—*cerebellum, urethra, syphilis, pneumonia,* and so on—were well represented, in an apparent effort to divorce appreciation of sound from sense.

These were my selections:

| | |
|---|---|
| diarrhea | murmuring |
| gossamer | onomatopoeia |
| lullaby | Shenandoah |
| meandering | summer afternoon |
| mellifluous | wisteria |

# 18 NOVEMBER

### Let the Ball Lay Where It Was Flang

There are strong verbs, and then there are weak verbs. *Weed* is a weak verb, because its root does not change with its tense: weed, weeded, weeded. But *Wede,* my nickname, is a strong verb, or would be if it were a verb; its tenses would go: wede, wed, divorced, re-wed, divorced, re-wed. . . . M. H. Greenblatt recalls that Dizzy Dean preferred the strong to the weak verb; thus:

> "The pitcher wound up and he flang the ball at the batter. The batter swang and missed. The pitcher flang the ball again and this time the batter connected. He hit a high fly right to the center fielder. The center fielder was all set to catch the ball, but at the last minute his eyes were blound by the sun and he dropped it."

The following is a classic parade of strong, even musclebound, verbs:

#### THE LOVERS

Sally Salter, she was a young teacher who taught,
And her friend, Charley Church, was a preacher, who praught;
Though his enemies called him a screecher, who scraught.

His heart, when he saw her, kept sinking, and sunk;
And his eye, meeting hers, began winking, and wunk;
While she, in her turn, fell to thinking, and thunk.

He hastened to woo her, and sweetly he wooed,
For his love grew until to a mountain it grewed,
And what he was longing to do, then he doed.

In secret he wanted to speak, and he spoke,
To seek with his lips what his heart long had soke;
So he managed to let the truth leak, and it loke.

He asked her to ride to the church, and they rode;
They so sweetly did glide, that they both thought they glode,
And they came to the place to be tied, and were tode.

Then homeward he said let us drive, and they drove,
And soon as they wished to arrive, they arrove;
For whatever he couldn't contrive, she controve.

The kiss he was dying to steal, then he stole;
At the feet where he wanted to kneel, then he knole;
And he said, "I feel better than ever I fole."

So they to each other kept clinging, and clung,
While Time his swift circuit was winging, and wung;
And this was the thing he was bringing and brung:

The man Sally wanted to catch, and had caught—
That she wanted from others to snatch, and had snaught—
Was the one she now liked to scratch, and she scraught.

And Charley's warm love began freezing, and froze,
While he took to teasing, and cruelly toze
The girl he had wished to be squeezing, and squoze.

"Wretch!" he cried, when she threatened to leave him, and left,
"How could you deceive, as you have deceft?"
And she answered, "I promised to cleave, and I've cleft."

—*Author Unknown*

# 19 NOVEMBER

## *A Flock of Ships*

A foreigner looking at a picture of a number of vessels, said, "See what a flock of ships." He was told that a flock of ships was called a fleet, and that a fleet of sheep was called a flock. And it was added, for his guidance in mastering the intricacies of our language, that a flock of girls is called a bevy, that a bevy of wolves is called a pack, and a pack of thieves is called a gang, and that a gang of angels is called a host, and that a host of porpoises is called a shoal, and a shoal of buffaloes is called a herd, and a herd of children is called a troop, and a troop of partridges is called a covey, and a covey of beauties is called a galaxy, and a galaxy of ruffians is called a horde, and a horde of rubbish is called a heap, and a heap of oxen is called a drove, and a drove of blackguards is called a mob, and a mob of whales is called a school, and a school of worshippers is called a congregation, and a congregation of engineers is called a corps, and a corps of robbers is called a band, and a band of locusts is called a swarm, and a swarm of people is called a crowd.

—*C. C. Bombaugh*

# 20 NOVEMBER

### *In Short, A Verse*

Adam
Had 'em

The drawback to very short verses is that they often require very long titles—at least mine do. For instance:

*A Genteel Exchange Between the British Ambassador's Wife, Who Speaks No Spanish, and the Spanish Ambassador's Wife, Who Speaks No English, During an Afternoon Call on the Former by the Latter; Written for Those with Some Knowledge of English, Spanish, and the Language of ABC*

"T?"
"C."

Or this:

*Conclusion After Studying a Cross Section of the Population, with Special Attention to Comeliness, Age, Health, Reputation, Accomplishments, Prospects, Temperament, Social Commitment, Fairness, Tolerance, Modesty, Wit, Courtesy, Honor, Compassion, Generosity, Life Expectancy, and Coolness Under Fire; Disregarding as Irrelevant Only Worldly Goods or Lack Thereof*

Who do I want to be? . . .
Me.

Have you ever seen a verse that reads the same upside down as right side up? Here is one:

M O M
S W I M S
W O W

—*Louis Phillips*

Written in longhand, this word too reads the same right side up or upside down:

# 21 NOVEMBER

### *The Strange Case of the Surplus Anagrams*

If a puzzle does not make me smile, I find it of little interest. By this criterion, is the five-anagram verse immediately below preferable to its nine-anagram enlargement?

*Five anagrams:*

A \*\*\*\*\*\* from \*\*\*\*\*\* named Boreas
As a \*\*\*\*\*\* for girls was notorious.
  When their answer was "Nay,"
  He would \*\*\*\*\*\* away;
When 'twas "yes," the \*\*\*\*\*\* was quite
  glorious

*Nine anagrams:*

A lady from \*\*\*\*\*\* her lute softly
  played;
A \*\*\*\*\*\* beside her made sweet
  serenade.
"O fairest of \*\*\*\*\*\*, take pity," he sang;
"Thou \*\*\*\*\*\* my heart into many a
  pang.
Thou \*\*\*\*\*\* me ever; I see in thine eyes
A \*\*\*\*\*\* unmatched in the earth or the
  skies.
Though ne'er was I \*\*\*\*\*\* for feminine
  flesh,
Thy gown's slightest \*\*\*\*\*\* my heart
  doth enmesh.

So sang the poor fellow, and so did he
  woo;
And what the \*\*\*\*\*\* was, I leave up to
  you.
                —W.R.E.

# 22 NOVEMBER

### Lines to Miss Florence Huntingdon

The place names of the state of Maine are even odder to read and hear than those of my native Washington. But they are not so suited to punning. This nineteenth-century verse gives the flavor of them:

Sweet maiden of Passamaquoddy,
  Shall we seek for communion of souls
Where the deep Mississippi meanders,
  Or the distant Saskatchewan rolls?

Ah no,—for in Maine I will find thee
  A sweetly sequestrated nook,
Where the far-winding Skoodoowabskooksis
  Conjoins with the Skoodoowabskook.

There wander two beautiful rivers,
  With many a winding and crook;
The one is the Skoodoowabskooksis,
  The other—the Skoodoowabskook.

(And so on for a total of twelve stanzas. Let us limit ourselves to the last two:)

Let others sing loudly of Saco,
  Of Quoddy, and Tattamagouche,
Of Kennebeccasis, and Quaco,
  Of Merigonishe, and Buctouche,

Of Nashwaak, and Magaguadavique,
  Or Memmerimammericook,—
There's none like the Skoodoowabskooksis,
  Excepting the Skoodoowabskook!
           —*Author Unknown*

# 23 NOVEMBER

### The Egg That Hen Belonged To

Some observations by Samuel Butler, the man who said, "A hen is only an egg's way of making another egg":

- Jones's Conscience. He said he had not much conscience, and what little he had was guilty.
- Dogs. The great pleasure of a dog is that you may make a fool of yourself with him and not only will he not scold you, but he will make a fool of himself too.
- Solomon in all his Glory. But, in the first place, the lilies do toil and spin after their own fashion, and, in the next, it was not desirable that Solomon should be dressed like a lily of the valley.
- From a worldly point of view there is no mistake so great as that of always being right.
- God is Love. I dare say. But what a mischievous devil Love is!
- A little boy and a little girl were looking at a picture of Adam and Eve. "Which is Adam and which is Eve?" said one. "I do not know," said the other; "but I could tell if they had their clothes on."
- Seasickness. How holy people look when they are seasick! . . . He [the seasick man] made a noise like cows coming home to be milked on an April evening.
- The Complete Drunkard. He would not give money to sober people, he said, because they would only eat it and send their children to school with it.
- Falsehood. If a man is not a good, sound, honest, capable liar there is no truth in him. Any fool can tell the truth, but it requires a man of some sense to know how to lie well. I do not mind lying, but I hate inaccuracy.
- Theist and atheist. The fight between them is as to whether God shall be called God or shall have some other name.
- All progress is based upon a universal, innate desire of every organism to live beyond its income.
- To live is like love, all reason is against it and all healthy instinct for it.
- Life is one long process of getting tired.

# 24 NOVEMBER

### *"There But for the Grace of God . . ."*

Nancy McPhee gathered hundreds of offensive remarks along the order of these into *The Book of Insults:*

- OSCAR WILDE: George Moore wrote brilliant English until he discovered grammar.
- ACTOR to OLIVER HERFORD: I'm a smash hit. Why, yesterday I had the audience glued in their seats! HERFORD: Clever of you to think of it.
- MARK TWAIN on CECIL RHODES: I admire him, I frankly confess it; and when his time comes I shall buy a piece of the rope for a keepsake.
- BENJAMIN DISRAELI on LORD JOHN RUSSELL: If a traveler were informed that such a man was leader of the House of Commons, he may well begin to comprehend how the Egyptians worshipped an insect.
- GYPSY ROSE LEE (on a pretentious chorus girl): She is descended from a long line that her mother listened to.

- JOHN MASON BROWN: Tallulah Bankhead barged down the Nile last night as Cleopatra—and sank.

### DISRAELI AND GLADSTONE

- GLADSTONE: I understand, sir, that you are a witty fellow.
- DISRAELI: Some people are under that impression.
- GLADSTONE: I'm told that you can make a joke on any subject.
- DISRAELI: That is quite possible.
- GLADSTONE: Then I challenge you—make a joke about Queen Victoria.
- DISRAELI: Sir, Her Majesty is not a subject.

(In the French version of this exchange, the protagonists are Louis XVI and the wit Marquis de Bièvre. LOUIS: Marquis, there is no subject you don't pun on. Make a pun about me. DE BIÈVRE: *Sire, le roi n'est pas un sujet.*)

# 25 NOVEMBER

## *Winchellese*

It must have been at about the time that the country tilted into the Great Depression that I first saw "celebrity" shortened to "celeb." The truncation occurred, naturally, in a Walter Winchell newspaper column. "Celeb" is one of the few Winchellisms that have endured. Many were only respellings or distortions of familiar words: "That's the sitch-ee-ay-shun," or "What producer gave his squaw a swelegant black orb after He Found Her Out?" or "Oakie's sensayuma is de-voon." Some Winchellisms were puns: "Girlesq"; "Things about a Restaurant I Never Noodle Now." Others were inelegant wordplay: "The neatest of squelches for bores, to wit: 'Oh, you're simply too, too, threesome.'"

The most famous Winchellisms were in the area somewhat misleadingly known as love. Winchell loved his celebs passionately, but not so passionately as he loved their love affairs. It is common knowledge that the course of true love seldom runs smooth: Winchell exploited the fact that the course of untrue love seldom runs smooth either. He flitted from nightclub table to nightclub table, on the watch for some hint of tumescence. When he saw the telltale, he told his readers, linking each confidence with a string of dots denoting breathlessness. He kept them informed as the balloon swelled, and he clapped his hands with public glee when it popped.

Having to tell the same story again and again about different people, he found that the best way to avoid monotony was to create a variety of arch words for a single meaning. The result was the repellent language known as Winchellese. It fascinates. Here are some examples of the tongue:

*They're in love:*
- "That rumor about Jed Harris being yowzuh over Margaret Sullavan is true."
- "Dorothy Parker is riding the skies again with Alan Campbell."

- "Drew Eberson and Betty Boyd have that droopy look in their orbs."
- "Prince George of Russia and Mary Hoyt Wiborg have the tremors."
- "Vincent Youman and Marjorie Oolricks are dueting."
- "Neva Lynn and E. Judson are On The Verge."
- "Eileen Wenzel and Nicholas Blair are plenty Voom Voom."
- "Mrs. J. Loose and V. P. Curtis are blazing."

*They're getting married:*
- "Charles Chaplin is about to announce his Secret Merger."
- "Jack Pickford and Mary Mulhern will probably middle-aisle it."
- "Jayne Shattuck and Jack Kirkland Blend on Friday."

*They're expecting:*
- "The Al Trahans are threeing."
- "The Jack Dempseys will be a trio in later July."
- "The John LaGattas are infanticipating."

*They're no longer in love:*
- "Two of the polo playing Hays tribe of Chicago are unwinding secretly."
- "The Robert Carses are unraveling."
- "They have placed it in the paws of their respective counsellors."
- "Lord and Lady Cavendish will have it melted soon."
- "Roberta Wells, the oil heiress, and I. Belasco, the baton juggler, have crashed."
- "Marion Batista and Tom Hamilton have phfftt." (How Winchell relished that phfftt!)
- "Stella Duna and the heart, Francis Lederer, are shrugging."
- "So the Fred Warings are having the handcuffs melted after all."
- "The Arthur Mays are Renovating it."

# 26 NOVEMBER

## *N'Heure Souris Rames*

In *Mots d'Heures Gousses Rames*, by the late Luis D'Antin Van Rooten, French words strung together evoke the sound of English-language nursery rhymes. (The elaborate scholastic footnotes are part of the jape.) Now comes poet Ormonde de Kay in a book called *N'Heure Souris Rames* to carry on the great tradition:

> Tu marques et tu marques et
>    Tu bailles, effet typique.[1]
> Heaume et gaine! Heaume et gaine!
>    Gigoté chic![2]
> Tu marques et tu marques et
>    Tu bailles, effet tac.[3]

Heaume et gaine! Heaume et gaine!
Gigoté Jacques!

[1]"You mark and you mark and you yawn, a typical effect." The speaker is evidently chiding, rather scornfully, an individual engaged in marking or writing something, perhaps a small merchant marking prices on merchandise for sale or totting up his take.

[2]"[My] helmet and sheath! [*bis*] [My] fine prancer!" (*Gigoté*—a horse strong in the hind legs.) It appears that the speaker is a horseman, very possibly a wandering knight, who longs for action, though the fact that both the items of military gear he apostrophizes are protective in function suggests that he is not really all that keen for a fight, the true purpose of his crying out being, one suspects, to proclaim his moral superiority, as a warrior, over his money-grubbing interlocutor. Incidentally, his steed is named Jacques (see last line).

[3]When the persistent marker yawns a second time the speaker notices a clicking sound (*tac*). While the first known mention of dentures occurs in a manuscript of the year 1728 by the French dental surgeon Pierre Fouchard, it is conceivable that Fouchard's compatriot, the persistent marker, an enterprising person clearly endowed with singleness of purpose, could centuries earlier have devised for himself a set of artificial teeth, which, by permitting him to smile broadly, would have made it easier for him to ingratiate himself with customers.

—*Ormonde de Kay*

# 27 November

## *A Zoological Romance*

### INSPIRED BY AN UNUSUAL FLOW OF ANIMAL SPIRITS

No sweeter girl ewe ever gnu
Than Betty Marten's daughter Sue.

With sable hare, small tapir waist,
And lips you'd gopher miles to taste;

Bright, lambent eyes, like the gazelle,
Sheep pertly brought to bear as well;

Ape pretty lass, it was avowed,
Of whom her marmot to be proud.

Deer girl! I loved her as my life,
And vowed to heifer for my wife.

Alas! a sailor, on the sly,
Had cast on her his wether eye—

He'd dog her footsteps everywhere,
Anteater in the easy-chair.

He'd setter round, this sailor chap,
And pointer out upon the map

The spot where once a cruiser boar
Him captive to a foreign shore.

The cruel captain far outdid
The yaks and crimes of Robert Kid.

He oft would whale Jack with the cat,
And say, "My buck, doe you like that?

"What makes you stag around so, say!
The catamounts to something, hey?"

Then he would seal it with an oath,
And say, "You are a lazy sloth!"

"I'll starve you down, my sailor fine,
Until for beef and porcupine!"

And, fairly horse with fiendish laughter,
Would say, "Henceforth, mind what giraffe ter!"

In short, the many risks he ran
Might well a llama braver man.

Then he was wrecked and castor shore
While feebly clinging to anoa;

Hyena cleft among the rocks
He crept, *sans* shoes and minus ox;

And when he fain would goat to bed,
He had to lion leaves instead.

Then Sue would say, with troubled face,
"How koodoo live in such a place?"

And straightway into tears would melt,
And say, "How badger must have felt!"

While he, the brute, woodchuck her chin,
And say, "Aye-aye, my lass!" and grin.

\* \* \* \* \*

Excuse these steers . . . It's over now;
There's naught like grief the hart can cow.

Jackass'd her to be his, and she—
She gave Jackal and jilted me.

And now, alas! the little minks
Is bound to him with Hymen's lynx.
—*Charles Follen Adams*

# 28 NOVEMBER

### *Jensen with Scotch in Hand*

Jensen with Scotch in hand was heard to say
That **Noontime** is the DEADWOOD of the day.
"Give me," cried he, "the **Glamour** of the dark;
A **Bembo** who will cuddle in the park!
Perhaps some **Oriental** with **Oblique**
Regard and dainty **MOLE** on **SHADED** cheek!
Some fair Amati, **DANDY** Nymphic peach
To show me *Boulevard*, BROADWAY or BOUL MICH
Some **Latin, Wide** Open for the marriage bell!
Suburban French! Parisian Mademoiselle!
In *Stygian Black* Schadow let me hold
An **Ultra Modern Venus Extra Bold**!
'Neath Stellar Light I'll *Charme* and *Fox* the maid
With SAPPHIRE CIRCLET, DIAMOND-INLAID;
Onyx and O PA L BRACELET drape upon her,
And write a **Novel Gothic** in her honor.
I'll woo her with **Typewriter** and with *Quill*
I'll take her to BURLESQUE and VAUDEVILLE;
To Barnum, P. T., and the CIRCUS too;
To *Zebra*, ZEPHYR, Zeppelin and zoo.
With KLONDIKE GOLD I'll *Signal* my desire;
With *Coronet* her MARBLE HEART I'll fire.
If she from all this **Artcraft Bold** should shrink,
Why then (says Jensen with Scotch in hand), I think
                    . . . I'll have another drink."

—*W.R.E.*

# 29 NOVEMBER

## Faultily Faultless

A cosmetic ad says, "Honest makeup!" One would think such an oxymoron would cancel itself out, but the effect seems to be synergistic. Claudio's oxymorons did not soften his indictment of Hero:

> But fare thee well, most foul, most fair! farewell,
> Thou pure impiety, and impious purity!

Swinburne described the archetypical poet as a "bird of the bitter bright grey golden morn," with "poor splendid wings." Erasmus made an oxymoron out of one word: "foolosophers."

I give you an oxymoronic jingle:

> *By yourself, you are:*
>
>> Faultily faultless,\*
>> Splendidly null,†
>> Politely insulting,
>> Brilliantly dull.
>
> *By myself, I am:*
>
>> A little bit big,‡
>> A bigger bit little;
>> Idly laborious,
>> Gummily brittle.
>
> *Together, we are:*
>
>> Modestly arrogant,
>> Sadly amused,
>> Cheerfully mournful,
>> Clearly confused.§
>>            —W.R.E.

# 30 NOVEMBER

## The Venom of Contented Critics

That is the way someone described dramatic criticism, and here are some drops of the venom:

Noel Coward on a play about an obnoxious schoolboy: "Both the boy's throat and the second act should be cut." A capsule criticism of *I Am a Camera*: "No Leica." Eugene Field on Creston Clarke's portrayal of King Lear: "Mr.

---

\* Tennyson.
† Tennyson.
‡ Thurber.
§ The British Foreign Office, reporting on the situation in Iraq.

Clarke played the king as though under momentary apprehension that someone else was about to play the ace." Howard Dietz on Tallulah Bankhead: "A day away from Tallulah is like a month in the country."

George Oppenheimer objected to a geriatric drama: "I don't like plays," he said, "in a varicose vein."

An aspiring playwright asked Carl Sandburg, "How could you sleep through my dress rehearsal when you knew how much I wanted your opinion?" "Young man," said Sandburg, "sleep *is* an opinion."

John Chapman predicted that a play starring Mae West would be a bust, "which," he said, "is one more than Mae West needs."

Banned from the Shubert theatres, Walter Winchell said, "I can't go to the openings, eh? Well, I'll wait three days and go to the closings."

None of those jeremiads appeared in the advertisements for the plays. Every producer, like every publisher, has a slavey behind the curtain who is charged with extracting a favorable word or phrase from even the most damning review. *New York Times* film critic Vincent Canby says an advertisement in the *Times* for Ingmar Bergman's film "The Touch" included a misleading endorsement, attributed to Mr. Canby, that said:

> INGMAR BERGMAN'S "THE TOUCH" TELLS A LOVE
> STORY FULL OF THE INNUENDOES OF HIS GENIUS

This, he says, is how they did it:

> They took the headline on the review that said simply "Berg-man's 'Touch' Tells a Love Story" and then skipped to the 10th paragraph of the review to ransack a sentence that said, in its entirety: "Bergman may occasionally make dull movies—as I believe 'The Touch' to be—but he cannot be stupid, and 'The Touch' is full of what might be called the innuendoes of his genius."

Book reviewers too are occasionally unkind, as witness this report by John Jay Chapman:

> Did you hear what Howells once said to a boring author who was trying to wring a compliment out of him? "I don't know how it is," said the author, "I don't seem to *write* as well as I used to do." "Oh, yes you do—indeed you do. You write as well as you ever did. But your *taste* is improving."

Keith Preston was one of the few reviewers without carbolic acid in his veins. I commend his point of view to other critics:

> We cannot bear to roast a book
> Nor brutally attack it.
> We lay it gently in our lap
> And dust its little jacket.

# DECEMBER

## 1 DECEMBER

*The Poodle Doodle Whitney D. Didn't Noodle*

Whitney D.
Noodles
Doodles.
Whitney D.
Promised he
Would noodle
A poodle
Doodle
For me.
Do you see
A poodle
Doodle
By Whitney D.?
Where can it be
That poodle

Doodle
Whitney D.
Promised me?
I'd give oodles
Boodles
Flapdoodles
Kiyoodles
Yankee doodles
Of boodles
To see
The poodle
Doodle
Whitney D.
Didn't noodle
For me—
            i.e.,
        —W.R.E.

# 2 December

## *Friend in the Middle*

J. Newton Friend invites you to make words by putting three letters on each side of the combinations below:

| | | | |
|---|---|---|---|
| 1. URAL | 5. CAUT | 9. REDI | 13. CTRO |
| 2. OCIA | 6. HEST | 10. DPEC | 14. HANI |
| 3. UPUL | 7. MENT | 11. OLUT | 15. USTR |
| 4. CINA | 8. IDEL | 12. EPHO | 16. GERH |

# 3 December

## *Pseudo-opposites*

| | |
|---|---|
| Night hawk | Mourning dove |
| Catwalk | Dogtrot |
| Ant hill | Uncle Sam |
| Water mark | Fire brand |
| Lowlands | High seas |

—*David L. Silverman*

| | |
|---|---|
| Undergo | Overcome |
| Hereafter | Therefore |
| Write ahead | Left behind |
| Piece work | War games |
| Rare coins | Common sense |
| Cargo | Bus stop |

—*Murray Pearce*

| | |
|---|---|
| Undertow | Overhaul |
| Hotheads | Cold feet |
| Creeping thyme | Walking space |

—*Les Card*

# 4 December

## *Ambivalence in the Oyster Beds*

Scientists are still arguing about what destroyed the native oysters in the bay off Oysterville. This double-dactyl explanation of their extinction is as good as any:

Evil days fell upon
Oysterville, Washington;
Oysters grew testy, no
More reproduced.

Theirs was a quandary
Hermaphroditical:
Which should be gander and
Which should be goosed.
—*W.R.E.*

Florence M. Platt understood the problem:

### THE BEWILDERED OYSTER

Oh me, Oh my, what shall I do?
Asked the oyster of its mother.
Yesterday I was just a girl but
Since I slept, I am her brother.
There's no sense in your complaining
I haven't time to bother;
You're not the only changeling here
Since I have just become your father.

# 5 DECEMBER

## *Alimentary Canals Abroad*

"Alimentary Canals Around the World" is a twelve-nation stew of palatable
verses, two of which I serve up here:

### FRANCE

Digestions of the Gallic school
are tuned to *escargots* and *moules,*
*terrine* and crusty bread and *mousse*
and *cassoulets* of pork or goose.
French mice will mutter "Quel dommage!"
if traps aren't set with fine *fromage*
while hens rinse off with *Chambertin*
to qualify as *coq au vin.*
For him you bore that bygone day,
our thanks, Madame Escoffier.

### GERMANY

The Germans fuel the body cavity
with fare of great specific gravity.
Digestive enzymes tilt and topple

under the threat of *hoppelpoppel,*
*hassenpfeffer* and *pfefferbrot*
thundering heavily down the throat.
Scarce is that gone (though not forgotten),
there follows a volley of *sauerbraten.*
"Watch out, watch out," the enzymes whine,
"Upstairs he's reached for *gänzeklein*
and, after a *bier* to quench his thirst,
no doubt we all can expect the *wurst.*"
—E. C. K. Read

# 6 DECEMBER

## *Green Red? Yes No*

Life is filled with paradoxes. So is language. So is *Word Ways,* quoted here:

- To walk down the street is to walk up the street.
- Since the hour hand is the first hand on a clock, and the minute hand is the second hand, the second hand is the third hand.
- Yesterday's tomorrow is tomorrow's yesterday.
- A day consisting of twenty-four hours, nighttime must be day-time.
- An inexperienced Communist is a green Red.
- If the left direction is right, then right is wrong.
- The king is dead, long live the king!
- You must slow down in a speed zone.
- An even number that is also a prime number is an odd number: the only one known is two.
- To fill out a form is to fill it in.
- "No" in Hawaiian is "yes."
- Shameless behavior is shameful, and vice versa.
- To stay within a budget, one must go without.
- A near miss is a near hit.
- A boxing ring is square.
- A tree must be cut down before it is cut up.
- A lawyer's brief is frequently lengthy.
- A slim chance is the same as a fat chance.
- To drink up, you down your drink.
- When a house burns up it burns down.
- When the bases are loaded, a walk is a run.

# 7 DECEMBER

## *Ounce Dice Trice*

"Words," says the poet Alastair Reid, "have a sound and shape, in addition to their meanings. Sometimes the sound *is* the meaning. If you take a word like BALLOON and say it aloud seven or eight times, you will grow quite dizzy with it."

Mr. Reid elaborated his point in a book called *Ounce Dice Trice*. (I am sorry I cannot reproduce Ben Shahn's illustrations.) Here is the source of the title:

> "If you get tired of counting *one, two, three,* make up your own numbers, as shepherds used to do when they had to count sheep day in, day out . . . : OUNCE, DICE, TRICE, QUARTZ, QUENCE, SAGO, SERPENT, OXYGEN, NITROGEN, DENIM."

The way to get the feel of words, says the poet, "is to begin with a sound and let it go. ZZZZ is the sound of someone sleeping. From it, you easily move to BUZZ and DIZZY, and soon you have a list: ZZZZ, BUZZ, FIZZLE, GUZZLE, BUZZARD, BAMBOOZLE. Or begin with OG and see what happens: OG, FROG, OGLED, GOGGLED, GROGGY, TOBOGGAN, HEDGEHOG."

Mr. Reid has *light words* (ARIEL, WILLOW, SPINNAKER); *heavy words* (DUFFLE, BLUNDERBUSS, GALOSHES); *words to be said on the move* (FLIT, FLUCTUATE, WOBBLE); *squishy words* (SQUIFF, SQUIDGE, SQUAMOUS); *bug words* (HUMBUG, BUGBEAR, BUGABOO). And many, many more.

I give you here a few of his Garlands, "odd words, either forgotten or undiscovered, with which you can bamboozle almost anyone."

## GARLANDS

*What is a Tingle-airey?*
A *tingle-airey* is a hand organ, usually played on the street by the turning of a handle, and often decorated with mother-of-pearl or *piddock* shells.

*What are Piddocks?*
*Piddocks* are little mollusks which bore holes in rocks and wood, or in the *breastsummers* of buildings.

*What is a Breastsummer?*
A *breastsummer* is a great beam supporting the weight of a wall, and sometimes of a *gazebo* above.

*What is a Gazebo?*
A *gazebo* is a round balcony with large windows looking out on a view, often of ornamental gardens and *cotoneasters*.

*What is a Cotoneaster?*
A *cotoneaster* is a kind of flowering shrub, a favorite of *mumruffins*.

*What is a Mumruffin?*
A *mumruffin* is a long-tailed tit which often visits bird tables in winter for its share of *pobbies*.

*What are Pobbies?*
*Pobbies* are small pieces of bread *thrumbled* up with milk and fed to birds and baby animals.

*What is Thrumbled?*
*Thrumbled* is squashed together. Ants thrumble round a piece of bread, and crowds in streets thrumble round *gongoozlers.*

*What is a Gongoozler?*
A *gongoozler* is an idle person who is always stopping in the street and staring at a curious object like a *tingle-airey.*

Alastair Reid goes on with more Garlands, but this seems a good place to cut off, since we are back at our beginning and can start again.

# 8 DECEMBER

### SUSAN SIMPSON

*S* starts more words than any other letter—including every word in this verse (as long as you consider *side-by-side* one word):

> Sudden swallows softly skimming,
>     Sunset's slowly spready shade,
> Silvery songsters sweetly singing
>     Summer's soothing serenade.
>
> Susan Simpson strolled sedately,
>     Stifling sobs, suppressing sighs.
> Seeing Stephen Slocum, stately
>     She stopped, showing some surprise.
>
> "Say," said Stephen, "sweetest sigher;
>     Say, shall Stephen spouseless stay?"
> Susan, seeming somewhat shyer,
>     Showed submissiveness straightway.
>
> Summer's season slowly stretches,
>     Susan Simpson Slocum she—
> So she signed some simple sketches—
>     Soul sought soul successfully.
>
> Six Septembers Susan swelters;
>     Six sharp seasons snow supplies;
> Susan's satin sofa shelters
>     Six small Slocums side-by-side.
>         —*Anonymous*

If "Susan Simpson" had been written 100 years earlier, the printer would have used an *f*-like font at the beginning and middle of the words. The extinct letter has a rather wide open top; the tail does not go below the line; and the little bar is confined to the left-hand side of the tail.

# 9 DECEMBER

### Stop Hissing, Belinda!

Barbara, does it bother you that your name has the same root as barbarous? Leah, when I say I love you do you realize that I am protesting my devotion to a cow?

Let me confine my point to the names of beasts. As the curtain rises, we find a cluster of these milling about the cradle of a newborn girl. Each wishes the babe to bear its own name.

*The Chorus speaks:*

*Hair and scale and wool and starling,*
*How shall mummy name her darling?*

*The Beasts speak:*

"Pick *Jemima*," DOVE suggests;
"*Lilith*, rather," SNAKE contests.
(He'd accept *Ophelia*, too;
Or *Belinda*, that would do.)

"*Ursula*," growls father BEAR;
"*Leah*," BOSSY doth declare;
"*Agnes, Agnes*," baas the LAMB;
"*Rachel, Rachel*," bleats her DAM.

"*Lupe, Lupe*," WOLF doth cry;
"*Vanessa*," answers BUTTERFLY.
"*Dorcas*" the GAZELLE doth please;
"*Deborah*," the HONEY BEES.

*The Chorus speaks again:*

*Hair and scale and wool and starling,*
*How shall mummy name her darling?*
—W.R.E.

# 10 DECEMBER

### Cork and Work and Card and Ward

I take it you already know
Of tough and bough and cough and dough?
Others may stumble, but not you
On hiccough, thorough, laugh, and through?

I write in case you wish perhaps
To learn of less familiar traps:
Beware of heard, a dreadful word
That looks like beard, and sounds like bird.
And dead: it's said like bed, not bead;
For goodness' sake, don't call it 'deed'!
Watch out for meat and great and threat
(They rhyme with suite and straight and debt).
A moth is not a moth in mother,
Nor both in bother, broth in brother.
And here is not a match for there,
Nor dear for bear, or fear for pear.
There's dose and rose, there's also lose
(Just look them up), and goose, and choose,
And cork and work, and card and ward,
And font and front, and word and sword,
And do and go and thwart and cart—
Come come, I've barely made a start!
A dreadful language? Man alive,
I'd mastered it when I was five!

—*Anonymous*

# 11 DECEMBER

### *I Kmnow Pfil Pfizer Pfomnebd Me, Though*

*Bdellium* is an aromatic gum resin similar to myrrh; the *bd* is pronounced *d*. *Ptisan* is a slightly medical infusion, such as barley water; the *pt* is pronounced *t*, as in *pterodactyl*. Likewise the *pf* in *Pfizer* sounds *f*, the *mn* in *Mnemosyne* sounds *n*, and the *ps* in *psychologist* sounds *s*. Therefore:

Pfil Pfizer pfomnebd me pto imparpt
Mnemosymne'ps amn amnciemnpt ptarpt,
   Amnd myrrh ips bdellium creamebd.
Psychiaptripstps, he mnexpt amnmnoumnceps,
Drepsps pterobdacptylps' youmng imn pfloumnceps,
   Amnd ptoabdps eapt ptisanps pspteamebd.
I bdo mnopt kmnow thapt thips ips pso;
I kmnow Pfil Pfizer pfomnebd me, though.

—*W.R.E.*

# 12 DECEMBER

### *Biographical Sketch*

Mrs. J. W. Haltiwanger writes that she is planning to discuss a book of mine at a meeting of her study club and needs biographical information. I have sent her the following verse, which might have been written with me in mind:

## ONCE—BUT NO MATTER WHEN

Once—but no matter when—
There lived—no matter where—
A man, whose name—but then
I need not that declare.

He—well, he had been born,
And so he was alive;
His age—I details scorn—
Was somethington and five.

He lived—how many years
I truly can't decide;
But this one fact appears:
He lived—until he died.

"He died." I have averred,
But cannot prove 'twas so;
But that he was interred,
At any rate, I know.

I fancy he'd a son,
I hear he had a wife:
Perhaps he'd more than one—
I know not, on my life!

But whether he was rich
Or whether he was poor,
Or neither—both—or which—
I cannot say, I'm sure.

I can't recall his name
Or what he used to do:
But then—well, such is fame!
'Twill so serve me and you.

And that is why I thus
About this unknown man
Would fain create a fuss,
To rescue, if I can,

From dark oblivion's blow,
Some record of his lot:
But, ah! I do not know
Who—why—where—when—or what.
                          —*Anonymous*

# 13 December

### \*\*\*\*\*\*\*\*\*\* *Drank for 969 Years*

I gave up any notion of abandoning liquor when I read that even if I stopped drinking altogether, my stomach would go right on brewing something like a gallon of beer a day.

Here is a set of bibulous anagrams on the name of a man who bibbed joyously for 969 years.

> Muse, say not I (tush \*\*\*\*!) \*\* \*\*\*\*
> That out of ale I make my meal.
> \*\*\*\*\*\*\*\*\*\*, it now appears,
> \*\*\* \*\*\*\* \*\*\* was of many beers.
> No gold a man might \*\*\*\* \*\*\* \*\*\*
> Gold as the \*\*\*\* \*\* \*\*\*\* would brew;
> And no \*\*\*\* \*\*\* \*\*\* kick those beers
> Supplied him for a thousand years.
> \*\*\*\*, \*\*\*\*\*\* waits in the glass! I pray
> Let ale \*\*\*\*; \*\*\*\* \*\* not away.
> —W.R.E.

# 14 December

## *The Quodlibets of Tom Aquinas*

Seventeen folio volumes, says Isaac Disraeli, testify to the industry and genius of Thomas Aquinas, the Angelical Doctor: "A great man, busied all his life with making the charades of metaphysics."

### I

### ON LOVE, DEMONS, SOUL, AND SINS

> Ne'er divine was so divine as
> Sainted Doctor Tom Aquinas,
> Who on LOVE wrote plus or minus
> Eight discursions and eight score;
> On DEMONS, five and eighty more;
> On SOUL, two hundred. Then he tore
> Into SINS, and from him sundered
> Thirty-seven plus two hundred,
> Who in batlike panic blundered
> Into this old debauchee.
> Tom, the sins you lodged in me
> Flourish like the green bay tree.
> —W.R.E.

II

## ON ANGELS

You'll find items infinite in
Tom on Angels. He has written
Fifteen score and ten and eight
On angelical estate.

Tom can tell you whether mange'll
Harm the feathers of an angel;
Whether angels moult, or shed;
How they fold their wings in bed;

Tell their substance, orders, natures,
Offices, and legislatures;
How they differ in their species;
If they're he's or she's or he-she's.

He can count the cherubin
Doing kick-ups on a pin
(But he keeps their numbers hidden,
Knowing dancing is forbidden).

More corporeal than God is,
Less corporeal than bodies,
Angels don't have matter where
Matter matters—they have air.
—*W.R.E.*

III

## A FUNDAMENTAL DISPUTE

The contradiction between man's corporeal and spiritual parts was a source of endless quodlibetting by Tom Aquinas and his fellow disquisitors in the seventeenth century. Today's more ardent ecologists can sympathize with their dilemma:

Shall good men on the Final Day
With Bowels be to Heaven sent,
To soil the very Seat of God
With Risen Human Excrement?
—*W.R.E.*

# 15 December

## *Holey, Holey, Holey, Holed Sox Almighty*

Homophonic puns, irresistible a couple of centuries ago, are showing signs of wear, but I still fall for them, as you see here:

I sought to hold a maiden,
As fair as any foaled,
With golden tresses laden—
Well heeled, and so well soled.
(I could not take the jade in
Because my sox were holed.)

I'd normally have sold her
With clever lies well told;
Or maybe bowled her over
With kisses overbold;
(But I could not enfold her,
Because my sox were holed.)

Quoth she, "I find you holy,
All-wise, and lofty-souled;
But I reject you wholly—
My goal depends on gold.
(Not just your sox are holey,
Your trousers too are holed.)"

"Though hotly coaled your stove be,"
Cried I, "your heart is cold;
I'd rather die and moulder
Than fit into your mold.
Let richer lovers hold you—
I like my sox well-holed."

*You dears whose arms enfold me,*
*Long, long may you be skoaled!*
*But as for you who scold me*
*Because my clothes are old,*
*I'll live to see you mould,*
*And when your death-bell's tolled,*
*I'll dance in sox still holed.*
                              —W.R.E.

# 16 December

## *Games for Insomniacs*

That's the name of a verbal kaleidoscope of a book drawn by John G. Fuller from his *Saturday Review* column, "Trade Winds." Mr. Fuller multiplies a thousandfold snippets like the following:

- BUSINESS SLOGANS. The Victor Refuse Company (to the Victor Belong the Spoils); the Macduff Linoleum Company (Lay On Macduff); the Mercy Baby Food Company (the Quality of Mercy is Not Strained).

- FRACTURED BOOK REVIEWS. *Webster's Dictionary:* Too wordy. *Hammond's Atlas:* Covers too much ground. *Handbook of Adhesives:* Couldn't put it down.
- BOOK TITLES. *Tender is the Knight:* Memoirs of a dragon who devoured Sir Galahad. *Gone to Pot:* Confessions of a Dope Addict.
- ANIMAL CRACKERS. As inflamed as a moth; as hidebound as a rhino; as canny as a sardine; as testy as a guinea pig; as chaste as a fox; as instinctive as a skunk.
- INVERTED ZOO. Whales that had a people of a good time; the sardines who felt like people in the subway; the cat who let the man out of the bag.
- FRACTURED GEOGRAPHY. Feeling, Ill.; Hoop, La.; Requiem, Mass.; Ding, Dong, Del.; Vita, Minn.; Dunno, Alaska; Nohitsnorunsno, Ariz.
- UNLIKELY LETTER COMBINATIONS. XOP (saxophone); DHP (jodhpurs); RIJU (marijuana); OMAHA (tomahawk); AGAMU (ragamuffin); HTH (eighth); RND (dirndl); RYG (drygoods).
- EXCLAMATION—Without Point. By Jerre Mangione: What, no mummy? Tut, Tut! What, no drama? Pshaw! What, no corn? Shucks! By Marvin Preiser: What, torn socks? Darn!
- MEANINGLESS NOTHINGS. By Kelley Roos: A chainless end; a pitless bottom; a gameless score; a bra-less strap; a gemless flaw; a jobless thank; a hatless brim; a caseless hope.
- TRANSITIONAL LOGIC. By Harry Kuris, to prove a sheet of paper is a lazy dog: (1) A sheet of paper is an ink-lined plane (2) an inclined plane is a slope up (3) a slow pup is a lazy dog.
- HAPPY BIRTHDAY. Mark Koppel and his roommates send greetings to Mary Ann Haste, Judy Obscure, Bella de Ball and others.
- NEWSMEN'S SELF-INTRODUCTIONS. Some of Bruce Fessenden's: I'm Cutt from the *Blade;* I'm Brown, from the *Sun;* I'm Justice, from the *Tribune;* I'm Tied, from the *Post.* Some of E. P. H. James's: I'm Ugley, from the *American;* I'm Shakespeare, from the *Globe;* I'm Trumpett, from the *Herald.*

Go ahead—anyone can play.


# 17 DECEMBER

## Manon? Mais Non!

The following ballade is built on a series of formidable quibbles by Boris Randal on operatic compositions and composers:

MANON? MAIS NON (*A Punning Ballade*)

Aida relish cymbal-smack,
   Horn-sweetness, shrill of piccolo
(To savor these, how Offenbach
   To Bach and Offenbach I go!) . . .

Or don't. I *hate* Manon Lescaut.
(You said, "Lescaut to hear Manon:
    I've Boito tickets, second row . . . ")
*Manon Lescaut a mauvais ton.*

We go. Of Korsakov, and hack,
    As old men Lakme do; I blow
My nose, and doze. I'm in the sack
    From Faust plucked string to last *bravo*
    I dream I'm Chopin up that shmo
Puccini: *C'est un sale cochon.*
    Most art (Mozart, say) leaves a glow;
*Manon Lescaut a mauvais ton.*

Manon is Verdi vulgar pack
    Hangs out. If Massenet should throw
A Mass in A, I'd lead the claque.
    (Giovanni hear Giovanni? So
Do I. It's not quite *comme il faut,*
But Gudenov. *Alors, allons!*)
    Indeed, I only hate one show:
*Manon Lescaut a mauvais ton.*

ENVOY

Prince, best of Gluck! . . .
                One final *mot:*
    Though opera is mostly *bon,*
For Bizet folk there's one *de trop:*
    *Manon Lescaut a mauvais ton.*
                                    —W.R.E.

I call puns that require elaborate buildups Puns in Perpetuity. Here are two
Puns in Perpetuity from Arnold Moss:

Chan was a Chinese gentleman who discovered the footprints of a
small boy in the sand that led to his prize collection of valuable
teakwood. Night after night, pieces had been stolen. One night he
discovered the culprit: a huge Siberian bear, wearing boy's shoes
as he stealthily approached the wood, in an upright position.
Whereupon Chan shouted: "I see who is the thief, boy-foot bear
with teak of Chan!"

A gentle Korean named Rhee worked for *Life* magazine. Sent out
on a dangerous investigative mission, he disappeared. After a year-
long search he was finally discovered by a staff member who, on
sighting him, said: "Ah, sweet Mr. Rhee of *Life,* at last I've found
you."

# 18 December

## GREEK, GREEK, GREEK

If for some unimaginable reason you wish to memorize the Greek alphabet, here is a yell for you:

> Gimme an Alpha Beta
> Gamma Delta
>   And Epsilon!
>
> Gimme a Zeta, Eta, Theta,
> Iota Kappa Lambda
> Mu Nu XI
>   And Omicron!
>
> Gimme a Pi!
> Gimme a Rho!
>   A Sigma Tau
>   An Upsilon!
>
> Gimme a Phi!
>           Chi!
>               Psi!
> O–M–E–G–A!
> And a piece of bread and butter.
> —W.R.E.

# 19 December

## The Faithful Connectors

John Alden, interceding with Priscilla for Miles Standish, was what is known in grammar as a Coordinating Conjunction—that is, a connector between two principals of equal rank. In Mr. Longfellow's poem, the Connector gets the girl; in the verse below, nobody gets anything.

> I summoned my Conjunctions;
>   They entered hand in hand,
> Obedient Connectors,
>   Awaiting my command.
>
> Subservient their greeting;
>   Respectful their hello;
> Their names were *And, But, For, Nor, Or,*
>   And part-time *Yes* and *So.*

I said, "Now do your duty
    As Seventh Parts of Speech!
Restore my darling to me!
    Connect us each with each!"

Said *And*, "And how! And also
    We'll make you man and wife!"
Said *But*, "But we forewarn you,
    You'll soon miss single life."

Said *For*, "For never woman
    To husband has been true."
Said *Nor*, "Nor is this maxim
    About to change for you."

"Yet we will do our duty,"
    Said *Yet*, and *Or* said, "Or
At least we'll do our damnedest."
    Said *So*, "So who asks more?"

\* \* \*

They crept back in the morning,
    Connectors brave and good,
With scratches on their faces,
    And noses dripping blood.

Their bumps and bruises told me
    Without a sentence spoken—
Between me and my darling,
    Connections had been broken.
                    —W.R.E.

# 20 December

## *Mistletoe Means Watch Out*

A child's-eye view of Christmas is not always what an older person might expect. Two of Mike Collins's fourth-grade boys lacked the traditional spirit when it came to mistletoe:

- Mistletoe means watch out for slobry girls.
- The most dangerous thing about Christmas is standing underneath the kissletoe.

The children who wrote the following comments may grow up to be poets:

- A star is for living in heaven when it is not for wearing in a Christmas tree's hair.
- Christmas trees gives me joy feels all over.
- Pine trees give us Christmas and turpentine.

Mr. Collins's favorite Christmas reflection:

- Santa Claus lives just north of the imagination.

\*   \*   \*   \*   \*

A Christmas card by a present-day master of word puzzles:

### DOOLEY'S HATS

I suspected, of course, when I accepted the invitation to Donald Dooley's Yule party, that he was keeping something under his hat. The man loves nothing more than springing puzzles on surprised friends.

The night arrived. The party was going with the sound of golden oldies. Inebriants and potations were being poured freely, and consumed in the same spirit. And then—Dooley ducked into a side closet, to reappear triumphantly with ten hats and a word taped to the front of each. "Uh-oh," I said.

"Friends, gather round," said he, with an eye's twinkle like Santa's but a smile like Satan's. "I have a puzzle." And situating us in a circle, he paced the perimeter placing a hat on each guest's head. I could not see the word on my headpiece—in fact no one could see his own word—but I could see every other. Around the circle the words read: TENNIS. PAINT. WHITE. GREASE. OFF. ELBOW. BRUSH. TABLE. CARD.

I thought one person grinned slightly when he glanced at my word.

"What's this nonsense about a puzzle?" asked one overpixilated lady.

"It is a puzzle of logic and word sense," Dooley responded, but speaking to all of us. "You each have a hat with a word and full view of everyone else. Your goal is to be the first person to guess his word successfully."

"Any clues?" asked the man next to me.

"Yes," Dooley said. "There is a pattern among the words which becomes apparent once they are placed in proper sequence. If you can discover that pattern and put the words in order, naming your own will follow naturally."

Reaching for paper and pencil on the center table before me, I prodded my besotted gray matter into action. Several minutes later I exultantly blurted out my answer.
WHAT WAS MY WORD?

—*Will Shortz*

# 21 DECEMBER

## *One Last Croak*

James I. Rambo and Mary J. Youngquist start with standard Croakers*:

- "You snake!" she rattled.
- "Someone's at the door," she chimed.

The next step is homonymic Croakers:

- "Company's coming," she guessed.
- "Dawn came too soon," she mourned.

Next, Croakers that use only part of the verb:

- "Ring the bell," she appealed.
- "I already did," he harangued.

Next, Croakers that involve the speaker's name in the pun:

- "I think I'll end it all," Sue sighed.
- "I ordered chocolate, not vanilla," I screamed.

Finally, Croakers involving both verb and adverb:

- "Your embroidery is sloppy," she needled cruelly.
- "Where did you get this meat?" he bridled hoarsley.

# 22 DECEMBER

## *Why the Heaths Didn't Have This Year's Christmas Carol Program*

Do you know what *afforient* is? Neither did I till I heard Priscilla, who is fifteen and who should know better, sweetly warble that she three kings afforient were, and I asked her. *Afforient*, if you are interested, is the state of being disoriented, or wandering, as one does over field and fountain, moor and mountain.

*See 2 February.

And has anybody ever wondered where the Ranger is on Christmas Eve? Well, Betsey Heath has. "*Away* is the Ranger," she will inform you, if you listen carefully. And obviously, he is away because there is no crib for his bed. After all, why should the Ranger stick around *here,* when he hasn't even got a crib much less a bed for Pete's sake!

Janet, canny little Janet, all of whose sins are premeditated and blatant, sang exactly what she intended to sing. "*No L, No L the angels did say.*" It was a matter of the angels' alphabet, she explained to me a little tiredly, "A B C D E F G H I J K M N O P Q R S T U V W X Y Z. No L, *get it, Mother? No L!*" I eyed her suspiciously, because more humor in the family we do not need, but I let it pass.

Jennifer settled my next problem, which had to do with the angels. Do you know how the angel of the Lord shone around? He shone around in a glowy manner, that's how. While shepherds watch'd their flock by night, she explained, the angel of the Lord came and glowy showed around. How else?

Pam, even Pam, kept announcing in her clear, sweet contralto that God and sin are reconciled, but she realized immediately, when it was pointed out to her, that God was far more likely to reconcile Himself to sinners than to sin.

Jim had to argue a little. He was the one who kept urging the shepherds to leave their "you's" and leave their "am's" and rise up, shepherds, and follow.

"What in heaven's name is this about you's and am's?" I asked him.

"Oh-h, rejection of personality, denial of self," said Jim grandly. "Practically the central thesis of Christian theology."

"I think that's Communist theory, not Christian theology," I told him. "In any case, could you come down from those philosophic heights and join us shepherds down here with our ewes (female sheep) and rams (male sheep)?"

But I was too weary to go on. "Children," I said. "Let's just do one thing absolutely *perfectly.* Let's concentrate on 'Silent Night,' because that's the one we know best anyway. Pam and Priscilla can do the alto, John can do the descant, the rest of you just sing nice and softly, and, Buckley, I don't want to hear one single *note* below middle C."

They lined up, looking very clean and handsome and holy.

"*Silent night, holy night,*" nine young voices chanted softly, and I noticed Jennifer and Betsey beginning to break up in twinkles and dimples. "*All is calm, all is bright,*" they went on, John's recorder piping low and clear. Buckley and Alison clapped their hands briefly over their mouths. "*Round John Virgin, Mother and Child,*" the chorus swelled sweetly, and I rapped hard on the piano. "Just *who,*" I asked in my most restrained voice, "is Round John Virgin?"

"One of the twelve opossums," the young voices answered promptly, and they collapsed over the piano, from the piano bench into the floor, convulsed by their own delicate wit.

And that's why we didn't have this year's Christmas carol program.

—*Aloïse Buckley Heath*

### TROPING THE TEXT

Altar boys have been known to sing "All wipe your noses" for "Ora pro nobis." This is known as "troping the text," and it is exactly what the wicked

Heath children were doing in the foregoing account. Mrs. R. E. Guppy sent me these tropes:

- Donzerly light.
- While shepherds washed their socks by night.
- Land where the pilgrims died, land where the pigeons flied.
- We three kings of Oregon are.
- Wreck the halls with boughs of holly.
- One for his master, one for his dame, one for the little boy who lives down the drain.

In the Episcopalian Collect which begins ". . . We pray thee that thy grace may always prevent and follow us," *prevent* is from Latin *prevenio*, "to go before." The Sunday before Advent is known as Stirrup Sunday because of the opening words of the Collect: "Stir up, we beseech thee."

*—Faith Eckler*

# 23 December

## *There Is a Needle in the Bag*

Nationality transforms truth, or at least it would appear so from these matching proverbs:

| ENGLISH | FRENCH | SPANISH | JAPANESE | ARABIC | GERMAN |
|---|---|---|---|---|---|
| Little drops of water make the mighty ocean. | Little by little the bird makes his nest. | Little by little the cup is filled. | Dust may pile to form a hill. | A hair from here and there makes a beard. | Steady dripping hollows a stone. |
| Everyone has a right to his own opinion. | Everyone to his own taste. | Everyone has his own way of killing fleas. | Ten men, ten colors. | Every person is free in his opinions. | Don't quarrel about tastes. |
| Look before you leap. | Turn the tongue seven times; then speak. | Think before speaking. | Have an umbrella before getting wet. | Before you drink the soup, blow on it. | First weigh; then dare. |
| There is something rotten in Denmark. | There is an eel under the rock. | There is a cat shut up. | There is a worm in the lion's body. | There is a snake under the hay. | There is something foul in Denmark. |

| ENGLISH | FRENCH | SPANISH | JAPANESE | ARABIC | GERMAN |
|---|---|---|---|---|---|
| Don't count your chickens before they're hatched. | Don't sell the bearskin before you kill the bear. | Don't saddle before bringing the horses. | Before you kill badgers, don't count their skins. | Don't say "lima beans" before they are weighed. | Don't hang people before you have caught them. |

# 24 DECEMBER

## *A Visit from St. Nicholas*

```
                              T
                             WAS
                            THENI
                          GHTBEFO
                         RECHRISTM
                        A SWHENAL L
                       THR OUGHT HEH
                      OUSEN OTA CREAT
                     UREWASS T IRRINGN
                    OTEVENAMO USETHESTO
                   C KINGSWE R EHUNGBY T
                  HEC HIMNE YWI THCAR EIN
                 HOPES THA TSAIN TNI CHOLA
                SSOONWO U LDBETHE R ETHECHI
               LDRENWERE NESTLEDAL LSNUGINTH
              E IRBEDSW H ILEVISI O NSOFSUG A
             RPL UMSDA NCE DINTH EIR HEADS AND
            MAMMA INH ERKER CHI EFAND IIN MYCAP
           HADJUST S ETTLEDD O WNFORAL O NGWINTE
          RSNAPWHEN OUTONTHEL AWNTHEREA ROSESUCHA
         C LATTERI S PRANGFR O MMYBEDT O SEEWHAT W
        HAT WASTH EMA TTERA WAY TOTHE WIN DOWIF LEW
       LIKEA FLA SHTOR EOP ENTHE SHU TTERS AND THREW
      UPTHESA S HTHEMOO N THEBREA S TOFTHEN E WFALLEN
     SNOWGAVEA LUSTEROFM IDDAYTOOB JECTSBELO WWHENWHAT
    T OMYWOND E RINGEYE S SHOULDA P PEARBUT A MINIATU R
   ESL EIGHA NDE IGHTT INY REIND EER WITHA LIT TLEOL DDR
  IVERS OLI VELYA NDQ UICKI KNEW WINAM OME NTITM UST BESTN
 ICKMORE R APIDTHA N EAGLESH I SCOURSE R STHEYCA M EANDHEW
HISTLEDAN DSHOUTEDA NDCALLEDT HEMBYNAME NOWDASHER NOWDANCER
N OWPRANC E RANDVIX E NONCOME T ONCUPID O NDONNER A NDBLITZ E
NTO THETO POF THEPO RCH TOTHE TOP OFTHE WAL LNOWD ASH AWAYD ASH
AWAYD ASH AWAYA LLA SDRYL EAV ESTHA TBE FORET HEW ILDHU RRI CANEF
LYWHENT H EYMEETW I THANOBS T ACLEMOU N TTOTHES K YSOUPTO T HEHOUSE
TOPTHECOU RSERSTHEY FLEWITHA SLEIGHFUL LOFTOYSAN DSTNICHOL ASTOOANDT
H ENINATW I NKLEIHE A RDONTHE R OOFTHEP R ANCINGA N DPAWING O FEACHLI T
TLE HOOFA SID REWIN MYH EADAN DWA STURN ING AROUN DDO WNTHE CHI MNEYS TNI
CHOLA SCA MEWIT HAB OUNDH EWA SDRES SED ALLIN FUR FROMH ISH EADTO HIS FOOTA
NDHISCL O THESWER E ALLTARN I SHEDWIT H ASHESAN D SOOTABU N DLEOFTO Y SHEHAD
LUNGONHIS BACKANDHE LOOKEDLIK EAPEDDLER JUSTOPENI NGHISPACK HISEYESHO WTHEYTWIN
K LEDHISD I MPLESHO W MERRYHI S CHEEKSW E RELIKER O SESHISN O SELIKEA C HERRYHI S
DRO LLLIT TLE MOUTH WAS DRAWN UPL IKEAB OWA NDTHE BEA RDONH ISC HINWA SAS WHITE AST
HESNO WTH ESTUM POF APIPE HEH ELDTI GHT INHIS TEE THAND THE SMOKE ITE NCIRC LED HISHE
ADLIKEA W REATHHE H ADABROA D FACEAND A LITTER O UNDBELL Y THATSHO O KWHENHE L AUGHEDL
IKEABOWLF ULLOFJELL YHEWASCHU BBYANDPLU MPARIGHTJ OLLYOLDEL FANDILAUG HEDWHENIS AWHIMINSP
I TEOFMYS E LFAWINK O FHISEYE A NDATWIS T OFHISHE A DSOONGA V EMETOKN O WIHADNO T HINGTOD R
EAD HESPO KEN OTAWO RDB UTWEN TST RAIGH TTO HISWO RKA NDFIL LED ALLTH EST OCKIN GST HENTU RNE
DWITH AJE RKAND LAY INGHI SFI NGERA SID EOFHI SNO SEAND GIV INGAN ODU PTHEC HIM NEYHE ROS EHESP
RANGTOH I SSLEIGH T OHISTEA M GAVEAWH I STLEAND A WAYTHEY A LLFLEWL I KETHEDO W NONATHI S TLEBUTI
HEARDHIME XCLAIMASH EDROVEOUT OFSIGHTHA PPYCHRIST MASTOALLA NDTOALLAG OODNIGHTP OEMBYCLEM ENTCHMOORE
                              1822    1972
                            THIS MOST
                             FAM OUS
                              YU LE
                              PO EM
                            OBSE RVES
                            THIS XMAS
                        ITS 150TH ANNIVERSARY
```

# 25 December

## *Take Back That Powdered Rhinoceros Horn, Santa!*

To decode the following acrostic sonnet, you must know that I first intended to call this book *The Oysterville Almanac* rather than *An Almanac of Words at Play*. On the basis of the earlier title, the verse contains my season's greetings to you.

Start decoding by listing the first letter of each line, but don't stop with that—the acrostic runs down the lines twice more.

> These presents are quite odd (I speak of mine):
> Hand-painted sox; linguini made of eel;
> Engraved cigars; mice from the river Rhine;
> One yak; and barbwire for my fishing reel.
>
> You meant no harm, I know, about that yak;
> Strange gifts arise from love. (Thus, I conject,
> The queer clock ticking in my haversack
> Expresses, though bizarrely, your respect.
>
> Really, won't it explode, though—or implode?)
> Venom's a *darling* thought. Now let me see . . .
> I never saw a better-looking toad.
> Land's sake! You say it's here to marry me?
>
> *Love sometimes overdraws and misses aim.*
> *Eject this useless stuff! Thanks all the same.*
> —W.R.E.

# 26 December

## *Showoff Words*

I pass on a formula of which I made good use in the days when I was writing promotion for the cover pages of *Reader's Digest:*

To communicate and convince, write pithily, in the active voice. But to impress your authority, throw in one longer, exotic word—for instance, *karimata,* a two-headed Japanese arrow that whistles while it works—even if it has nothing to do with the point you are making. More than one showoff word, though, can become counterproductive, as you see here:

### IF FROM HYPOBULA YOU USE

> If from Hypobula you use
>   A Dysphemism to
> Engross your love's attention,
>   The gesture you may rue;

Should your Hircismus bait her nose,
She'll drive you from love's feasts
To crowd into a Savssat
With all the other beasts.
—W.R.E.

# 27 December

## The Assination of English

It is an article of faith with politicians, professors, and editorial writers that each new generation of boys and girls is handsomer, brighter, and more honest than the one before. If I ever doubted that proposition, I doubt it no longer. Here, from essays of recent school years, is the proof:

- "Henry VIII found walking difficult because he had an abbess on his knee."
- "In *A Streetcar Named Desire* the climax is when Blanche goes to bed with Stella's husband."
- "In *Mrs. Warren's Profession*, her profession is the Oldest Profession, but she is not really a Lost Woman. She is just mislaid."
- "Abstinence is a good thing if practiced in moderation."
- "Today every Tom, Dick, and Harry is named Bill."
- "A virgin forest is a place where the hand of man has never set foot."
- "It was the painter Donatello's interest in the female nude that made him the Father of the Renaissance."

—*Temple G. Porter*

# 28 December

## More Odd Ends

None of these jottings deserves a separate entry, but I like the way they bubble together in the pot. In this game for a quiet evening, the first player asks a question, to be defined by the answer:

- Do you know what procrastination is?
  I've been meaning to look it up.
- Do you know what conciseness is?
  Yes.
- Do you know what irritability is?
  Stop bothering me with silly questions.

—*Jane R. Barliss*

*Time* magazine here defines *Btfsplkian,* as in this quotation from the magazine: "Yakubovsky has a Btfsplkian habit of turning up just before something big happens":

> Btfsplkian (unpronounceable) *adj.* [Neologism, from Joe Btfsplk, a cartoon character in Al Capp's *Li'l Abner* who is accompanied by a little black cloud of disaster wherever he goes] 1: Full of bad luck and imminent mishap for anyone in the vicinity. 2: Baleful; calamitous; pernicious; unpropitious; as in "Joe Btfsplk attended a sailing party for the *Andrea Doria.*"

Dr. Johnson said he advised young people to rise early, but slept in until noon himself. He would have admired Hungarian author Ferenc Molnàr, so unaccustomed to early rising that when called for morning jury duty, he gawked from his hansom cab at the thronged streets of Budapest, marveling, "Are they *all* jurors?"

John K. Spencer copied these reflections from the wall of a men's room at a divinity school:

> (The first)  Eternity is forever.
> (The second) Better bring an extra pair of socks.

Kim Garretson says these graffiti were written in three hands:

> To do is to be. *John Stuart Mill*
> To be is to do. *Jean Paul Sartre*
> Do be, Do be, Do. *Frank Sinatra*

"I have just turned sixty," writes Elizabeth L. Stanley, "and am referred to as an 'older' woman. Yet an 'old' woman is actually someone older than that. And the word *oldest* can refer to a child of five who has younger siblings."

New dictionary definitions might help:

old: older than older
oldest: younger than older, but older than younger
You're looking very well: has the date been set for your funeral service?

# 29 DECEMBER

## *With Fading Breath*

It was 1635, and the sorrowers grouped about the bedside of dying Spanish dramatist Lope de Vega warned him that he was slipping away fast. "All right, then," he whispered, "I'll say it. Dante makes me sick."

A priest asked Ramón María Narváez, statesman-general to Queen Isabella of Spain, whether he forgave his enemies. "I don't have to," he replied. "I've had them all shot."

Herbert Hoover, celebrating his eightieth birthday at the Dutch Treat Club, declared he felt no remnants of bitterness toward the political enemies who had savaged him in the White House. "I am reminded," he went on, "of the old man who got shakily to his feet when the preacher asked, 'Is there anyone in this congregation with no bitterness in his heart for a single human being? Behold, my dear brethren,' exclaimed the preacher, 'a man whose heart holds only love! Tell me, sir—how did this happen?' 'I outlived the sons of bitches,' quavered the old man."

It is not true, as often stated, that Oscar Wilde called for champagne and said, "I am dying as I lived—beyond my means." A more likely account is that he breathed his last in a miserable room, with a priest imploring him to recant his past wickedness. Wilde turned his face to the peeling wallpaper, and said, "One of us has to go." With that he expired.

I have heard, but doubt extremely, that the last words of Gertrude Lawrence, star of *The King and I*, were: "See that Yul Brynner gets star billing. He deserves it."

Nor would I place too much credence in the last words given here:

- Boswell: I believe, if I could again visit Corsica, I might recover.
- Jane Austen: I wish I had someone to smile with me.
- Berkeley: What matter, my friends, that I must leave you? There is no matter.
- Dr. Bowdler:  A. I have purged.
              B. Had I but lived to purify the scriptures!
              C. Macbeth: Three, One, Twenty-nine, delete "bloody."
- Mae West: Turn off that red light.
- Casanova: Your lips are cold, madam.
- Donne: I am un-Done!
- Nero: I shall burn while Rome fiddles.
- Stalin: Doctor, quick, another purge!
- Sullivan: I must compose myself.
- Shakespeare:  A. Don't let Ben mess around with my plays.
              B. My second-best bed! The rest is silence.
  (dies, chuckling)

# 30 DECEMBER

## *Year-End Interview*

Q. Looking at yourself objectively, Mr. Espy, sir, what would you say is your outstanding characteristic?
A. Oh—modesty.
Q. And what has held you back most?
A. Modesty.

Q. Who would you say is the finest writer in English?

A. No comment. Modesty, you know.

Q. Let me broaden the question, sir. Of all the books you have ever read, which do you consider the finest?

A. Sorry, it is not quite finished.

Q. And the finest writer?

A. Won't you reporters ever allow a fellow any privacy?

Q. Would you name your favorite composer—Bach, Beethoven, Handel, that sort of thing?

A. I have never taken up that line of work. But to answer your question—Dick Hyman, the jazz man. No doubt of it.

Q. Would you explain?

A. He is putting my verses to music. Once I have heard them, I will be glad to tell you my favorite musical composition.

Q. What is your favorite city, Mr. Espy?

A. Oysterville, Washington. Subject of one of the outstanding books of our time.

Q. Who is the author?

A. No comment. Modesty, you know.

Q. Which Broadway play have you enjoyed most this season?

A. It has been a bad year. But did you see me on Johnny Carson?

Q. Is it true that you have proposed your birthday be made a national holiday?

A. Someone had to suggest it.

Q. Let us turn to matters of national concern, sir. Are you worried about the size of the deficit?

A. You should see *my* bills.

Q. Do you make New Year resolutions, Mr. Espy?

A. One. Every year.

Q. Would you mind telling me what it is?

A. It is "Let sleeping dogs lie."

Q. Forgive me for mentioning this, sir, but you look a bit seedy. Who will speak at your memorial service?

A. No problem. I will.

Q. One last question, sir. Are you going to a New Year's Eve party tonight?

A. No. Nobody has invited me.

Q. I see. Thank you, sir.

A note on years past and years to come:

## BUZZ AND BIZZ

Buzz and bizz and bizz and buzz,
Bee and mee, that's how it was.
Bizz and buzz and buzz and bizz,
Bee and mee, that's how it izz.
No more bizz-buzz, bee or mee;
That's the way that it will bee.
—W.R.E.

# 31 December

*Fee, Fi, Fo, Fum—I Smell the Blood of Frank Sullivan, Etc.* *

<table>
<tr>
<td>Happy New Year to my contributors:</td>
<td>1. Let bells of bronze with tongues of gold<br>Ring in the new, ring out the old<br>For wags and wits, alive and dead,<br>Whose bones I've ground to make my bread!</td>
</tr>
<tr>
<td>the nameless . . .</td>
<td>2. A happy New Year I propone<br>For Auth. Anon. and Auth. Unknown.</td>
</tr>
<tr>
<td>and the defunct . . .</td>
<td>3. It isn't quite the thing, perhaps,<br>To bring up New Year to you chaps<br>Who sit in bliss, exchanging toasts<br>With Fathers, Sons, and Holy Ghosts.<br>Instead, I wish for your Fraternity<br>A healthy, prosperous Eternity.</td>
</tr>
<tr>
<td>including those listed here . . .</td>
<td>4. To Mencken, Prior, de la Mare;<br>To Sitwell (Edith); Osbert (frère);<br>To Coleridge and Sackville-West—<br>To Housman, Belloc, Gay—my best!<br>May Keats till Judgment Day stay squiffed<br>With Herrick, cummings, Stupp, and Swift!</td>
</tr>
<tr>
<td>here . . .</td>
<td>5. Beside your Stygian river snore well,<br>Cowper, Shelley, Eliot, Orwell!<br>On Lander, Thackeray, and Lawrence<br>May joy celestial pour in torrents!<br>Shakespeare, Riley, Butler, Lardner,<br>Thurber, Benchley—prosit, pardner!</td>
</tr>
<tr>
<td>and here . . .</td>
<td>6. Swinburne, Leacock, Wordsworth, Donne,<br>F.P.A., Yeats, Tennyson,<br>Goldsmith, Bishop, Blake, and Proetz—<br>Season's greetings, perished poets!</td>
</tr>
<tr>
<td>and those who are still alive . . .</td>
<td>7. For you who yet are overground,<br>May royalties next year abound!</td>
</tr>
</table>

---

*This poem was written for *An Almanac of Words at Play* and thanks the contributors to that volume. —*Ed.*

*these Word Ways contrib-*
*utors, for instance . . .*

8. May rave reviews, with nary heckler,
   Greet Borgmann, Bergerson, and Eckler!
   May Youngquist, Porter, Ashley, Mercer,
   Find each day better, no day worser!
   May Francis, Silverman, and Lindon
   (And Cohen, too!), have medals pinned on!

*certain sots of my ac-*
*quaintance . . .*

9. May Cole and Niven live in style,
   And laughing walk the final Miall!
   May banners wave, may hearts be all-astir
   For Morris, Hellman, Read, and Hollister!
   May some kind Angell ease your way,
   Bendiner, Harrison, de Kay!

*word players I know or*
*would like to know . . .*

10. My wish for Pei and for Ciardi's
    Starlets of their choice at Sardi's;
    For Levin, Schur, and Richardson,
    *Paillard de boeuf* at Twenty-one;
    For Baker, Lauder, and McCord,
    Wine picked by George of Perigord.

*more of the same . . .*

11. May juices this year flow not thinly
    Along MacLean, McCrum, McGinley.
    Rosten, Ransom, Harrold, Tidwell,
    Creamer, Harris, Pope, I bid well;
    Bronowski,* Berger, Brien, Stoppard,
    May your winning cards be coppered!

*and still more . . .*

12. This year set afire the Thames,
    Hitchcock, Hickerson, and James!
    Joy shine through your window pane,
    Bainbridge, Updike, Minogue, Caen!
    May no toe of yours be gouty,
    Jacobs, Bongartz, Starbuck, Dowty!

*perhaps too many.*

13. Take your ease in summer haycock,
    Dunphy, Considine, and Laycock!
    Farmer, Hollander, and Deal,
    Sound the New Year campanile!
    Fuller, Gilliatt, and Lewis,
    Reed and Mockridge, sock it to us!

---

*Dr. Bronowski left the present for the past category after this verse was written. Vale!

*Repeat now the Happy New Year chorus:*

14. *Let bells of bronze with tongues of gold*
    *Ring in the new, ring out the old*
    *For wags and wits, alive and dead,*
    *Whose bones I've ground*
    *Whose bones I've ground*
    *Whose bones I've ground*
    *To make my bread.*

    —*W.R.E.*

I have left out some contributors, I know. To them no less than to those named above—and to you, too, O reader, my rod and my staff—a Happy, Prosperous New Year!

# ANSWERS AND SOLUTIONS

## 2 January: *An ABC Proposal Comes to O*

1. You sigh for a cipher, but I sigh for you;
   Oh sigh for no cipher, but oh sigh for me;
   Oh let not my sigh for a cipher go,
   But give sigh for sigh, for I sigh for you so.

2. Naughty Otto thought he ought
   To own an auto. Otto bought
   An auto but he never thought
   He'd owe the auto dealer aught
   For the auto Otto bought.
   Say, has Otto's auto brought
   Otto aught that Otto sought?
   Otto's auto's good for naught.

## 6 January: *My S's Grow S's*

The word Mr. Canning had in mind was cares.

## 8 January: *What's Yours, Fella?*

1. A cup of coffee.
2. An order of Jello.
3. French fried potatoes added.
4. Corned beef and cabbage.
5. Salt and pepper.
6. Doughnut and coffee.
7. A glass of buttermilk.
8. Hash with catsup.
9. A glass of water.
10. One hot dog.
11. An Italian hero sandwich.
12. Bacon, lettuce and tomato sandwich without mayonnaise.
13. Beans with two frankfurters.
14. Beef stew.
15. Scrambled eggs with whole wheat toast.
16. Vanilla ice cream in a chocolate soda or milkshake (sometimes also coffee with cream).
17. A glass of orange juice.
18. A glass of water.
19. Nova Scotia smoked salmon on a bagel.
20. Poached eggs on toast.

## 11 January: *Clitch, Clitch, Clitch*

1. destruction (Proverbs 16:18) 2. paint (Shakespeare, *King John*) 3. learning (Pope, *An Essay on Criticism*) 4. thought (Heywood, *Proverbs*) 5. savage breast (Congreve, *The Mourning Bride*) 6. of (Colton, *The Lacon*) 7. fibs (Goldsmith, *She Stoops to Conquer*) 8. an ell (Ray, *English Proverbs*) 9. very spice (Cowper, *The Task*) 10. The love of money (1 Timothy 6:10) 11. nor any (Coleridge, *The Ancient Mariner*) 12. one life to lose (Nathan Hale)

## 12 January: *First Lines*

Tom Sawyer, *by Mark Twain*

| | | |
|---|---|---|
| 1. L | 8. C | 15. A |
| 2. J | 9. S | 16. K |
| 3. M | 10. H | 17. T |
| 4. I | 11. D | 18. U |
| 5. O | 12. B | 19. Q |
| 6. P | 13. F | 20. R |
| 7. N | 14. E | 21. G |

## 14 January: *One Man's Abdomen*

You misunderstood me. I said polo pony.

## 20 January: *A Squirming of Snakes*

1. Apes
2. Wolves
3. Boars
4. Chickens
5. Badgers
6. Birds
7. Leopards
8. Pheasants
9. Bears
10. Swine
11. Fish
12. Cats
13. Kine
14. Hares
15. Monkeys
16. Foxes
17. Peacocks
18. Geese
19. Partridges
20. Whales, or young seals. (A grown male seal is a *bull*, his females *cows*, their offspring *pups*, an immature male a *bachelor*, a colony of seals a *herd*, and their breeding place a *rookery*.)

## 22 January: *John Hancocks*

1. Andrew Young
2. Marlene Dietrich
3. Moshe Dayan
4. Robert Redford
5. Henry A. Kissinger
6. H. R. Haldeman
7. Alexandre Dumas
8. Marshal Tito
9. Yul Brynner
10. Rudolf Nureyev
11. Al Pacino
12. Walter Mondale
13. David Niven
14. Cary Grant
15. Guy Lombardo
16. Sophia Loren
17. Marcel Marceau
18. James Cagney

## 25 January: *Be Friendly, Borgmann*

*Mr. Friend's anagrams:*
1. I got a rat
2. Cannot stir
3. I mean to rend it
4. Violence run forth
5. Spare him not
6. Partial men
7. It ran

*Mr. Borgmann's:*
1. Attaineth its cause: freedom!
2. They see
3. Positively!
4. Hear Dante! oh, beware you open hell!
5. Faces one at the end
6. Has to pilfer
7. Can ruin a selected victim
8. "Time's running past," we murmur
9. No city dust here!
10. Ars magna
11. Sly ware
12. Nine thumps
13. Stamps one as so nice
14. Voices rant on
15. A rope ends it
16. Tender names
17. Get a "no" in
18. A step-in

## 29 January: *Vile Vodka*

FAREWELL, A LONG FAREWELL
TO ALL MY PROTESTANT ETHIC

Today's misfortunes John ignores, to wait
Tomorrow's joys, which he foresees as great;
Forgets that if his forties were a curse,
His seventies and eighties must be worse.
The future he foretells sounds fine; but he
Foregoes for its sake present ecstasy—
Forbids himself all actions apt to please.

*My* rule is this: Time's forelock's meant to seize.
What's here for use I mean to use; I reach
For surf that phosphoresces on the beach
No less than sweet forays and foragings;
All are for wise men's use to ease life's stings.
John's foresight's not for me; I give my praise
To pleasures not tomorrow's but today's.

### MITIGATION

So tender's the night,
So tender's the voice of the dove,
Who can blame the young wight
If he tenders his lady his love?

## 8 February: *Mots d'Heures: Gousses, Rames*

The sounds of the first verse approximate "Old Mother Hubbard"; of the second, "Hickory Dickory Dock."

## 9 February: *Variable Verbs*

1. The batter flied out to center field.
2. They hanged the cattle rustler.
3. When spring arrived, the trees leaved.
4. Chris Evert letted three consecutive serves.
5. An enthusiastic crowd ringed the speaker.
6. The aspiring executive shined his shoes every morning.
7. They spitted the pig and then roasted it.
8. The farmer sticked the vines so that they would grow straight.
9. He treaded water until help arrived.
10. The car weaved its way through heavy traffic.

## 12 February: *Spaghettibird Headdress*

Lincoln's Gettysburg Address scarcely needs repeating.

### A POEM

When first you scan this silly rhyme
   To try to make the meaning clear,
You think 'twould but be wasting time
   You say, "It's simply nonsense sheer!"
No matter; analyze a line!
   Nay, shun my slender verses not—
For cryptic poetry like mine,
                                  means a lot.

## 17 February: *Shipwreck*

Row, row, row your boat
   Till the prow go down;
Fie on him who borrows sorrow:
All must sink and drown tomorrow;
   All must sink and drown.

Let no wailing crowd your throat;
   Bar your brow from frown;
Bare your breast to Cupid's arrow,
Gnaw the bone and suck the marrow,
   Ere you sink and drown.

Plait the blossoms life has grown,
   Wear them as a crown;
Many a crow shall flee from sparrow,
Many a lad his row shall harrow
   Ere you sink and drown.

**21 February:** *To My Greek Mistress*

| | |
|---|---|
| With many a sigh I ate a pie | PSI PI |
| That you had baked, my dear; | |
| This torpor new I owe to you— | NU IOTA |
| I'm feeling very queer. | |
| | |
| O fie O fie upon your pie!— | PHI PHI PI |
| You dealt a cruel blow! | DELTA |
| Your dreadful pie has made me cry; | PI CHI |
| My tears fall in a row. | RHO |
| | |
| I would have lammed another lass | LAMBDA |
| Who baked that pie, I vow; | PI |
| But still I moo and moo for you, | MU MU |
| As sick as any cow. | |

**25 February:** *Bless the Shepherd*

APPROACH OF EVENING

Idling, I sit in this mild twilight dim,
Whilst birds, in wild, swift vigils, circling skim.
Light winds in sighing sink, till, rising bright,
Night's Virgin Pilgrim swims in vivid light!

INCONTROVERTIBLE FACTS

Dull humdrum murmurs lull, but hubbub stuns.
Lucullus snuffs up musk, mundungus* shuns.
Puss purrs, buds burst, bucks butt, luck turns up trumps;
But full cups, hurtful, spur up unjust thumps.

**27 February:** *Cats, Cats, Cats, Cats!*

The initial letters of the lines of Mr. Lindon's verses spell out the titles. The initial words of the lines of "Forecast: Chilly," strung together, read "Time for warm clothes, man; this looks like one long cold winter."

**29 February:** *Twisted Proverbs*

1. Every dog has his day.
2. Don't put all your eggs in one basket.
3. Least said soonest mended.
4. The proof of the pudding is in the eating.
5. When in Rome do as the Romans do.
6. Birds of a feather flock together.
7. The pot calls the kettle black.

**22 March:** *Re: Rebuses*

Mr. Manheim's rebus: The envelope went to John Underwood, Andover, Mass. Mrs. Youngquist's rebuses:

| | | |
|---|---|---|
| 1. Much ado about nothing | 3. Frameup | 5. Six of one, half a dozen of another |
| 2. World without end, amen | 4. All in one | 6. Square meal |

**25 March:** *Up and Down Counting Song*

Dear ewe, dear lamb, I've won thee: we
Will tootle through the fields together;
With reed and pipe we'll jubilee;
We'll gambol back and forth in glee;
If I've your heart, who gives a D.
How raw and sick's the weather?
In seventh heaven me and thee
Will late and soon find ecstasy—
My ewe benign is tied to me,
And tender is the tether!

*Mundungus is an obsolete word meaning trash. It once had something to do with black pudding.

Yet there may be a tendency
(Someday when I no more know whether
You wait for me still longingly
Or find our love less heavenly)
For you in classic sulk to flee—
Off I've no doubt to new bellwether
And fresher forage . . . It may be
We'll both require a style more free,
And find the Bird of Love to be
Reduced to one Pinfeather.

## 28 March: *Schizophrenic Words*

*Infantry* means "a body of children." *Infatuate* means "frustrate." *Inhabited* means "uninhabited." *Inroad* means "raid," and so does *outroad*. *Invaluable* means both "priceless" and "worthless."
*Jack* means "quarter pint" but also "half pint." *Juror* means "false witness."
*King* means "queen bee."
*Lap* means "bosom" (2). *Law* means "thieving." *Let* means "prevent."
*Mahound* means "Mohammed," but also "the devil." *Maness* means "woman." *Mankind* means both "mad" and "savage." *Midmorn* means "9 A.M." *Moody* means "brave." *Mythometer* means "a measure for judging myths."
*Nephew* means "niece" (2b). *Nice* means "foolish," "silly," "stupid," "simple," "ignorant," "lewd," "lascivious," "wanton," "strange," "uncommon," and "weak." *Noon* means "midnight" (3a). *Novantique* means "new, yet old." *Nutty* means "fascinating."
*Orient* means both "blue" and "bright red."
*Palace* means "cellar." *Peculiar* means "wife" (1d). *Philematology* means "the science of kissing." *Politician* means "schemer." *Practical* means "unscrupulous." *Precious* means "worthless," "poor," and "bad."
*Rat* means "cat." *Ravel* means both "entangle" and "disentangle." *Resolute* means "firm" but also "infirm." *Restive* means "inactive," but also "fidgety." *Riddle* means "unriddle." *Rout* means "assemble." *Ruffian* means "paramour."
*Sad* means both "satisfied" (1) and "bad" (9). *Scot* means "Irishman." *Sevenbark* means "ninebark." *Several* means "single," "an item," and "an individual." *She* means "he." *Shower* means "drops about 1/25 inch in diameter and falling at the velocity of 10 to 25 feet per second." *Sinople* means both "blood red" and "green." *Sinus* means "bosom." *Sit* means "stand." *Sleeveless* means "bootless." *Snob* means "one not an aristocrat." *Snug* means "sizable." *Stand* means "lie flat" (17). *Supermuscan* means "above the power of a fly." *Sweat* means "dry thoroughly."
*Thrill* means "bore." *Tickle* means "whip" and "chastise." *Tonight* means "last night." *Twosome* means "single."
*Undercool* means "supercool." *Undercreep* means "overreach." *Undertake* means "overtake." *Undoctor* means "to make unlike a doctor." *Universal* means "local." *Unrelentless* means "relentless." *Unremorseless* means "remorseless." *Unrude* means "rude." *Unslip* means "slip." *Upright* means "supine."
*Vile* means "great."
*Wan* means "dark black." *Widow* means "widower." *Wonder* means "admiration," but also "evil." *Wrist* means "ankle."

*—Tom Pulliam*

## 4 April: *Anagrams from* Punch

*Animal Fare:* Stable, bleats, tables, ablest
*Pre-parental Plaint:* Aspired, praised, despair, diapers
*A Cleric of Antic ******:* Stripe, priest, ripest, tripes, sprite
*Gastronomically, Cranes Act Comically:* Crate, react, cater, carte, trace
*Make That Ghost Stop Peeking, Honey!:* Sacré, scare, cares, acres, races
*Royal Pick-me-up:* Large, lager, regal, glare

## 6 April: *Biblical Fruitcake*

The Bible verses cited refer to: 1. flour 2. butter 3. sugar 4. raisins 5. figs 6. almonds 7. honey 8. eggs 9. salt 10. baking soda 11. spices (Mrs. Harrold suggested ½ tsp. cloves, ½ tsp. nutmeg, 1 tsp. cinnamon and 1 tsp. mace, but one should choose among them, not use them all.) 12. beat well

## 10 April: *What Is the Word for #?*

1. Number.
2. Pounds.
3. Space.
4. Sharp.
5. Tic-tac-toe.
6. Octothorp.
7. Non-add.
8. Fracture.

### 14 April: *Up Here in the (9)*

    A.  (1) a (2) pa (3) ape (4) peas (5) sepia (6) praise (7) despair (8) paradise (9) disappear
    B.  (1) O (2) on (3) one (4) nose (5) stone (6) honest (7) thrones (8) another's (9) northeast

### 17 April: *Private? No!*

    1.  Said I, "I said you said I said 'said.' " Said he, "Who said I said you said 'said?' I said said is said *'said.'* Said is not said 'Said' like Said."*
    2.  That that is, is; that that is not, is not. Is not that it? It is.
    3.  The murderer protested his innocence. An hour after, he was put to death.
    4.  He said that that 'that' that that man said was correct.

### 28 April: *Don't Quote Me*

    1.  Backward, turn backward, O Time, in your flight.—*Elizabeth Akers Allen*
    2.  How dear to this heart are the scenes of my childhood.—*Samuel Woodworth*
    3.  Nor any drop to drink.—*Coleridge*
    4.  I knew him, Horatio.—*Shakespeare*
    5.  Tall oaks from little acorns grow.—*David Everett*
    6.  Breathes there the man, with soul so dead.—*Sir Walter Scott*
    7.  'Twas the night before Christmas, when all through the house.—*Clement Clarke Moore*

### 4 May: *Odd Ends*

Mercury, Jupiter.

### 5 May: *Era Uoy a Diamrab?*

    1.  A backward barmaid fell in love,
        And wed her backward guest.
        Of all Earth's backward children
        Theirs were the backwardest.

    2.  When I was young as you are
        I bled the system white
        When reading verse and novels
        By starting from the right.

        When you are old as I am
        And equally bereft
        . . . Take comfort then as I do
        *By reading right from left.*

### 8 May: *Where Did That Poisoned Pawn Come from, Mr. Fischer?*

NxB!? = Knight captures Bishop. Strong, but risky.
O–O = castles to the King's side.
QxQ = Queen captures Queen.
!! = The move is powerful, and winning.
PxP = Pawn captures Pawn.
RxN = Rook captures Knight.
R = Castle, or, as above, Rook.
Q = Queen.
R = Rook.
B = Bishop.
P = Pawn.
– = moves.

So the verse, in the clear, reads as follows:

    The match begins; the breaths are bated.
    Will Black resign? Will White be mated?
    White's Ruy Lopez circumvents

*Said, the Egyptian port, is pronounced Sah-eed.

Black's Nimzo-Indian defense.
Now White (intent) and Black (intenter)
Maneuver to control the center.

White moves. Too bold? Perhaps from whisky?
Knight captures Bishop. Strong, but risky.
Now Black, to plaudits from the ringside,
Correctly castles to the King's side.
Queen captures Queen (White's ranks are thinning).
The move is powerful, and winning.

The mating net is drawing tight:
Pawn captures pawn, rook captures knight.
White, backed against his castle wall,
In vain seeks check perpetual.
Of Queen, Rook, Bishop, Pawn bereft,
He moves to right, he moves to left.

*Poor White in Zugzwang sealed his fate;*
*His Fianchetto came too late.*
*He pondered a Maroczy Bind,*
*Could see no future, and resigned.*

## 11 May: *Philander Is a Wallaby*

If you marked every one of the definitions correct, you were 100 percent right.

## 23 May: *Four Kate, Won Eye a Door*

### ANT SONG

Next week offer me romance
Hold me, dance and dance and dance
Answer, answer, answer do
Let us turn a pace or two.

### ANN DREW

Ann drew Andrew, Andrew drew Ann
Andrew drew Ann Ann drew Andrew

### A CYST ME TWO

Assist me to pursue you, Kate;
My sentiment for you is great.
My heart is melancholic, Kate;
Ah, would that I might germinate
In you also this cancer, Kate!
Ah, would that I might inculcate
Idolatry of me in Kate!
When I see you my eyes dilate.
Yet you appear inviolate;
To no avail do I placate
You, Kate.

My purpose for you I relate,
And mention how I daily wait
For you before your mansion gate;
But this annoys you, for you hate
Romance, dear Kate.
Insensate opals coruscate
And scintillate
No more than you, inhuman Kate.

Diurnally I supplicate
You, Kate,

My charismatic Kate.
Oh Kate, abate
My sordid state!
Deplore my fate!
Communicate
Affection, Kate!
Be not cantankerous, dear Kate—
Capitulate!
Say you will be my candidate
For matrimonial estate.
Pray, answer, Kate!

#### KNOT TWO KNOT FOUR WON EYE A DOOR

'Tis not amiss a miss to find
With promise in her glance, sir;
If miss with mister be combined,
Then mischief is the answer.

A lass to idolize I sought
In some secluded section;
The noble lass alas would not
Accede to my affection.

If you some maiden would acquire,
She may avoid you also;
All lads are frequently afire,
All lasses oft are false, O.

## 25 May: *Recovered Charades*

1. The first six lines are answered by the words *Bed, Oh, Sin, Tobacco, Oak,* and *Noun.* The initial letters of the word spell *Boston,* the name of the city where the magazine was published.
2. Mite, time.

## 4 June: *When Baby Gurgles Guam and Georgia*

When baby gurgles goo and gah,
Then how I envy baby's pa,
As slapping knee with loud huzzah
He sings in key or cries, "Hurrah!
My tad's OK, oh tra la la!"
But when the sound is wah wah wah
He loudly shouts, "Where are you ma,
Our Al is ill, oh pish, oh bah!
The M.D.'s off at baccarat!
Oh ma go hie you in our cah
And fetch him to me, near or fah!"
Then I don't envy pa at a'.

## 14 June: *Jack Be Nimble*

| | | |
|---|---|---|
| 1. Jack-of-all-trades | 7. Lumberjack | 13. Jackrabbit |
| 2. Applejack | 8. Union Jack | 14. Straitjacket |
| 3. Jackknife | 9. Crackerjack | 15. Jackhammer |
| 4. Hit the jackpot | 10. Jackson Five | 16. Jumping jacks |
| 5. Blackjack | 11. Jackstraws or jacks | 17. Jack-in-the-pulpit |
| 6. Jack-in-the-box | 12. Jack Frost | 18. Flapjack |

## 15 June: *He Beat You to That One, Too*

The plays quoted from are, in order: *Cymbeline, Antony and Cleopatra, The Tempest, The Merry Wives of Windsor, The Taming of the Shrew, The Winter's Tale, King Henry VI, Measure for Measure, The Comedy of Errors, Much Ado about Nothing, A Midsummer Night's Dream, As You Like It, Julius Caesar.*

## 17 June: *Collegiate Quiz*

| | | | |
|---|---|---|---|
| 1. | Purdue | 11. | Vassar |
| 2. | Columbia | 12. | Amherst |
| 3. | Rutgers | 13. | Oberlin |
| 4. | Bryn Mawr | 14. | Howard |
| 5. | Villanova | 15. | Yeshiva |
| 6. | Bowdoin | 16. | Barnard |
| 7. | Harvard | 17. | Berkeley |
| 8. | Mount Holyoke | 18. | Swarthmore |
| 9. | Duke | 19. | Vanderbilt |
| 10. | Yale | 20. | Wellesley |

## 19 June: *Y Is X a Y of Y?*

1. Ilk is a kind of a kind. [I prefer a name of a name.—*W.R.E.*]
2. House construction is the building of a building.
3. Greta's clothes are the garb of Garbo. (A little tricky?)
4. An ale steward is a porter of porter.
5. Paying the check is a tender of tender.
6. Bunches of partly eaten apples are corps of cores.
7. Policemen hiding in the woods are a copse of cops.
8. A silver-covered dish is a plate of plate.
9. Clothing storage for undergarments is drawers for drawers.
10. Putting mother's sister up for a gambling stake is ante of Auntie.

## 1 July: *A Troop of Tropes*

1. . . . without benefit of clergy (euphemism).
2. . . . curio (apocope). Loss of a final letter or syllable; *curio* shortens *curiosity*.
3. . . . Crown (metonymy). Substitution of a suggestive word for the name of the thing meant, as "The White House" for the Administration or the President.
4. . . . the Borscht Circuit (periphrasis). A circumlocution, as "The year's penultimate month."
5. . . . said Tom, meteorologically (Tom Swifty).
6. . . . carried away by elation and a large airplane (zeugma or syllepsis). The use of a verb or adjective with two different words, to only one of which it strictly applies.
7. . . . calling her Ducky (hypocorism). Use of pet names, nursery rhymes, diminutives, etc.
8. . . . boondocks (exoticism; from the Philippines). Other familiar exoticisms (oxymoronically speaking) are *pajamas* and *jungles.*
9. . . . how pleasant so ever (tmesis). Slicing a word or phrase to insert something: "I saw her some bloody where."
10. . . . "threads" (synecdoche). The use of a part for a whole, or the reverse: "hands" for "workmen," "purple" for "royal," etc.
11. . . . naïvely (diaeresis). The pronunciation of two successive vowels as separate sounds rather than as a single vowel or dipthong. Viz., "Chloe."
12. . . . their limbs (Bowdlerism). Prudish expurgation, so called after Thomas Bowdler, who published an expurgated Shakespeare.
13. . . . it's a beautiful world (hysteron proteron). Reversal of natural order of ideas, as in "For God, for Country, and for Yale."
14. . . . not bad, eh? (litotes). Affirming a thing by denying its contrary, as when a father comments on his son's straight A average at college, "that's pretty fair."
15. . . . forever grateful (hyperbole). Use of exaggerated terms to emphasize rather than deceive.
16. . . . the old bag (dysphemism). Use of a disparaging term to describe something inoffensive.
17. . . . she'd turn over in her grave if she were alive today (catachresis). Deliberately paradoxical figure of speech.
18. . . . a wave like a watery giant (simile). A figurative comparison, usually introduced by "like" or "as."
19. . . . 'way (aphesis). Loss of an initial syllable or letter.
20. . . . the gull's territory (kenning). Almost synonymous with periphrasis, as in Scandinavian "the sea of the blood" for "body" and "wound-engraver" for "the point of a sword."
21. . . . hissed (onomatopoeia). The fitting of sound to sense: *buzz, moo, choo-choo,* etc.
22. . . . the Sunday punch of an expert (metaphor). A figure in which a comparison or identity is implied: "She is a tigress."
23. . . . Well, I never! (ellipsis). Omission of a word or words necessary to complete the sense. The full expression might have been: "Well, I never did see such a thing!"

## 3 July: *Cockney Alphabet*

A.  Hay for horses, aphorism
B.  Beef or lamb, beef or mutton
C.  Sea for sailors, see for yourself
D.  Differential, deef or dumb, deformity
E.  Eve or Adam, heave a brick, Eva Peron, evolution
F.  Effervescent, ever so nice, ever been had, efficacious
G.  Chief of Police
H.  Age for mellowness
I.  Highfaluting, eye for an eye, hyphenated, Eiffel Tower
J.  Jaffa oranges, d'ja ever hear about . . . ?, juvenile delinquent, d'ja ever see a dream walking
K.  Cain and Abel, Kay Francis, cafeteria
L.  Hell for leather
M.  Emphasis, emphasize
N.  Hen for a cockerel, enforcer, envelope
O.  Over the garden wall, overpopulated, over my dead body, oversexed, overcoat
P.  Pee for relief, perfidious Albion, performing fleas
Q.  Queue for the pictures, queue for tickets, cutie pie.
R.  "'Arf a mo'" ("Half a moment—wait a minute!"), half a crown
S.  As far as I'm concerned
T.  Tea for two, T formation
U.  You forgot, euphoria, euphemism
V.  Vive la France, vivisection, vive la différence
W.  Double your money, trouble you for a match? double ewe for a Siamese ram
X.  Eggs for breakfast
Y.  Wife or mistress, why for heaven's sake
Z.  Zephyr breezes

## 8 July: *Omak Me Yours Tonight*

Provenance of the Place Names Used in *Omak Me Yours Tonight*

(To sniff out the sense of the ballad, one must not hesitate to mispronounce some of the place names. The correct pronunciation is indicated below.)

Omak, OH-mak. From omache, "good medicine."
Ilwaco, il-WAW-koh. Name of a chief.
Acme. The town was named for a hymn book.
Tolt. From H'lalt. Mr. Phillips does not give the meaning of the word.
Fife. Name of the founder of the town.
Toutle. From Hullooetell, a tribe on the Cowlitz River.
Dabob, Dah-BAHB. A tidal estuary on Puget Sound.
Spee-Bi-Dah. Phonetic spelling of a word for "small child."
Walla Walla, WAW-luh WAW-luh. From Walatsa, "running water."
Duwamish, doo-WAH-mish. From dewampsh, "the people living on the river."
Wollochet, WAH-luh-chet. From walatchet, "squirting clams."
Wenatchee, wuh-NACH-ee. From wenatchi, "river flowing from a canyon."
Elochoman, ee-LOH-ku-min, name of an Indian village on the Columbia River.
Latah, LAY-tah. From lahtoo, "the stream where little fish are caught."
Lilliwaup, LIL-uh-wahp. "Inlet."
Olalla, oh-LAL-uh. From olallie, "many berries."
Palouse, puh-LOOS. From the Palus tribe.
Lummi, LUHM-ee. From the Lummi tribe.
Asotin, uh-SOH-tin. "Eel Creek."
Chetlo, CHET-loh. "Oyster."
Auburn. After Auburn, N.Y.
Quilcene, KWIL-seen. "Salt-water people."
Chesaw, CHEE-saw. Name of a Chinese miner.
Dewatto, de-WAH-toh. "Home of evil spirits who make men crazy."
Tatoosh, ta-TOOSH. Perhaps from to-tooch, "thunderbird."
Tumtum. From thum(p)-thum(p), "heart."
Whatcom. WHAHT-kuhm. "Noisy water," the name of a chief.
Attalia, a-TAL-liuh. Named after an Italian hamlet.
Hamma Hamma, HAM-uh HAM-uh. From hab'hab, a swamp reed.
Klickitat, KLIK-i-tat. Either "robber" or "beyond."

Malott, muh-LAHT. Name of a pioneer.

Wynoochee, weye-NOO-chee. "Shifting," as the course of a river.

Mattewa, MAT-a-wuh. "Where is it?"

Startup. Named for an early manager of a lumber company.

Anacortes, an-uh-KOR-tis. A husband's romanticization of his wife's maiden name, Anna Curtis.

Thurston. Named for Oregon Territory's first delegate to Congress.

Havermale, HAV-er-mayl. The name of an early minister.

Tonasket, tuhn-AS-kuht. Honoring Chief Tonascutt.

Ohop, OH-hahp. From owhap, "water rushing out."

Naselle, nay-SEL. From the Nasal tribe.

Algona, al-GOH-na. From algoma, "valley of flowers."

Malone, muh-LOAN. Named for a New York community.

Methow, MET-how. From an Indian tribe.

Sekiu, SEE-kyoo. "Calm water."

Alava, AH-lah-vuh. Named for Jose Manuel de Alava, commissioner for Spain at the Nootka convention of 1790.

Spokane, spoh-KAN. From an Indian who identified himself as "chief of the sun people."

Canby. Named for Maj. Gen. Canby of the U.S. Army.

Olequa, OH-luh-quah. "Where salmon come to spawn."

Sauk, SAWK. From the Sah-kee-ma-hu tribe. No meaning is given.

Satsop, SAT-suhp. From sachap or sats-a-pish, "on a stream."

Tacoma, tuh-KOH-muh. The Indian name for Mount Rainier. The meaning is not given.

Mowich, MOH-ich. "Deer."

Touchet, TOO-she. From tousa, "curing salmon before a fire."

Scatchet, SKA-chit. Variant of Skagit. The meaning is lost.

Offut. Family name of two brothers who were early settlers.

Coulee, KOO-lee. From French couler, "to flow."

Pysht, PISHT. "Fish."

Skagit, SKA-jit. The meaning is lost.

Newaukum, noo-AW-kuhm. "Gently flowing water."

Yellepit, YEL-uh-pit. The name of a chief.

Yelm. From chelm, "heat waves rising from the earth."

Taholah, tuh-HOH-luh. Name of a Quinault tribal chief.

Tahuyah, tuh-HOO-ya. From ta and ho-i, "that done," referring to some notable but forgotten occurrence.

Yacolt, YA-kawlt. "Haunted place." "A small band of Indians," says Mr. Phillips, "mysteriously lost their children while picking huckleberries, and after a futile search concluded that they had been stolen by Yacolt, the evil spirit."

Sucia, SOO-shuh. In Spanish, "dirty," or, nautically, "foul," a fair description of the reefs and hidden rocks surrounding the island.

Vashon, VASH-ahn. After Captain James Vashon, a British naval officer who fought the Americans in the Revolution.

Moran, mor-ANN. Named for Robert Moran, the shipbuilder and onetime mayor of Seattle who donated the land for this park.

Vader, VAY-der. In honor of an early settler "who was not honored, but outraged, and promptly moved to Florida."

Leland. An acronym from the name of Mrs. Laura E. Andrews, the first white woman there; originally spelled Lealand.

La Push, luh POOSH. Indian adaptation of French la bouche, "the mouth" (of a river).

Twisp. From twitsp, the meaning of which is not given.

Chuckanut, CHUHK-uh-nut. The definition is unknown.

Lebam, li-BAM. J. W. Goodell created the town's name by spelling his daughter Mabel's name backward.

Bangor, BANG-gawr. Presumably named by former down easters after the city in Maine.

Kapowsin, kuh-POW-suhn. From the Indian name, origin not recorded, for the lake on which the town is situated.

Memaloos, MEM-a-loos. "Dead." Memaloos, an island in the Columbia River, was used by the Indians as a cemetery.

Mohler. Named for a mail-stage driver.

Dosewallips, dhohs-ee-WAH-lips. From the name of a legendary Indian who turned into a mountain.

Kickit, KICK-uht. A peninsula jutting into Puget Sound.

Wawawai, wuh-WAH-ee. "Council ground."

Queets. From the Quaitso tribe.

Klipsan, KLIP-suhn. "Sunset."

Moclips, MOH-klips. A Quinault word for a place where maidens underwent puberty rites.

Elwha, EL-wah. "Elk."

Ione, eye-OHN. For Ione, niece of the town's first postmaster.

Wauna, WAW-nuh. "Strong and mighty."

Semiahmoo, sem-ee-A-moo. Perhaps from a word for "half moon."

Doughty, DOW-tee. Named for John Doughty, a petty officer aboard the Wilkes expedition's vessel *Peacock*.

Anatone, AN-uh-tohn. Name of a legendary Indian woman.

Colfax. In honor of U. S. Grant's Vice-President.

Snohomish, snoh-HOH-mish. Name of an Indian tribe.

Neah, NEE-uh. Nasal pronunciation of Deeah, chief of the Makah tribe.

Willapa, WIL-uh-pah. From Ah-whil-lapah, the name of the Chinook tribe that dwelt on the banks of the river.

Utsalady, uht-suh-LAD-ee. "Land of berries."

Liplip. Chinook jargon for "boiling."

Kachess, kuh-CHEES. "More fish."

Coweman, kow-EE-muhn. From Cowlitz ko-wee-na, "short man," after a dwarf-sized Indian who lived on the bank of the Cowlitz river.

Ruff. Named for the man on whose property the town was located.

Flattery. At the southern entrance of the Strait of Juan de Fuca, noted Captain James Cook in 1778, "there appeared to be a small opening that flattered us with hopes of finding a harbour there." The hope proving vain, he named the point Cape Flattery.

Vail. Named for the family that donated the townsite land to the Weyerhaeuser Company.

Towal, TOW-al. Name of a chief.

Blaine. Named in 1885 for James C. Blaine, unsuccessful Republican candidate for President.

Seattle, see-AT-uhl. Name of a chief.

Azwell, AZ-well. Named for A. Z. Wells, a prosperous orchard farmer.

## 15 July: *Last Request*

I'll die, my devious sins to expiate,
   Where canine, snake and avian
     'Mid murmurs apian
     Exuviate;
While you, by foreign springs artesian,
Achaian deities assimilate,
And for the water in the cooking pan
     To estuate
     Wait.

*Dear entity, from whom doth emanate*
*The essence of euphoria for me;*
*You opium benign, you opiate . . .*
*Ideal agency of ecstasy . . .*

These decencies pray grant: no elegies,
No dolorous paeans to extenuate
    My sins; no sigh for my sad state.
Nay—raise Te Deums; cheer for my decease;
   Then help some new ephemeral mate
    To ease
His tedium, and all his senses sate
    And tease.
    Please.

### ON MORES AND MORALITY

The verses my hurrays are for
Are verses of a tedious mor-
Al decency, to ease us chaps
Who occasionally lapse.

## 27 July: *Hitchcock Steers a Bull*

Alan Whitney reports in John G. Fuller's "Trade Winds" column (*The Saturday Review*) that the people listed attained fame under the following names:

1. Douglas Fairbanks
2. Leon Trotsky
3. Mary Pickford
4. George Eliot
5. Irving Berlin
6. Jack Benny
7. Edward VII
8. Mike Todd
9. Cary Grant
10. El Greco

## 28 July: *More John Hancocks*

1. Frédéric Chopin
2. Charles Dickens
3. Napoleon
4. Mussolini
5. Mary Queen of Scots
6. Arturo Toscanini
7. John F. Kennedy
8. Lord Byron
9. Adolf Hitler

## 29 July: *Young Johnny and Ugly Sal*

Young Johnny, chancing to discover
That everybody loves a lover,
Concluded it would be his pleasure
To wed in haste, repent at leisure.
He said to ugly Sal, "I'm bound,
My dear, love makes the world go 'round.
Your looks, that make an angel weep,
Are only epidermis-deep.
Who says men seldom passes make
At girls with glasses?—a mistake!
Appearances deceive, 'tis true;
Yet better *they* deceive, than *you*.
It's not immortal beauties that
Make mortal hearts go pitty-pat;
You're wealthy, Sal, per my research:
A rich bride goeth young to church."

Sal felt her laggard pulses start.
Cold, cold her hands; warm, warm her heart.
She thought, "Each day it truer gets:
Men wink at blondes, but wed brunettes!
Though gray my hair beneath the dye,
No older than I feel am I;
This hand shall soon the cradle rock,
And rule the world (per Doctor Spock)!"
Who takes a wife, he takes a master;
For John, the marriage was disaster.
Love makes time pass away, I guess,
But t'other way around no less.
Who weds for love, his nights are great,
But daytime is the normal state;
And marriages, in heaven made,
On dusty earth are soon decayed.
The lewdest bride may pass for chaste
Unless too soon she goes to waist.
And when such fruits begin to show,
The cuckold is the last to know.

*Now one last, sad reminder to end John's dreary tale:*
*The female of the species is more deadly than the male.*

## 30 July: *The Nicknaming of States*

1. Missouri, Arkansas.
2. New Mexico, New York, Maryland.
3. Illinois, Georgia.
4. Louisiana.
5. Connecticut, Oklahoma.
6. New Hampshire.
7. North Carolina, Minnesota, Alabama.
8. Maryland, Texas, Delaware, Massachusetts.
9. Connecticut, Colorado.
10. Nevada; Florida and South Dakota; Pennsylvania.
11. Virginia, Massachusetts.
12. California, Montana, Wyoming.
13. Indiana, Hawaii, Tennessee.
14. Nebraska, Rhode Island.

15. Iowa, North Carolina, North Dakota.
16. Delaware, Kentucky.
17. Montana, Vermont (I reversed "green" and "mountain" for the rhyme).
18. West Virginia, Maine, Michigan.
19. Arizona, Ohio.
20. Mississippi, New Jersey, Georgia.
21. Ohio, Nevada, Washington.
22. Delaware, Nebraska, Alabama, Illinois.
23. Kansas, Idaho.
24. Utah.
25. South Carolina.
26. Wisconsin, Oregon, South Dakota.
27. North Dakota, Minnesota.
28. Alaska, Alabama.

The nicknames used in "The Nicknaming of States" were derived from various annual almanacs—the *World*, *Reader's Digest, Associated Press*, and so on. After writing the verse I came across a list of additional state nicknames in William Rose Benet's *The Reader's Encyclopedia*. I lacked energy to incorporate them into my verse, but include them here for whatever use you may wish to make of them:

*Battle-born State*. Nevada, so called because it was admitted into the Union during the Civil War.
*Bayou State*. Mississippi, because of its bayous.
*Bear State*. Arkansas, formerly a haunt of the beasts.
*Big Bend State*. Tennessee, an Indian name meaning "River of the Big Bend."
*Blue Law State*. Connecticut, for obvious reasons.
*Border Eagle State*. Mississippi, from the border eagle in its coat of arms.
*Bullion State*. Missouri, whose Congressman, Thomas Hart Benton, was known as "Old Bullion."
*Cockade State*. Maryland, from the cockades worn by Maryland Revolutionary troops.
*Corn-cracker State*. Kentucky, perhaps from its corn-cracker birds. Crackers are "poor whites."
*Cracker State*. Georgia. More "poor whites."
*Creole State*. Louisiana.
*Equality State*. Wyoming, first to grant women suffrage.
*Everglade State*. Florida, from its marshes.
*Excelsior State*. New York, from its motto *Excelsior*.
*Freestone State*. Connecticut, from its freestone quarries.
*Grizzly Bear State*. California.
*Jay Hawk State*. Kansas, where Jay Hawks (anti-slavery guerrillas) were active before and during the Civil War.
*Lake State*. Michigan, which abuts a number of the Great Lakes.
*Live Oak State*. Florida.
*Lumber State*. Maine.
*Peninsular State*. Florida, because it juts into the ocean.
*Sucker State*. Illinois, for the "suckers" who worked in the lead diggings of Wisconsin but returned to Illinois for the winter.
*Turpentine State*. North Carolina, a producer of the oil.
*Land of Steady Habits*. Connecticut.
*Sunset Land*. Arizona.

# 1 August: *Fifty English Emigrants*

1, Certificate (Yiddish); 2. beefsteak (French); 3. cold cream (Italian); 4. striker (Slovak); 5. blind pig (Swedish); 6. operation (Danish); 7. love letter (Pennsylvania Dutch); 8. telephone (Chinese); 9. television (Polish); 10. newspaper (Dutch); 11. pay day (Yugoslavian); 12. so long (Malay); 13. picnic (Japanese); 14. bear in mind (Swedish); 15. blackboard (Norwegian); 16. atom bomb (Finnish); 17. smoking jacket (French); 18. streetcars, financed by bonds, (Brazilian); 19. pretty good (Norwegian); 20. engine (French); 21. depot (Icelandic); 22. Yankee (Gaelic); 23. racketeer (Italian); 24. frankfurter (Spanish); 25. basketball (Greek); 26. quarter, or 25¢ (Portuguese); 27. gambling house (Icelandic); 28. mockingbird (Czechoslovak); 29. riding coat (French); 30. quay (Cuban Spanish); 31. haircut (Ukrainian); 32. nylon (Italian); 33. ice cream (Polish); 34. baby (Finnish); 35. old country (Hungarian); 36. cowboy films (Lithuanian); 37. goddamn (Syrian); 38. city hall (Greek); 39. coffee (Chinese); 40. wild western movie (Swedish); 41. moving pictures (Lithuanian); 42. proletariat (Chinese); 43. sidewalk (Italian); 44. watchman (Panamanian Spanish); 45. screened (German); 46. glycerine (Japanese); 47. shake hands (Italian); 48. rail bus made in Kalamazoo (French Canadian); 49. vacuum cleaner (French Canadian); 50. enough (Rumanian).

# 3 August: *Drinking Song of a Hard-Hearted Landlord*

Though my tenant's a lass who's a loner,
So many contenders are milling
About with pretensions to own her,

They'd be dear at ten ha'pence the shilling.
(CHORUS: They'd be dear at, *etc.*)

The tendrils that frame her sweet forehead
Would merit Tenniel's attentions;
But her tenement's mine, and *I'm* horrid:
I jeer at romantic intentions.
(CHORUS: I jeer at, *etc.*)

If she tenders her payments, I heed not
How tender's this lass when unbent;
Treat tenants as humans? Indeed not;
Their tendency's not to pay rent.
(CHORUS: Their tendency's, *etc.*)

## 20 August: *Word Belt*

Supple • Plentiful • Fuller Brush man • Manful • Fulsome • Omega • Egad • Gadget • Geth-
semane • Anecdotage • Agent • Entire • Irenic

## 23 August: *Swiftly Speaking*

Who, what, *where*. Young M.D.: *interne*. Gold leaf: *gilt*. John in Spanish: *Juan*. Elec. unit: *amp*. Elmo Roper's
poll: *Poll lightly*. Coda, in music, is a *final passage*. Shirtwaist: *blouse*. Maid's night off: *helpless*. K-: *K-rations*.
Pass the cards: *I deal*. Quiet meadow: *silent lea*. Zero: *naught*. Lose a few, *win some*. Drei, *vier*, fünf. Brothers,
*Grimm*. Oriental gift: *pleasant*. One pair: *a brace of*. X's and: *Y's*. Bequeath: *will*. Newsweek, *Time*. Tripod: *easel*.
Pope, *Pius*. Furn., *apt*.

## 24 August: *Charades Again*

1. Cats 'n' dogs, Datsun cogs.
2. Saturday night, satyr denied.
3. Schenectady, da neck ta ski.
4. Precipitation, prissy potation.

## 26 August: *Back and Forth*

| | | | |
|---|---|---|---|
| 1. BIB | 6. NOON | 11. MADAM | 16. TENET |
| 2. EVE | 7. TOOT | 12. REFER | 17. CIVIC |
| 3. ANNA | 8. PEEP | 13. SHAHS | 18. HANNAH |
| 4. DEED | 9. RADAR | 14. SOLOS | 19. REDDER |
| 5. OTTO | 10. LEVEL | 15. KAYAK | 20. REPAPER |

## 28 August: *Doublets*

1. Eye, dye, die, did, lid.
2. Pig, wig, wag, way, say, sty.
3. Ape, are, ere, err, ear, mar, man.
4. Army, arms, aims, dims, dams, dame, name, nave, navy.
5. Cain, chin, shin, spin, spun, spud, sped, aped, abed, Abel.
6. Wheat, cheat, cheap, cheep, creep, creed, breed, bread.
7. River, rover, cover, coves, cores, corns, coins, chins, shins, shine, shone, shore.
8. Winter, winner, wanner, wander, warder, harder, harper, hamper, damper, damped, dammed, dimmed, dimmer, simmer, summer.

## 29 August:

1. B is m arc K = Bismarck.
2. O, high O = Ohio.
3. You are too good to me to be forgotten.

4. Man for all seasons.

— Hail Caesar!
— Peace to you, O foreigner! Rise! You are?
— I am Aristes, Excellency, an Arabian exile.
— Why are you an exile, Aristes?
— I used to be a spy, O Caesar.
— A messy business! Have you eaten?
— Yes, thank you, sire, I ate a cheese and veal pie—excellent, too. O Caesar, I have one desire. I foresee easy forays for you, sire, if I am a spy for you. I have an eyepiece to use to spy.
— An eyepiece! Have you seen an enemy army?
— Yes, Excellency, in a secure city, adjacent to a forest, two armies.
— I have seen your city, and I say your city is empty! Are you a spy for anyone else? Seize him, men!
— O Caesar, you are too wise to use force! I am innocent! I see two cities: One is empty, and one two armies occupy. I am your ally, and I have a double use, sire. You see, I am a spy and I am a seer, too.
— If you are a seer, I ask you, are you a teller of fortunes?
— Yes, Caesar, I foresee nine seasons of easy success for you before you expire.
— Nine seasons! And am I to expire in nine seasons? Why? Will I be sick, spy?
— O Caesar, you will expire before you are ill of a disease, to my sorrow. Have you any enemies?
— A few, a few.
— I foresee you will have two eulogies, O Caesar; one orator to accuse your enemies and one to excuse them; one to expiate and one to extenuate; one to say "Peace, Peace," and one to argue for "an eye for an eye"; one to attest to your tyranny, and one to attest to your energy and excellence; a forum for forensics, Caesar, before your enemies' demise. Yes, eventually your enemies will expire, too—Excellency, are you OK? Excuse Aristes, Caesar, if I have foreseen too far!
— O hell, I say to arms! A sea of enemies awaits, Aristes! To arms!

## 31 August: *Garbled Geography*

| | | |
|---|---|---|
| 1. Wash. | 5. O. | 9. Tenn. |
| 2. Ark. | 6. Md. | 10. Ala. |
| 3. Pa. | 7. Miss. | 11. Penn. |
| 4. Me. | 8. Mass. | 12. Del. |

## 11 September: *Last Lines*

| | | |
|---|---|---|
| 1. F | 7. E | 13. L |
| 2. G | 8. C | 14. P |
| 3. A | 9. N | 15. M |
| 4. B | 10. I | 16. R |
| 5. H | 11. O | 17. Q |
| 6. D | 12. K | 18. J |

## 13 September: *English Is Unamerican*

1. Ad, advertisement
2. Boulevard, main road
3. Bath
4. Beet
5. Scab, or fink
6. Ticket agent
7. Trunk
8. Recess
9. Taxi stand
10. Catalogue
11. Parking lot
12. Express company
13. Catnip
14. French fries
15. Closed season
16. Clothespin
17. Master of ceremonies
18. Cone
19. Cruising
20. Potato chip
21. Delegation
22. Flop house
23. Extension wire
24. Fraternal order
25. Period
26. Gingersnap
27. Box car
28. Installment plan
29. Vacationist
30. Horn, or siren
31. Eraser
32. Domestic mails
33. Pantry
34. Editorial
35. Checkroom
36. Truck farmer
37. Game
38. Pot pie
39. Highway patrolman
40. Pen point
41. Bellboy, or bellhop
42. Hall
43. Baby carriage, baby buggy
44. Gasoline

45. General delivery
46. District attorney, or state's attorney
47. Holdup man, stickup man, highjacker
48. Sirloin
49. Operating cost
50. Commuter
51. Sell out
52. Dumbwaiter
53. Hash
54. Thriller
55. Stenographer
56. One-way ticket
57. Soda fountain
58. Hot water bottle
59. Distributor
60. Scholarship
61. Rutabaga
62. T.V.
63. Parole (for a criminal)
64. Can
65. Lumber
66. Flashlight
67. Hike
68. Transport
69. Night club, or nightstick
70. Touchdown
71. Street corner
72. Rare
73. Watch crystal
74. Witness stand
75. Excelsior

## 15 September: *The Song of Snohomish*

The players' names, in order of appearance in the poem, are: Catfish: George Metkovich. Mudcat: Jim Grant. Ducky: Joe Medwick. Coot: Orville Veale. The Babe: George Herman Ruth. The Barber: Salvatore Maglie. The Blade: Jack Billingham. The Brat: Eddie Stanky. Windy: John McCall. Dummy: William Hoy. Gabby: Charles Hartnett. Hoot: Walter Evans. Big Train: Walter Johnson. Big Six: Christy Mathewson. Big Ed: Edward Delehanty. Fat: Bob Fothergill.

Greasy: Alfred Neale. Sandy: Sanford Koufax. Muddy: Herold Ruel. Rocky: Rocco Colavito. Bunions: Rollie Zeider. Twinkletoes: George Selkirk. Footsie: Wayne Belardi. The Hat: Harry Walker. Fuzzy: Al Smith. Dizzy: Jay Hanna Dean. Buddy: John Hassett. Cocky: Eddie Collines. The Bull: Al Ferrara. The Stork: George Theodore. The Weasel: Don Bessent. The Cat: Harry Brecheen.

Schoolboy: Lynwood Rowe. Preacher: Elwin Roe. Rajah: Rogers Hornsby. Duke: Edwin Snider. General: Alvin Crowder. Major: Ralph Houk. Spaceman: Bill Lee. Spook: Forrest Vandergrift Jacobs.

Shoeless Joe: Joseph Jefferson Jackson. Cobra Joe: Joe Frazier. Bullet Joe: Leslie Bush. Bing: Edmund Miller. Old Hoss: Charles Radbourne. Mule: George Haas. Country: Enos Slaughter. Rube: George Waddell. Smokey Joe: Joe Wood. Fireman Joe: Joe Beggs. Jersey Joe: Joe Stripp. Ping: Frank Bodie. Bulldog: Jim Bouton. Squirrel: Roy Sievers. Puddin' Head: William Jones. Boob: Eric McNair.

The Georgia Peach: Ty Cobb. The Fordham Flash: Frank Frisch. The Flying Dutchman: Honus Wagner. Cot: Ellis Deal. The People's Cherce: Fred Walker. The Blazer: Wade Blassingame. Crash: Lawrence Davis. The Staten Island Scot: Bobby Thompson.

Skeeter: James Webb. Scooter: Phil Rizzuto. Pepper: Johnny Martin. Duster: Walter Mails. Ebba: Edward St. Claire. Bama: Carvell Rowell. Booms: Ron Blomberg. Buster: Calvin Coolidge Julius Caesar Tuskahoma McLish.

Specs: Billy Rigney. The Grey Eagle: Tris Speaker. The Toy Cannon: Jim Wynn. Tex: James Carleton. The Earl of Snohomish: Earl Torgeson. The Duke of Tralee: Roger Bresnahan. Art the Great: Arthur Shires. Gorgeous George: George Sisler. Ox: Oscar Eckhardt. Double X: Jimmie Foxx. The Nashville Narcissus: Charles Lucas. The Phantom: Julian Javier. The Flea: Freddie Patek. The Little Professor: Dominic Paul DiMaggio. The Iron Horse: Lou Gehrig. Cap: Adran Anson. Iron Man: Joe McGinnity. Iron Mike: Mike Marshall. Iron Hands: Chuck Hiller. Hutch: Fred Hutchinson. Jap: William Barbeau. The Mad Russian: Lou Novikoff. Irish: Emil Meusel. Swede: Charles Risberg. Nap: Napoleon Lajoie. Germany: Herman Schaefer. Frenchy: Stanley Bordagaray. Big Serb: John Miljus. Dutch: Emil Leonard. Turk: Omar Lown. Tuck: George Steinback. Tug: Frank McGraw. Twig: Wayne Terwilliger. Spider: John Jorgensen. Birdie: George Tebbets. Rabbit: Walter Maranville. Pig: Frank House.

Three-Finger: Mordecai Peter Centennial Brown. No-Neck: Walt Williams. The Knuck: Hoyt Wilhelm. The Lip: Leo Durocher. Casey: Charles Dillon Stengel. Dazzy: Clarence Vance. Hippity: Johnny Hopp. Zim: Don Zimmer. Flit: Roger Cramer. Bad Henry: Henry Aaron. Fat Freddie: Frederick Fitzsimmons. Flip: Al Rosen. Jolly Cholly: Charles Grimm. Sunny Jim: James Bottomley.

Shag: Leon Chagnon. Schnozz: Ernesto Lombardi. King Kong: Charlie Keller. Klu: Ted Kluszewski.

Boog: John Wesley Powell. Buzz: Russell Arlett. Boots: Cletus Elwood Poffenberger. Bump: Irving Hadley. Boo: David Ferriss.

Baby Doll: William Jacobson. Angel Sleeves: Jack Jones. Pep: Lemuel Young. Sliding Billy: Billy Hamilton. Buttercup: Louis Dickerson. Bollicky: Billy Taylor. Boileryard: William Clarke. Juice: George Latham. Colby Jack:

Jack Coombs. Dauntless Dave: Dave Danforth. Cheese: Albert Schweitzer. Gentle Willie: William Murphy. Trolley Line: Johnny Butler. Wagon Tongue: Bill Keister. Rough: Bill Carrigan. What's the Use: Pearce Chiles.

Ee-yah: Hugh Jennings. Poosh 'Em Up: Tony Lazzeri. Skoonj: Carl Furillo. Slats: Marty Marion. Ski: Oscar Melillo. Ding Dong: Bill Bell. Ding-a-Ling: Dain Clay. Dim Dom: Dominic Dallesandro. Dee: Wilson Miles.

Bubbles: Eugene Hargrave. Dimples: Clay Dalrymple. Cuddles: Clarence Marshall. Pinky: Mike Higgins. Poison Ivy: Ivy Paul Andrews. Vulture: Phil Regan. Stinky: Harry Davis.

Jigger: Arnold Statz. Jabbo: Ray Jablonski. Jolting Joe: Joseph Paul DiMaggio. Blue Moon: Johnny Lee Odom. Boom Boom: Walter Beck. Bubba: Wycliffe Nathaniel Morton. Bo: Robert Belinski.

## 25 September: *Address Unknown*

The place names, as you, clever reader, saw at once, are Baton Rouge, Santa Fe, Pend Oreille (though this is really a lake and river, not a town), Corpus Christi, Des Moines, and Amarillo. Have you ever shot craps at The Swans NE?

## 27 September: *Wacky Wordies*

1a. Just between you and me. 1b. Hitting below the belt. 1c. Head over heels in love. 1d. Shrinking violets. 1e. Bermuda Triangle. 1f. A mixed bag.

2a. Cry over spilt milk. 2b. Lying in wait. 2c. *Unfinished Symphony*. 2d. Pineapple upside-down cake. 2e. You're under arrest. 2f. Split-second timing.

3a. Nothing on TV. 3b. Fly-by-night. 3c. Raise a big stink. 3d. Add insult to injury. 3e. Railroad crossing. 3f. A person after my own heart.

4a. At the point of no return. 4b. The inside dope. 4c. Long underwear. 4d. Ostrich with its head in the ground. 4e. Lucky break. 4f. Corner the market.

## 7 October: *Yknits Seiknip*

| | | | |
|---|---|---|---|
| 1. | mad dam | 11. | rap par |
| 2. | made Edam | 12. | redo Oder |
| 3. | cod doc | 13. | Tao oat |
| 4. | diaper repaid | 14. | nomad Damon |
| 5. | reed deer | 15. | mined denim |
| 6. | mar ram | 16. | pin nip |
| 7. | Reno oner | 17. | Roma amor |
| 8. | Lodi idol | 18. | lee eel |
| 9. | Edom mode | 19. | emir rime |
| 10. | pacer recap | 20. | lamina animal |

## 10 October: *What Is the Question?*

The questions:

1. What is your full name, Dr. Presume?
2. What's a Grecian urn?
3. How can you recognize a brass band?
4. What is so rare as a day in June?
5. What have rainbow trout got that no other trout has?
6. What's Nu?
7. What was the final score of the Strontium-Carbon game?
8. What was the slogan of that airline that went out of business?
9. What are all those cherry pits doing in my bed?
10. Where the hell did all these rocks come from?
11. What do you use to beat up a stork?
12. What would Oliver Wendell Holmes, Jr., have been had he had his father's talent for writing verse?

## 13 October: *"Hark to the Mewsicians of Bremen!"*

Cervine is deerlike; colubrine, snakelike; hircine, goatlike; larine, gull-like; lutrine, otterlike; meline, badgerlike; mephitine, skunklike; musteline, weasellike (or martenlike, or minklike); ovine, sheeplike; phocine, seallike; sciurine, squirrellike; viverrine, civetlike.

## 16 October: *A Collection of Crocks*

From a Collection of Sources
I bring you this curious Collection of Facts.
One day a Collection of Gallants
A Collection of Jews
And a Collection of Hicks
Who included a Collection of Cals
And a Collection of Dicks
Left their Collection of Flats
To walk on a Collection of Docks
With a Collection of Monsters.
There they met a Collection of Gals
Among whom were a Collection of Janices
A Collection of Sals
And a Collection of Mses.
The Collection of Hicks
Had brought a Collection of Hens
And the Collection of Hens
Had brought a Collection of Chicks.
The Collection of Gals
Agreed to dance a Collection of Jigs
On the Collection of Docks
With the Collection of Gallants
The Collection of Jews
And the Collection of Hicks
But not the Collection of Monsters.
This enraged the Collection of Monsters.
Who loosed in the Collection of Jigs
A Collection of Bats
And made off in the confusion with the
Collection of Hens
And the Collection of Chicks.
With the prodigious Collection of Curses
The Collection of Hicks
Sic'ed a Collection of Curs
A Collection of Collies
And a Collection of Bears
On the fleeing Collection of Monsters
But the clever Collection of Monsters
Ran into a Collection of Stores
Where they sold the Collection of Hens
And the Collection of Chicks
For a Collection of Cents.
With a quick Collection of Pecks
The Collection of Hens
And the Collection of Chicks
Ate a Collection of Pills
And a Collection of Bugs.
When the Police caught the Collection of Monsters
They rode them on a Collection of Rails
And in a Collection of Cells
Rapped a Collection of Skulls.
The Judge imposed a Collection of Fines.
But the poor Collection of Hicks
Never got back the Collection of Hens
Or the Collection of Chicks,
For the Collection of Hicks
Were a Collection of Fools.

## 17 October: *Puzzle School*

PARTWORDS

*Possible answers*

ROWBOAT
STRAWBERRY

OVERWORK
LOBSTER
EMPHASIS
DEFTNESS
BOATSWAIN

FILL-IN STATION

*Possible answers*

| | | | |
|---|---|---|---|
| SCOUT | SCOUR | FLOUR | FLOUT |
| CLOUT | CLOUD | GROUP | SHOUT |
| SPOUT | SNOUT | STOUT | GHOUL |
| TROUT | GROUT | CROUP | KNOUT |

MATCH-UPS

| | |
|---|---|
| NERVES | THEMES |
| IMPALE | INGOTS |
| SHORES | CLOSET |
| CURSES | MANSION |

## 25 October: *Stinky-Pinkies*

1. Fervent servant
2. Prosaic mosaic
3. Truculent succulent
4. Granite planet
5. Raucous caucus
6. Dire choir
7. Puerile mural
8. Saline praline
9. Helot zealot
10. Fecund second

## 29 October: *Double Trouble*

1. Flipper, flivver
2. Scuttle
3. Mission
4. Feeling
5. Drizzle
6. Barrage
7. Gazelle
8. Connect, correct
9. Haddock, hassock
10. Aggress
11. Chattel
12. Bassoon

## 30 October: *Caught in the Middle*

The completed words are solecism, breviary, adjutant, and meridian.

## 16 November: *Double Duty*

1. Backward, Wardrobe
2. Barren, Render
3. Border, Derive
4. Common, Money
5. Curtain, Tainted
6. Doorkey, Keystone
7. Explain, Plaintive
8. Fireside, Sideways
9. Footstep, Stepson
10. Fretsaw, Sawmill
11. Hamlet, Lettuce
12. Handsome, Somebody
13. Housework, Workman (or Houseboat, Boatman)
14. Mischief, Chieftain
15. Present, Sentence
16. Prowess, Essence
17. Pursuit, Suitable (or Purport, Portable)
18. Sunset, Settee
19. Tasty, Tyrant
20. Warfare, Farewell

**21 November:** *The Strange Case of the Surplus Anagrams*

The missing words in the five-anagram verse:
Sutler, Ulster, luster, rustle, result.
The missing words in the nine-anagram verse:
Ulster, sutler, luters, lurest, rulest, lustre, luster, rustle, result.

**2 December:** *Friend in the Middle*

1. Naturalist
2. Associated
3. Scrupulous
4. Fascinated
5. Precaution
6. Orchestral
7. Commentary
8. Infidelity
9. Ingredient
10. Woodpecker
11. Revolution
12. Telephones
13. Electronic
14. Mechanical
15. Illustrate
16. Loggerhead

**11 December:** *I Kmnow Pfil Pfizer Pfomnebd Me, Though*

Phil Pfizer phoned me to impart
Mnemosyne's an ancient tart,
    And myrrh is bdellium creamed.
Psychiatrists, he next announces,
Dress pterodactyls' young in flounces,
    And toads eat ptisans steamed.
I do not know that this is so;
I know Phil Pfizer phoned me, though.

**12 December:** *Biographical Sketch*

Alastair Reid would have made the last line of the limerick read: "Or my name is not Alastair Reid."

**13 December:** *Methusalah Drank for 969 Years*

Muse, say not I (tush tush!) am heel
That out of ale I make my meal.
Methusalah, it now appears,
The hale sum was of many beers.
No gold a man might melt has hue
Gold as the meal he thus would brew;
And no mule has the kick those beers
Supplied him for a thousand years.
Muse, health waits in the glass! I pray
Let ale heal; shut me not away.

**20 December:** *Mistletoe Means Watch Out*

TABLE TENNIS. ELBOW GREASE. PAINT BRUSH.
OFF WHITE. CHRISTMAS CARD

**25 December:** *Take Back That Powdered Rhinoceros Horn, Santa!*

Read in order the first letter of the first word of each line of the sonnet ("hand-painted" is one word); the first letter of the third word of each line; and the first letter of the last word of each line. It comes out:

The Oysterville Almanac bids
you Merry Christmas.

And most sincerely.

**26 December:** *Showoff Words*

HYPOBULA: neurotic haste in decision-making.
DYSPHEMISM: the deliberate use of a disparaging or offensive term for shock value.
HIRCISMUS: stinky armpits.
SAVSSAT: animals crowded around a hole in the Arctic ice.

# PERMISSIONS

*Ways.* Used by permission of *Word Ways.* Jean B. Boyce, "Alpha and Omega," from *The Wall Street Journal.* © 1979 Dow Jones and Company, Inc. Permission, Cartoon Features Syndicate. Maxey Brooke, "Isograms," from *Word Ways.* Used by permission of *Word Ways.* Pat Bullen, "I Love That Woodsy Mensy Smell," from *The New Statesman.* Reprinted by kind permission of *The New Statesman.* Betsy Burr, Rebuses, from *Word Ways.* Used by permission of *Word Ways.* Leslie E. Card, Pseudo-opposites, from *Word Ways.* Used by permission of *Word Ways.* John Ciardi, "The Lesson," from *Saturday Review/ World* magazine. © Ciardi Family Publishing Trust. Used by its permission. William Cole, "What a Friend We Have in Cheeses." © 1972 William Cole. William Cole, "Just Dropped In." © 1955 *The New Yorker* magazine. William Cole, "Verse Aid." William Cole, "Dirty Work on the Appellation Trail." © 1966 William Cole. All used by permission of William Cole. Robert A. Creamer, "Petersonese," from *Sports Illustrated,* December 4, 1972. Reprinted courtesy of *Sports Illustrated.* Copyright © 1972, Time Inc. All rights reserved. Kim Dammers, "Manicdepressant," from *Poems One Line and Longer.* Original publication in *Gallery Series III—Poets (Levitations and Observations).* Whitney Darrow, Jr., "Poodle Doodle" illustration. Used by permission of Whitney Darrow, Jr. Ormonde de Kay, "Bowwow, Dingdong, Pooh-Pooh." © Ormonde de Kay. Peter Donchian, "Quote or Misquote," from *Reader's Digest.* © Estate of Peter Donchian. Joe Ecclesine, "Measure for Measure," from *Saturday Review/World* magazine. Used by permission of Joe Ecclesine. Faith Eckler, "Troping the Text," from *Word Ways.* Used by permission of *Word Ways.* A. Ross Eckler, "Mary Had a Lipogram," from *Word Ways.* Used by permission of *Word Ways.* R. Merrill Ely, Isogram, from *Word Ways.* Used by permission of *Word Ways.* William E. Engel, "Thumb Fun." © William E. Engel. Enigma, Anagrams, from *Enigma* magazine. Used by permission of the National Puzzlers League. Jim Everhart, Excerpts from *Illustrated Guide to the Texas Language,* Cliffs Notes. © The Estate of Jim Everhart. Used by permission of Gail Everhart, Executrix. A. S. Flumenhaft, "Can We Write This Wrong," from *Verbatim* magazine. Used by permission of *Verbatim,* www.verbatim-mag.com. Wilson Follett, Excerpt from *Modern American Usage* (Hill and Wang, 1966). © Wilson Follett. Darryl Francis, "British and Scottish Pronunciation," "Chain States." Both from *Word Ways.* Used by permission of *Word Ways.* John G. Fuller, Excerpts from *Games for Insomniacs.* Copyright © 1966 by John Fuller. Used by permission of Doubleday, a division of Random House, Inc. Games, "Wackie Wordies," from *Games* magazine. © Games Publications, Inc., 1979. Reprinted by permission of *Games* magazine. M. H. Greenblatt, "Opposite Proverbs," from *Word Ways.* Used by permission of *Word Ways.* Virginia R. Hager, List of book titles, List of saints. Both from *Word Ways.* Used by permission of *Word Ways.* Sidney Harris, "Mini, Minu," from *Saturday Review/World* magazine. Used by permission of Sidney Harris. Aloïse Buckley Heath, "A Heath Christmas Carol," from *National Review.* © 1980 by National Review, Inc., 215 Lexington Avenue, New York, NY 10016. Reprinted by permission. Christine Heffner, "A Scoop of Reporters." Reprinted with permission from *Reader's Digest.* Copyright © 1975 by The Reader's Digest Association, Inc. Geoffrey Hellman, "Dynastic Tiff." © Geoffrey Hellman. Ted Hipple, "The Traditional Grammarian as Poet." Used by permission of

# ABOUT THE AUTHOR

**Willard R. Espy** was born in Olympia, Washington, in 1910. He grew up in the town of Oysterville, which was founded on the Long Beach Peninsula in southwestern Washington by his grandfather, R. H. Espy, in 1854. Espy graduated from the University of Redlands in California in 1930, and spent a year abroad before returning to work as a reporter in California. In 1941, after other journalistic endeavors, he was hired by *Reader's Digest*. Espy spent the next 16 years at the magazine, including as promotion director. In the late 1960s he began a long and prolific career as a wordsmith, writing verse for such publications as *Punch* and eventually turning out 15 books on language. Among these are the almanacs from which the entries in the present volume are collected, as well as *The Game of Words* (1971), *Thou Improper, Thou Uncommon Noun* (1978), and *Words to Rhyme With* (1985). His life in the publishing world of New York, and his long love affair with language, did not, however, cause Espy to forget his deep roots in the sands of Washington, as shown by his moving local history, *Oysterville: Roads to Grandpa's Village* (1977); *Skulduggery on Shoalwater Bay* (1998), which consists of verse "whispered up from the graves of the pioneers"; and other works on the Evergreen State. Willard Espy, who continued to divide his time between Manhattan and Oysterville, passed away in New York City in February 1999.